THE TRANSFORMATION OF ISLAMIC LAW IN GLOBAL FINANCIAL MARKETS

The role of global capital in relation to human social systems has assumed enormous proportions in liberalised, deregulated markets. States attempt to nationalise it, financial centres spring up in its wake, and INGOs attempt to deal with its de-territorialising, supranational characteristics. A global adjudication system (arbitration) has been introduced to safeguard and buttress its flow.

The power of Islamic capital has generated numerous sites of legal contestation and negotiation, ranging from gateway financial centres, international law firms and transnational financial institutions, all of which interact in the production of Islamic financial law (IFL). The process of producing IFL illustrates complex fields of action driven by power dynamics, neoliberal paradigms and the institutional momentum of the global economy. The municipal legal systems under study in this book (the United Kingdom, Bahrain, United Arab Emirates and the Dubai International Financial Centre) illustrate globalisation's acceleration of legal, economic and social production.

JONATHAN G. ERCANBRACK is Lecturer in the Law of Islamic Finance and Deputy Director of the Centre for Islamic and Middle Eastern Law at SOAS, University of London.

THE TRANSFORMATION OF ISLAMIC LAW IN GLOBAL FINANCIAL MARKETS

JONATHAN G. ERCANBRACK

CAMBRIDGE
UNIVERSITY PRESS

CAMBRIDGE
UNIVERSITY PRESS

University Printing House, Cambridge CB2 8BS, United Kingdom

Cambridge University Press is part of the University of Cambridge.

It furthers the University's mission by disseminating knowledge in the pursuit of education, learning and research at the highest international levels of excellence.

www.cambridge.org
Information on this title: www.cambridge.org/9781107061507

First published 2015

A catalogue record for this publication is available from the British Library

Library of Congress Cataloguing in Publication data
Ercanbrack, Jonathan, author.
The transformation of Islamic law in global financial markets / Jonathan Ercanbrack.
pages cm
Includes bibliographical references and index.
ISBN 978-1-107-06150-7 (hardback)
1. Finance–Law and legislation. 2. Finance (Islamic law) 3. Finance–Law and legislation–Great Britain. 4. Finance–Law and legislation–Persian Gulf States. I. Title.
K1066.E73 2015
343′.03–dc23
2014032051

ISBN 978-1-107-06150-7 Hardback

CONTENTS

ACKNOWLEDGEMENTS

This book was written over the course of seven years in which my principal research interest resided in understanding the role of law in inspiring, facilitating and regulating Islamic finance. I began researching the book as a doctoral student at the School of Oriental and African Studies (SOAS), where Werner Menski had agreed to supervise my work. Werner's 'blue bible' or magnum opus on comparative law presented a wide spectrum of possibilities for understanding law and the diverse ways in which it originates, interacts, transforms and governs. Werner's work, as well as that of other legal pluralists, impressed upon me the importance and usefulness of legal pluralism, a comparative law concept. It has become an essential conceptual tool in terms of the way in which I approach the research of dynamic and interactive normative systems in the global economy.

The commercial nature of my work required additional expertise and as fate would have it I was very fortunate to receive it from Peter Muchlinski and Nicholas Foster. Peter's work on the role of transnational corporations as originators of law (and foreign direct investment), as well as their ability to influence and disseminate legal standards on a global basis, has played an important role in how I view financial law. Nick, on the other hand, could not have been a better supervisor, despite his demanding standards. Nick's extraordinary attention to detail, his love of the law and rigorous academic scholarship inspired me to develop my own abilities as an academic lawyer. Furthermore, his comparative work on English law and the commercial aspects of the sharia provided necessary grounding in the fundamental commercial concepts of Islam and English law as well as the complex interplay between these and modern systems of law.

My PhD thesis, entitled 'The Law of Islamic Finance in the United Kingdom: Legal Pluralism and Financial Competition' dealt mostly with the challenges of articulating and implementing Islamic finance in the United Kingdom. As with all my research, however, I quickly realised its limitations and indeed the limitations of my understanding of the global and theoretical dimensions of the subject. I have attempted to augment these with this book. The book advances a conceptual argument concerning the nature of Islamic financial law (IFL) that was developed by examining a much broader set of jurisdictions, international actors and transformative legal processes than was possible in the thesis.

I am grateful for the inspiration I received to embark upon this project from many other esteemed scholars in the field. In particular, I have found sustenance in the writings of and discussions with Haider Ala Hamoudi concerning the importance of practice and context in understanding IFL and Islamic law more generally. I have also benefited greatly from the work and ideas of many fine scholars and wish to note just of few of the most influential here: Wael Hallaq, Mahmoud El-Gamal, Saskia Sassen, Timur Kuran, Joseph Schacht and Rodney Wilson.

I would also like to thank my talented research assistants (Margarita Dimova and Hamza Zaveri), whose assistance was indispensable in producing this book in a reasonable period of time. I would also like to give especial thanks to Carmen Hofmann for her abiding support as well as her technological savvy!

I owe thanks to SOAS for its institutional support and financial assistance. In addition to helping me with numerous small research grants, SOAS provided a research environment in which heterodoxy is encouraged. At SOAS I was able to introduce a course on the Law of Islamic Finance at both the master's and LLB levels, which to my knowledge, is the first of its kind in the North Atlantic.

Finally, I wish to thank my beloved children, Saskia and Matias for whom I wish happiness, love and a profound interest in life. I dedicate this book, the fruits of my labour, to them.

CASES AND LEGISLATION

English case law

Amin Rasheed Shipping Corp v. *Kuwait Insurance Co, the Al Wahab* [1984] AC 50, [1983] 2 All ER 884, [1983] 3 WLR 241, HL 326

Antaios Cia Naviera SA v. *Salen Rederierna AB* [1984] 3 All ER 229, 233, [1985] AC 191, 201 121

Halpern v. *Halpern* [2006] EWHC 1728 (Comm), [2006] 3 All ER 1139, [2006] 2 All ER (Comm 484, [2006] 3 WLR 946, [2006] NLJR 1137, (2006) Times, 18 July, [2006] All ER (D) 20 (Jul), QB; [2007] EWCA Civ 291, [2008] QB 195, [2007] 3 All ER 478, [2007] 2 All ER (Comm) 330, [2007] 3 WLR 849, [2007] 2 Lloyd's Rep 56, (2007) Times, 14 May, [2007] All ER (D) 38 (Apr), [2007] QB 88, CA 228, 327

The Investment Dar Company KSCC v. *Blom Developments Bank SAL* [2009] EWHC 3545 (Ch), [2009] All ER (D) 145 (Dec) 233

Investors Compensation Scheme v. *West Bromwich Building Society* [1998] 1 WLR 896, [1998] All ER 98 120

Islamic Investment Co Ltd v. *Symphony Gems NV* [2002] All ER (D) 171 (Feb), QB; [2009] EWHC 2378 (Comm), [2009] All ER (D) 07 (Oct), [2008] All ER (D) 141 (Mar), (2008) Times, 4 April, CA 224

Kleinwort Benson Ltd v. *Malaysia Mining Corp Bhd* [1989] 1 WLR 379 121, 205

Law Debenture Trust Corp Plc v. *Elektrim Finance BV* [2005] EWHC 1412 (Ch) 323

Musawi v. *Re International Ltd* [2007] EWHC 2981 (Ch), [2007] All ER (D) 222 (Dec) 327

Nea Agrex SA v. *Baltic Shipping Co Ltd* [1974 N. No. 2011] – [1976] QB 933, [1976] 2 All ER 842, [1976] 2 WLR 925, [1976] 2 Lloyd's Rep 47, [1976] 120 Sol Jo 351 229, 230

Petroleum Development Ltd v. *Sheikh of Abu Dhabi* [1953] 47 AJIL 156. 317

Ruler of Qatar v. *International Marine Oil Company Ltd.* [1952] 1 Int Comp LQ 247 [1953] 20 Int LR 534 231, 316

Sanghi Polyesters Ltd v. *the International Investor KCSC* [2000] WL 389643, [2000] All ER (D) 93, [2000] 1 Lloyd's Rep 480, [2001] CLC 748 324

Saudi Arabia v. *Arabian American Oil Co (Aramco)* [1958] 27 Int LR 117 231

Schuler AG v. *Wickman Machine Tool Sales* [1974] AC 235 120

UAE case law

US case law

International case law

Statutes and statutory instruments, Bahrain

Statutes and statutory instruments, Dubai International Financial Centre (DIFC)

Statutes and statutory instruments, Dubai

Statutes and statutory instruments, France

Statutes and statutory instruments, United Arab Emirates (UAE)

Statutes and statutory instruments, United Kingdom

European Union treaties and legislation

Treaties, conventions and model laws

ABBREVIATIONS

AAA	American Arbitration Association
AAOIFI	Accounting and Auditing Organization for Islamic Financial Institutions
AFIB	Alternative finance investment bond
ALI	American Law Institute
BCBS	Basel Committee on Banking Supervision
BCDR-AAA	Bahrain Chamber for Dispute Resolution
BD	Bahraini Dinar
BFH	Bahrain Financial Harbour
BIS	Bank for International Settlements
BRIC	Brazil, Russia, India and China
CAR	Capital Adequacy Requirement
CBB	Central Bank of Bahrain
CE	Common Era
CDO	Collateralised Debt Obligation
CIS	Collective Investment Scheme
CIS	Commonwealth of Independent States
CISG	United Nations Convention on Contracts for the International Sale of Goods
CRCOM	credit risk capital requirement
DCR	displaced commercial risk
DFSA	Dubai Financial Services Authority
DIFC	Dubai International Financial Centre
DIFX	Dubai International Financial Exchange
ECAI	external credit assessment institution
EEA	European Economic Area
ESCA	Emirates Securities and Commodities Authority
ESFS	European System of Financial Supervisors
ESRB	European Systemic Risk Board
ESUA	Exchange in Satisfaction and User Agreements
EU	European Union
FCA	Financial Conduct Authority
FDI	Foreign Direct Investment
FSA	Financial Services Authority
FSCS	Financial Services Compensation Scheme

FSMA	Financial Services and Markets Act 2000
GCC	Gulf Cooperation Council
GDP	Gross Domestic Product
HJ	*hamish jiddiyyah*: a security deposit that is held as collateral by the bank
HMRC	Her Majesty's Revenue and Customs
HPP	Home Purchase Plan
HSA	higher sharia authority
IAH	investment account holders
IBB	Islamic Bank of Britain
ICC	International Chamber of Commerce
ICDR	International Centre for Dispute Resolution
ICG	individual capital guidance
ICTA	Income and Corporations Tax Act
IFI	Islamic financial institution
IFL	Islamic financial law
IFRS	International Financial Reporting Standards
IFSB	Islamic Financial Services Board
IFSL	International Financial Services London
IIC	Islamic investment company
IIFM	International Islamic Financial Market
IILM	International Islamic Liquidity Management Centre
IINGO	Islamic International Non-governmental Organisation
IMF	International Monetary Fund
INCEIF	International Centre for Education in Islamic Finance
INCOTERMS	International Commercial Terms
INGO	International Non-governmental Organisation
IOSCO	International Organization of Securities Commissions
IRB	internal ratings-based
IRR	investment risk reserve
ISA	Individual Savings Accounts
ISDA	International Swaps and Derivatives Association
LIBOR	London Interbank Offered Rate
LLR	lender of last resort
LMA	Loan Market Association
LMC	Liquidity Management Centre
MATP	master agreement for treasury placement
MENA	Middle East and North Africa
MPO	*murābaḥah* to the purchase orderer
NASDAQ	National Association of Securities Dealers Automated Quotations (second-largest stock exchange in the world by market capitalisation, after the New York Stock Exchange)
NS&I	National Savings & Investments
OECD	Organization for Economic Cooperation and Development
OPEC	Organization of the Petroleum Exporting Countries
PER	profit equalisation reserve

PLS	profit- and loss-sharing
PLSIA	profit- and loss-sharing investment account
PRA	Prudential Regulatory Authority
QFC	Qatar Financial Centre
RAO	Regulated Activities Order
SDLT	Stamp Duty Land Tax
SG	Symphony Gems
SOAS	School of Oriental and African Studies
SPL	Sanghi Polyesters Ltd
SPV	special purpose vehicle
SSB	Sharia Supervisory Board
SSM	Single supervisory mechanism
TID	The Investment Dar Company
TII	The International Investor
TMA	*Tahawwut* Master Agreement
TNC	Transnational Corporation
UAE	United Arab Emirates
UCC	Uniform Commercial Code
UK	United Kingdom
UNCITRAL	United Nations Commission on International Trade Law
UNIDROIT	International Institute for the Unification of Private Law
US	United States of America
VAT	Value Added Tax
WTO	World Trade Organisation

ARABIC-ENGLISH GLOSSARY

Note: The transliteration of Arabic words into the Roman script has been undertaken according to the Library of Congress transliteration standard. For the sake of simplicity, most singular Arabic words have been given an English 's' to denote the plural form. Words such as *sukuk*, however, which are often used in modern financial markets, are used in the plural. Finally, Arabic words that, according to the Oxford English Dictionary, have been borrowed into the English language have not been transliterated or italicised. Such words include the sharia, fatwa, Hadith and Sunna.

'Ādat at-tujjār	practice of the merchant/trader
'Adhāb	punishment, chastisement
Aḍ'āfan muḍā'afatan	(sum that is) doubled and multiplied
Aḥad	solitary
'Ahd	obligation, covenant, treaty, agreement
Ahkām	legal rules
'Amal	labour; action, performance
Amānah	trust, faithfulness
'Aqd	contract, covenant
Ārbāb al-māl	a group of financial institutions
'Ariyah	loan
Arkān (pl.)	component(s), pillar(s) (of a contract)
'Ayn	a corporeal matter, substance
Bāṭil	void (legal)
Batīn	inner meaning or interpretation
Bay'	sale
Bay' al-dayn	sale of debt
Bay' al-dayn bi al-dayn	sale of a debt for a debt
Bay' al-salam	a forward sale in which the price of a commodity is paid upfront
Bay' bithaman ajil	deferred payment sales
Bay' ghā'ib	contract of sale for an absent thing or object
Bay' al-'īnah	double sale used to circumvent the prohibition of lending with interest
Bay' al-wafā'	a contract in which the owner of property (house or land) sells it, with the condition that he will repurchase the property for a larger sum than the original price
Bayān	a legal method used to reveal or elaborate legal rules on the basis of the holy texts (Quran and Sunna)

bi-kayfīyah la yaqūl bihā mujtahid	a rule of law that no qualified legal interpreter teaches
Dalīl	sign, indication
Dar al-ḥarb	abode of war
Dar al-islām	abode of peace
Ḍarūrah	necessity, need
Darūrīyāt	'the essentials' (type of *maṣlaḥah*)
Dayn	obligation, debt; also expresses the idea of 'claim' or right
Diyet	blood money
Dīwān	historical records including court registers
Dhimmah	capacity, personal responsibility or obligation
Fā'idah	interest; growth
Faqīh (sg.) /*Fuquhā'* (pl.)	expert in Islamic jurisprudence (*fiqh*)
Farḍ	obligatory
Farḍ kifāyah	divine communal obligation
Fāsid	defective (legal)
Faskh	rescission of a contractual bond
Fiqh	Islamic jurisprudence
Fiṭra	the native ability to know of God's existence
Furū'	branches of jurisprudence; whereas the *uṣūl al-fiqh* indicates the roots of the law
Gharar	risk/speculation
al-gharar al-kathīr	excessive risk/speculation
al-gharar al-yasīr	minimal risk/speculation
Hadith	narration of the words and deeds of the Prophet Muhammad
Ḥājah	a need
Hājīyat	'the complementary' (type of maṣlaḥah)
Halakha	Jewish law
Ḥalāl	lawful
Ḥarām	forbidden
Ḥawālah	transfer of debt
Hibah	gift
Hijra	the emigration of the Prophet Mohammed from Mecca to Medina in 622 CE
Hikmah	God's infinite wisdom
Ḥīlah (sg.)/*ḥiyal* (pl.)	legal stratagem
Hukm	underlying cause of the legal ruling
'Ibādāt	devotional worship (e.g. prayer, fasting)
Ibāhah	permissibility
'idah	promissory
Ījāb	offer
Ijārah	lease
Ijārah wa-iqtinā'	financial lease
Ijmā'	scholarly consensus

Ijtihād	independent reasoning
Ikhtilāf	disagreement, difference of opinion
Ikhtiyār	option, choice, preference
'Illah	effective cause. The element utilised in establishing a connection between the holy sources, the Quran and Sunna, and a novel case requiring independent juristic reasoning (*ijtihād*)
Insidād bāb al-ijtihād	'the closing of the gate of *ijtihād*'
Irādah	human will
Isnād	chain of authorities (of a Hadith)
Istiḥsān	juridical or personal preference
Istiṣlaḥ	public benefit (technical legal term)
Istiṣnā'	contract of hire, manufacture
jā 'iz	permissible contract
Jāhilīyah	time of ignorance; pre-Islamic
Jahl	want of knowledge; ignorance
Jawāz	basic legality
Jins	Saleh's definition of genus
Ju'ālah	reward
Kafālah	guarantee
Kanun	the laws of the Ottoman rulers
Khiyār al-'ayb	the option of voiding a contract due to a defect
Khiyār al-ru'yah	the option of inspection
Khultah	mixed type of partnership
Kitāb	book
Kitāb al-ḥiyal	book of ḥiyal
Kuffār	unbelievers
Ma'dūm	non-existent subject matter
Madhhab/Madhāhib	schools of law (Sunni schools of law: Shāfi'i, Mālikī, Ḥanafī, and Ḥanbalī)
Mafsadah	evil
Majallah	gazette
Majlis	(noun of place) indicating a session or meeting, assembly
Majlis al-hukm	sharia court(less frequently: *majlis al-qaḍā*)
Makhraj (sg.)/*Makhārij* (pl.)	exit(s); Ḥanafī term for *ḥiyal*
Makrūh	reprehensible
Māl	property
Mandūb	meritorious, recommended
Manfa'ah	usufruct
Maqāṣid al-sharī'a	objectives of the sharia/ of the law
Maqṣad (sg.)/*maqāṣid* (pl.)	God's purpose
Masālik al-'illah	method devised by jurists to identify God's true intentions
Maṣlaḥah	public interest
Maṣlaḥah mursalah	unattested *maṣlaḥah*

Maysir	gambling
Mohatra	from the Arabic, *mukhāṭarah*, meaning risk
Mu'āmalāt	transactions
Mubāh	permissible, licit
Muḍārabah	an investment partnership; also known as muqarāḍah and qirāḍ
Muḍārib	investment agent
Mujma' 'alayh	law in which unity prevails
Mujtahid	Islamic scholar who possesses the aptitude of performing ijtihād
Mukhāṭarah	legal stratagem (ḥīlah), commonly associated with bay' al-'īnah
Mukhtalaf fīh	law in which there is disagreement
Murābaḥah	a sale with a mark-up (profit)
Mushārakah	contractual partnership; participation financing
Mustaḥabb	recommendable
al-muta'ārif	the usual practice of the people
Muzabana	the sale of fresh fruit without measure for another commodity of unknown weight/value
Muzāra'ah	agricultural partnership
nakaḥa	to marry
Namā	extension, growth
Naṣṣ	a text whose presence in the Quran or Hadith must be demonstrated
Nīyyah	intention
Nizām	parallel body of secular law in Saudi Arabia ('regulations')
Pashas	governors
Qabḍ	possession
Qabūl	acceptance (contractual relation)
Qāḍī	judge
Qarḍ	loan
Qarḍ ḥasan	loan, a charitable loan (without interest)
Qaṣd	human intention
Qirād	sleeping partnership, also known as *muḍārabah* and *muqarāḍah*
Qiṣāṣ	right of retaliation
Qiyās	analogical reasoning (one of the four sources of Islamic law according to orthodox Sunni Islam)
Rabb al-māl	investor (a partner in the *muḍārabah* contract)
Ra'y	discretion (legal reasoning)
Ribā	usury
Ribā al-faḍl	*ribā* of excess
Ribā al-jahiliyyah	the *ribā* (doubled and multiplied)
Ribā al-nasī'ah	*ribā* by delay
Ribāwī	*ribā*-based; illicit
Riḍā	the fact of being pleased or contented; approval

Rukn (sg.)	component(s), pillar(s) (of a contract)
Sabab	cause
Sadaqah	voluntary charitable contribution
Sadd al-dharā'i'	blocking the means (legal principle) (literally: closing the gates to evil)
Sakk (sg.)/sukuk (pl.)	cheque; Islamic bond; Islamic investment certificate
Salam	a forward sale (fungible commodity)
Ṣaḥīḥ	valid (legal)
Shahādah	witness; the declaration by which a believer professes belief in the Islamic faith
Sharia	literally, the way; Islamic law
Sharik	partner
Shirkah/Sharikah	partnership
Shurūṭ (sg. *sharṭ*)	legal formularies; also conditions or appendages to contracts
Sīghah	form of a contract
Sukuk	Islamic bonds
Sukuk al-ijārah	Islamic securitisation based on a lease
Sunna (pl. *sunan*)	the living tradition; the sayings and doings of the Prophet Muhammad (holy source)
Sūrah	chapter or segment indicating the way in which the Quran has been organised
Taḥawwuṭ	a profit-rate derivative product
Taḥsin	improvement
Taḥsīnīyāt	'the embellishments' (type of *maṣlaḥah*)
Takāful	Islamic insurance
Takhayyur	eclectic choice (legal)
Ṭalāq	pronunciation of divorce (by the man)
Talfiq	patching (a legal technique used to derive a novel legal opinion)
Tanzimat	series of rapid reforms in the Ottoman Empire
Taqlīd	juristic conformity in the period after the 'gates of *ijtihād*' were said to have been closed
Tashrī'	refers to modern statutory legislation that incorporates elements of the sharia
Tawarruq	sale and re-sale transaction used to generate cash/liquidity
Tawātur	requirement of multiple transmission or recurrence in order to lower the uncertainty surrounding a hadith's origins
Thaman	price
Thawāb	merit; compensation offered where not required
'Ulemā'	religious scholars
'Umlah	commission
Ummah	community
'Urf	custom
'Urbun	downpayment sale
Uṣūl al-fiqh	the principles of jurisprudence (methodology)
Wadi'ah	safekeeping, deposit

wa'd	promise
Wadī'ah yad ḍamānah	guaranteed safekeeping
Wājib	acts that are obligatory in the second degree; these acts are established by probable knowledge
Wajīh al-tijārah	general manner of commerce
Wakīl	agent
Wakālah	agency; investment contract in which agent represents investor(s)
Waqf	charitable endowment
Waṣf	attribute
Wūjuh	credit
Zakāh	obligatory charitable contribution (Islamic law)
Ẓāhir	outward meaning of a word, language or event
Ẓahir al-riwāya'	basic texts of Ḥanafī jurisprudence, which include the *Kitāb al-Aṣl*, *al-Jāmi' al-kabīr* and *al-Jāmi' al-ṣaghīr*. The *ẓahir al-riwāya* contains the three major scholars of the Ḥanafī school: *Abū Ḥanīfah* (eponym of the school), *Abū Yūsuf*, and *Shaybānī*
Zawwāja	to marry
Ziyādah	increase, augmentation

1

Introduction

1.1 Sharia and the nation state

The modern alternative banking and financial system, known as Islamic finance, caters to the religious conscience of Muslims by creating modern financial products that are premised upon the principles and commercial rules of the sharia or Islamic law.[1] Yet the sharia is no longer the sovereign law of most countries in the Muslim world.[2] By the end of the nineteenth century Muslim rulers had almost wholly discarded it throughout Muslim territories.[3] Traditionally, lawmaking authority in sharia legal systems presided with the class of jurists known as the *'ulemā'*, who sought to determine what God's law was on the basis of the Quran and Sunna. The Muslim ruler or caliph oversaw the enforcement of the law and the administration of the polity. Theoretically, the state was careful not to overstep the limits assigned to this role.[4] By the mid-nineteenth century, however, this *modus vivendi* had come to an abrupt end. Modernity and demands for social change had undermined the *'ulemā's'* authority and the state assumed the power to determine all the enacted laws of its sovereign territory.[5] This led to an unprecedented transformation in the relationship between the state and the jurists as the hitherto exclusive repository of legal authority.

[1] I use the term 'classical' to denote the long period stretching from the first Quranic revelations in 623 CE until the early nineteenth century when Islamic law was displaced by Western-based legal systems. The term 'medieval' has been avoided as it generally refers to a European periodisation of history.

[2] Saudi Arabia is the sole exception.

[3] See Wael B. Hallaq, *Shari'a: Theory, Practice, Transformations* (Cambridge University Press, 2009), 443.

[4] Joseph Schacht, 'Problems of Modern Islamic Legislation' (1960) 12 *Studia Islamica*, 113.

[5] Ann Elizabeth Mayer, 'The Shari'ah: A Methodology or a Body of Substantive Rules?' in Nicholas Heer (ed.) *Islamic Law and Jurisprudence* (University of Washington Press, 1990), 182.

The rise of the nation state, inextricably linked with the development of European imperialism, came to be felt throughout the entire Muslim world. Some European legal orders were superimposed upon traditional legal systems. For example, in British colonial territories English common law was imported as the supreme law and yet it continued to recognise traditional norms and institutions within its own legal structure.[6] In British India this situation is said to have created an independent legal system known as Anglo-Muhammadan law, which was substantially different from classical Islamic law, but comprised elements of each legal system.[7]

Other aspects of this epochal transformation involved sheer European military, political, economic and scientific might, which by the nineteenth century had become so dominant that the then Ottoman Empire instigated a series of rapid reforms known as the *tanzimat* to strengthen its relative position.[8] The *tanzimat* included wide-sweeping reforms in both civil and criminal law. For example, the Ottomans promulgated a Commercial Code in 1850, a penal code in 1858, a Code of Commercial Procedure in 1861 and a Code of Maritime Commerce in 1863. All of these were almost entirely based on French law.[9]

In the Middle East the introduction of these codes was seen as the abandonment of any pretence of adhering to Islamic law and a concerted secular drive to import Western-made law.[10] In 1877 the last of the *tanzimat* reforms, the Mejelle,[11] was billed as a civil code, encompassing nearly all areas of private Hanafī Islamic law except family law.[12] The Mejelle paved the way for a broader effort to codify Islamic law throughout the Muslim world.[13] Yet even before efforts had commenced to codify highly circumscribed areas of Islamic law, the adoption of European legal codes

[6] Gordon R. Woodman, 'The Idea of Legal Pluralism' in Baudouin Dupret, Maurits Berger and Laila al-Zwaini (eds.), *Legal Pluralism in the Arab World* (The Hague: Kluwer Law International, 1999), 8.

[7] Joseph Schacht (n 4) 112.

[8] Albert Hourani, *The Emergence of the Modern Middle East* (London: Macmillan Press in association with St Antony's College, Oxford, 1981), 14.

[9] *Ibid.*, 385; and James Norman Dalrymple Anderson, *Islamic Law in the Modern World* (London: Stevens & Sons Limited, 1959), 21–4.

[10] Ann Elizabeth Mayer (n 5) 181.

[11] Turkey, '*The Mejelle, Being an English Translation of Majallah el-Ahkam-i-Adliya and a Complete Code of Islamic Civil Law*' (Lahore: Law Publishing Company, 1967).

[12] Haider Ala Hamoudi, 'The Death of Islamic Law' (2010) 38 *Ga.J.Int'l.& Comp.L.*, 308.

[13] *Ibid.*, 306.

had the cumulative effect of dismantling the sharia legal system and with it the social fabric of lands under Ottoman rule.[14]

This historical background informs the contemporary position of the sharia in the legal systems of nation states. Among contemporary Muslim-majority states Saudi Arabia is the only one in which the sharia has not been wholly displaced by the introduction of European legal codes.[15] This is due to three key facts: Saudi Arabia was the country least affected by European colonialism; it hosts the two holiest cities of Islam – Mecca and Medina; and it largely subscribes to an ultra-conservative strain of Sunni Islam known as Wahhabism.[16] In 1992 Saudi Arabia did enact a Basic Law of Governance, a constitution of sorts, in response to political pressure.[17] The Basic Law declares in Article 1 that the constitution of the country is the Quran and the Sunna of the Prophet Muhammad. Moreover, the Saudi monarchy claims a traditional hereditary right to rule the country from the Quran and Sunna in Article 7 and sees its role as the guardian of the two holy mosques (Article 24), as well as the enforcer of sharia (Article 23).[18] However, even Saudi Arabia has enacted a parallel body of secular law, which it conveniently refers to as 'regulations' (*nizām*) so as not to offend its conservative religious elements. Commercial matters dealing with banking, companies, intellectual property and capital markets are all governed by modern regulations. Although subject to the Board of Grievances, whose judges are trained in Ḥanbalī *fiqh* (Islamic jurisprudence), disputes in these commercial areas are usually settled by separate, specialist dispute resolution bodies outside the jurisdiction of the sharia courts.[19] In fact, many, if not most, financial institutions conduct purely conventional transactions despite the fact that aspects of these

[14] Nicholas H. D. Foster, 'Using Comparative Commercial Law in the Study of Legal Transformation: Commercial Aspects of the Early Stages of Ottoman Legal Transition' in Ron Shaham and Aharon Layish (eds.), *Islamic Law Facing the Challenges of the 21st Century* (The Van Leer Jerusalem Institute, 2011), 14–15.

[15] Ann Elizabeth Mayer (n 5) 181.

[16] Peter D. Sloane, 'The Status of Islamic Law in the Modern Commercial World' (1988) 22 *Int'l L.*, 743, 751.

[17] See Kingdom of Saudi Arabia, 'The Basic Law of Governance' (Saudi Embassy, Ministry of Affairs, 1 March 1992).

[18] For an interesting examination of the development of the Saudi legal system, see Abdulaziz H. Al-Fahad, 'Ornamental Constitutionalism: The Saudi Basic Law of Governance' (2005) 30 *Yale J.Int'l L.* 375.

[19] Esther Van Eijk, 'Sharia and National Law in Saudi Arabia' in J. M. Otto (ed.), *Sharia Incorporated: A Comparative Overview of the Legal Systems of Twelve Muslim Countries in Past and Present* (Leiden University Press, 2010), 167.

may conflict with the sharia.[20] If found to conflict with the sharia, these transactions and the secular regulations that govern them would almost certainly be overturned in a sharia court, thus confirming the holy law's spiritual ascendancy in the kingdom.[21]

Other states including Iran, Pakistan, Sudan, Afghanistan, the northern states of Nigeria[22] and to some extent Libya, have re-islamised their legal systems by introducing Islamic law codes to their previous Western-derived systems after Islamists came to power.[23] The influence of the sharia in almost all Muslim-majority jurisdictions, however, is not usually dominant, clearly defined or consistent. For example, Middle Eastern states such as Kuwait, Bahrain and the United Arab Emirates (UAE) cite the sharia as 'a' source of their constitutions, whereas Qatar and Egypt designate the sharia as 'the' source.[24] Yet these states' legal systems comprise a secular mixture of western-style civil or common law with only a highly circumscribed role for the sharia in family, inheritance and personal status matters. Even in those areas of law where the influence of the sharia is still felt, it has been modernised in ways that clearly distinguish it from classical Islamic law.[25]

As a result, there is considerable uncertainty surrounding what role the sharia will play in solving a legal problem, let alone a commercial one, which generally requires a high degree of certainty, transparency and uniformity. Whereas the sharia may not impact upon a commercial dispute tried in Kuwait (for reasons associated with the principles of its Civil Code) and the sharia plays a prominent role in Saudi Arabia, other juris-

[20] Frank E. Vogel and Samuel L. Hayes, *Islamic Law and Finance: Religion, Risk and Return* (Kluwer Law International, 1998), 12.

[21] William Ballantyne, *Commercial Law in the Arab Middle East: The Gulf States* (London: Lloyd's of London Press, 1986), 46.

[22] Olaf Koendgen, 'Shari'a and National Law in the Sudan' in J M Otto (ed.), *Sharia Incorporated: A Comparative Overview of the Legal Systems of Twelve Muslim Countries in Past and Present* (Leiden University Press, 2010), 221.

[23] Rudolph Peters, 'From Jurists' Law to Statute Law or What Happens When the Shari'a Is Codified' in B A Robertson (ed.), *Shaping the Current Islamic Reformation* (London: Frank Cass, 2003), 92.

[24] *Ibid.*, 49. According to Egypt's provisional constitution. See Constitutional Declaration of the Supreme Council of the Armed Forces (Almajlis al-Ala Lil-quwwat Almussallaha Yasdaru Al-iilaan Aldustoori) [Egy const.] of March 30, 2011, Art. 2 http://egyptelections.carnegieendowment.org/2011/04/01/supreme-council-of-the-armed-forces-constitutional-announcement. Accessed 24 March 2014.

[25] Joseph Schacht (n 4) 114.

dictions range in the degree of uncertainty somewhere between these two extremes.[26]

Reflecting this reality, legal practitioners of Islamic finance almost never use the sharia as the governing law of Islamic financial contracts unless they choose Saudi law. And even Saudi sharia law (Ḥanbalī *fiqh*) is not viewed by legal practitioners as an advantageous governing law because it is commercially disadvantageous as compared to secular legal systems.[27] In fact, English law and New York law are the legal systems most often chosen to govern Islamic financial transactions for the reason that they comprise systems of well-developed jurisprudence, objectivity and a history of upholding parties' contractual interests.

Furthermore, Islamic financial transactions, which entail legal structures that differ from conventional transactions, in practice almost always depend upon secular municipal legal systems for their facilitation.[28] This requirement has led interested states to undertake legislative and regulatory reforms so as to integrate the industry into their municipal legal frameworks. Indeed, most states have chosen the path of integration, while a select few have created dual or industry-specific financial systems (Malaysia, Bahrain and Brunei). Others have attempted to completely transform their financial systems into Islamic ones (Iran, Pakistan and the Sudan).

In every mode of facilitation mentioned above the modern state's authority to determine the law has significantly changed the Islamic legal substance of transactions given effect in municipal legal jurisdictions. This may be partly attributable to the effects of codifying Islamic law, which many learned scholars have long considered as distorting.[29] The much more important aspect of this change, however, involves the simple fact that Islamic law, in particular rules concerning commerce, has not been a functioning legal system for over 150 years. The reintroduction of Islamic law in a highly globalised world economy is thus not only revolutionary but subject to a whole host of structural forces that have

[26] *Ibid.*

[27] See *National Group for Communications and Computers* v. *Lucent Technologies Intl.*, No. 00-86 (JLL), 2004 WL 1825228 (D.N.J. Mar. 21, 2004) in which a US District Court applied the Saudi version of the sharia, which led to a disadvantageous commercial outcome.

[28] A municipal legal system is the law of a jurisdiction or area in which a legal system is operative, e.g. England and Wales, France and New York state. Terms such as 'national law' are defective, as they do not take account of the fact that many nation states such as the United Kingdom and the United States are divided into various jurisdictions.

[29] See, for example, Joseph Schacht (n 4).

no classical example and now determine both the substance and letter of the law. The globalisation of commercial law indicates that the analysis of Islamic law in modern financial markets cannot be reduced to the study of the jurists' law or the discourse among Islamic jurists (*fuquhā'*). To do so would deprive the analysis of the most important factors relating to causation and effect. An analysis rooted in the objective examination of context must approach the law of Islamic finance (IFL), as well as other non-national normative systems, as the product of the global context in which it is conceived and practised. This includes its formulation and implementation by investment banks, accountancy firms, multinational law firms, sharia consultancies, nation states, regulatory authorities, international Islamic non-governmental organisations (IINGOs) and other market practitioners.[30]

1.2 The globalisation of commercial law

Three principal characteristics of modernity exert significant influence over traditional societies. Taken together, these characteristics have a major impact on the nature and design of global commercial law, including the modern variant known as Islamic financial law. First, modernity has set in motion an unprecedented pace of social change, which has rapidly increased with the development of new technologies. Second, the global scope of this change is unparalleled as it draws the most far-flung areas of the world together in hitherto unimaginable ways. Third, aspects of this change have generated wholly novel institutions such as the nation state, the corporation, and the specialisation of production and knowledge.[31]

Globalisation as a broader concept embodies these aspects of modernity, but evidences an unprecedented shrinking of time and space, which modern technologies continue to make possible with increasing speed. This means that social activity can be dis-embedded from particular contexts and times, so that 'manifold possibilities of change' arise in contexts where customary usages and local habits have been relatively closed-off from outside influences.[32] Technologies minimise distances and allow

[30] Kilian Bälz, 'Sharia Risk? How Islamic Finance Has Transformed Islamic Contract Law' (Occasional Publications no. 9, Islamic Legal Studies Program, Harvard Law School, September 2008) 3, www.law.harvard.edu/programs/ilsp/publications/balz.pdf. Accessed 25 March 2014.

[31] Anthony Giddens, *The Consequences of Modernity* (Stanford: Polity Press, 1990), 6.

[32] *Ibid.*, 20.

instantaneous communication with people around the world.[33] And yet the concept of globalisation is more systematic, comprehensive and methodologically useful than the mere notion that the world is becoming more interconnected.[34]

One of the most important ways in which globalisation has made itself felt is in the activities of transnational corporations and other transnational actors.[35] Transnational actors' dealings beyond the borders of the nation state have provoked a lively debate concerning the sovereign authority of the nation state in the globalised economy. It is argued that the global reach of economic activity including regional and global systems of trade has undermined the state's authority, which is socially and territorially delimited.[36] But, in fact, the state is one of the most crucial actors in the global economy. So as to secure and maintain sovereign power, states actively participate in the implementation of the global economy and in doing so have undergone considerable transformations. These transformations take place in the negotiations between states, transnational corporations and foreign investors in which states accommodate the interests of these actors. The promulgation of law and regulations, and the enforcement of foreign judgments and arbitral awards are the means by which municipal legal systems accommodate the needs of global capital within their national territories.[37]

The nature of the globalised economy should prompt legal scholars to reconceptualise the role of the nation state in promulgating legal norms, from viewing modern societies and legal systems as relatively closed-off, impervious entities that can be adequately studied in isolation to understanding a wide range of 'legalities' that affect societies' relations

[33] Robert O'Brien and Marc Williams, *Global Political Economy* (3rd edn, Basingstoke: Palgrave MacMillan, 2010), 425.

[34] I disagree that globalisation cannot be used as an analytically useful concept. However, the concept should not replace searching analysis of the structures of global integration. For a counterargument see Frederick Cooper, 'What Is the Concept of Globalization Good For? An African Historian's Perspective' (2001) 100 *Afr.Aff.*, 189.

[35] Silvia Fazio, *The Harmonization of International Commercial Law* (Alphen aan den Rhine: Kluwer Law International, 2007), 2.

[36] There is a large and growing body of literature on this subject. See Saskia Sassen, *Globalization and Its Discontents* (New York: New Press, 1998), xxvii; and Susan Strange, *The Retreat of the State: The Diffusion of Power in the World Economy* (Cambridge University Press, 1996), 4. For a good overview of the debate see Stephen Gill and David Law, 'Global Hegemony and the Structural Power of Capital' in Stephen Gill (ed.) *Gramsci: Historical Materialism and International Relations* (Cambridge University Press, 1993), 279–80.

[37] Saskia Sassen, *A Sociology of Globalization* (New York: W.W. Norton & Co, 2007), 51.

both internally and externally.[38] If one takes stock of the legal reality of daily life, then the impact of a wide range of normative influences on our internal legal relations becomes apparent. Consider, for example, the impact of European Union law, the European Court of Human Rights, transnational religious law (e.g. sharia) or international standards such as the Basel capital adequacy requirements (CARs).[39]

Another aspect of the globalised legal environment is the proliferation of official and unofficial legal orders in any given polity. Known theoretically as legal pluralism, the concept describes a situation in which two or more bodies of law coexist in the same social field.[40] The concept originated from studies of hybrid legal systems created by European colonisation as discussed above. European countries superimposed their state-based law on native legal systems, resulting in a situation in which different bodies of law were available for different population groups.[41]

From the 1970s, the concept has been used to analyse non-colonised industrial states. In this context it is used to examine relations between dominant and subordinate groups, such as ethnic, cultural and religious minorities, as well as unofficial normative orders[42] in institutional and social networks.[43] Contemporary views of legal pluralism see the interaction of highly complex normative orders in virtually every society and social field. As a result, the focus of scholars of legal pluralism has shifted from the effect that law had on society, and vice versa, towards the interaction of highly complex official and unofficial normative orders in the same social field.[44]

Importantly, the interaction of social fields, which comprise the analytical object of all legal systems, introduces the powerful insight that the 'semiautonomous social field is one that can generate rules and customs and symbols internally, but that ... is also vulnerable to rules and

[38] William Twining, *Globalisation and Legal Theory* (London: Butterworths, 2000), 51. See also Boaventurade Sousa Santos, *Toward a New Common Sense* (New York: Routledge, 1995), 385.

[39] William Twining (n 38) 51.

[40] Gordon R. Woodman (n 6) 10.

[41] Sally Engle Merry, 'Legal Pluralism' (1998) 22 *Law.Soc.Rev.*, 869, 870.

[42] The boundary between normative orders that can and cannot be called law has not been decided and will not be attempted in this book. The problem persists because of the great diversity amongst normative orders and the particular social fields in which they are present. The normative orderings examined in this book are relatively uncontroversial in that Islamic law is generally accepted as 'law', and other legal systems are either state-based or globally accepted as normative standards, i.e. Basel CARs.

[43] Sally Engle Merry (n 41) 872.

[44] *Ibid.*, 873.

decisions, and other forces emanating from the larger world by which it is surrounded'.[45] Social fields such as a country's political system, economy, culture and traditions, are not confined by impermeable boundaries. Local, national and global normative orders interact with each other simultaneously. Cultures or social orders are never impervious or sealed off from outside forces. They are dynamically evolving sub-systems which interact with other referents in highly complex and heterogeneous ways;[46] and which may come to mimic, resemble or define themselves in opposition to each other.

Global legal pluralism is not merely a legal or even a political phenomenon. It results from the collision between all spheres and practices of our global society. These collisions originate in the contradictions between 'society-wide institutionalised rationalities',[47] which are both structural and ideological.[48] Legal pluralists view the resulting fragmentation of global law as giving rise to innumerable heterogeneous legal orders, a so-called 'poly-contextualisation of the law'.[49] Arguably, this view overemphasises growing diversity in global law by underestimating the role of power dynamics and the ways in which leading states exercise regulatory power. Structure and mechanisms of power can be understood as denoting a relationship between agents in which modes of action act indirectly upon others and their actions in an ongoing process.[50]

The structure and regulation of the global economy is powered by the most dominant region in the world, namely the North Atlantic region comprising the United States, the European Union and Canada.[51] The economy of the North Atlantic region is the largest and wealthiest market in the world, accounting for more than 50 per cent of world Gross

[45] *Ibid.*, 878. The concept of semi-autonomous spaces was first conceived by Sally Falk Moore, *Law as Process* (London: Routledge & Kegan Paul, 1978).

[46] William Twining (n 38) 85. See also Boaventura de Sousa Santos (n 38) 270.

[47] Andreas Fischer-Lescano and Gunther Teubner, 'Regime-Collisions: The Vain Search for Legal Unity in the Fragmentation of Global Law' (2004) 25 *Mich.J.Int'l L.*, 1004.

[48] Terence C. Halliday and Bruce G. Carruthers, 'The Recursivity of Law: Global Norm Making and National Law-making in the Globalization of Corporate Insolvency Regimes' (2007) 112 *Am.J.Soc.*, 1189.

[49] Andreas Fischer-Lescano and Gunther Teubner (n 47) 1007–8.

[50] For an in-depth examination of power see Michel Foucault, 'The Subject and Power' (1982) 8 *Crit. Inq.* 777.

[51] Globalisation is also attributed to the early expansion of European states across the globe including early European settlement and colonisation patterns. See Katherine Lynch, *The Forces of Economic Globalization: Challenges to the Regime of International Commercial Arbitration* (The Hague: Kluwer Law International, 2003), 40.

Domestic Product (GDP).[52] This region dominates the single most important force powering the globalisation of the economy: foreign direct investment (FDI) in the form of global capital markets and cross-border mergers and acquisitions. The region accounts for 57 per cent of the inward stock of FDI and a staggering 71 per cent of the outward stock of FDI. Importantly, countries comprising the region have invested a great portion of that stock in each other's economies.[53] With some exceptions for the volume of capital resources available to Japan and China's holdings of US dollars, the North Atlantic region vastly outweighs other major regions in these economic processes.[54]

North Atlantic economic predominance has created strong global forces for legal harmonisation in financial markets, which mirrors the financial standards and best practices developed in the leading financial centres (New York and London). In the area of financial services law, North Atlantic economic predominance delimits legal diversity to the neoliberal market paradigm.[55] However, the harmonisation of legal standards and best practices is more than just a functional requirement of capitalism. Market actors and government authorities assign qualitative meanings to economic processes (regulation, taxation, social welfare systems) and states' adoption of particular neoliberal policy measures is affected by this subjectivity. The range of financial market activities examined in this book underscores a diverse set of qualitative policy responses to the global capital of Islamic finance. Such responses, however, originate from within the neoliberal economic paradigm, which circumscribes the choices available to market actors.

A legal pluralistic perspective of global law differs from traditional comparative law in the sense that it is not concerned with locating the functional equivalent of different legal orders, despite vast differences in

[52] Daniel S. Hamilton and Joseph P. Quinlan, *The Transatlantic Economy 2013*, vol I (Washington, DC: Paul H. Nitze School of Advanced International Studies, 2013) v.

[53] *Ibid.*

[54] Saskia Sassen (n 36) 60.

[55] Neoliberal theory is a strongly law-centred economic paradigm in which an identifiable set of laws, regulations, best practices and institutions are thought to constitute an optimal strategy for economic development and prosperity. The implementation of these laws, best practices and institutional reform strategies are designed to enable private entrepreneurial activity and investment, the engine of economic growth. State intervention must be highly circumscribed if growth is not to be impeded. See Kerry Rittich, *Recharacterizing Restructuring: Law, Distribution and Gender in Market Reform* (The Hague: Kluwer Law International, 2002) 30. Chapter 4 deals with the nature of the neoliberal global economy in greater detail.

social, economic or political conditions.[56] Rather, the study of global law highlights the normative appearance of legal systems by focusing analysis on the process in which global law is generated. Therefore, the methodology of global law places less emphasis on locating legal structure and hierarchy,[57] since they are in constant flux in a globalising world. Viewing the law in this fashion enables the scholar to perceive the modes of connection between 'multiple networks of legal orders',[58] which intersect in dynamic, unstable and generative ways.

These types of 'inter-legalities' can be relatively autonomous from the political principle of territoriality,[59] a quality that may be amenable to the non-national requirements of IFL. The new *lex mercatoria* is an example often used to argue that an emerging global legal order has arisen via a self-generating legal process, which does not depend on the authority of state-based legislative mechanisms for the enforcement of contracts.[60] It is said to be spontaneously created in global commercial practices, 'unitary directives, standardised contracts, activities of global economic associations, codes of conduct and the awards of international arbitration courts'.[61] Indeed, a large number of quasi-independent, sectorally specialised legal authorities can be easily identified. Among many others, these include the International Court of Justice, the European Court of Human Rights, the European Court of Justice, various international criminal courts, trade and investment judicial bodies and convention-derived bodies.[62] International Islamic financial standard-setting and regulatory institutions such as the Accounting and Auditing Organization for Islamic Financial Institutions (AAOIFI) and the Islamic Financial Services Board (IFSB) are examples of non-national standard-setting institutions.

[56] Kilian Bälz (n 30) 6.

[57] Andreas Fischer-Lescano and Gunther Teubner (n 47) 1007–8.

[58] Boaventura de Sousa Santos, 'Law: A Map of Misreading. Toward a Postmodern Conception of Law' (1987) 14 *J.L.& Soc.*, 279, 298.

[59] Andreas Fischer-Lescano and Gunther Teubner (n 47) 1009.

[60] Gunther Teubner, '"Global Bukowina": Legal Pluralism in the World Society' in Gunther Teubner (ed.), *Global Law Without A State* (Aldershot: Dartmouth Publishing Company, 1997), 4. The new *lex mercatoria* represents a modern version of medieval *lex mercatoria* or merchant law, which is to have been a relatively uniform and autonomous legal system used by merchants at fairs such as those of St. Ives. However, most legal historians now agree that merchant law never solely relied on arbitration and ad hoc private tribunals. Instead, merchants availed themselves of a mixture of the law of the state, merchants' customs and private dispute resolution mechanisms.

[61] *Ibid.*, 9.

[62] Andreas Fischer-Lescano and Gunther Teubner (n 47) 1000–1.

The findings of this book indicate an even more complex picture. Global law results not from a wholly autonomous non-national law-making process, but from a complicated interaction between state-based and non-national norm-making processes.[63] This conceptual recalibration transgresses the artificial division between state and non-state legal systems,[64] and highlights the complex ways in which legal variants of global commercial law such as IFL are created and continuously adapted. The porosity of semi-autonomous social systems in a globalising world does not enable social systems, no matter their type or size, to operate as closed-off silos.[65] Empirical evidence indicates that purely private legal systems in fact are rare. Particularly in global commerce, a highly complex cocktail of pragmatic solutions emerges in which all types of governance mechanisms are invoked.[66]

Such processes generate legal properties both similar and different from those associated with legislatures. An example concerns the quasi-legislative UNIDROIT (International Institute for the Unification of Private Law) principles,[67] which are considered to be a codified version of the *lex mercatoria*. Another involves sharia standards issued by AAOIFI, one of Islamic finance's most respected global standard-setting bodies. AAOIFI standards evince properties very similar to codified legal systems, which is unlike the traditional expression of law as found in the books of *fiqh*. Some aspects of law-making processes do not resemble positive legal systems, whose norm creation is legitimised by institutional authority and legal hierarchies. Consider, for example, the law-making processes of sharia scholars or the drafting of private contracts by international lawyers, most of which never require state intervention. In sum, our understanding of the way in which global commercial law is formulated is advanced

[63] Gralf-Peter Calliess and Peer Zumbansen, *Rough Consensus and Running Code: A Theory of Transnational Private Law* (Oxford: Hart Publishing, 2010), 110.

[64] The most persuasive account of this perspective is by Ralf Michaels, 'The True Lex Mercatoria: Private Law Beyond the State' (2007) 14 *Ind.J.Global Legal Studies*, 447.

[65] An example of a contrary methodology is presented by Gunther Teubner, *Law as an Autopoietic System* (Oxford: Blackwell Publishers, 1993). See also Niklas Luhmann, *Soziologische Aufklaerung: Aufsaetze Zur Theorie Sozialer Systeme* (Koeln und Opladen: Westdeutscher Verlag GmbH, 1970).

[66] Gralf-Peter Calliess and Peer Zumbansen (n 63) 120.

[67] UNIDROIT, '*UNIDROIT Principles of International Commercial Contracts 2010*' (International Institute for the Unification of Private Law, Rome 2010), www.unidroit.org/english/principles/contracts/principles2010/blackletter2010-english.pdf Accessed 26 March 2014. UNIDROIT is a non-governmental organisation dedicated to harmonising international private law.

by critically assessing the processes that give rise to legal systems and continue to transform them.

1.3 The role of context in the analysis of IFL

This book examines the creation of IFL in modern financial markets. It is concerned with the context and process in which sharia principles are articulated and applied in municipal legal systems and the ways in which they are transformed in modern financial markets. Literally translated, the sharia is the road to the watering place, the clear path to God.[68] It originates from the primary source of Islamic law, the Quran, which, according to Muslims, is the word of God, revealed by the Prophet Muhammad; and the second revealed source of law, the Sunna, which are the sayings and doings of the Prophet Muhammad. The sharia sets forth numerous comprehensive social obligations and ideals in all facets of life, which, at its greatest extent, encompasses a 'totality of life-ways'[69] among Muslims everywhere, and practical consequences and ultimate sanctions attached to these.[70] *Fiqh* literally means 'understanding'. *Fiqh* represents Islamic jurists' interpretation of the holy sources of Islamic law. It was implemented in Muslim territories as the positive law, as the sources themselves were insufficient to govern Muslim polities (*ummah*). In practice, the *fiqh* is often included under the umbrella term of Islamic law and this practice will be followed in this book. The sharia encompasses Islamic commercial law, although classical jurists did not distinguish between commercial and other types of law.

The sharia is a jurists' law or a law developed by jurists in the early centuries of Islam. Traditional Islamic legal discourse is heavily focused on jurists' application of a rigorous legal methodology (*uṣūl al-fiqh*) and derived principles and rules (*fiqh*) to solve legal problems. By contrast, the modern variant of Islamic commercial law, IFL, is a product of global financial markets, in which jurists' role in developing it is marginal. IFL, in contrast to traditional approaches to the sharia, cannot be reduced to juristic discourse, in which the classical sharia is the point of reference, without missing the factors and processes which underlie the creation and transformation of the law.

68 William Ballantyne, *Essays and Addresses on Arab Laws* (Richmond, VA: Curzon, 2000), 33.

69 M. G. S. Hodgson, *The Venture of Islam*, vol I. (The University of Chicago Press, 1961), 75.

70 *Ibid.*, 74.

Undoubtedly, the modern resurgence of Islamic principles in commerce and trade underscores the unyielding importance with which Muslims regard the sharia. The application of sharia principles in markets otherwise known for their uniformity illustrates an effort to develop cultural diversity in global commerce that challenges our understanding both of Islamic law and the global commercial environment.

On a global level, Islamic finance has thrived in secular jurisdictions where law and religion are mostly separate such as Dubai, London and Kuala Lumpur. Religion-based jurisdictions have had less success in developing Islamic finance (such as Pakistan, Sudan and Iran).[71] Part of the reason for this discrepancy may lie in the simple fact that a secular legal environment makes Islamic financial products attractive as alternative products whereas a sharia-based legal system would be expected to offer such products by default. Another reason is that relatively liberal and legally certain regulatory frameworks have been more attractive to international investors, whereas jurisdictions in which Islamic legal rules are sometimes enforced in the area of commercial law (Saudia Arabia, Pakistan and Sudan) are considered less so.[72] Such jurisdictions have resisted economic globalisation, have not sought to develop regional financial centres (Saudi Arabia changed tack and is now the largest financial centre in the Gulf) and have been somewhat reticent to adopt the regulatory standards and best practices that structure the global economy.

Another observation of the developing system of law concerns the industry's heavy reliance on English common law.[73] Due to the colonial

[71] Kilian Bälz (n 30) 7. Saudi Arabia is something of an exception as it has been reticent to develop Islamic finance for fear of acknowledging that other financial institutions are not Islamic. It, nonetheless, claims to have the largest assets by volume in the world.

[72] *Ibid.*, 10.

[73] English Law is the law of England and Wales. England and Wales, Northern Ireland and Scotland are the three legal jurisdictions that comprise the United Kingdom. Each jurisdiction has a separate judiciary and contains bodies of substantive and procedural law that are applicable only to that jurisdiction. Common law is the basis of the English and Welsh legal system. Wales, Northern Ireland and Scotland have developed constitutional codes for regional governance in the form of devolution statutes. These statutes are: the Northern Ireland Act 1998; the Government of Wales Act 2006; and the Scotland Act 1998. As a result, these three countries have developed distinct legislative and executive institutions that are separate from the central government of the United Kingdom. England has no 'English Parliament' or 'English government' that can be distinguished from the United Kingdom as a whole. The UK Parliament, as the supreme legislative body of the United Kingdom, is the sole body with power to enact statutes for England and/or Wales.

legacy of the British Empire, the United Kingdom's continuing role as one of the world's leading economies, and the tried and tested characteristics of the English common law system as described above, the predominance of English law, English law firms, and even English judges, in the financial centres of the Gulf Cooperation Council (GCC) states is unmistakeable. These actors create transnational networks that allow the flow of ideas, skills and expertise to the municipal legal systems of these states. The networks they create are not necessarily cosmopolitan, however, in that these actors often remain embedded in the localised environments from which they originate.[74] These networks nonetheless represent the vanguard of Western-led globalisation by disseminating English financial and legal expertise (US and increasingly EU standards also predominate) to the municipal legal systems of these states. These financial and legal interactions constitute a type of global frontier in which carriers of economic globalisation interact with national economies, altering institutional structures and producing entirely new ones.[75]

Not only are most Islamic financial transactions governed by English common law, the new and rapidly emerging financial centres of Arab Gulf states including the Bahrain Financial Harbour (BFH), the Dubai International Financial Centre (DIFC), and the Qatar Financial Centre (QFC) were established as offshore, mostly English common-law based jurisdictions.[76] Market liberalisation has allowed a large increase in the number of cities eager to join the financial club. These financial centres operate as gateways to increased flows of international capital and sites of operation to international law firms and transnational financial and accounting corporations.[77] The interactions between these firms and states' municipal legal systems spurn the globalisation of these states' national economies. For example, in the last decade many GCC states have modernised their financial centres so as to accommodate these firms. Modernisation measures include the abolition of rigid currency controls, the privatisation of assets, new laws permitting foreign ownership and a concerted drive to harmonise municipal law with international standards. Paradoxically, these same firms have taken an active role in these

[74] Saskia Sassen (n 37) 74. [75] *Ibid.*

[76] Dubai International Financial Centre, 'Laws and Regulations', www.difc.ae/laws-regulations. Accessed 26 March 2014. Qatar Financial Centre Authority, 'Why QFC' (QFCA, 1 July 2013), www.qfc.com.qa/en-US/About-qfc/Why_QFC.aspx. Accessed 26 March 2014.

[77] Saskia Sassen, 'Global Financial Centers' (1999) 78 *Foreign Affairs* 75, 75–6.

modernisation efforts as their skills, knowledge and experience have been crucial to the enterprise.

Most major transnational professional services firms have established affiliates or other types of collaborative arrangements with local firms in the new financial centres of the Middle East, including some of the most prominent law firms, investment banks, accountancies and business consultancies.[78] These linkages correspond to a global trend in which a sharp increase in the demand for professional services has coincided with a slowdown in manufacturing.[79] The ascendance of professional services, especially financial services, has led to a restructuring of the global economy in which finance towers above all other sectors of the economy. The superprofits of the financial sector have had the effect of devaluing manufacturing because manufacturing does not generate the same level of profit.[80]

The North Atlantic region is by far the largest provider of services in the world across a wide range of professional services. For example, in 2010 the North Atlantic provided 83.5 per cent of all financial services exports; 72.1 per cent of all communication services exports; and 63.2 per cent of all computer and information service exports.[81] In particular, New York and London lead the world in producing and exporting legal, financial, accounting, advertising, management consulting and other business services.[82] The affiliates, subsidiaries and other business linkages providing these services operate according to western standards and practices, and these are imposed on transactions involving firms from other parts of the world.[83] As a result, the Arab Gulf states have developed an increasingly westernised business and legal environment which has been conducive to the growth and development of Islamic finance.[84]

States are repositioning their agendas and policy prescriptions towards a new non-national normativity in which the *raison d'état* is not always the master normativity. Economic globalisation encourages privatisation of the public realm and a denationalisation of what were once national institutions and policy prerogatives. A reformulation of the role of the nation state is intimately connected to the powerful dynamics of global capital and capital markets.[85] For instance, non-national Islamic organisations

[78] Saskia Sassen (n 36) 174–5.
[79] Saskia Sassen, *Cities in a World Economy* (Thousand Oaks, CA: Pine Forge Press 2006), 84.
[80] *Ibid.*, 82. [81] Daniel S. Hamilton and Joseph P. Quinlan (n 52) x.
[82] Saskia Sassen (n 79) 86–93. [83] *Ibid.*, 69.
[84] Kilian Bälz (n 30) 11. [85] Saskia Sassen (n 36) 39–40.

such as AAOIFI and the IFSB have assumed policy work that states have assumed in the past. And the growth of international arbitration largely excludes the jurisdiction of states' municipal legal systems in the regulation of private law affairs. It offers parties the choice of non-state legal systems to govern arbitrations. The liberalisation of the nation state and contemporary patterns of de-territorialisation are intimately connected with the development and function of IFL.

The first case study of this book examines the United Kingdom. The United Kingdom is a catalyst of economic globalisation (it hosts the City of London, the largest international financial centre), English law has outsized weight in international commerce and finance and as a result, the United Kingdom is a pioneer in its facilitation of Islamic finance. It is the ninth largest market for Islamic banking and financial assets and plays an even larger role in terms of commodity *murābaḥah* or *tawarruq*,[86] used for interbank lending and financing. Other systems under study include Bahrain, the UAE and the DIFC. These municipal systems have developed regional financial centres, which operate as gateways for global capital. This is easily established by the fact that two of the three municipal systems have developed offshore financial centres (Bahrain and the DIFC).[87] The municipal legal systems of these polities facilitate, regulate and adjudicate Islamic finance in different ways. Their experiences with Islamic finance provide convincing evidence that IFL is developed beyond, between and within states' regulatory systems. The legal and economic substance of the particular type of IFL that emerges reflects the neoliberal economic paradigm in which the global economy operates.

1.4 Structure

Apart from this chapter the book consists of nine chapters and a conclusion. The analysis of IFL is conceptually organised according to some of

[86] *Tawarruq* is a product comprising a series of sale transactions, transacted individually, which together generate inter-bank and other types of financing.

[87] Offshore financial centres are designed to attract FDI by eliminating taxes and burdensome regulation and by providing banking secrecy and anonymity. This may include no capital tax, no withholding tax on dividends or interest, no corporation tax, no capital gains tax, no tax on transfers, no exchange controls, less stringent reporting requirements and trading restrictions, and a light-touch regulation and supervisory approach. See International Monetary Fund, 'Offshore Financial Centers' (IMF Background Paper, Monetary and Exchange Affairs Dept, 2000).

the economic and legal processes that contribute to the transformation of sharia in modern financial markets.[88]

Chapter 2 demonstrates that modern Islamic financial jurisprudence derives some of its pragmatism and flexibility from the broad range of legal tools used to adapt and extend the sharia. The chapter introduces the sharia, its sources, its legal theory and the role of *ijtihād* (independent reasoning) in solving new legal problems. It situates the development of these legal principles within the historical context with a view to understanding the way in which jurists developed and applied Islamic law in practice. It contains a discussion of custom as an unofficial source of law and the important role of rationalising legal tools and legal stratagems (*ḥiyal*) in finding solutions to legal challenges in traditional economies. On the basis of Ottoman court records the chapter investigates the way in which these diverse legal sources and tools were harnessed in classical sharia legal systems. Moreover, records from the Cairo Geniza provide some general indications as to how such tools enabled traders and merchants to meet commercial requirements.

Chapter 3 tries to come to grips with the general nature of classical Islamic commercial law (*fiqh*), which is markedly different from commercial notions of western secular law. In particular, the chapter examines the system of Islamic nominate contracts and the prohibitions of *gharar* (uncertainty) and *ribā* (interest). Despite most modern scholars' claims to the contrary, classical sharia restricts considerably parties' freedom to contract, particularly as understood from the concept's western origins. Moreover, the Islamic law of contract does not comprise a general theory of contract, since the notion of will theory is largely absent from theoretical conceptions about the formation of contract. However, jurists made many exceptions to the classical system, and in practice, these, combined with the use of various legal tools, enabled merchants and traders to meet parties' commercial requirements in a sharia-appropriate manner.

Chapter 4 examines the dynamics and normative underpinnings of economic globalisation and Islamic finance's position in the global economy. The chapter deals with a range of transnational actors and market-driven processes involved in the legal transformation of sharia. Transnational financial corporations are most active in deploying considerable resources to develop IFL. These commercial drivers of the Islamic finance industry

[88] Nicholas H. D. Foster, 'Islamic Finance Law as an Emergent Legal System' (2007) 21 *ALQ* 170. Foster's scholarship provided the first conceptualisation of IFL as an emerging legal system.

exert powerful influence on the way in which sharia principles are conceptualised, innovated and applied. Islamic international standard setters play a role in relation to the commercial, transnational pull of the industry that states are unable to do. Some of their most important activities concern the standardisation of IFL and the development of cross-border regulatory standards. Western-trained lawyers play an often overlooked role in this transformational project. For instance, they develop and apply standard terms and conditions to Islamic contracts, infusing them with English-style cross-border uniformity. This type and nature of interaction between commercial objectives and religio-ethical principles is a particular focus. Many writers represent sharia scholars, in their capacity as sharia supervisory board members, as among the most important organs in developing the legal and substantive aspects of IFL. The jurisprudential strategy of sharia scholars is analysed with a view to gaining a better understanding of their input in the transformational process.

Legal transformation of the sharia is controversial since it challenges traditional discourses concerning the nature of the law and poses religious and ethical questions that may rattle the markets. An analysis of an Islamic derivative structure developed by Deutsche Bank underscores the transformational input of a wide range of mostly non-national practitioners.

Chapter 5 examines the legislative and regulatory approach of the United Kingdom towards Islamic finance. It is concerned with the ways in which English law acts as a carrier system for IFL and with the nature of this legal interaction. The chapter deals with the particular type of legislative accommodation given to IFL in the United Kingdom. In particular, legislative measures for facilitating commercial *sukuk* (Islamic bonds) in UK wholesale markets are examined.

Chapter 6 analyses the regulatory approach taken by the now disbanded Financial Services Authority (FSA) to Islamic financial institutions (IFIs). In April 2013 the FSA was split into the Prudential Regulation Authority (PRA) and the Financial Conduct Authority (FCA). The chapter examines multiple tiers of regulatory requirements imposed on all UK financial institutions, with little, if any, distinction made for the differences of conventional and Islamic institutions. These include municipal laws (English law), UK financial services law, European Union directives and global banking standards (Basel). The regulatory authority's treatment of Sharia Supervisory Boards (SSBs) is also examined, preceded by an analysis of an SSB's function, process and risks. An examination of the adjudication of Islamic financial transactions in English courts rounds up the analysis by demonstrating the role that English courts have played in resolving sharia-based transactions.

Bahrain's offshore financial services framework was designed to function as a regional gateway for the region's oil surpluses in the mid-1970s. The country's pioneering approach to Islamic finance is also structured to appeal to international investors. Bahrain has circumscribed the sharia to a few specific non-commercial areas of law, and unusual among jurisdictions, has developed an industry-specific regulatory framework for Islamic finance. The presence of numerous IINGOs in the country adds depth, expertise and commercial pull to Bahrain's Islamic financial centre. Chapter 7 examines Bahrain's regulation of Islamic finance. It highlights a number of critical regulatory processes in relation to Islamic finance in which legal inputs from a range of legal and other non-national normative systems are nationalised in Bahraini financial services law.

The UAE has become the regional leader in the provision of financial services in the Gulf region. The country has gone to great efforts to attract FDI, despite the challenges its opaque and conflicting legal system poses for international investors. Its ambition to become the global centre of an Islamic economy outpaces its development of a transparent and legally certain regulatory framework. As such, the country provides an interesting example of a country, which has retained much of its post-colonial hybrid legal system, while also taking gradual steps to become a modern, transparent and competitive financial services centre in the neoliberal global economy. As with other case studies, Chapter 8 is concerned with understanding the ways in which its legal and regulatory structures affect the central bank's regulation of IFIs.

The Dubai International Financial Centre is the focus of Chapter 9. It is a financial free zone located in the Emirate of Dubai, which largely conducts wholesale business with institutional clients and high net-worth investors. Created from scratch to attract global capital, its legal and regulatory systems comprise English common law, international standards and best practices. As such, the DIFC epitomises the legal and regulatory trends of the global economy. The chapter examines the DIFC's approach to the regulation of Islamic finance and places particular focus on understanding the ways in which its neoliberal legal and regulatory systems interact with Islamic finance.

Chapter 10 examines an alternative method of contract enforcement known as arbitration, which Western states developed as a means of safeguarding FDI in developing countries with weak legal systems. Arbitration, among other advantages, allows parties to choose whatever law they wish to govern an arbitral dispute. It paves the way for Islamic financial transactions to be enforced according to sharia or any other normative system agreeable to the parties. The Middle East has had a complex and sometimes troubled relationship with modern arbitration practices: culturally; in relation to the sharia; and with regard to historic arbitrations involving Middle Eastern states. The chapter examines this relationship and lays emphasis on understanding the ways in which the courts of the municipal legal systems under study in this book approach contemporary arbitration, and, in particular, the enforcement of foreign arbitral awards.

Chapter 11 draws some general principles from the findings of the chapters. In general, these concern the trends of legal and regulatory development in the neoliberal, globalised economy and its implications for developing alternative financial or development models. The role and meaning of context in understanding legal systems is examined in relation to IFL and the sharia authenticity problem.

1.5 Technical matters

Dates used throughout the book correspond with the Gregorian calendar, although effort has been given to providing the Islamic calendar, where appropriate.

Arabic words will be used as noted in the foreword to the Arabic–English glossary at the front of this book.

2

The sharia: sources, legal theory and unofficial sources of law

Unlike modern legal systems the sharia is rooted in religious sources that imbue the law with a religious and ethical spirit, and which continue to shape it as it develops over time. Yet various legal tools enable the law to be developed according to its underlying principles. The balance between these two modes of legal development is a topic of lasting importance to the viability and religious authenticity of the sharia.

This chapter contains a discussion of the sharia, its sources and legal theory, the role of custom, 'rationalising legal principles' and legal stratagems known as *ḥiyal*. It also examines the historical development of the four formal sources of the sharia according to Sunni Islam and its legal theory.

The analysis of Islamic legal literature is not sufficient to determine the way in which the law was applied, which sometimes can be different from its written form. An understanding of the applied law is critical since it reveals the ways in which context and time alter the law. Unfortunately, very few court records, which would illustrate the application of the law, have been found or have survived the ravages of the centuries. Ottoman court records known as *sijill* are, in fact, the only 'found' court records from the pre-modern Islamic era. The *sijill* provide fascinating insights into the application of the sharia and the larger legal culture in which the sharia was predominant.

2.1 The formal sources of Islamic law

Four formal 'sources' underlie the body of Islamic jurisprudence. These include the Holy Quran and the Sunna, which constitute the wellspring of Islamic jurisprudence. The third and fourth sources are *ijmāʿ* (scholarly consensus) and *qiyās* (analogical reasoning) which jurists used to develop the nascent law. *Qiyās* will be addressed first in order to emphasise its importance in developing the law.

The Quran is the first and most sacred source of legal and moral guidance to the Muslim faithful. It contains revelations to the Prophet Muhammad, believed to have emanated directly from God. These were embodied in permanent written form in the Quran shortly after the death of Muhammad in 632 CE. The Quran is concerned with a broad range of circumstances in the believer's life, which extend from matters of prayer, ritual and belief to the family, transactions and commerce, criminal acts and much more. Unlike secular legal systems the Quran does not differentiate between law and morality but sees the two as inextricably linked; in fact, one cannot possibly exist without the other.[1]

It is generally accepted that Islamic law, envisioned as a system of rules and standards that impose order and sanction malfeasance, existed outside the sphere of religion, even during the Prophet's lifetime. As far as there were no religious or moral objections to specific transactions or modes of behaviour, Muslims remained largely indifferent to the more technical aspects of the law.[2] Muhammad may have only realised in the fifth year of the *Hijra* – after the migration to Medina – that his revelations also contained legal matter of significant import for the community.[3] Indeed, it is generally agreed that the Quran itself contains relatively few technical legal verses that Muslim jurists were able to readily apply as the foundation for a growing body of Islamic law.[4] This is particularly the case concerning the Quran's commercial aspects, wherein it is estimated that only seventy to eighty verses involved contracts, trade and other economic matters.[5]

The early jurists of the Umayyad dynasty did not have a polished and ready 'Islamic law' at their disposal from which legal rulings could be taken. Foreign and pre-Islamic Arab customary practices constituted

[1] Gotthelf Bergsträsser, 'Anfänge und Charakter Des Juristischen Denkens Im Islam. Vorläufige Betrachtungen' (1925) 14 *Der Islam*, 76, 78.

[2] Joseph Schacht, 'Pre-Islamic Background and Early Development of Jurisprudence' in Majid Khadduri and Herbert J. Liebesny (eds), *Law in the Middle East* (Washington, DC: The Middle East Institute, 1955), 35. While Schacht argues that law did not exist in the technical meaning of the term, he omits the fact that pre-Islamic customary practices were, in essence, nothing other than law.

[3] S. D. Goitein, 'The Birth-Hour of Muslim Law? An Essay in Exegesis' (1960) 50 *Mus.World*, 23, 27.

[4] Joseph Schacht, 'Fiḳh' in P. Bearman, Th. Bianquis, C. E. Bosworth, E. van Donzel and W. P. Heinrichs (eds.), *Encyclopaedia of Islam* (2nd edn, Brill Online 2014), referenceworks.brillonline.com/entries/encyclopaedia-of-islam-2/fikh-SIM_2364. Accessed 25 April 2014.

[5] Knut S. Vikor, *Between God and the Sultan: An Historical Introduction to Islamic Law* (London: Hurst, 2004), 33.

the raw material of the budding law that the religious specialists and caliphs of Islam shaped according to their discretion (*ra'y*) or sound opinion and with respect to the unique practices or customs of the jurisdiction in which the law was to be applied.[6] In large part, the early law did not derive from the Quran. Apart from areas of family law and inheritance, as well as cult and ritual, the norms taken from the Quran were reintroduced to the law during the second/eighth century.[7]

Early jurists adhered to the ancient Sunna of their ancestors, and later to the 'living tradition' of their respective schools.[8] The Sunna (pl. *sunan*), an ancient Arab concept, describes an exemplary mode of conduct that is meant for others to emulate. Persons renowned for their charisma, rectitude and distinguished status in the pre-Islamic period were seen as the providers of Sunna or normative practices that should be followed.[9] Adherence to traditional Sunna constituted the ethical, social and religious framework around which Arabian life revolved and found its meaning.[10]

Much of the material comprising prophetic Hadith was derived from the ancient Sunna and *ra'y*. Prophetic hadith were endowed with a legitimacy, however, that these sources of law did not possess.[11] In fact, many of the hadiths put into circulation were blatant fabrications. They reflected

[6] The raw material from which Islamic law originated was comprised of a wide range of foreign and pre-Islamic borrowings including Mesopotamia, Judaism, Christianity, and the Hellenistic and Roman civilisations. See Joseph Schacht, 'Foreign Elements in Ancient Islamic Law' (1950) 32 *J.Comp.Leg.*, 9; and Joseph Schacht, 'From Babylonian to Islamic Law' (1994) 1 *Yrbk Islam Mid East L.*, 29. For a critical examination of these influences as well as an assessment of Western-based research on the subject see Patricia Crone, *Roman, Provincial and Islamic Law* (Cambridge University Press, 1987). See also Seymour Vesey-Fitzgerald, 'The Alleged Debt of Islamic to Roman Law' (1951) 67 *L.Q.R.*, 81. For an analysis of common legal institutions, language and stylistic patterns in Middle Eastern legal texts see Chibli Mallat, 'From Islamic to Middle Eastern Law: A Restatement of the Field (Part I)' (2003) 51 *Am.J.Comp.L.* 81, 704.

[7] Joseph Schacht (n 2) 41–2.

[8] *Madhhab* is conventionally translated as school or doctrine. It usually refers to a jurist's opinion concerning a particular case or to the opinion of an entire school. See, in general, Christopher Melchert, 'The Formation of the Sunni Schools of Law' in Wael B. Hallaq (ed.), *The Formation of Islamic Law* (Aldershot: Ashgate, 2004). Sunni Islam is composed of four doctrines or schools of law (pl. *madhāhib*) which bear the name of distinguished jurists associated with them: the Ḥanafī, Mālikī, Shafi'i and Ḥanbalī schools. Other Islamic sects include the Shia, which are predominantly represented in today's Iran and large parts of Iraq. The Shia comprise three schools including the Zaydīs, the Jaafaris (Twelvers) and the Ismā'īlīs.

[9] See Wael B. Hallaq, *Shari'a: Theory, Practice, Transformations* (Cambridge University Press 2009), 443.

[10] Joseph Schacht (n 2) 34–5. [11] Wael B. Hallaq (n 9) 45.

the ideal wishes of the present and were projected back to the Prophet so as to endow them with authority.[12] Jurists faced the difficulty of establishing the connection between a text and the Prophet. The discovery of dubious personages or a defective chain of transmission (*isnād*) rendered hadiths devoid of any legal effect. Furthermore, hadiths were scrutinised for their linguistic traits as well as their chain of transmission before they could be utilised as valid sources of legal reasoning.[13]

The uncertainty surrounding a hadith's origins led jurists to devise the requirement of multiple transmission or recurrence known as the principle of *tawātur*. Islamic theology views the recurrent transmission of texts from multiple sources as a type of knowledge that is immediate, subconscious and innate.[14] On the other hand, texts transmitted via channels fewer than that of *tawātur* are termed *aḥad* (solitary). The vast majority of Hadith belong to this latter category, which Muslim theologians generally view as a source of probable knowledge. The important point is that the large body of Islamic law – which mostly derives from hadith narratives – reflects a *probable* interpretation of God's commands.[15]

The epistemic importance of prophetic hadith, the great authority and legitimacy that such narratives inspired, is probably the reason why the prophetic Sunna gradually eclipsed the authority of ancient Arab practices. Prophetic hadith were endowed with a unique legitimacy that allowed jurists to shed light on what the law was.[16] Jurists eventually came to realise that the prophetic Sunna comprised an important aspect of Quranic hermeneutics; it gave them clues as to the meaning of the Quran with respect to a particular case.[17] It enabled the construction of a body of Islamic law known as *fiqh*.

The great jurist and systematiser of the law, al-Shāfi'ī (d. 204/820), is considered to be the originator of the theory of Sunna – the endowment of Sunnaic authority in the Prophet Muhammad – in classical Islamic law.[18] Al-Shāfi'ī considered *ra'y* to be an arbitrary form of reasoning that threatened to taint the holy texts with human judgment.[19] His unerring insistence upon the sole authority of traditions originating directly from the Prophet, and his dismissal of 'practice' and 'consensus' as embodied

[12] Ignaz Goldziher, 'Muhammedanisches Recht in Theorie und Wirklichkeit' (1888) 8 *Zeit vergl Rechtswiss*, 180.
[13] Wael B. Hallaq (n 9) 92.
[14] *Ibid.*, 93. [15] *Ibid.* [16] *Ibid.*, 41. [17] *Ibid.*, 406, 418.
[18] Joseph Schacht, *The Origins of Muhammadan Jurisprudence* (Oxford: Clarendon Press, 1950), 77.
[19] Wael B. Hallaq (n 9) 51. See also Joseph Schacht (n 18) 20.

in the living Sunna eventually established prophetic hadith as the second exclusive source of law.[20] The authoritative establishment of prophetic hadith allowed religious scholars less freedom to exercise their juridical discretion (*ra'y*). Al-Shāfi'ī had achieved a means of conformity in the law that would help to preserve it from human meddling.[21] The eventual triumph of hadith over *ra'y* towards the middle of the third/ninth century saw the emergence of six 'canonical' hadith collections.

Long before non-textual *ra'y* was outlawed, however, jurists had foreseen the great value of certain types of reasoning that were too important to discard. In a long process that stretched from the middle of the second/eighth century and continued well into the next, the concept of *ra'y* underwent a largely semantic transformation that established several different categories of legal tools that derived from the same principle. These were *qiyās*, *ijtihād* and *istiḥsān*.

Qiyās signified a disciplined form of reasoning that was rooted in the holy texts, i.e. the Quran and Sunna. Its primary typology is analogy although it also includes the *a fortiori* argument in both of its forms, namely the *a maiore ad minus* and the *a minore ad maius*.[22] The textual authority for *qiyās* was found in prophetic Sunna and the practice of the Companions.[23] Eventually, *qiyās* came to be accepted as the fourth formal source of law.

Of the three categories *ijtihād* represented the most general type of reasoning. Prior to the disapproval of *ra'y* it had been known as *ijtihād al-ra'y*. Sometime in the second/eighth century the *ra'y* was dropped – it had become untenable – but the concept retained the same meaning, namely: 'the total expenditure of effort in the search for an opinion as to any legal rule in such a manner that the individual senses (within himself) an inability to expend further effort'.[24]

The third category, *istiḥsān*, represents a mode of reasoning that overrides strictly logical inferences derived from *qiyās*, which may present undue hardship. A more reasonable, preferred solution may be chosen in its stead. Therefore, *istiḥsān* appeals to a general sense of fairness, conscience and common sense.[25] However, it lacked any textual authority and was the subject of much criticism. Its usefulness clearly outweighed

[20] Joseph Schacht (n 18) 20. [21] Wael B. Hallaq (n 9) 49.

[22] *Ibid.*, 50. [23] *Ibid.*, 80.

[24] Bernard Weiss, 'Interpretation in Islamic Law: The Theory of Ijtihad' (1978) 26 *Am.J.Comp.L.* 199, 207.

[25] Mohammad Hashim Kamali, *Principles of Islamic Jurisprudence* (Cambridge: Islamic Texts Society 2003), 323.

such criticism in the end, however, and consequently was adopted by the Ḥanafī, Mālikī and Ḥanbalī schools, while Shāfi'ī jurists rejected it altogether.[26] The principle of *istiḥsān* was lent considerable weight by allowing the jurist to reject *qiyās* in favour of *istiḥsān*, in response to the flexibility it provided.[27] Citing Al-Shaybānī, Al-Sarakshi wrote that '*[I]stihsan* is the renunciation of analogy and the adoption of what is more fitting for people. Some say: *istiḥsān* seeks to introduce more lenience in laws in connection with difficulties encountered by the individual and the general public (viz., everyone). Some say: it is to give wide latitude and to solicit comfort.'[28]

Therefore, the strict textual adherence demanded by the proponents of prophetic hadith was not complete and unconditional. In fact, by the end of the third/ninth century jurists are reported to have arrived at a 'great synthesis', a methodological recognition that combined the different approaches to the law.[29]

The third formal source of Islamic law is known as consensus *(ijmā')*. Consensus provided jurists with an all-important juristic tool for safeguarding the entire structure of the law, including the learned opinions (fatwas) of jurists.[30] It can be defined as 'the agreement of the community as represented by its highly learned jurists living in a particular age or generation'.[31] The concept establishes the epistemological certainty of any particular law based upon probable textual evidence and agreed upon by the *mujtahids* (the highest class of jurists). In fact, once consensus was agreed on any particular point of law it became 'an infallible expression of the divine law' and could not be cast aside by any future *mujtahid*.[32] As a result, the law was divided into two spheres, namely that in which unity prevails (*mujma' 'alayh*) and that in which there is disagreement (*mukhtalaf fīh*). Within the sphere of disagreement diversity in the law is given free reign so that the schools of law and their body of doctrine can be justified as equally valid representations of the law.[33]

Like all sources of law, with the exception of the Quran whose divine origins are grounded in a broad consensus that pre-dates the juristic

[26] Wael B. Hallaq (n 9) 50. See also Hallaq, 324.
[27] Wael B. Hallaq, *Islamic Legal Theories* (Cambridge University Press 1997), 109.
[28] Gideon Libson, 'On the Development of Custom as a Source of Law in Islamic Law' (1997) 4 *I.L.& S.* 131, 151.
[29] Wael B. Hallaq (n 9) 56. [30] *Ibid.*, 100.
[31] Wael B. Hallaq, *An Introduction to Islamic Law* (Cambridge University Press, 2009), 21.
[32] Bernard Weiss, *The Spirit of Islamic Law* (Athens: University of Georgia Press 1998), 122.
[33] *Ibid.*

notion of *ijmāʿ*, authority for *ijmāʿ* as a source of law had to be found in the revealed texts. While fatwas evince probable knowledge, the sources of law – which uphold the faith – must be absolutely certain. However, the Quran did not have a lot to offer in this regard. Therefore, around the end of the third/ninth century a hadith was promulgated that established, once and for all, that Muhammad's community (*ummah*) as a whole could never agree upon an error.[34] Needless to say, the textual proof (Sunna) that legitimised consensus as a source of law had itself only recently attained certitude.[35]

Consensus can only be established on the basis of revelation and with respect to a textual indicant (*dalīl*). Importantly, consensus from the past must be assumed to have located the textual indicant whether or not the present generation has discovered it.[36] Once consensus has been established it may act as a driver of further *ijtihād*. As *ijtihād* yields new law, consensus can continue the process of law making by enshrining the law to the realm of God. Hence, consensus has been likened to the common law concept of *stare decisis* or doctrine of precedent, although its formulation does not take place in the courtroom.[37]

The absolute certainty bestowed by consensus, coupled with the authority it derives from the revealed texts, endows consensus with a superior authority over the Sunna and the Quran. Essentially this means that whenever consensus has been established with respect to a particular matter, the textual evidence used to arrive at a consensus trumps any other conflicting evidence. The reasoning behind this is circular. Evidence set aside as a result of consensus is deemed irrelevant insofar as the community of Muslims would not have agreed on other evidential indications.[38]

The development of the *fiqh* was gradual and marked by great debate and decisive theological developments. A clearly delineated set of legal sources grew out of this process, as well as a number of legal tools used to provide flexibility. In the following section the legal theory of Islamic law, the *uṣūl al-fiqh*, is examined.

2.2 The theory of Islamic law

The substantive body of Islamic jurisprudence known as *fiqh* was developed prior to the *uṣūl al-fiqh*, the legal theory that is rooted in the four

[34] Wael B. Hallaq (n 9) 80.
[35] *Ibid.* [36] Wael B. Hallaq (n 27) 76.
[37] Bernard Weiss (n 24) 208–9.
[38] Wael B. Hallaq (n 27) 76–7.

sources of Islamic law.[39] Moreover, the *fiqh* that had developed by the end of the second/eighth century was not modified as a result of the genesis of the new legal methodology. Rather the creation of the *uṣūl al-fiqh* seemed to mark a culmination in how the law should be developed but it also sought to endow the law with an ideal character.[40] From around the middle of the fourth/tenth century, however, the *uṣūl* adopted a more prescriptive nature, while maintaining its normative and descriptive functions.[41]

The theory of *uṣūl al-fiqh* required jurists to know which cases were subject to consensus so as not to work outside the existing school doctrine or the larger community of jurists. Cases not subject to consensus – those having remained subject to disagreement (*ikhtilāf*) – or novel legal problems were subject to the theory.[42] *Qiyās* was to provide the legal tool that was to elicit new law. It comprised four elements: (1) the novel case requiring a legal solution; (2) the established rule, which can be found in the revealed texts or among those established by consensus; (3) the *ratio legis* (*'illah*), also known as the 'effective cause', which can be found in both of the aforementioned elements; (4) the legal norm found in the established case, which, on the basis of similarity between the two cases, can be transposed to the novel legal problem.[43] Consequently, the determination of the *'illah* became the jurist's principal task. Some *'illahs* were quite explicit and thus easily deciphered, while most could only be gleaned from inference and interpretation.[44]

The *uṣūl al-fiqh* created a juristic *modus operandi* by which only the most highly qualified Muslim jurists (*mujtahid*) were to exercise *ijtihād* concerning legal problems for which the texts were silent or ambiguous.[45] In fact, the practice of *ijtihād* was seen as a divine communal obligation (*farḍ kifāyah*) that all competent jurists had to perform as a means of worship and belief in God.[46] There is no single mode of *ijtihād* and, indeed, *mujtahids* over the course of centuries developed their own methodologies. However, several common methodological concerns can be identified.

The first and most important prerogative of the *mujtahid* is to look for the meaning of words and texts within the holy sources, i.e. the Quran and Sunna. A legal method used to reveal or elaborate legal rules (*ahkām*) on the basis of these texts is known as *bayān*. It is used where different

39 This research is limited to an investigation of Sunni Islam and its four formal sources.
40 Wael B. Hallaq (n 9) 74. 41 *Ibid.*, 75.
42 *Ibid.*, 100–1. 43 *Ibid.*, 101. 44 *Ibid.*
45 Imran Ahsan Khan Nyazee, *Islamic Jurisprudence: Usūl al-Fiqh* (Herndon, VA: International Institute of Islamic Thought 2000), 267.
46 Wael B. Hallaq, 'Was the Gate of Ijtihad Closed?' (1984) 16 *Int'l J.Mid.E.Stud* 3, 5.

types of *bayān* are present in the texts.[47] Furthermore, two broad methodologies have been developed that are concerned with interpreting the meaning of the texts. However, these could just as easily be characterised as a number of independent methodologies, each comprised of complex interpretive taxonomies, which share an overlapping methodological concern for discerning God's law.[48]

The second mode of *ijtihād* concerns the extension of the law via the use of *qiyās*, the fourth source of law that has been described above. The primary objective of the jurist is to discover the underlying cause of the legal ruling (*ḥukm*) without which analogical *qiyās* is not possible. The methodological concern was to develop methods for identifying the *'illah* that were true to God's intentions. Jurists devised a number of methods towards this end, known as the *masālik al-'illah*,[49] which, however, fall outside the principal concern of this study.

The third mode of *ijtihād* relies on the general principles of the sharia, which derive from God's infinite wisdom (*ḥikmah*).[50] In cases where a textual indication is completely absent, this mode enables a jurist to make rules on the basis of generally agreed principles or even those that he discerns. Yet the wide discretion that this mode permits creates risks that the lawgiver's intentions will be diluted, particularly over the course of time. Different methodologies were devised to systematise this mode so that the jurist's absolute discretion could be restricted.[51] A subsequent analysis concerning the *maqāṣid al-sharī'a* (objectives of the law) will demonstrate the issues associated with this mode of reasoning.

2.2.1 *The epistemology of acts*

The process of *ijtihād* highlights the probable nature of the jurist's fatwa. It is a central epistemic challenge, since a true and certain rendering of God's law is the basis of the law's legitimacy and authority. The problem was solved by viewing the law two-dimensionally: namely, via the *forum internum* or religious conscience; and the *forum externum*, which accepted the contingency of all legally valid decisions based on probable assertions concerning the facts of the case or the probability that the law had been extracted from the holy sources pursuant to God's intentions.[52]

[47] Imran Ahsan Khan Nyazee (n 45) 275–6.

[48] For a detailed treatment of these methodologies see *ibid.*, chapters 15–17.

[49] *Ibid.*, 305. [50] *Ibid.*, 312. [51] *Ibid.*, 313.

[52] Baber Johansen, *Contingency in a Sacred Law: Legal and Ethical Norms in the Muslim Fiqh*, vol. VII, Studies in Islamic Law and Society, edited by Ruud Peters and Bernard

If probable assertions turn out to be false, the jurist's error does not annul the legal validity and binding nature of his decision so long as sincere and diligent scrutiny of the revealed texts has been given.[53] In the *forum internum*, however, the absolute veracity of one's decisions in one's relationship with God cannot be shirked – the eternal Law of God remains an absolute obligation for the individual concerned. The concept demonstrates the underlying epistemological scepticism of the jurists towards the *fiqh*. However, this is necessary for a religious law, in which the absolute truth and validity of revelation is upheld, on the one hand, and the fallibility of the jurists' interpretation of those texts, is acknowledged on the other.[54]

The Islamic judge, on the other hand, was forced to evaluate individual acts, dispositions and statements of human beings. The intentions and motives of human beings (the 'invisible and interior' (*bāṭin*)) can only be deciphered from their acts and statements (the 'apparent and exterior' (*ẓāhir*)).[55] Only God knows the minds of His subjects and thus only He is in a position to punish them for their innermost convictions (which He shall do in the hereafter). Human judges are not in a position to judge, as God would do. The human judge must arbitrate according to the appearance that legal acts and dispositions produce.[56] Thus the legality of an act or disposition in the temporal world is emphasised in a textual materialism in which the form of the law takes on greater relevance. This salient point re-surfaces in Chapter 4 in connection with the jurisprudence of Islamic financial transactions, which evinces a formal or textual adherence to the sharia but may not adhere to religious and ethical prerogatives. The two-dimensionality of the law may be a helpful clue in understanding some of the juristic motives and justifications underlying the creation of Islamic financial law.

Islamic law does not always attach legal consequences to relevant legal acts. Rather it is often more concerned with laying down moral norms that distinguish between forbidden and allowed transactions.[57] Accordingly, acts are classified according to whether their objects are spiritual or secular. The performance of acts with secular objects, such as the performance

Weiss (Leiden: Brill 1999), 36–7. While the two spheres of law – the religious and ethical and the strictly juridical – are agreed to characterise the corpus of Islamic law, their relationship cannot always be united in legal practice. See Baber Johansen, 'Die Sündige, Gesunde Amme. Moral Und Gesetzliche Bestimmung (Hukm) im Islamischen Recht' (1998) 28 *Die Welt des Islams*, 264, 282.

53 Bernard Weiss (n 24) 205.

54 Baber Johansen, *Contingency in a Sacred Law* (n 52) 7.

55 *Ibid.*, 70–1. 56 *Ibid.*, 24.

57 Joseph Schacht, *An Introduction to Islamic Law* (Oxford: Clarendon Press, 1964), 121.

of certain devotional acts, secures the release of the believer from the obligation of that act. On the other hand, acts performed with a spiritual objective in mind secure a spiritual reward for the believer in the hereafter.[58]

Some acts should be performed as the omission of such acts is prohibited. These acts are either obligatory in the first degree (*farḍ*); this is the case when the rule is established in a clear and conclusive text. Other acts are *wājib* and thus obligatory in the second degree; these acts are established by probable knowledge. The payment of *zakāh*, prayer five times daily, fasting and pilgrimage are obligatory acts of the second category. Muslims must perform both classes of obligatory acts. They secure spiritual merit (*thawāb*) by performance, and spiritual punishment (*'adhāb*) by omission. Furthermore, some acts are beneficial and yet not required. These acts are supererogatory and commended (*mandūb, mustaḥabb*). They include the creation of a religious or charitable endowment (*waqf*), *ṣadaqah* (charitable contribution), and giving gifts and attending to the sick. A further category of acts are forbidden and prohibited (*ḥarām*); these acts are regarded as abominable and condemned (*makrūh*). A final category of acts are neither favoured nor prohibited but are regarded with indifference. Such acts are *mubāh* (permissible) and include transactions of sale, pledge, lease and so forth.[59]

2.2.2 *The textualism of the* Uṣūl Al-Fiqh

The *uṣūl's* emphasis upon visually apparent material attributes endowed the law with a formalistic rationality, although it was an abstract formalism. Islamic law is not concerned with the abstraction of general principles and systemic logic.[60] Rather the sharia illustrates a casuistic approach to the law that eventually gave rise to an elaborate superstructure of rules; these too were developed and based on rulings, which, for their part, were derived from other original rulings and the influx of new subject matter.[61] In the subsequent chapter an examination of the system of nominate

[58] Abdur Rahim, *The Principles of Islamic Jurisprudence* (New Delhi: Kitab Bhavan 1994), 187–9.

[59] *Ibid.*

[60] Joseph Schacht, 'Zur Soziologischen Betrachtung Des Islamischen Rechts' (1935) XXII–XXIII *Der Islam* 207, 214.

[61] Joseph Schacht (n 57) 113.

contracts provides a clear example of how this approach affected the corpus of Islamic jurisprudence in the field of commercial law.

The superstructure of law created by the unrestricted use of analogical reasoning tends towards the creation of rules, originally restricted to a single description of acts, which are then extended to all acts of the same class.[62] For example, because wine is prohibited in the Quran, all intoxicants are prohibited. Or less rational: a provision ensuring general cleanliness is extended into long ceremonies of ritual purification, and so forth. Such an increasingly rigorous systematisation may preclude practical considerations of the law and limit society's ability to function. It reflects a conscious effort to systematise the law or to produce a doctrine, which was free of all presuppositions (or any contextual considerations), Arab and non-Arab, and could be restricted to the observable characteristics of the revealed language, Arabic.[63]

The necessity to return to the original texts in all matters of faith, society, religion and law in order to generate doctrine is an enduring and meaningful quality that is indicative of the development of the sharia and its unique religious and ethical spirit. And yet the essentially static nature of this requirement betrays the greatest challenge to its continuing relevance as time evolves and society progresses. Social necessities and opinion create the terms and circumstances to which law must respond. Indeed, even in those instances in which the law creates new sets of circumstances, human invention and nature tend to catch up and overwhelm the law by finding any number of evasions of or loopholes in the literal interpretation of the law. All of these responses to legal stimuli are a result of the natural progression of social and human development. Legal rules are essentially static, and inherently indeterminate; they are created at a particular time and context, and effective only to the extent that their underlying norms are highly specific and can be applied to a particular set of factors.[64]

[62] Henry Sumner Maine, *Ancient Law: Its Connection with the Early History of Society and Its Relation to Modern Ideas* (10th edn, London: John Murray, 1885), 17.

[63] Sherman Jackson, 'Fiction and Formalism: Toward a Functional Analysis of Usul Al-Fiqh' in Bernard Weiss (ed.), *Studies in Islamic Legal Theory* (Leiden: Brill 2002), 195.

[64] Julia Black, *Rules and Regulators* (Oxford: Clarendon Press, 1997), 199. By the beginning of the fourth/tenth century many modern scholars argued that the activity of *ijtihād* had ceased to take place; that, in fact, Muslim jurists had agreed to practice *taqlīd* or juristic conformity with the already established doctrines of the *madhhab* and the legal theory (*uṣūl al-fiqh*) that had developed up until that time. For example, Joseph Schacht argued that jurists 'felt that all essential questions had been thoroughly discussed and finally settled, and a consensus gradually established itself to the effect that from that time onwards

The *uṣūl al-fiqh* came to fruition only after a body of Islamic jurisprudence had been developed. Yet legal theory played more than just a rhetorical and descriptive role. It established a strict textual hermeneutic that, nonetheless, was not free from human error. While its epistemological difficulties could be overcome, jurists' subscription to the hermeneutic created a highly casuistic law built upon the edifice of analogical reasoning. The following section examines a further unofficial source of Islamic law, namely, custom.

2.3 *Maṣlaḥah* and rationalising legal tools

This section focuses on the principle of *maṣlaḥah* (public interest) and the legal tools created to give it effect. *Maṣlaḥah*, referred to as *istiṣlaḥ* in technical legal terms, literally means a source of something beneficial or good.[65] More generally, it refers to 'prohibiting or permitting a legal act or disposition on the basis of public interest'.[66]

Fatwas based on considerations of *maṣlaḥah* are found in some of the earliest legal writings from the second/eighth and third/ninth centuries. However, the principle attained widespread acceptance only in the late fifth/eleventh century when the Shāfi'ī jurist al-Ghazālī (d. 505/1111) established that the '*maṣlaḥah* was God's purpose (*maqṣad*, pl. *maqāṣid*) in revealing the divine law'.[67] Al-Ghazālī asserted that God's revelation of divine law was designed to preserve the five essential elements of human welfare, namely: religion, life, intellect, offspring and property. The protection of these essential elements or what averts harm from them is considered a *maṣlaḥah*; the endangerment of these elements constitutes its

no one might be deemed to have the necessary qualifications for independent reasoning in law, and that all future activity would have to be confined to the explanation, application and, at the most, interpretation of the doctrine as it had been laid down once and for all'. See Joseph Schacht (n 57) 70–1. Known as the 'closing of the gate of *ijtihād*' '(in Arabic: *insidād bāb al-ijtihād*), *taqlīd* was to have demanded an unquestioning acceptance of the school doctrines. The *mujtahid* or the jurist entitled to perform *ijtihād* was no longer said to exist. However, Hallaq convincingly demonstrates that jurists capable of exercising *ijtihād* existed at all times, in all centuries. Moreover, *ijtihād* contributed to developing the positive law of school doctrine (*fiqh*) in the period of *taqlīd*. For more see Wael B. Hallaq (n 46).

[65] Felicitas Opwis, 'Islamic Law and Legal Change: The Concept of Maslaha in Classical and Contemporary Islamic Legal Theory' in Abbas Amanat and Frank Griffel (eds.), *Shari'a: Islamic Law in the Contemporary Context* (Stanford University Press,2007), 62.

[66] Nicolas P. Aghnides, *Mohammedan Theories of Finance* (Lahore: Premier Book House 1961), 97.

[67] Felicitas Opwis, 'Maslaha in Contemporary Legal Theory' (2005) 12 *I.L.& S.* 182, 187–8.

opposite, namely, *mafsadah* (evil).[68] *Maṣlaḥah* is generally categorised according to three types: these are the 'essentials' (*ḍarūrīyāt*); the 'complementary' (*ḥājīyat*); and the 'embellishments' (*taḥsīnīyāt*).[69]

The use of *maṣlaḥah* as a means of creating legal change was and still is controversial. The controversy centres on whether or not the human intellect is able to discern *maṣlaḥah* without a concrete textual indication (*dalīl*) in the revealed sources. Known technically as *maṣlaḥah mursalah* or unattested *maṣlaḥah,* this type of *maṣlaḥah* pertains to matters in which no textual authority can be located. The challenge for jurists was and still is to devise legal strategies in which *maṣlaḥah* can be utilised in a legally valid manner.[70]

Amongst the eponymous founders of the *madhhabs* Al-Malik is the most outspoken supporter of *maṣlaḥah* as 'a proof and basis of legislation (*tashrīʿ*)'.[71] Al-Malik held that not upholding *maṣlaḥah* when it is compatible with the objectives of the law or falls within the categories or genus of what God has expressly permitted would be to neglect God's law. As such *maṣlaḥah* constitutes an integral norm of the sharia.[72] The Ḥanbalīs adopted a similar position.[73] On the other hand, the Ḥanafīs and Shāfiʾīs held that *maṣlaḥah* constitutes a valid ground for legislation only in the presence of a textual indication as pointed out in the *ʿillah* of a given text or in the general objectives of the revealed texts. This requires the type of enquiry used in determining the *ʿillah* in *qiyās* and is thus designed to limit arbitrariness in the formulation of the law.[74] Despite their different approaches to the principle, however, all four schools of law agreed that an instance of *maṣlaḥah,* which did not conflict with the objectives of the revealed sources, should be upheld.[75]

Rationalising legal tools such as *istiḥsān, istiṣlāḥ* and *ṣadd al-dharāʾiʿ* (blocking the means) were created by the scholars to give effect to the general interest (*maṣlaḥah*) of the Muslim community.[76] Although each term is denoted differently, their varying nomenclature merely serves to identify their particular method but, in essence, they all are designed to promote

68 *Ibid.* 69 Mohammad Hashim Kamali (n 25) 356.

70 Felicitas Opwis (n 67) 191.

71 Mohammad Hashim Kamali (n 25) 355.

72 *Ibid.* 73 *Ibid.*, 364. 74 *Ibid.*, 362.

75 *Ibid.*, 365.

76 'Rationalising legal tools' are those legal instruments that are used in the practice of *ijtihād*. They are 'rationalising' because they allow jurists to use their individual discretion (*raʾy*) in determining a solution to a novel legal problem. Some writers have referred to them as 'legal scaffolding' 'or 'legal fictions'.

maṣlaḥah.[77] For example, *ṣadd al-dharā'i'*, (literally: closing the gates to evil), prevents a lawful act from taking place that may eventually lead to an unlawful act. Its ultimate objective is to establish *maṣlaḥah*.[78]

Rationalising legal tools serve as an important vehicle in adapting and extending the law. In essence, they are designed to limit the damage and inconvenience of a formalist interpretation.[79] They satisfy society's desire for progress and improvement while, at the same time, not offending sacred or other authoritative instances disinclined towards change.[80] They are constructed to conceal, or affect to conceal, the fact that a law has been altered, its letter remaining true, but its spirit wholly modified. These and other mitigating effects were particularly necessary in the post-formative phase of jurisprudence in which jurists operated under a regime of *taqlīd* (conformity), since they were charged with maintaining a genetic connection with the *mujtahids* of old. It became necessary to invent new exceptions and classifications, to manipulate the wording and scope of legal injunctions to accommodate a changed reality and thereby erect a sort of 'legal scaffolding'.[81]

However, the pursuit of rationality in the interpretation of the sharia is at odds with the *uṣūl al-fiqh*'s strict procedures for deriving legal rulings. Yet the predominance of Ash'arī textualism left unanswered the problem of how jurists were to know God's law when a novel legal problem came to light and a scriptural indicant was not available.[82] Rationalist legal tools provided an indispensable means of adapting and extending the law to new and changing circumstances where a strict adherence to the *uṣūl al-fiqh* would have stymied the applicability and relevance of the law as time and circumstances changed.

Yet such tools possess the distinct disadvantage of creating a law lacking a guiding coherence expounded in logical deduction and which is subject to arbitrariness, subjectivity and legal uncertainty.[83] Furthermore, when any novel problem can be decided by human reasoning, unaided

[77] Mawil Izzi Dien, 'Maslaha in Islamic Law: A Source or a Concept?' in Ian Richard Netton (ed.), *Studies in Honour of Clifford Edmund Bosworth* (Leiden: Brill, 2000), 348.

[78] *Ibid.*, 351.

[79] Sherman Jackson (n 63) 195. Jackson refers to these as 'safety-net' principles.

[80] Henry Sumner Maine (n 62) 26.

[81] Alan Watson, *The Nature of Law* (Edinburgh University Press, 1977). Watson is the first to have used the concept of 'legal scaffolding'. Sherman Jackson has applied the concept with respect to Islamic jurisprudence in Sherman Jackson, *Islamic Law and the State: The Constitutional Jurisprudence of Shihab Al-Din Al-Qarafi* (Leiden: Brill, 1996), 98–9.

[82] Felicitas Opwis (n 67) 190.

[83] *Ibid.*, 191–2.

by indicants located in the scriptural sources, the body of jurisprudence that is attributable to revelation will consistently decrease over time.[84] The resulting secularisation of the law is an unviable alternative for a religious law.[85] The following section concerns the use of legal stratagems designed to circumvent the substance of the sharia.

2.4 Legal stratagems (*ḥiyal*)

Islamic jurisprudence also makes use of legal stratagems known as *ḥiyal*, (sg. *ḥīlah)*. Ibn Qayyim al-Jawzīyah (d. 751/1350) wrote that *ḥiyal* represent the subtle management of aspects of a legal transaction in ways for which they were not intended.[86] However, for those who ascribed to these means, one could utilise *ḥiyal* to make lawful that which otherwise is unlawful; to create what the Ḥanafīs called '*makhārij* ' (sg. *makhraj*) or 'exits'.[87] *Ḥiyal* represent an attempt by the jurists to ease the difficulties posed by scrupulous adherence to the sharia without having to trespass the divine laws on account of the exigencies of everyday life.

Ḥiyal are devised to seek a compromise between theory and practice, between ideals and reality.[88] Schacht has made the largest contribution so far to contemporary understanding of *makhārij* with his translation of four published works dedicated to expounding these 'ruses', as he called them; these included those by Abū Bakr Aḥmad al-Khaṣṣāf (d. 874), Abū Ḥātim Maḥmūd al-Ḳazwīnī (d. 440/1048–49) and Muhammad Ibn al-Ḥasan al-Shaybānī (d. 189/805).[89] Three of the works are by Ḥanafīs and the fourth by al-Ḳazwīnī, a Shāfi'ī jurist. Shaybānī was one of Abū Ḥanīfah's most brilliant disciples. His writings constitute some of the basic texts of Ḥanafī jurisprudence, which include the *Kitāb al-Aṣl, al-Jāmi' al-kabīr* and *al-Jāmi' al-ṣaghīr* – the so-called '*ẓahir al-riwāya*', i.e. the authoritative and faultless transmission of Ḥanafī doctrine. The *ẓahir al-riwāya* contains contributions by the three major scholars of

[84] *Ibid.*, 191.

[85] For more on this process see, in general, Aharon Layish, 'The Contribution of the Modernists to the Secularisation of Islamic Law' (1978) 14 *Middle E.Stud.* 263; and Noel J. Coulson, 'The Concept of Progress and Islamic Law' (Jan–Mar 1964) 40 *Quest* 16, 25.

[86] C.f. Satoe Horii, 'Reconsideration of Legal Devices (Hiyal) in Islamic Jurisprudence: The Hanafis and Their "Exits" (Makharij)' (2002) 9 *I.L.& S.*, 312, 312–13.

[87] *Ibid.*

[88] Joseph Schacht, *Das Kitab Al-Hijal Fil-Fiqh (Buch der Rechtskniffe) Des Abu Hatim Mahmud Ibn Al-Hasan Al-Qazuini* (Hanover: Orient-Buchhandlung Heinz Lafaire, 1924), 6.

[89] Maxime Rodinson, *Islam and Capitalism* (London: Allen Lane 1974), 36.

the Ḥanafī school: Abū Ḥanīfah (eponym of the school), Abū Yūsuf, and Shaybānī.[90] It is therefore evident that the *makhārij* are an authoritative and illustrative feature of Ḥanafī jurisprudence, and not merely obscure works by less well-known authors whose views bore little impact.

Ḥiyal were employed in nearly all facets of life. They were not reserved for those areas of social transaction that, for the Western reader, are more closely associated with legal transactions. However, the chapters of the *fiqh* devoted to spiritual matters *('ibādāt)* comprise a much smaller proportion of *ḥiyal*,[91] which probably indicates that the practice of ritual worship is more closely aligned with the ideals of the law.

Hence the Ḥanafīs acquired a well-earned reputation for the systematic use of *makhārij*, although the Shāfi'ī s were known to have utilised them as well.[92] Abū Ḥanīfah is said to be the founder of the genre despite the fact that he did not compose a treatise on the subject. Many statements concerning *ḥiyal* in standard Ḥanafī texts are attributed to him.[93] A book of *ḥiyal (kitāb al-ḥiyal)* written by al-Shāfi'ī or one of his early disciples would have been unthinkable inasmuch as a lively polemic was directed by this school against the Ḥanafī works devoted to the subject. The Shāfi'ī experiment with *ḥiyal* seems to be more of an intellectual exercise of competition with the Ḥanafīs after the schools had consolidated their authority and legitimacy as a recognised *madhhab*.[94] In this regard, their devices are not as practically oriented as are the Ḥanafī *ḥiyal*.

The Ḥanafīs' recommendation of their use stretches far beyond a limited exercise. Ḥanafīs encouraged the faithful to utilise them, even to avoid merely undesirable situations, since the law provides for these exits for those who seek them. Ibn Qayyim al-Jawzīyah confirmed this claim in his description of the Ḥanafī view regarding the sharia as a body of exits that envisioned the exigencies of human life.[95] It is apparent, therefore, that the Ḥanafīs regarded the law in terms of its utility. *Makhārij* were devised to help the faithful seek remedies for 'oppressive' or inconvenient situations that 'prejudiced' them.

The Mālikī or Medinese position on *ḥiyal* invoked the principle of *ṣadd al-dharā'i'*. It has been described as the antithesis of *ḥiyal* in the sense

[90] Satoe Horii (n 86) 327.

[91] Joseph Schacht, 'Die Arabische Hijal-Literatur: Ein Beitrag Zur Erforschung Der Islamischen Rechtspraxis' (1926) XV *Der Islam* 211, 213.

[92] Nabil A. Saleh, *Unlawful Gain and Legitimate Profit in Islamic Law* (Cambridge University Press, 1986), 61. Also Satoe Horii (n 86) 312–18.

[93] Satoe Horii (n 86) 319. [94] Joseph Schacht (n 88) 6.

[95] Satoe Horii (n 86) 321.

that it seeks to block unlawful acts for presumably illegal purposes despite their otherwise lawful appearance.[96] The principle became instrumental to later criticism of *ḥiyal*.

A well-known example of *ḥiyal* is one of the oldest of its kind, the *bay' al-inah* or the double-contract sale. An object is sold on a deferred payment basis, but then bought back for a sum less than the original deferred price, payable on the spot. This is, in essence, an interest-bearing loan. The transaction was so successful and widespread that Europeans of the Middle Ages adopted its use under the name of *mohatra* (from the Arabic, *mukhāṭarah*, meaning risk).[97] Most jurists found the transaction impermissible but, interestingly, Muzanī notes that al-Shāfi'ī treated the sale as valid.[98] This particular *ḥiyal* plays a very important role in many sales-based Islamic financial transactions.

Therefore, the Ḥanafīs justified the incorporation of *ḥiyal* into their legal doctrine not as an attempt to circumvent the law but rather sought to utilise the law according to its underlying spirit, which provided for 'exits'. *Ḥiyal* were, by definition, legitimate, and were thus transmitted as a special genre of Ḥanafī doctrine.

2.5 The role of custom as a legal source

Custom has been defined as a form of life rooted in a people's sense of propriety,[99] and as a whole body of usages, practices or conventions, be they social, economic or other, which regulate social life from the grassroots level.[100] These tend to be established practices, a usual way of doing things, and adherence to these folkways is an expression of membership to a particular community. The more homogenous a society is, in terms of its racial, ethnic and cultural background, the stronger such a tendency is likely to be.[101] Custom, unsurprisingly, is not one of the classically

[96] *Ibid.*, 343.

[97] Joseph Schacht, 'Ribā' in M. Th. Houtsma, T. W. Arnold, R. Bassett, R. Hartmann (eds.), *Encyclopaedia of Islam, First Edition* (1913–1936) (Brill Online, 2014), referenceworks.brillonline.com/entries/encyclopaedia-of-islam-1/riba-SIM_3700. Accessed 25 April 2014.

[98] Satoe Horii (n 86) 346.

[99] Clifford Geertz, *Local Knowledge: Further Essays in Interpretive Anthropology* (New York: Basic Books 1983), 210.

[100] 'Custom' (*Merriam-Webster's Online Dictionary*, 2009), www.merriam-webster.com/dictionary/custom. Accessed 25 April 2014.

[101] Peter Stein, *Legal Institutions: The Development of Dispute Settlement* (London: Butterworths, 1984), 3.

recognised sources of Islamic law; yet it is employed and called upon to such an extent that, in actuality, it is not only a major source of law, but an aspect of social life that the sharia has often left to its own devices.

The refusal to recognise custom as a formal source is grounded in the doctrine of the spiritual essence of the sharia which is fundamentally opposed to human tampering with God's law. The juristic methodology sought to distance the law from the bedrock of customary practices which had bequeathed to the new community the very foundations of the sharia.[102] Paradoxically, however, it is the universal claim of Islam, its willingness to envelop and acquire the novel mosaic of customary practices that it met through siege and conversion, that enabled Islam to accept customs and imbue them with the Islamic spirit.[103] It is this universal legitimising claim, on the one hand, and the divinely inspired doctrine, on the other, which have enabled Islam to straddle the sometimes uneasy chasm between theoretical ideals and the law applied.

Yet it would simplify the relationship of customary practices to the sharia, and vice versa, by viewing their enmeshed relationship in discreet categories or institutionalised identities the authority of which lies in their struggle with each other for legitimacy and identity.[104] The authority and influence of the sharia extended to every domain of Muslim social and religious life. It permeated all other conceptions of knowledge and practice so as to render impracticable the absolute distinctiveness of the sharia and custom.[105] Thus the demand for universality rendered Islamic all sorts of practices and these, in turn, reciprocated by allowing indigenous social practices to flourish within the broader confines of Islamic doctrine. It is probably the inclusiveness of Islam's universal values that accounts for the rapid spread of Islam amongst disparate local traditions and that enabled Muslim rulers to retain their subjects' obedience. In sum, drawing too fine a line between custom and theory, between the formal and informal, may distort the nature of Islam to the extent that its distinctiveness as a universalising religion is lost to the observer.

102 Gideon Libson (n 28) 135.

103 Abraham L. Udovitch, 'The Constitution of the Traditional Islamic Marketplace: Islamic Law and the Social Context of Exchange' in S. N. Eisenstadt (ed.), *Patterns of Modernity: Beyond the West* (London: Frances Pinter Publishers, 1987), 166.

104 Max Gluckman, *The Judicial Process among the Barotse of Northern Rhodesia* (University of Manchester Press,1955), 261–2.

105 Lawrence Rosen, 'Law and Custom in the Popular Legal Culture of North Africa' (1995) 2 *I.L.& S.* 194, 201.

Substantial historical evidence underscores the controversy concerning custom's role as a formal source of law in the classical period, and yet a de facto recognition of its importance is revealed in Muslim legal literature. Quasi-recognition of certain customs was made possible by resorting to other more legitimate legal tools such as *istiḥsān* or by linking these to *ijmā'*, both of which became a common means for assimilating popular custom into the law. Likewise the principle of *ḍarūrah* (necessity) was utilised for the same purpose.[106]

The introduction of hadith collections in the latter part of the third/ninth century proved to be an essential means of incorporating age-old and recent customary practices into the sharia without diverging from the principles of the *fiqh*. Because the Sunna is, in essence, the living custom or tradition of the Prophet Muhammad, customs originating elsewhere could be identified with the Sunna and accorded divine legitimacy.[107] However, the incorporation of foreign elements was not limited to customary usages. All sorts of ideals and common adages reflective of the then contemporary scholars' wishes for the developing doctrine were projected back to the time of the Prophet and given religious legitimacy.[108]

Some evidence of this incorporation exists in the fact that legal literature does not mention custom as a material source, i.e. its association with *istiḥsān*, as long as the redaction of the hadith collections was taking place. Once the standard hadith collections had been finalised at the beginning of the third/ninth century, discussion of custom as a material source becomes frequent and was subsequently woven into the fabric of the law.[109] This is particularly the case in commerce and trade, wherein jurists without qualm or hesitation invoked the domain of custom (*'urf*) or the 'practice of the merchant' *('ādat at-tujjār)* in the formulation of contracts and in the settlement of disputes. Indeed, large swathes of commercial conduct and the legality of its practical details are left untouched and unchartered due to the omnipresence of the inherently amorphous notion of custom.[110]

Early Muslim legal literature underscores the supremacy of the concept of 'custom' in commercial exchange as a decisive feature of the laws of commerce.[111] The prevalence of custom was not relegated or confined

106 Gideon Libson (n 28) 151.

107 *Ibid.*, 138. 108 Ignaz Goldziher (n 12) 423.

109 Gideon Libson (n 28) 139. 110 Abraham L. Udovitch (n 103) 160.

111 Chibli Mallat, 'Commercial Law in the Middle East: Between Classical Transactions and Modern Business' (2000) 48 *Am.J.Comp.L.* 81, 95–6.

to the details of the law, but permeated the form and general character of the central institutions of commercial activity.[112] With respect to an entire corpus of commercial practice, such as the all-important and ubiquitous use of weights and measures, the means of transportation, the appointment of agents for the purchase and sale of commodities, even the semantic definition of descriptive terms when applied to certain commodities, the final arbiter of commerce is none other than custom. Thus it is the habitual practice of the merchants, the general manner of commerce (*wajīh al-tijārah*) or the usual practice of the people *(al-muta'ārif bayna al-nās)* that busied the minds of jurists, who clearly sought to enable Muslim entrepreneurs and merchants to succeed in meeting the material and subsistence concerns of the community.[113] In many ways the commercial elaborations of the sharia reflect a diverse set of customary business practices – many derived from ancient foreign origins – in the medieval Middle East.

Commercial customs were also introduced into the law through the framework of dispositive law, i.e. via contract and stipulation by the parties. Thus custom has the authority to determine the rights and duties of contracting parties when these have agreed stipulations to that extent. Even in the absence of such stipulations, scholars representing nearly all the *madhabs* voiced support for the interpretation of contracts with a view to the customary practices prevalent in the area in which they were carried out.[114]

With the passing of time and the increasing complexity of commercial exchange, custom has come to be recognised as a quasi-source of law, particularly within the Ḥanafī school. The post-classical period was witness to this transformation in the formulation of the *Mejelle*, whose authors' compiled rulings on custom in ten articles.[115] Following this break with the theory of classical jurisprudence, the gradual inculcation of custom as a formal source has been adopted by modern Muslim jurists who have attempted to legitimise their position through a revisionist view of the primary sources.[116]

112 Abraham L. Udovitch, 'The "Law Merchant" of the Medieval Islamic World' in G. E. von Grunebaum (ed.), *Logic in Classical Islamic Culture* (Wiesbaden: Otto Harrassowitz 1970), 124–5.

113 Abraham L. Udovitch (n 103) 162.

114 *Ibid.*, 153.

115 *Ibid.*, 141.

116 For an example of modern revisionism that seeks to adapt the sharia to modern circumstances see Tariq Ramadan, *Western Muslims and the Future of Islam* (Oxford University Press, 2004).

2.6 The sharia in pre-modern legal practice

Understanding the role of custom in legal literature provides an important basis for examining the legal pluralistic system of law that characterises the practice of law in pre-modern Islamic societies. Yet the authoritative works of *fiqh* are not historical records of actual transactions or the way in which the law was practised. *Fiqhi* literature or doctrine may, in fact, reflect a partly idealistic conception of the law. The task of examining legal practice is made difficult by the fact that the historical record suffers from the almost 'complete absence of any actual documents or records from the first few centuries of the Islamic era'.[117] Historical records of classical trade and commerce prior to the fourth/tenth century are almost non-existent or are yet to be discovered.[118] The situation is even worse with regard to sharia court (*majlis al-ḥukm*, less frequently: *majlis al-qaḍā*) records known as *dīwān* or *sijill*. Despite a convincing range of evidence that such records were meticulously kept, none have been found from all the centuries leading up to the Ottoman conquests and their centralisation of judicial administration.[119] This is not to infer that classical legal literature dating from the third/ninth century has not provided valuable insights into the social and economic institutions of the classical Islamic world. Indeed, such literature provides an invaluable resource and has helped scholars piece together an otherwise poorly documented canvas of Muslim social life.[120] Yet the absence of historical records including court registers (*dīwān*) leaves many questions unanswered concerning the ways in which legal doctrine was actually put into effect by the law courts.

Ottoman court records are the exception to this rule. Court records stretching from the sixteenth century and ending in the nineteenth from several different locations across the empire confirm a complex judicial tradition notable for its flexibility and pragmatism. Records also offer extraordinary insights into the role of sharia courts as a centralising nexus of multiple normative systems, which sometimes became mixed in the process. Sharia courts were the pre-eminent adjudicatory courts in all of the cities from which records have thus

[117] Abraham L. Udovitch, 'At the Origins of the Western Commenda: Islam, Israel, Byzantium?' (1962) 37 *Speculum* 198, 202.

[118] Robert S. Lopez and Irving W. Raymond, *Medieval Trade in the Mediterranean World: Illustrative Documents* (London: Oxford University Press, 1955), 18.

[119] Wael B. Hallaq, *The Qadi's Diwan (sijill) before the Ottomans* (Bulletin of the School of Oriental and African Studies, 1998), 434.

[120] Abraham L. Udovitch (n 103) 152.

far been analysed. As the law of the land, the 'sharia was in principle valid and binding in its entirety'.[121] The degree to which sharia courts functioned as the legal and administrative centre of these communities is remarkable. Despite this prominence, however, sharia courts made exceptions to their monopoly over legally binding rules by allowing space for the application of *kanun* (the laws of the Ottoman rulers) as well as customary law.[122]

Imperial law comprised individual sultanic decrees, law books specifically made for a particular region or important town, and a comprehensive law book for the entire empire. The responsibility for seeing that these sources of law were applied belonged to both the *qaḍīs* and provincial governors.[123] Imperial law functioned as a type of administrative law. It laid out a blueprint for the organisation and administration of the vast territories of the Ottoman Empire. But it also comprised a wide variety of laws concerning crime, market organisation, urban and agricultural taxes, regulations dealing with the peasantry, and those concerning the infantry corps and provincial cavalry.[124]

The extent of its application is heard in the oft-repeated phrase of the fifteenth and sixteenth centuries, 'by *kanun* and sharia', which indicates that people recognised the application of both legal regimes. Over the course of centuries, however, the *kanun* and sharia became mixed to some degree, making a sharp distinction between the two difficult if not impossible. For example, Süleyman's comprehensive penal code prescribed punishments for crimes committed under both sharia and those ignored by the sharia.[125] Moreover, sharia laws concerning the payment of blood money (*diyet*) and the right of retaliation (*qiṣāṣ*) were incorporated into *kanun*.[126]

Customary law, already an important source of law in legal doctrine, figured prominently in dispute resolution. Customary law is an unwritten law that places primary importance on the use of witnesses. Witnesses' testimony is considered to be an authoritative statement of the law concerning the particular circumstances of the case.[127] In Aintab customary law was not required to be used in written form so long as a

[121] Haim Gerber, 'Sharia, Kanun and Custom in the Ottoman Law: The Court Records of 17th Century Bursa' (1981) 2 *Int'l Journ.Turk.Stud.*, 132.

[122] *Ibid.*

[123] Leslie P. Peirce, *Morality Tales: Law and Gender in the Ottoman Court of Aintab* (Berkeley, CA: University of California Press, 2003), 116.

[124] *Ibid.*, 117. [125] *Ibid.*, 119.

[126] Haim Gerber (n 121) 139. [127] *Ibid.*, 140.

trustworthy witness could speak authoritatively on a matter, which the *qadī* could use to facilitate his ruling in a dispute involving circumstances unfamiliar to him.[128] In seventeenth-century Bursa the legal principle that every practice of old was legally binding and deserved application by the court demonstrates the veneration for 'the old' that must have underpinned pre-Islamic societies' adherence to customary practices.[129] In mid-eighteenth century Aleppo the practice of recognising customary law in sharia courts, where 'established custom' could be proven, led to the formulation of an oft-used dictum: 'the old custom must stand undisturbed'.[130]

Yet the concept was also fluid and highly adaptable. In fact, 'old custom' included rules that were not static at all, nor were they old or universal and could be 'made and unmade daily'.[131] The court's accommodation of custom became one of the principle ways in which people were able organically to shape legal norms according to their interests and the changing social and economic conditions of their community. Considerable legal space was available for people to resolve disputes according to a wide range of intermeshed laws, regulations and customs.[132]

These records indicate that the *qāḍī* must have had considerable leeway in his application of the law. A *qāḍī* could reach a different decision for the same recurring legal problem or set of facts.[133] Yet the appearance of variability in law making may be misleading. Legal procedure in sharia courts was highly informal and arbitrary. Although not unjust, disputants in Bursa may not have been able to decipher the reasoning underlying the judge's ruling. For example, an authority for the decision was not cited by the court in the majority of cases.[134] However, the reason for this may have to do with the fact that, unlike modern times, the general public, not merely the educated elite, had an intimate knowledge of the legal doctrines of the four schools and the legal procedures of sharia courts.[135] In fact, people knew what to expect from the court in matters of personal status, transactions and so forth. It was not unusual for a 'person

[128] Leslie P. Peirce (n 123) 120. [129] Haim Gerber (n 121) 141.

[130] Abraham Marcus, *The Middle East on the Eve of Modernity: Aleppo in the Eighteenth Century* (New York: Columbia University Press, 1989), 104.

[131] *Ibid.* [132] *Ibid.*, 105.

[133] Nelly Hanna, 'The Administration of Courts in Ottoman Cairo', in N. Hanna (ed.) *The State and Its Servants: Administration in Egypt from Ottoman Times to the Present* (Cairo: American University in Cairo Press, 1995), 52.

[134] Haim Gerber (n 121) 145. [135] Nelly Hanna (n 133) 53.

to buy a house one day according to Ḥanbalī law and get married next day according to Maliki or Shafi'ī law'.[136]

Numerous other mechanisms for communal problem-solving regulated pre-modern Islamic societies, which relied on these to maintain order where the state's surveillance mechanisms were limited relative to those of the modern state.[137] An example concerns non-Muslim minorities, who were granted a degree of legal autonomy under the Ottoman Empire. Christian archbishops and rabbinical courts (*beth din*) allowed religious communities to decide over certain limited matters, although they encouraged their flock to follow the law (sharia) whenever possible.[138]

Court records indicate that people almost always sought to solve their problem in less formal venues first before bringing their claims to court. Most cases, in fact, were resolved in other venues by mediation or arbitration and informal law courts. Only in the final instance did disputants bring their claims to court.[139] A known example concerns *pashas* (governors), who acted as administrative judges involving matters of public order and security. Yet people often raised claims in the governor's court that exceeded this narrow remit. Claimants brought forward a wide variety of matters including theft, assault, fraud, violations of public morals, obscenity, inheritance disputes, debts and property rights.[140]

Some areas of the sharia were necessarily displaced by this intermixing nexus of laws. This is evident in the example of contractual formulae, the *shurūṭ*, for use in formal, private transactions. Islamic legal practice denied the validity of the use of written documents in a sharia court, despite an explicit ruling in the Quran at *sūrah* 2:282, which commanded: 'When you contract a debt for a fixed term, record it in writing. Let a scribe record it in writing between you … Be not averse to writing down [the contract], whether [the amount] be small or great, with its term'. Yet oral testimony provided the only form of formal proof inasmuch as the personal testimony of an upright Muslim was deemed much more worthy than a written document, which may have been falsified and/or have dubious origins. A private contract required at least two male witnesses, or two female witnesses for every male, and public documents required court-hired witnesses.[141] Every case heard in court required the use of witnesses,

[136] *Ibid.* [137] Wael B. Hallaq (n 9) 159.

[138] Abraham Marcus (n 130) 108.

[139] Leslie P. Peirce (n 123) 123. See also Wael B. Hallaq (n 9) 159.

[140] Abraham Marcus (n 130) 108.

[141] Jeanette A. Wakin, *The Functions of Documents in Islamic Law* (Albany, NY: University of New York Press, 1972), 6–7.

some who performed the role for the court regularly, and usually totalled three or four in number. Their role was to review the correctness of the legal procedures employed in the case and to retain memory of the case for the benefit of the community.[142] This distinctive characteristic seems to have reaffirmed the moral connection between the community and the court and may have contributed to consistency in judges' rulings.

The use of witnesses (*shahādah* in the wider sense) was not an Islamic invention, but was common throughout the pre-Islamic Near East. In pre-Islamic Arabia the use of witnesses for giving evidence was almost certainly the most common form of proof, and ceremonies may have been performed for their reception.[143] The legal invalidity of written documents in sharia courts may simply highlight an aspect of the law that – despite the religious and ethical imprint of the *shahādah* – remained procedurally immune.

Despite the complex range of legal sources in pre-modern legal practice and the wide flexibility available to the *qāḍī* in his judicial reasoning, a surprising legal consistency characterises the judicial law making of North Africa and the eastern Mediterranean regions under the Ottomans.[144] This may be partly due to the fact that no major changes took place with regard to the sources of law or the methodologies by which society made its rules as well as enduring conceptions of justice and law enforcement.[145] It also likely stems from Islam's unchallenged presence and prominent stature in nearly all legal and social institutions of the state. For example, the sharia court and its actors were deeply embedded in the social morality of premodern society to the extent that people were legally mindful of everyday realities.[146] The legally minded tight-knit culture in which the sharia was practised took place in a context of 'morally grounded social relations' within which certain modes of conduct were known as acceptable.[147]

The state's backing of the sharia legal system was critically important in buttressing this institutional structure. It was necessary to foster the conditions for legal consistency. Part of the Ottoman state's support involved a formalised administration of the courts by which the Ottomans sought to standardise procedures across the empire.[148] As a result, legal transactions

142 Leslie P. Peirce (n 123) 97. 143 *Ibid.*

144 Marcus argues this point with regard to eighteenth-century Aleppo. See Abraham Marcus (n 130) 110. Hallaq argues that pre-modern judicial decision making under the Ottomans can be characterised in these terms. See Wael B. Hallaq (n 9).

145 Abraham Marcus (n 130) 110.

146 Wael B. Hallaq (n 9) 173.

147 *Ibid.*, 168–9. 148 Nelly Hanna (n 133) 45.

developed a degree of uniformity and could be recognised across the empire. This made the transfer of records to the Aintaban court from other courts in the region (and vice versa) a frequent practice.[149] Another aspect of legal standardisation involves the assignment of judges to a post via a centrally organised administration and their rotation every two or three years.[150] The standardisation of the Ottoman legal system created many similarities between the courts of Cairo, Istanbul, Damascus and Hums so that the deeds issued in one could be recognised in another: 'A person could, in one of the courts of Cairo, buy a house in Damascus'.[151] All of these reforms resulted in increased public certainty concerning the way in which a court would rule on a particular matter.

2.7 Concluding remarks

The detailed hermeneutic known as the *uṣūl al-fiqh* typifies jurists' efforts to derive God's law in strict conformity with the literal meaning of His revelations. Yet the Quran contained little 'strictly' legal material that early religious specialists could use to develop a body of Islamic law. However, there was more legal content in the Sunna. It added to the legal content and helped to clarify the meaning of Quranic verses. Yet these two principal sources of law did not lay down rules for the infinite number of legal problems Muslims would eventually encounter as time and context evolved. To meet these challenges a wide variety of legal instruments were developed. Furthermore, jurists gave a wide berth to customary practices in their legal writings, despite not acknowledging them as a formal source of law. Together jurists' invocation of these instruments infused legal doctrine (*fiqh*) with a considerable degree of flexibility and pragmatism.

Court records originating during Ottoman rule of North Africa and the Eastern Mediterranean reveal a highly pluralistic legal culture in which the sharia constituted the social and moral centre of the community. Sharia courts regularly gave effect to customary law and left space for *kanun* in a wide range of legal matters. Other informal (pre-trial) dispute mechanisms were, in fact, a more likely avenue for people to settle their disputes. The courts' willingness to embrace this normative order demonstrates a striking degree of flexibility and adaptive capacity in the sharia. Evidence indicates that over the course of time the interaction

[149] Leslie P. Peirce (n 123) 110. [150] Abraham Marcus (n 130) 111–12.
[151] Nelly Hanna (n 133) 49.

of normative systems led to changes in the substance and procedure of each.

Records also indicate that a surprising degree of legal consistency characterised pre-modern law making. A number of reasons contributed to this outcome but perhaps none so important as the legal mindfulness and moral fabric of tightly knit Muslim communities. People understood what to expect from the law across a wide range of legal problems and these expectations were buttressed by a pronounced moral framework.

The degree to which these attributes of the pre-modern sharia legal system are or can be replicated in Islamic financial law requires a multifaceted examination. The next chapter takes a step towards answering this question by examining the commercial rules of the sharia. Knowledge of these is critically important in conceptualising the way in which jurists formulate Islamic financial law.

3

Islamic commercial doctrine and classical commercial transactions

Islamic commercial doctrine generally restricts contracting parties' freedom to contract. In particular, the prohibitions of *ribā* (usury) and *gharar* (risk) strongly affect the types of transaction in which a party may engage. Furthermore, the modus operandi by which the jurist is able to sanction novel contracts depends on a conservative tradition of textual interpretation. For these reasons and others it is important to investigate what the sacred texts say concerning the principal prohibitions and to understand the ways in which contract making can be lawfully undertaken.

The chapter begins with an analysis of the theological conception of the Islamic contract and the derived system of nominate contracts. Second, the definitional aspects of the prohibitions of *gharar* and *ribā* are considered in detail. Finally, Cairo Geniza records are analysed as a means of illuminating the way in which the law was applied in the classical period.

3.1 God's covenant with mankind

Classical Muslim thought is unanimous with respect to a human being's native endowment, a God-implanted ability, to know with absolute certainty of God's existence. Known as *fitra,* this universal concept describes one's ability to reason one's way to an unshakeable knowledge of God and to its attendant obligations. The pursuit of the knowledge of God ushers one into a covenantal encounter with Him. To know God is to stand before Him in a covenantal relationship.[1] This relationship is enunciated in the seminal passage detailing the covenant: 'And [remember] when your Lord brought forth from the Children of Adam, from their loins, their seed, and made them testify against themselves [saying]: Am I not

[1] Bernard Weiss, *The Spirit of Islamic Law* (Athens, GA: University of Georgia Press, 1998), 26–31.

your Lord? They said: Yes, verily. We testify. [This was] lest you should say at the Day of Resurrection: Lo! Of this we were unaware'.[2]

The orthodox interpretation of divine revelation insists that all obligations to which human beings are subjected arise out of the covenantal encounter between God and mankind. This relationship is vastly unequal as befits the superiority of God vis-à-vis His subjects. Thus, the passage is descriptive of two parties to the covenant: God, the Lord, who dictates the terms of the relationship, and mankind, an inferior, who submits to those terms.[3] The covenant describes the rights and responsibilities of mankind and enunciates the consequences both of compliance and non-compliance.[4]

The Muslim believer owes his obedience to God. His faithfulness or loyalty (*amānah*) to his pledged word is made in His presence so that God is witness to the conclusion and binding nature of all contracts. Several verses in the Quran highlight the divine importance of keeping one's oaths and agreements. For example: 'Verily those who swear allegiance to thee, swear allegiance really to God, the hand of God is above their hands; so whoever breaks faith, to his own hurt he breaks it, and to those who fulfil what they have pledged to God, he will one day give a mighty reward'.[5] Likewise, oft-cited verses that remind believers to hold tight to their pledge illustrate the general tenor of such commandments: 'Ye who believe! Fulfil all obligations'[6] and 'Fulfil the covenant of God when ye have entered into it and break not your oaths after ye have confirmed them'.[7] Jurists developed the Islamic law of contract from the primordial covenant. Thus, the sharia, not unlike the Western legal principle of *pacta sunt servanda*,[8] underscores the sanctity of contract.

However, the ever-present ethical concerns of Islamic law differ from the Western legal principle, as contracting parties are given the means to cancel unilaterally a validly concluded contract, if necessary. Known as the option of rescission (*faskh*), they are designed to ensure that the agreement between the parties is real and not just apparent and that the parties

[2] Quran, trans. by M. A. S Abdel Haleem (Oxford University Press, 2008), 7:172.
[3] Bernard Weiss (n 1) 31–2. [4] *Ibid.*, 93.
[5] Quran (n 2) 48:10. [6] Quran (n 2) 5:1.
[7] Quran (n 2) 16:91.
[8] William Ballantyne, 'The Shari'a and Its Relevance to Modern Transnational Transactions' in *Arab Comparative & Commercial Law: The International Approach* (Proceedings IBA First Arab Regional Conference: Cairo 15–19 February 1987), vol. I (London: Graham & Trotman, 1987), 12; William Ballantyne, 'Commercial Law: The Conflict in Shari'a and Secular Law', in Sohrab Behdad and Farhad Nomani (eds.), *International Review of Comparative Public Policy* (Greenwich, CT: JAI Press 1997), 228.

are satisfied and committed to the fulfilment of their mutual obligations.[9] Hence, the principal ethical aspiration embedded within the Islamic law of contracts seeks to extract the highest degree of certainty in the rights and obligations amongst the parties. The extinguishment of the option, either by agreement or forfeit, triggers the mechanism whereby the contract is endowed with binding legal force.[10]

The option may only be attached to contracts that involve consideration and are to be legally binding. Where these criteria do not exist, the option to rescind does not come into play. Straightforward contracts such as sale (*bay'*) and hire (*ijārah*) fulfil these criteria, while valid but not binding contracts such as partnership (*sharikah*), agency (*wakālah*) and reward (*ju'ālah*) are revocable by either party.[11] The system of options is varied and complex and will not be pursued further here. However, it is one of several features of Islamic commercial law that distinguish its underlying ethical impetus from the absolute binding nature of the Western maxim.

3.2 The role of intention (*Qaṣd*)

Muslim scholars agree that human will alone (*irādah*) does not create rights and obligations, the central elements resulting from the conclusion of a contract. While they agree that human intention (*qaṣd*) is responsible for triggering the commencement of the contractual process, the effects of the contract are produced immediately and irrespective of what the parties have agreed. Thus the contract becomes a mere exchange of rules, wherein the role of human will (*irādah*) is curtailed dramatically.[12] The will of the author of a contractual declaration has almost no place in the Islamic scheme of nominate contracts. Chehata, the famous Egyptian jurist, emphasises: 'If the spirit of the person making the declaration is to have in view the effects of the declaration, his will is in no way attached one way or another to the contents of the declaration. This content, by which is meant the signification of the declaration, is realised

9 Noel J. Coulson, *Commercial Law in the Gulf States* (London: Graham & Trotman, 1984), 57–8.

10 *Ibid.*

11 *Ibid.*, 61. Kuran has stirred controversy by arguing that the Islamic laws of partnership stifled the economic development of Middle Eastern civilisation. See Timur Kuran, *The Long Divergence: How Islamic Law Held Back the Middle East* (Princeton University Press, 2011).

12 Nayla Comair-Obeid, *The Law of Business Contracts in the Arab Middle East* (London: Kluwer Law International, 1996), 6.

by virtue of the law. The will cannot by its own virtue create rights and obligations'.[13]

Seen in this light, the contract in Islamic law is a cause (*sabab*) that flows from the sharia. It produces effects (*aḥkām*) in terms of rights and obligations, equally foreseen by the law.[14] Most contemporary Muslim theorists perceive the element of intention (*qaṣd)* as a choice (*ikhtiyār*) at the moment of declaration, a primordial element in the formation of the contract. Thus, according to theology, freedom in contracting exists only at the level of the *ikhtiyār.*

The emphasis placed upon the role of intention (*nīyyah*), rather than will, has led to the wilful underdevelopment of cause (*sabab*) as a juridical structure in Islamic law.[15] In its stead jurists stress the important role that Islam places on the detailed nature of the rules concerning parties' contractual consent, and most especially, concerning the subject matter of the legal act. The richness of this legal matter, they argue, is sufficient to determine which legal acts should be cancelled.[16]

Consequently, the reduced role of intention in secular transactions (*mu'āmalāt*) as opposed to the realm of worship (*'ibādāt*) – where the importance of intention is undisputed – is evidenced in the differential treatment applied to the concept by the four schools of law. Al-Shāfi'i, writing in his famous *al-Umm* (the Mother), emphasised the appearance of validity of the contract which cannot be cancelled based on the suspicion or previous practices of the parties. An unlawful intention is reprehensible (*makrūh*) but it does not cancel an agreement or disposition so long as it is not expressed.[17] Likewise, the Ḥanafīs stressed the validity of a contract based upon its appearance even despite circumstantial evidence indicating an act's unlawfulness.[18] The Ḥanbalīs and Mālikīs, however, foresee a greater role for the will, and hence the intention (*niyyah*) of the parties receives greater emphasis when assessing the validity of contracts.[19] Therefore, Ḥanbalī and Mālikī jurists annul any agreements or unilateral dispositions of which the authors' intentions are suspected to be unlawful.[20] This is also the reason why the Hanbalīs do not condone *ḥiyal* or legal stratagems, which were examined in the previous chapter.[21]

13 *Ibid.* 14 *Ibid.*

15 Nabil Saleh, 'Are the Validity and Construction of Legal Acts Affected by Cause (Sabab)?' (1992) 7 *ALQ* 116, 117.

16 *Ibid.*, 120–1. 17 *Ibid.*, 123. 18 *Ibid.*, 125.

19 Nabil Saleh, 'The Role of Intention (Niyya) Under Saudi Arabian Hanbali Law' (2009) 23 *ALQ*, 469, 474.

20 *Ibid.* 21 *Ibid.*, 474.

The importance of contractual intention (*niyyah*) in assessing the validity of contracts is perhaps an even more prominent issue today than in the early Islamic centuries. It is critical to Islamic financial law making, in particular, because the adaptability of the sharia can be used for illegitimate purposes. In the next section the system of Islamic nominate contracts, the building blocks of Islamic financial contracts, is explored.

3.3 The system of Islamic nominate contracts

The term *'ahd* is used frequently throughout the Quran and seems at times to be a synonym of *'aqd* (pl. *'uqūd*), although the latter is normally used to refer to bilateralism,[22] or to a bilateral economic exchange between parties. From the covenant or *'ahd* flow all other obligations, i.e. commandments and rules, which God also demands of his slaves. The Arabic word for contract, *'aqd*, is invoked only once in the Quran, in *sūrah* 5:1, cited above. However, *'aqd* appears consistently in the classical works of Islamic law[23] and is thus commonly used to denote the juridical operations concluded between parties.

In its more secular interpretation the Islamic contract is a legally recognised undertaking or juridical act, which is not necessarily used to denote an agreement. The term also describes unilateral juridical acts and dispositions by will (*mortis causa*) such as gifts, bequests, gratuitous loans, guarantees and so forth that do not require the consent of any other party. Moreover, the system of contracts includes mere juristic acts that do not require consideration, such as the repudiation of marriage by the husband (*ṭalāq*) and the manumission of a slave.[24]

Jurists laid down no less than thirty specific nominate contracts, nearly all of which were modelled on the contract of sale. In fact, some modern scholars of Islam view the contract of sale as a substitute for a general theory of contract, which itself is 'probably too occidental and systematic an approach' to impose upon the Islamic body of law.[25] In fact, the exceptions between the nominate contracts far outweigh the generalities amongst them.[26]

[22] Wael B. Hallaq, 'Contracts and Alliances' in Jane Damen McAuliff (ed.), *Encyclopedia of the Qur'an* (Brill Online, 2008), 1–4.

[23] Susan E. Rayner, *The Theory of Contracts in Islamic Law* (Arab and Islamic Laws Series, London: Graham & Trotman 1991), 88.

[24] *Ibid.* [25] *Ibid.*, 89.

[26] Noel J. Coulson (n 9) 27–31.

The jurist's casuistic approach to the law was inclined to elicit subtle rules pertaining to specific contracts rather than formulating broad theories.[27] In particular, *qiyās* was used to elicit additional contracts and the development of intricate rules pertaining to each commercial contract. The resulting category of contract was subsequently authorised by hadiths or other legal sources.[28]

A scheme of nominate contracts emerged in which contracting parties could seek out a valid and effective nominate contract heading amongst an array of basic and exceptional contract types. So for example, a contract of sale for agricultural commodities that had not yet been sown would be deemed null and void as it involved uncertainty as to the existence of the object of contract – comprising the central element of the prohibition of *gharar*. However, parties could choose another contract heading such as the *salam* (forward purchase), in which the non-existence of the commodity is permissible, and proceed with the exchange. Hence the rigid formality of the nominate contract system was minimised to a considerable extent.[29]

Classical jurists generally categorised the system of contracts into four branches, based on a classification as to whether the exchange is of the corpus or the usufruct, and whether it is for a consideration or not. These four contract types are often mentioned in the *fiqh* literature but, as seen, the contract of sale receives greatest emphasis as it tends to act as a hypothetical model from which other contracts originate. The four classifications are: (1) *bay'*, which denotes the transfer of the corpus for a consideration; (2) *hibah* (gift), the transfer of a corpus without consideration; (3) *ijārah* (lease, hire), the transfer of the usufruct for a consideration; and, finally, (4) *'arīyah* (loan), the transfer of the usufruct without consideration.[30] Despite their chief importance as foundational contracts, a much greater number of contracts constitute 'exceptions' to the basic scheme. The *'ulemā'* cite as 'standard practice' that by strict analogy or *qiyās* with the relevant prototype contract these exceptions would be invalid; in other words, their *'illah* would not correspond with the prototype contract. This is the case with exceptional contracts such as *istiṣnā'* and *salam*, which are examined below. It also applies to *bay' al-wafā'* – a financing contract in which a house or land parcel is sold for a cash price with the condition that the seller can repurchase the house at a later date. Agricultural tenancies such as the *muzāra'ah*, and, most importantly for modern Islamic

[27] Susan E. Rayner (n 23) 91. [28] *Ibid.*, 100.
[29] Noel J. Coulson (n 9) 30. [30] *Ibid.*, 19.

banking transactions, the *muḍārabah*, are all seen as exceptions to the relevant prototype contracts.[31] As a rule of thumb, all contracts for which a consideration as a fixed percentage of the profits is determined as a condition to the contract fall into this latter category.

Although such contracts did not meet the rigid standards of Islamic legal theory, classical jurists came to regard 'exceptional' contracts' as 'vital and integral parts of the total system'.[32] In fact, these exceptions far outnumbered the foundational structures,[33] which can be seen as further proof of the law's flexibility.

3.4 The conditions necessary for the general validity of contracts

The Islamic contract of sale contains four critical cornerstones or factors that apply to all other contracts. These are the seller, the buyer, the form (*ṣīghah*) and the object of the contract.[34] Jurists disagree whether it is necessary to combine all of these elements as a matter of principle. In all contracts, however, jurists do agree that the form of the contract must include an acceptance (*qabūl*) and corresponding offer (*ījāb*).[35] Further, a sale is valid if its fundamental components (*arkān*) and ancillary attributes (*waṣf*) are legal and are not connected to a third party. Moreover, a valid sale must not contain options. Properly concluded, a valid sale commences the immediate exchange of ownership of the object of sale and the price. Therefore, a sale without options would transfer immediate ownership of the object of sale to the buyer and the price to the seller.[36]

The legal status of a contract is either valid or invalid as a result of the degree to which the cornerstones and conditions of the contract are satisfied. A valid (*ṣaḥīḥ*) contract satisfies all of its conditions and cornerstones, while an invalid (*bāṭil*) contract violates one or more of its conditions and cornerstones. A sale is invalid if it is defective (*fāsid*) according to the majority. However, the Ḥanafīs categorise contracts according to three criteria: namely, (1) valid (2) defective and (3) invalid. Therefore, they distinguish between contracts that are defective and those that are invalid. A forbidden contract, although sinful, could be engaged in without invalidating the contract. Thus Ḥanafīs differentiated between the fundamental

[31] *Ibid.* [32] *Ibid.*, 29. [33] *Ibid.*, 28–9.

[34] Wael B. Hallaq, *Shari'a: Theory, Practice, Transformations* (Cambridge University Press, 2009), 443, 240.

[35] Wahbah Al-Zuhayli, *Financial Transactions in Islamic Jurisprudence*, trans. by Mahmoud A. El-Gamal, vol. I (Damascus: Dar al-Fikr, 2003), 22.

[36] *Ibid.*, 72–3.

components (*arkān)* of a contract, which invalidate it; and the prohibition of a general characteristic (*waṣf*) that only leads to it being defective.[37]

However, the majority of jurists ruled that a prohibited contract is invalid and that whoever utilises such a contract has committed a sin. Furthermore, the prohibition of a main component (*rukn*) of a contract 'is equivalent to a prohibition of a general characteristic that is satisfied in that particular contract'.[38] Any action, whether a fundamental component or a general characteristic, that disagrees with God's commands, is both defective and invalid.[39]

With respect to the form of a contract, the law's overriding concern is that the quality of *riḍā*, i.e. unconditional consent, is present between the parties. *Riḍā* can be obtained in different ways.[40] With respect to contracts orally concluded, Muslim jurists regard the exchange of offer and acceptance not as an exchange of promises or even implied promises, but rather as performative utterances, that is, as oral statements that have legal effects. In keeping with the sacrosanct nature of the utterance, both offer and acceptance are generally to be expressed in the past tense to indicate finality, rather than in the future tense, which is promissory (*'idah*).[41] The past-tense expression of the dispositive utterance reflects the contracting parties' establishment of immediate rights and obligations, so that the contract of sale is envisioned as an immediate transfer of counter-values.[42] However, the Ḥanafīs allow the exchange of offer and acceptance in the present tense as it indicates immediate or future action depending on the context.[43] An offer made in the present tense requires further clarification so that there is no uncertainty with respect to the way in which such language may be construed.[44]

With respect to the object or effects of the contract, a series of overarching principles must be satisfied that imply that every category of acts or contracts has an end it itself. Generally, the objective must be morally

[37] *Ibid.*, 71–2. [38] *Ibid.*, 71. [39] *Ibid.*, 72.

[40] Wael B. Hallaq (n 34) 240.

[41] Aron Zysow, 'The Problem of Offer and Acceptance: A Study of Implied-in-Fact Contracts in Islamic Law and Common Law' (1985–1986) 34 *Clev.St.L.Rev.* 69, 75. The contract of marriage is exceptional in that it requires specific language, namely the utterance of *zawwāja* and *nakaḥa* (both meaning to marry).

[42] In the majority of contracts offer and acceptance must be exchanged in the same session (*majlis*). However, the *majlis* requirement does not mean that contracts cannot be concluded in written form. The acceptance of a written offer is deemed to be binding in the same manner as if the parties had concluded the agreement in the *majlis*. See Wael B. Hallaq (n 34) 243.

[43] Wahbah Al-Zuhayli (n 35) 9. [44] Wael B. Hallaq (n 34) 242.

attainable and accord with other religious requirements; otherwise it is declared illicit (*ḥarām*). In particular, the contract must be linked to the holy texts and the effects must necessarily conform to the principles of the sharia. Any transgression of these effects or the creation of new ones that do not conform to sharia principles is unlawful. For example, sale has been deemed permissible on the basis of supporting evidence from the Quran, the Sunna, and *ijmāʿ*.[45] The Quran is explicit on this matter: 'But Allah has permitted trade'[46] and 'But let there be among you traffic and trade by mutual good will'.[47] The second criterion pertains to the determination of what the religion of Islam forbids. This list could comprise numerous illicit objects including the sale of alcohol, pork or *ribā* (usury).[48]

Furthermore, several necessary conditions are attached to the object of contract for it to be valid. Most jurists agree that four principal requirements must be met. First, the object of the sale must be in existence. Thus the sale of a non-existent object or an object that may cease to exist is not permitted. Exceptions to this general rule are made for the contracts of *bayʿ al-salam* (a forward sale in which the price of a commodity is paid upfront) and *istiṣnāʿ* (the sale of a manufactured product/contract of hire, with payments made at varying stages). Second, the object of sale must be owned and must be temporarily non-perishable, i.e. available for future use or consumption. Third, the article of sale must be owned privately and be in the possession of the seller. This stipulation prevents the sale of publicly owned lands, waters, wildlife and so forth. Finally, the object of sale must be deliverable upon conclusion of the sale. Therefore, the sale of an undeliverable good may not be concluded.[49] The existence of countervalues in a contract of sale is given further consideration below.

3.5 Appending *shurūṭ* (conditions) to contracts

As discussed above, free will has a limited scope in the formation of the Islamic contract. Each nominate contract produces its own effects and the degree to which these may be modified or altered by appending special conditions (pl. *shurūṭ*; sg. *sharṭ*) illuminates the object of the present discussion. Despite the theological limitations that have been discussed, the religious scholars (*fuquhāʿ*) concede that parties are free to contract

[45] Wahbah Al-Zuhayli (n 35) 6. [46] Quran (n 2) 2:275.
[47] Quran (n 2) 4:29. [48] Nayla Comair-Obeid (n 12) 16–17.
[49] Wahbah Al-Zuhayli (n 35) 15–16.

as they see fit as long as they do not add new effects to the contract or contravene the criteria with respect to the essence or finality of the act as established above.[50] Jurists perceive a danger in allowing parties to remove or, much less likely, add effects to their contracts as these may create abuses which involve illicit profit or *ribāwi* (*ribā*-based) transactions. An imbalance of benefits amongst contracting parties may ensue that undermines the essential reciprocity of exchange and the principles of equity and justice that underpin the law. Jurists legitimate this ruling with the well-known hadith from the Bukhārī compendium in which the Prophet expressed his opinion on the subject in front of his wife Aisha: 'What do they think of, those men who lay down conditions not to be found in the Book of God? Any stipulation not to be found in the Book of God is null and void. Were there a hundred such conditions of this sort, the one rule of God will be more equitable and more sure'.[51]

Of course, parties to a commercial transaction need to add stipulations or other conditions to a contract to fulfil commercial objectives. Recall that some modern jurists perceived a margin of freedom for doing so only in the formation of the option (*ikhtiyār*). At the moment of the option parties may choose different modalities with respect to the execution of the contract as long as these do not offend the essence of its structure.[52] However, the positions of the schools of law with respect to these criteria differ as considered below.

3.5.1 Conditions and the four schools of law

Two general strands of thinking underlie the *madhhab* positions with respect to the appendage of ancillary conditions to an Islamic contract. The first is typified by the Ḥanafī position, which is almost identical in every point of detail to the Mālikī and Shāfi'i viewpoint. Ḥanafīs categorise *shurūṭ* into two classes: clauses that are valid or *ṣaḥīḥ*; and clauses that are null and void (*bāṭil*). The following examines those conditions that do not conflict with the sharia. First, clauses that confirm the effects of contracts already established in the *fiqh* do not occasion controversy as no additional obligation is imposed on either party. An example would be for a seller to deliver a sale object to the buyer as this is an obligation that resides with the seller whether explicitly mentioned or not. Second, Al-Kāsānī notes that clauses that establish effects that agree

[50] Nayla Comair-Obeid (n 12) 32. [51] *Ibid.*, 32–3.
[52] *Ibid.*, 33.

with the effects of acts to which they are attached are also deemed valid. According to Ibn Qudāma, these are known as stipulations 'connected with the legitimate interests of the parties'. These include: a pledge; a security or bond in a sales transaction to secure payment;[53] the determination of the period over which payment is to be made; and specification of the quality of services to be performed. These stipulations are valid and binding.[54]

Finally, many clauses are deemed lawful due to their customary usage or practice. These tend to be services of little import that a purchaser may require of a seller when conducting a transaction. This latter class of *shurūṭ* is seen as an exception and granted permissibility on the basis of *istiḥsān*. Al-Kāsānī explains that 'according to *qiyās* the clauses are not valid because they involve a supplementary advantage for one of the contracting parties. They are null and void just like a clause by which the purchaser of some cloth required the seller to make him a shirt of it. But such clauses have been accepted in practice; the *qiyās* has given ground in the face of such practice and these stipulations have been admitted by *istiḥsān*'.[55] Notably, Shāfi'is and Mālikīs admit the use of clauses that reflect customary commercial practice as a matter of principle.

As noted above, Ḥanbalīs take a decidedly more liberal view of the role of human will in the contracting process. Unsurprisingly, Islamic financial law often avails itself of the Ḥanbalī doctrine. Ḥanbalī liberalism extends beyond the sphere of the option even to the actual effects of the contract. Yet clauses and stipulations must not contravene general prohibitions or consensus (*ijmā'*). In fact, few new contracts are able to avoid this legal web.[56] Still, the general sentiment is that parties are able to contract according to their requirements. The influential Ḥanbalī jurist, Ibn Taymīyah, went so far as to state that 'the parties decide as they wish the content of their juridical acts and determine the effects on the condition that these effects are not contrary to public order and morals'.[57]

The Ḥanbalī *madhhab* adopted several areas of overlapping restrictions with other schools that are worth noting because of Ḥanbalī doctrinal prominence in IFL. First, as is the case with the Ḥanafīs, Shāfi'is and

[53] *Ibid.*, 35–6. [54] Noel J. Coulson (n 9) 51.

[55] Nayla Comair-Obeid (n 12) 36.

[56] Frank E. Vogel and Samuel L. Hayes, *Islamic Law and Finance: Religion, Risk, and Return* (London: Kluwer Law International, 1998), 99.

[57] Nayla Comair-Obeid (n 12) 38.

Mālikīs, a single contract may not comprise two agreements or stipulate a condition the fulfilment of which is necessary to enact the other. A famous dictum from the Prophet declared that 'a loan coupled with a sale is not lawful'.[58] This prohibition is ostensibly designed to avoid the uncertainty surrounding the apportionment of consideration or price. Therefore, the sharia forbids the creation of two contracts for a single price. This is a significant problem for Islamic financial transactions since they combine nominate contracts and wholly novel legal structures to achieve a single financial objective. The solution has been to create 'promise to purchase/ sale' undertakings, which enable individual contracts to be transacted separately. This strategy is examined in detail in Chapter 5.

Second, a contract of sale may not impose two ancillary conditions imposing supplementary obligations upon the same contracting party. So, for example, a buyer who purchased corn or wheat and required the seller to both grind and deliver the commodity to him would be unlawful.

Finally, conditions may not be imposed that run counter to the juridical purpose of the act to which they are attached.[59] For instance, a seller could not forbid a buyer from disposing of his property as he wishes and so forth. While these rules place restrictions upon the contracting parties' liberty to contract to some extent, particularly as seen in the modern sense of the concept, the Ḥanbalī position is nonetheless relatively unencumbered as compared to other *madhhabs.*

The Ḥanbalī stance on contractual liberty is supported with textual evidence from the Quran which, as noted, includes exhortations to fulfil one's contracts. From these verses Ḥanbalīs deduce that every contract or condition that God has not declared *ḥarām* is licit in the absence of any divine textual references that speak otherwise.[60] Hence, the Ḥanbalī position clearly views a larger role for human will in choosing the effects and conditions of contracts. There is a presumption of permissibility (*ibāhah*) in transactions because 'nothing in them is forbidden,' as Ibn Taymīyah enunciated. According to Ḥanbalī jurists, an attempt to declare something forbidden on merely speculative grounds, or to impose hardship or unnecessary rigidity upon people, violates the spirit of tolerance and well-being that God wishes for His believers.[61] The following Quranic verse is

[58] Noel J. Coulson (n 9) 54. [59] *Ibid.*, 39.

[60] Muhammad Yusuf Musa, 'The Liberty of the Individual in Contracts and Conditions According to Islamic Law' (1955) 2 *Islam.Quarterly* 79, 84.

[61] Mohammad Hashim Kamali, *Islamic Commercial Law* (Cambridge: Islamic Texts Society, 1999), 67–9.

cited as proof: 'God desires for you ease, He does not desire for you difficulty'.[62] Every people and epoch develops customary manners of business practice for which it would impose hardship were people required to provide explicit textual support (*naṣṣ*) from the Quran or Sunna to vindicate the legality of every commercial exchange.[63]

3.6 *Gharar*

The complex regime of Islamic contracts is subject to additional rules that have wide-reaching effects. The following examination begins with the prohibition of *gharar* as it relates to the existence of the subject matter of the contract, which was discussed above. The prohibition of *gharar* (risk, uncertainty, or speculation) is concerned with the issue of the existence of the counter-values at the time of contract; their qualities, quantities, ownership and presence.[64] Islamic law is averse to transactions which blindly award one person's good fortune at the expense of another's bad luck. It is considered an unjust result for which the *fuquhā'* sought to devise a systematic principle that required equality and fairness between the transacting parties in the formulation of contract. A just profit should be the result of one's labour, time and expenditure.[65]

Aleatory contracts, both pre-modern and contemporary, consist of financial products that seem to typify the probabilistic inequality the jurists so vehemently opposed. These contracts entail an uncertain outcome for one of the transacting parties whose benefit or loss from the transaction is impossible to predict. Parties to an aleatory contract stipulate the possibility of gain or else they seek to insure themselves against loss as a result of some unforeseeable circumstance. Yet gains and losses are not calculable beforehand as a result of this uncertainty. Thus the element of uncertainty on which these contracts rest necessarily results in the benefit of one party at the expense of another's loss.[66] Nonetheless,

[62] Quran (n 2) 2:185.

[63] Muhammad Al-Amine and Muhammad Al-Bashir, 'Istisna' and Its Application in Islamic Banking' (2001) 16 *ALQ* 22, 27.

[64] Some authoritative works on the subject are: Nayla Comair-Obeid (n 12); Nabil A. Saleh, *Unlawful Gain and Legitimate Profit in Islamic Law* (Cambridge University Press, 1986), 61; and Ahmad Hidayat Buang, *Studies in the Islamic Law of Contracts: The Prohibition of Gharar* (Kuala Lumpur: International Law Book Services, 2000).

[65] Hussein Hassan, 'Contracts in Islamic Law: The Principles of Commutative Justice and Liberality' (2002) 13 *Journ.Islam.Stud.* 257, 280.

[66] Nayla Comair-Obeid (n 12) 55. For a very interesting analysis in which the author has applied game theory to the concept of *gharar*, see Sami Al-Suwailem, 'Towards

jurisprudence ceded ground to the necessities of commerce in numerous instances, which resulted in a philosophical rendering of exceptions and qualifications to the general prohibition. These differed according to the jurist's *madhhab*, and the context and time of his writing.

The prohibition of *gharar* has widened in scope and detail over the centuries. The Quran warns humans to take care with regard to their own folly and extravagance, which may interfere with the believers' ritual and worship. Games of hazard or gambling (*maysir*) – a favourite pastime of pre-Islamic Arabs – are proscribed: 'You who believe, intoxicants and gambling, idolatrous practices, and [(divining with) – a pagan Arab custom] arrows are repugnant acts – Satan's doing – shun them so that you may prosper'.[67] These foundational verses do not specifically mention *gharar* but provide a general idea or principle that is subsequently broadened and elaborated in the Sunna.

3.6.1 *The sale of a non-existent object*

Ibn Ḥanbal, eponym of the Ḥanbalī *madhhab*, relates a well-known tradition that typifies the attributes of the prohibition. One should 'not buy fish in the sea, for it is *gharar*',[68] i.e., because one does not know with certainty what one is buying. Moreover, Ibn Māja's recounting of the following hadith continues to shape the concept of *gharar*, despite an acknowledged weak chain of transmission (*isnād*). He recites, 'The Prophet forbade sale of what is in the wombs, sale of the contents of the udders, sale of a slave when he has run away, ... and [sale of the] "stroke of the diver" [*ḍarbat al-ghā'is*, sale in advance of the yield of a diver's dive, whatever it was]'.[69] The message of these hadiths, according to Muslim scholars, is to protect the weak against exploitation by the strong. The general rule is that any transaction devoid of uncertainty and speculation facilitates the parties' complete and perfect knowledge of the counter-values to be exchanged.[70]

Ibn Rushd, a Mālikī scholar, wrote in his *Bidāyat Al-mujtahid* that *gharar* in sale transactions causes the buyer to suffer damage as a result of a want of knowledge (*jahl*), which affects either the price or the object of

an Objective Measure of Gharar in Exchange' (2000) 7 *Islam.Econ.Stud.*, 61–102. Al-Suwailem explains that the Quranic concept of *gharar* was to prevent enmity by prohibiting outcomes in which one party wins everything (zero-sum) at the expense of the other party.

[67] Quran (n 2) 5:90 and 2:219.

[68] Frank E. Vogel and Samuel L. Hayes (n 56) 88.

[69] *Ibid.* [70] Nabil A. Saleh (n 64) 62–3.

purchase. He specified several conditions that must be met for *gharar* to be averted: (1) both the price and the subject matter must be in existence; (2) the characteristics of these must be known; (3) their amount must be determined; (4) the parties must have control over these factors so as to ensure that the transaction can take place; (5) and, finally, the date of future performance, if any, must be defined.[71]

Subject matters that are non-existent at the time a bilateral transaction takes place have been declared void by an overwhelming majority of traditional Muslim scholars.[72] A non-existent subject matter (*ma'dūm*) epitomises the risk and speculation of a transaction based on a want of knowledge, and the eventual qualities and condition a subject matter may possess. A non-existent subject matter in contractual relations is often equated with debt (*dayn*). Yet the meaning of *dayn* is more general in that it relates to something not present, which is yet to be paid or completed at a future date, but which is already owned by the creditor pursuant to the contract. While a *dayn* is not yet in the possession of the creditor, it is embedded within his or her human capacity (*dhimmah*). Therefore, despite its incorporeal nature, *dayn* is described metaphorically in physical terms, leading some contemporary scholars to equate it with the English common law concept of 'chose in action', or a thing not in possession of the creditor.[73]

*3.6.2 The sale of debt (*bay' al-dayn*)*

Consensus surrounds the opinion that the sale of a debt for another debt at a discount (*bay' al-dayn bi al-dayn*) is not valid since it results in *ribā*.[74] The right to payment is considered to be money (a *ribāwi* good) and thus constitutes a *dayn* in the *dhimmah* of the debtor. Money can only be traded at par value or else it violates the rules pertaining to both *ribā* and *gharar*. An oft-cited hadith supported this prohibition: 'The Messenger of God forbade sale of the delayed obligation [*al-kālī*] for a delayed obligation'.[75]

[71] Ibn Rushd, *The Distinguished Jurist's Primer, a Translation of Al-Bidayat Al-Mujtahid*, trans. by Imran Ahsan Khan Nyazee, vol. II (Reading: Garnet Publishing Limited, 1996) 148 and 172.

[72] *Ibid.*; Mohammad Hashim Kamali (n 61) 99–102. See also Wahbah Al-Zuhayli (n 35) 74.

[73] Nicholas H. D. Foster, 'Transfers of Rights and Obligations in the UAE: A Comparative Analysis in the Light of English Law, French Law and the shari'a' in Eugene Cotran (ed.), *Yearbook of Islamic and Middle Eastern Law*, vol. VII (The Hague: Brill, 2000–2001), 41.

[74] Wahbah Al-Zuhayli (n 35) 81.

[75] Nicholas H. D. Foster (n 73) 43.

The transfer of a debt from one debtor to another (*ḥawālah*) at par value could be undertaken subject to a number of strict rules that ensure that instances of *ribā* and *gharar* do not arise. Suppose that X (a transferee) owes a debt to Y (transferor) and Y owes a debt to Z (creditor). By transferring Y's right to payment to Z, Y is freed from his obligation and Z has a right against X. Different rules pertain to the schools of law including who requires consent, whether a pre-existing debt owing to the transferor from the transferee is required, and to whom the creditor has recourse in case the transferee is unable to pay.[76]

Modern Islamic finance, in principle, prohibits the sale of a debt at a discount to third parties, although there is controversy concerning some types of transactional practices, which in economic terms replicate the transfer of debt. Controversy also surrounds the development of modern proprietary rights such as patents and copyrights and whether these should be considered as dependent on corporeal matter (*'ayn*) or whether they should be seen as incorporeal rights in the *dhimmah* of the debtor.[77] In the former case the transfer of such rights could be exchanged with a profit while the latter require equivalence according to the rules of *ribā al-faḍl*. These issues are considered below.

3.6.3 Gharar *and the four schools of law*

Commercial requirements are almost certain to have led many prominent scholars to qualify their objections to *gharar* transactions. Ibn Rushd wrote that in case of necessity (*ḍarūrah*), and when the future existence of the subject matter is certain, a sale contract could be valid. For example, a sale contract involving the harvest of fruit prior to full ripening was permitted by the Mālikīs as long as such fruit can be harvested in continuing succession. The majority opinion proscribed the sale of fruit prior to its full ripening.[78]

Ibn Rushd skilfully pointed out that each school of law's position with respect to a contract of sale for an absent thing or object (*bay' ghā'ib*) was unique and certainly not homogeneous. In a *bay' ghā'ib* the vendor has title over the subject matter, but the subject matter is either not available

[76] Nicholas Dylan Ray, 'The Medieval Islamic System of Credit and Banking: Legal and Historical Considerations' (1997) 12 *ALQ* 43, 61.

[77] Mughees Shaukat, *Sale of Goods and Sale of Debt: A Comparative Analysis* (INCEIF Paper, INCEIF, 2010), 9–10.

[78] Ibn Rushd (n 71) 182.

or not present at the meeting of the parties. Historically, the *bay' ghā'ib* served an important role in regional and long-distance trading in the far-flung Islamic provinces, as needed commodities were imported from trading partners without the buyer having inspected the goods prior to their importation.[79] Al-Malik and his disciples permitted the sale of an absent commodity so long as it was accompanied by description and was of the nature or kind of good the essence of which did not alter prior to the buyer taking possession. If the object conformed to the description, the sale became binding. On the other hand, Al-Shāfi'i and his disciples prohibited the *bay' ghā'ib* due to the buyer's failure to inspect the goods prior to purchase. Whether the unavailable object was accompanied by description was immaterial to their reasoning.[80]

The Ḥanafīs deemed the transaction valid by requiring the vendor to indicate the location of the good and by describing the object in detail. Known as the *khiyār al-ru'yah* (the option of inspection), it entitled the purchaser to inspect the subject matter after the purchase whereupon he could decide to proceed with or rescind the sale. Likewise, the Ḥanafīs held that the buyer always had a right to *khiyār al-ru'yah* – even when the subject matter mirrors the seller's description – and were thus more lenient with respect to *bay' ghā'ib*.[81] The point of contention concerned the issue of whether the degree of knowledge gained through description of the object for sale is equal to that gained by one's sensory perception of an object at hand.[82] Thus the eponyms of the schools debated the degree of uncertainty (*gharar*) in any given transaction, which, of course, can never be entirely risk-free.

According to al-Nawawī, Shāfi'īs tolerated *gharar* in case of need and when *gharar* could only be averted with exceptional difficulty.[83] Ibn Taymīyah argued vehemently that the sale of a non-existent object is unlawful only if it involves gambling and the misappropriation of the property of others, as there is neither a textual ruling (*naṣṣ*), nor a general consensus to support the view that such a sale is unlawful.[84] His interpretation allowed a large degree of risk. His disciple, Ibn Qayyim al-Jawzīyah, defended his mentor's argument by asserting that no reference, either specific or general, exists in the Quran or the *Sunna* of the Prophet or his companions to the effect that the sale of something non-existent is

[79] Nabil A. Saleh (n 64) 85–9.
[80] Ibn Rushd (n 71) 187–8. [81] *Ibid.*
[82] *Ibid.*, 188. [83] Nabil A. Saleh (n 64) 67.
[84] Mohammad Hashim Kamali (n 61) 100.

unlawful. The essential feature of sale is the delivery of the item sold; if the seller is unable to deliver, then this is the risk and speculation – the gambling – of which the Quran clearly speaks.[85] These scholars may have recognised that the tendency to define *gharar* in terms of non-existence of the subject matter had become deeply entrenched, and had outgrown the early substance of the principle as depicted in the Quran, i.e. risk, speculation and uncertainty associated with gambling. The concept of *gharar* had evolved by virtue of *qiyās* into a question of the existence of the subject matter in a contract of sale.

Contemporary interpretations of *gharar* have sought to interpret the prohibition in the larger legal context. The Lebanese jurist, Maḥmaṣānī, qualifies the general requirement of existence of the subject matter by making a distinction between the subject matter as a specific piece of property (*'ayn*) and the subject matter in the form of labour (*'amal*) or use (*manfa'ah*). The subject matter as an *'ayn* must meet the requirements as discussed above; whereas subject matters in the form of labour and use are necessarily non-existent at the time of contract and only come into being with the gradual implementation of the contract.[86]

A lease contract (*ijārah*), for instance, in which the usufruct of an object is hired for a specific term, only materialises with usage over a period of time. A contract of manufacture (*istiṣnā'*), in which a specialist's labour is employed to produce a subject matter, is included amongst these exceptions. Other kinds of transaction such as a guarantee of debts (*kafālah*) or agency (*wakālah*), which also involve use, are equally applicable to this distinction.[87] Accordingly, these exceptional contracts and others offer an analogical basis (*ḥukm*) by which the prohibition can be made more flexible.

3.6.4 *Avoiding the rigidities of* gharar

In practice the exigencies of trade and commerce required the *fuquhā'* to find solutions to the rigidity of the *gharar* prescription. *Ḥiyal* were employed to enable transactions that had appreciable benefits for the people. These included cases in which the value of the commodity was not precisely known, as in *muzabana* contracts,[88] or in the barter of livestock for meat, which on the basis of its unknown differences in counter-values

[85] *Ibid.*, 101.
[86] Nabil A. Saleh (n 64) 69. [87] *Ibid.*
[88] Susan E. Rayner (n 23) 291.

would violate both the prohibition of *ribā* and *gharar*. In sum, Islamic jurisprudence has yielded over time to the pressures of commerce and the needs of human existence, shielding merchants and traders from the sin of *ribā* and *gharar* by formulating exceptions to rules.

All commercial transactions, including those that took place in the early Islamic period, contain a certain element of risk or uncertainty with regard to some attribute of the transaction. In the classical period jurists seem to have agreed that excessive *gharar* (*al-gharar al-kathīr*) was prohibited whereas minimal *gharar* (*al-gharar al-yasīr*) was not. However, they continued to disagree about what constituted these categorisations.[89] Several modern jurists sought to establish a sort of doctrine of *gharar* that establishes legal effects and creates a viable framework for the assumption of risk. Maḥmaṣānī, for example, differentiated between excessive and trivial *gharar* with respect to legal effects. Excessive *gharar* renders a contract null and void (*bāṭil*), or it may be cause for indemnity and compensation. Slight *gharar* may be deemed to be tolerable (*mubah*) and, if so, would not invalidate a given transaction.[90] Al-Sanhūrī advocated that a distinction should be made between instances in which the subject matter of a transaction is non-existent but will come into existence with certainty, and other cases in which the subject matter is also non-existent, but the probability involving its existence is uncertain – thus invoking *gharar*. He accepted the notion of a scale of *gharar* in which excessive *gharar* is outlawed while slight *gharar* allows the transaction to be valid.[91]

Both scholars recognised the necessity of aleatory contracts in modern commerce and thus found ways to accommodate degrees of *gharar*. The following section addresses the other major prohibition in the law of Islamic contracts, namely, the prohibition of *ribā*.

3.7 The prohibition of usury: *ribā*

The practice of forbidding interest took place as early as 1750 BCE, if not earlier. King Bocchoris of the Egyptian 24th Dynasty (730–715 BCE) forbade the receipt of interest in excess of the principal amount owed. And the great Egyptian jurist, al-Sanhūrī pointed out the significance of the moment when Egypt decreed – after a three-thousand-year hiatus – that modern Egypt should forbid compound interest in Article 232 of the Civil Code.[92] However, the levying of interest is equally ancient and is likely to

[89] Ibn Rushd (n 71) 186.
[90] Mohammad Hashim Kamali (n 61) 85–9.
[91] Nabil A. Saleh (n 64) 68. [92] *Ibid.*, 12.

be a more prevalent form of money lending. Ancient Greeks and Romans charged exorbitant interest with the peculiar aspect of securing debt in the form of the person. If a debtor was unable to repay the loan in kind, he became the creditor's slave. In Rome, slavery for debt existed well into the fourth century CE.[93]

To understand Islam's position with regard to interest it is necessary to examine the economic context in which the prohibition was revealed and later developed. At the inception of Islam money was generally hoarded, for it was regarded as unproductive in the sense that a money economy did not yet fully exist. Instead, goods and services were bartered. Meccans are known to have bartered commodities in more settled agriculturalist societies such as Syria with the objective of returning to Mecca laden with precious goods. Goods transported and sold in Syria were hides, leather goods, skins, clothing and perhaps also animals, clarified butter, and perfume, on occasion.[94] Furthermore, workers did not receive money wages for their labour, and production was not the chief focus of hoarded wealth.[95] Instead the economy was generally premised on subsistence.

Goitein's meticulous scholarship of the Geniza records[96] shows that gold and silver were still traded as commodities three centuries later (approx. 1200 CE). However, by then they were also widely used as means of payment.[97] At each transaction, coins, like goods, had to be weighed and their value, including their fineness and state of preservation, had to be determined. One must bear in mind that coinage was not of uniform consistency and rulers often debased coinage so as to stretch limited resources. Money was generally handled in sealed purses of coins whose value was attached to the outer purse. As a rule, merchant-banker accounts indicated the real value or the value in weight of the dinars in consideration. Therefore, a document indicates that a purse of 76 and 1/6 dinars most probably contained 80 gold pieces.[98] The written value reflected the material value of the coinage rather than the numerical value. A similar system prevailed in Roman and Jewish societies and, subsequently, in Christian

93 *Ibid.*, 68.

94 Patricia Crone, *Roman, Provincial and Islamic Law* (Cambridge University Press, 1987), 149.

95 Ziaul Haque, *Islam and Feudalism: The Economics of Riba, Interest and Profit* (Lahore: Vanguard Books, 1985), 95.

96 These shall be discussed in a later section of this chapter.

97 S. D. Goitein, 'The Cairo Geniza as a Source for the History of Muslim Civilisation' (1955) 3 *Stud. Islam.*, 82.

98 *Ibid.*, 231 and 239.

Europe.[99] These characteristics of the classical money system may provide clues for the legal impetus in developing highly differentiated legal doctrines such as *ribā al-faḍl*.

3.7.1 *The Islamic origins of the prohibition of* ribā

In the Muslim tradition the prohibition of *ribā* is a central factor affecting all obligations and contracts in Islamic law due to its influence on the shape and contours of all commercial activity. *Ribā* has been simply defined to convey an unjustified enrichment in which a party receives a monetary advantage without giving a counter-value in return.[100] Yet scarcely is there a principle the meaning of which has been as vehemently contested over centuries of commercial practice and jurisprudential thought.

The Arabic root of *ribā* is *rbw*, which means to increase, grow or augment. It is used twenty times in the Quran. As a noun *ribā* denotes excess (*ziyādah*), increase, augmentation, expansion or growth (*namā'*), which for its part is used eight times in the Quran.[101] A consensus that the general meaning of *ribā* is synonymous with 'increase' is one of the few areas where there is little or no controversy.

The prohibition of *ribā* in *fiqh* seems to have developed gradually in successive revelations, likely beginning with the Meccan revelation from the *sūra al-rum* (references the defeat of the Byzantines at the hands of the Persians (613–614 CE)), which declares: 'Whatever you lend out in usury to gain value through other people's wealth will not increase in God's eyes, but whatever you give in charity, in your desire for God's approval, will earn multiple rewards'.[102] The Meccan verses are replete with denunciations of the economic injustices of Meccan society such as widespread profiteering and commercial exploitation by a small group of wealthy patricians at the expense of the poor.[103]

Tradition indicates that a debtor who could not repay the capital (money or goods) with accumulated interest at the time it came due was allowed an extension on the condition that the sum was 'doubled and multiplied' – *aḍ'āfan muḍā'afatan*. In his *Muwatta'*, al-Mālik Ibn Anas (d. 179/795–6)

[99] S. D. Goitein, *A Mediterranean Society* vol. I, Economic Foundations (Berkeley, CA: University of California Press, 1967), 231.

[100] Joseph Schacht, *An Introduction to Islamic Law* (Oxford: Clarendon Press, 1964), 145.

[101] Abdullah Saeed, 'Islamic Banking and Interest' in Ruud Peters and Bernard Weiss (eds.), *Studies in Islamic Law and Society*, vol. II (Leiden: E. J. Brill, 1996), 20.

[102] Quran (n 2) 30:39.

[103] Fazlur Rahman, 'Riba and Interest' (1964) 3 *Islam.Stud.* 1, 3.

recites this loan-*ribā* tradition, as follows: 'Zayd ibn Aṣlam relates that the *ribā* of *jāhilīyah* [pre-Islamic times] was that the creditor, who had given a loan for a certain period to a debtor, used to demand from the other when the time for its repayment came [saying]: "Will you return the loan, or give an increase [over the loaned capital)?"'[104]

The custom of doubling one's debts was categorised by some authors, including the renowned Ḥanbalī scholar, Ibn Qayyim al-Jawzīyah, as a so-called third category of *ribā* known as *ribā al-jāhilīyah*.[105] *Jāhilīyah* is a time of 'ignorance', denoting the period before the successive revelations from God to his Prophet Muhammad and in which polytheistic belief and worship were predominant. Al-Jawzīyah reported that Ahmad Ibn Ḥanbal confirmed that the *ribā al-jāhilīyah* was the *ribā* as to which there was no doubt. For his part, al-Jawzīyah considered this 'manifest *ribā*' and noted that besides this there are many unfair forms of commercial practice that are not explicitly *ribā*, but which he labelled as 'concealed *ribā*'. The breadth and range of this usage of the term was confirmed by the great expert on hadith, Ibn Ḥajar al-'Asqalānī, who said that 'the term *ribā* can be applied to every forbidden commercial practice'.[106]

The Quran seems to testify to an increasing awareness of the division between rich and poor and a diminished social morality vis-à-vis the poor and orphans.[107] For example, the Quran lays stress on acts of generosity and juxtaposes these with *ribāwī* transactions (see *sūrah*30:39 above). The general interpretation of this verse is seen as evidence that the meaning of *ribā* is concerned with avoiding practices that exploit the less well-off and/or most vulnerable members of society. By prohibiting *ribā* just and equitable transactions take the place of those in which only one party wins or loses.

The practice of doubling the principal sum of a debtor in the event that the debtor was unable to pay is a historically corroborated and persuasive account of this interpretation of the prohibition. The Quran's disdain for exploitative commercial practices resonates with its clear message of

[104] Ziaul Haque (n 95) 36.

[105] Joseph Schacht, 'Ribā' in M. Th. Houtsma, T. W. Arnold, R. Bassett, R. Hartmann (eds.), *Encyclopaedia of Islam, First Edition* (1913–1936) (Brill Online, 2014), referenceworks.brillonline.com/entries/encyclopaedia-of-islam-1/riba-SIM_3700. Accessed 25 March 2014.

[106] Fazlur Rahman (n 103) 36.

[107] See, for example, William Montgomery Watt, *Muhammad at Mecca* (Oxford University Press, 1953).

social responsibility and mutuality in which the wealthy have a moral obligation to provide for the poor, widows, divorcees, slaves and others.

The Quraysh's[108] zeal for usurious profit making is admonished in two separate passages in the Quran that deal specifically with this practice.[109] Quran 3:130 is thought to be an early Medinan passage, which would thus have been revealed after Muhammad and his followers' emigration (*hijra*) from Mecca and the subsequent Muslim defeat at the battle of Uḥud.[110] The verse, from the *sūra al 'Imrān* – the family of 'Imrān – is sharper in its admonition against the consumption of *ribā*, perhaps reflecting the Muslim community's increased political stature. Muhammad commands: 'You who believe, do not consume usurious interest, doubled and redoubled. Be mindful of God so that you may prosper – beware of the Fire prepared for those who ignore [Him] – and obey God and the Prophet so that you may be given mercy'.[111] The revelation is no longer a recommendation but a command and warning to the believers to desist in usurious lending typified by doubling the principals of the debtor's debt. Some Western scholars, including Schacht and Rodinson, associate this gradualism with Muhammad's experience with money lending as practised by the Medinan Jews after the *hijra*, but this assertion has not been substantiated.[112]

The third and last *sūra*, *sūra al-baqarah* or the cow, revealed before the fifth year of the *hijra* and the exile of the last Jewish tribe of *banū* Qurayzah, delineates the consequences of transgressing the prohibition: 'But those who take usury will rise up on the Day of Resurrection like someone tormented by Satan's touch'.[113] The Quran is adamant that those who disregard the ban on *ribā* merit the hell fires of the afterlife; these unbelievers (*kuffār*) commit perhaps the gravest sin that one may commit – it was said to have been worse than murder, idolatry and incest.[114]

It is true that monotheistic faiths, in particular, have often advanced the time-worn theme that the good things of this world divert men's

[108] The Quraysh were an affluent and powerful Meccan tribe that controlled access to the Kaaba, the most sacred site of Islam. The building predates Islam and at one time was the object of polytheistic worship. Muslims now turn to the Kaaba in prayer, five times a day; prayer is considered to be a pillar of Islam.

[109] Quran (n 2) 3:30 and 30:39.

[110] Abdullah Saeed (n 101) 21–2.

[111] Quran (n 2) 3:130.

[112] Joseph Schacht (n 105); Maxime Rodinson, *Islam and Capitalism* (London: Allen Lane, 1974), 15.

[113] Quran (n 2) 2:275.

[114] Th. W. Juynboll, *Handbuch Des Islamischen Gesetzes* (Leipzig: Otto Harassowitz, 1910), 270.

hearts from God and expose one to the danger of sin. The burden of guilt is automatically placed upon the well-to-do; the wealthy and powerful are often seen as unjust and oppressive.[115] However, the Quran clearly distinguishes between its hatred of oppression and exploitation, on the one hand, and its unequivocal support for trade, profit making and progress on the other. *Sūra* 2:275–6 is explicit: 'That is because they say, "Trade and usury are the same," but God has allowed trade and forbidden usury'.

In fact, the Quran has been described as the embodiment of the relations between man and God of a 'strictly commercial nature'. God is the merchant and the universe his reckoning, where all is counted and everything measured. His institution is the Quran and He establishes a pattern of honest dealing. Life is a business in which man gains or loses.[116] Furthermore, a number of traditions attest to the merchant's exalted role in the afterlife, such as Muhammad's proclamation that: 'the merchant who is sincere and trustworthy will (at Judgment Day) be among the prophets, the just and the martyrs'.[117] In fact, before his prophetic mission, Muhammad was a successful trader in his own right.

In sum, the Quranic verses clearly enunciate the usurious aspects of *ribā*, while they do not specifically denounce interest (*fā'idah*). The following discussion highlights another aspect of the prohibition, which resulted from jurists' efforts to decipher the meaning of *ribā*.

3.7.2 The differentiation of the ribā *concept: money, time and commodities*

Despite quranic evidence indicating that *ribā* constitutes usurious commercial practices, some of the earliest available historical documents indicate that people understood the concept as simply prohibiting interest on loans, chiefly in money and foodstuffs. This fact is attested by numerous documents from the Geniza indicating that not only were loans without interest extended on the basis of kinship or partnership but documentation completely failed to mention any increase for such transactions despite the detailed nature of such records.[118] In fact, few documents openly describe lending practices with interest, although the taking of loans on interest from members of other faith groups was regarded as legal. The

[115] Maxime Rodinson (n 112) 24.

[116] Charles C. Torrey, *The Commercial-Theological Terms in the Koran* (University of Strasbourg, Ph.D. thesis, 1892), 48.

[117] (Darimi, Sunan XVIII, 8) c.f. Maxime Rodinson (n 112) 16.

[118] S. D. Goitein (n 99) 254.

main point, however, is that the records indicate that dealing in 'interest' was equated with the trespassing of God's law; whether or not it was, in fact, the *ribā* of which the Quran speaks, is less important than the way in which Muslims, and Jews for that matter, understood and practised the scriptural sources.

Not unlike the process by which jurists enlarged the meaning of *gharar* in their efforts to decipher God's intentions, the quranic ban on usury was considerably extended in scope. A strongly influential hadith cited by al-Muslim and all the major *ṣaḥīḥ* (valid) compilations provided the textual material that enabled jurists to do so. It declared: 'Gold for gold, silver for silver, wheat for wheat, barley for barley, dates for dates, salt for salt, like for like, equal for equal, hand to hand. If these types differ, then sell them as you wish, if it is hand to hand'. The majority of jurists of the *madhhabs* agreed that although the items mentioned in the hadith are very particular, its meaning could be extended to other goods. However, they disagreed about the effective cause (*'illah*) of the hadith, the underlying rationale on the basis of which these species were prohibited.[119]

Consequently, a more technical systematisation of *ribā* developed in which unlawful gain is expressed in two forms. The first is *ribā al-faḍl*. It is accurately described as being 'derived from the quantitative inequality of the counter-values in any transaction purporting to effect the exchange of two or more species, and which belong to the same genus and are governed by the same efficient cause'.[120] The second, *ribā al-nasī'ah* (*ribā* of delay), is the 'deferred completion of the exchange of such species, or even of species which belong to different genera but are governed by the same *'illah* ... whether or not the deferment is accompanied by an increase in any one of the exchanged counter-values'.[121]

The 'equivalence' hadith – the influential tradition cited above – forms the basis of these distinctions. It mentions two precious metals (gold and silver) and four basic commodities (wheat, barley, dates and salt). By analogy to these items the prohibition was extended to all species governed by the same *'illah*; or which jointly belonged to any one of the genera to which the six articles named in the hadith are subordinated. Saleh's definition of genus (*jins*) comprises a class of articles in which several subordinate classes or species are extant. Likewise, species may be defined as a group of articles that contain several common attributes or qualities, and, for their part, are subsumed under the broader category of genus. Consonant

119 Ibn Rushd (n 71) 159.
120 Nabil A. Saleh (n 64) 17.
121 *Ibid.*

with most aspects of Islamic law, the *madhhabs* offered diverse interpretations of the nature and specificities of genera.[122]

It is hardly surprising, then, that the four *madhhabs* in Sunni Islam define the *'illah* of the equivalence hadith differently. Shāfi'īs detect two causes – that of currency and food; Mālikīs expand upon the traits of food – those foods being basic foodstuffs or essential nutrients and others which are able to be preserved and stored; the Ḥanbalī and Ḥanafī schools see only goods sold by weight or by volume, which are subdivided into three classes: (1) measure by weight; (2) measure by volume; (3) and highly precise measure (for gold and silver only). For their part the Ḥanafīs stressed equivalence as the aim of prohibiting *ribā* as justice demands that transactions are fair and equitable. When the differing nature of things made the determination of equivalence difficult, if not impossible, a money system of dinars and dirhams was established for the assessment of their values. A money system allows things differing in nature to be related to each other proportionately. That is, the ratio of the price of an object with respect to its own genus should be equivalent to the ratio of the price of another object relative to its genus.[123] Proportional valuation entails fairness and just commercial practices.

All *madhhabs* are unanimous that the *ribā* prohibition applies to goods that share a single subdivided class,[124] e.g. by weight, by volume, or by precise measure. Importantly, all the various eponyms based their rulings on different hadiths, and sometimes, like Al-Mālik, sought to reconcile two hadiths to express a certain principle.[125]

Yet the detailed systematisation of the prohibition made its functionality questionable. For example, the Ḥanafī *'illah* has two characteristics: the circumstance in which exchanged articles belong to the same genus and the fact that the same articles are either measured or weighed as a function of the exchange. In the case that one of these two characteristics arises in the course of a transaction, i.e. evincing properties susceptible to the *ribā* prohibition, the counter-values must be exchanged on the spot

[122] *Ibid.*

[123] Ibn Rushd (n 71) 162; Mahmoud A. El-Gamal, *An Economic Explication of the Prohibition of Riba in Classical Islamic Jurisprudence* (Houston, TX: Rice University, 2001). El-Gamal believes that the prohibition – when seen from this viewpoint – emphasises the efficiency of trading rather than exploitation by the rich. In other words, by taking to market the goods and services to be exchanged, parties are able to maximise their respective utilities.

[124] Frank E. Vogel and Samuel L. Hayes (n 56) 72–5.

[125] Ibn Rushd (n 71) 165.

and without delay. Gain or profit from the exchange is permissible only in a hand-to-hand transaction.[126] If the articles to be exchanged are either both measurable or both weighable and belong to the same genus, i.e. both characteristics of the *'illah*, a deferred transaction is strictly prohibited as is any gain in the exchange. When one of the exchanged counter-values is measurable and the other is not or when one of the exchanged counter-values is weighable and the other is not, gain is permissible in either a spot-sale or deferred transaction. Yet this reasoning leads to an unreasonable result, namely that the exchange of commodities such as sugar, cotton, iron and copper for a deferred payment of gold or silver (more generally, the sale of weighable articles for deferred payment) would be deemed unlawful because gold and silver are also weighable commodities.[127] The Ḥanafīs solved this problem by dividing weighable articles into those with a highly precise measure and all the rest, which clearly reflects the necessity of this type of transaction. The distinction between weighable qualities was considered to be of enough significance as to permit deferred sales transactions.

The famous traditionist Abū Bakr al-Bayhaqī catalogued a detailed record of different categories, forms and nuances of *ribā* transactions in his forty-chapter book, *al-Sunan al-Kubrā*, which dealt with loans and sales involving general commerce and agriculture.[128] Likewise, al-Mālik's *al-Muwaṭṭa'* describes in detail the contemporary forms of *ribā* in loans, sales and exchanges of commodities. Both works underline the notion that the loan of basic foodstuffs (*ribāwi* goods), other commodities or money for a certain period for an increase is *ribā*.[129] Thus the development of *ribā al-faḍl* expands upon the meaning of *ribā al-nasī'ah* considerably. The concept of *ribā al-nasī'ah* offers a more precise formulation for the prohibition of lending money at interest over a period of time.

However, the content and meaning of *ribā al-faḍl* has been controversial throughout Muslim history. As has been identified, this form of *ribā* is not clearly demarcated, nor is there a broad consensus on what is meant by the term. It seems to be a juristic hair-splitting exercise that involves the exchange of goods, some fresh, others old, some refined by craftsmanship and some in their raw state, with little, if any, economic consequences. After all, a system of bartering for goods and services is no longer relevant in the modern economy.

[126] Nabil A. Saleh (n 64) 26.
[127] *Ibid.* [128] Ziaul Haque (n 95) 68–9.
[129] *Ibid.*, 13–14.

Modern scholars, clearly aware of the economic problems associated with the prohibition of interest, have noted that some hadiths have contradictory messages. Consequently, the definitional claims made by classical jurists should be reconsidered. For example, Muslim, al-Bukhārī, al-Dārimī, al-Nasāʿī, Ibn Mājah and Ibn Ḥanbal recorded hadiths narrated through chains of transmitters whose general claim is '*ribā* is on loans' or as al-Bukhārī emphatically expressed: 'There is no *ribā* except on loans'.[130] However, many of these same authors, including al-Bukhārī, Muslim and other canonical collections also report the equivalency hadith that is the basis of *ribā al-faḍl*: Abū Sa'īd al-Khudrī reported God's Messenger as saying, 'Gold is to be paid for by gold, silver by silver, wheat by wheat, barley by barley, dates by dates, and salt by salt, like for like, payment being made "hand to hand". If anyone gives more or asks for more he has dealt in *ribā*. The receiver and the giver are equally guilty'.[131] Apparently, this obvious contradiction in meaning did not go unnoticed and each of the schools had its own supporting hadith.

In sum, the body of hadith material on this particular subject, which includes many other hadiths dealing with the topics of excess and delay, indicates a marked trend toward a more rigid and conservative definition of *ribā*.[132] It is also evident that a clear and unanimous definition of the term did not exist, especially amongst the learned jurists. Furthermore, historical evidence of commercial transactions in the earliest Muslim centuries is completely missing in these discussions. A more in-depth appreciation of the way in which the term was understood by early Islamic traders and merchants impedes a more pragmatic discussion of how the law was put into practice. It is true that the Geniza documents point to a general understanding that all interest – no matter how small or usurious – constituted the forbidden *ribā*. Yet our understanding of the concept is partial and ultimately unsatisfying in light of the total absence of commercial records from the earliest Islamic centuries, which would be likely to indicate the way in which the concept was practised. Furthermore, even in extant commercial records almost no evidence exists concerning the application of specialised concepts such as *ribā al-faḍl*'. The following sections attempt to provide a general analysis of the ways in which classical commerce was actually practised.

130 Fazlur Rahman (n 103) 13.
131 *Ibid.* 132 *Ibid.*, 17.

3.8 Historical commercial practices

The Cairo Geniza records are a rare occurrence of discovered records from the early Islamic era. They contain documentary material describing classical Middle Eastern civilisation from the fourth/tenth to the tenth/sixteenth centuries (the Fatimid and Ayyubid dynasties)[133] and comprise the largest single store of records concerning pre-modern Islamic life of this period. Research of these documents demonstrates that Hanafī jurists' detailed treatises and other legal works elaborated the primary classical institutions of commerce, including partnerships (*shirkah*) such as the *muḍārabah* in surprising conformity with the way in which medieval commerce was actually practised. Scholarly writings reflect a very detailed and elaborate discussion of commercial practices prevalent in the Near East in the medieval period.[134]

These findings have overturned the earlier Orientalist consensus that a pattern of Islamic belief developed in which believers took little notice of the sharia with respect to the transactions (*mu'āmalāt*) of daily life. In contrast, these same believers were to have placed great emphasis upon the uncompromising ideal doctrine,[135] particularly in those areas of private law associated with the institutions of the family, ritual and inheritance. On the contrary, these findings indicate that the sharia, far from being a static and inflexible law in *mu'āmalāt* matters, evinces a long history of pliability and contextual adaptation.

The practice-oriented nature of Islamic commercial law is more easily understood as a result of an interesting analysis which determined that over 75 per cent of the jurists from the third/ninth and fourth/tenth centuries either engaged in commerce or the handicrafts or originated from families whose members engaged in these professions.[136] In fact, the eminent scholar and eponym of the Ḥanafī *madhhab*, Abū Ḥanīfah, was a dealer and exporter of Khazz silk from Kufa to his partner in Baghdad.[137]

133 See S. D. Goitein (n 97) and (n 99).

134 Abraham L. Udovitch, 'The "Law Merchant" of the Medieval Islamic World' in G. E. von Grunebaum (ed.), *Logic in Classical Islamic Culture* (Wiesbaden: Otto Harrassowitz, 1970), 115.

135 Christiaan Snoucke Hurgronje, 'Islamic Law and Custom' in G. H. Bousquet and J. Schacht (eds.), *Selected Works* (Leiden: E. J. Brill, 1957), 290.

136 Hayyim Cohen, 'The Economic Background and the Secular Occupations of Muslim Jurisprudents and Traditionists in the Classical Period of Islam' (1970) 13 *J. Econ.& Soc. Hist.Orient*, 16, 39–40.

137 *Ibid.*, 26.

An influential number of pious scholars who contributed to the formulation of the law had an in-depth and personal knowledge of the commercial requirements of the marketplace. Evidently, these demands found their way into the law. The following discussion concerns the partnership (*shirkah*), which was one of the primary tools of commercial exchange in the classical Near East.[138]

3.8.1 The partnership (sharikah)

The *shirkah* or *sharikah* is an ancient form of business association that has been practised in the Near East since the days of Babylon, as evidenced by its mention in the Code of Hammurabi, the Talmud, its treatment in the *Corpus Iuris Civilis* of Justinian and in the Gaonic *responsa* of the ninth and tenth centuries.[139] Another credit institution, the *qirāḍ* partnership, seems to have originated with the pre-Islamic Arabian tribes in their pursuit of the trans-Arabian caravan trade.[140] With the Islamic conquests the *qirāḍ* was introduced to outlying provinces of the Near East, North Africa, and eventually to Southern Europe where it became known as the *commenda*.[141] The *qirāḍ* is, in fact, the earliest example of a commercial association and is similar to the later *commenda* in all its essential features.[142] The structure also became known as the *muqarāḍah, or muḍārabah*, depending on the region in which the contract was exercised and the preferences of the *madhhab*. The distinctive form of partnership known as *qirāḍ* and *muqarāḍah* originated in the Arabian Peninsula while the *muḍārabah* is of Iraqi provenance.[143]

The Geniza records attest to the surprising fact that at least one-half of international trade was based on a series of highly complex, informal business partnerships, which spanned the Near East from Morocco to Mesopotamia, and could last a lifetime. This fact is in keeping with our understanding of custom, of the proximate and trusted partners and agents, and locally available information which typify the 'local knowledge' criteria of successfully conducting commerce in the classical Near

[138] Abraham L. Udovitch, *Partnership and Profit in Medieval Islam* (Princeton University Press, 1970), 8.

[139] *Ibid.*, 8; Chibli Mallat, 'From Islamic to Middle Eastern Law: A Restatement of the Field (Part I)' (2003) 51 *Am.J.Comp.L.* 699, 706.

[140] Abraham L. Udovitch (n 138) 172.

[141] *Ibid.*

[142] Abraham L. Udovitch, 'At the Origins of the Western Commenda: Islam, Israel, Byzantium?' (1962) 37 *Speculum* 198, 207.

[143] Abraham L. Udovitch (n 138) 172–4.

East.[144] Thus the Mediterranean and Indian trade, the most important trade routes of the period, were largely based on informal relationships rooted in mutual trust and friendship, and lacked any formal legal instrumentation.[145] Moreover, an *'umlah* or commission was only rendered for a special service; no compensation was given for extraordinary expenditures of time and effort that these informal undertakings often required. Instead these partnerships flourished in reciprocity as the sources confirm that 'he serves there and I serve here', and 'you are in my place there, for you know well that I am your support here'.[146]

Formal partnerships tended to be of shorter duration and limited to specific undertakings, although many long-term business relationships seemed to have combined the two. Partnerships encompassed practically every economic activity in the Geniza period due to the fact that they substituted for large fields of economic activity that would subsequently be housed in alternative contractual forms: namely, employment and loans on interest. Partnerships ran the gamut from industrial pursuits such as: the running of workshops, wine production and the building of homes; to commercial projects in both wholesale and retail trade; projects related to the administration of the state such as tax farming (the fiscal basis of the state), and to occupations in the royal mint or exchange.[147] Money, goods, work, or any combination of the three, could form the basis of a partnership and records detail a number of diverse arrangements. There are two general vehicles of partnership that encapsulate this commercial activity, one of which has been discussed. The second, which is, in fact, an overarching concept of partnership, is known as the *shirkah* (also *sharikah)*, or perhaps more commonly as the *khultah* (literally, the mixing of the investments). It describes investors who mix their investment and share the profit or loss in proportion to their investment.[148]

The popularity and widespread usage of the more specialised *qirāḍ* reflect the unique character of the contract. An investor could harvest the advantages of a loan as the *qirāḍ* entailed no liability for the investor

144 Clifford Geertz, *Local Knowledge: Further Essays in Interpretive Anthropology* (New York: Basic Books, 1983), 210.

145 Avner Greif, 'Reputation and Coalitions in Medieval Trade: Evidence on the Maghribi Traders' (1989) 49 *J.Econ.Hist.*, 857, 859.

146 S. D. Goitein, 'Commercial and Family Partnerships in the Countries of Medieval Islam' (September 1964) 3 *Islam.Stud.*, 315, 316.

147 S. D. Goitein (n 99) 170.

148 Imran Ahsan Khan Nyazee, *Islamic Law of Business Organization: Partnerships* (Islamabad: The International Institute of Islamic Thought and Islamic Research Institute, 1997), 36.

beyond the sum of money or quantity of merchandise extended to the agent. In the event of a successful venture, the agent was to return the capital plus a share of the profits. Meanwhile the agent could claim complete indemnity from any liability for the capital, in the event of a partial or total loss.[149] Furthermore, the investor reduced the cost of trade by using partners and/or agents to undertake business dealings on his behalf. Finally, risk allocation could be better managed through trade diversification with respect to goods, location and time.[150]

In the contract of *qirāḍ* one of the most crucial issues was in determining the legitimate cost to the seller of any given commodity so as to determine the profit in excess of total cost. According to Ḥanafī law the single most important guideline in making this determination was the customary practices of the locale in which the transaction was to take place.[151] It is a definitive example of how the sharia incorporated local business practices.

Moreover, the enforcement of the ban on investment in the form of goods or merchandise would have dealt a severe blow to medieval commerce, particularly for those engaged in long-distance trade. It was common that merchants had nearly all their capital invested in goods and merchandise, which could not always be sold advantageously in a certain locale. A number of quite simple legal devices (*ḥiyal*) were developed to circumvent this prohibition. The merchants were to make frequent use of them, so that these subsequently were incorporated into the legal manuals and the earliest legal formularies (*shurūṭ*).[152] The assimilation of the *ḥiyal* in the *fiqh*, including contractual formularies, was so complete and without reservation that their extra-judicial quality was eventually forgotten and omitted from the texts.[153]

The *qirāḍ* was often the source of partnership between Muslims and Jews and could be formed by a variable number of partners and partnership stakes, while profit, loss and expenditure were divided in proportion to the investment. So, for example, a Tunisian merchant had a one-sixth stake in a 365-dinar partnership in which lacquer was transported from Egypt, while he maintained a five-sixths stake in a shipment of indigo and sal ammoniac dispatched from the same country.[154] So adept and practical in the field of commercial exchange were the Arabs that their

[149] Abraham L. Udovitch (n 142) 200.
[150] Avner Greif (n 145) 863.
[151] Abraham L. Udovitch (n 134) 120–1.
[152] *Ibid.* [153] *Ibid.*
[154] S. D. Goitein (n 146) 321.

widespread use of complex credit facilities throughout the Islamic territories predated a similar European development of credit by at least three or four centuries.[155]

The *qirāḍ* partnership was the subject of lengthy discussion in the earliest Islamic legal literature (late second/eighth century), and the refinement and tone with which it is treated indicates its historical antiquity. In addition to citing a number of hadith relating to the Prophet and his companions, al-Sarakhsī justifies the permissibility of the *qirāḍ* contract on the grounds of commercial necessity: 'in relation to this contract, the requirements of the law yielded in face of the people's need for it'. Furthermore, when commercial practice was stymied by the broad restrictions relating to analogical reasoning, Ḥanafī jurists were inclined to exercise the prerogative of *istiḥsān* and thereby suspend the rigid application of strict analogy.[156] In addition to enhancing the flexibility and efficiency of market players, these principles succeeded in adopting large swathes of commercial customary practices into the Islamic fold.

Although the Quran does not mention the *qirāḍ*, traditions attribute it to the practice of the Prophet and his leading Companions. One tradition places Muhammad as an agent in a *qirāḍ* investment with his future wife, Khadīja, and 'Umar and 'Uthmān, the second and third, respectively, of the rightly guided caliphs, are known to have participated in these ventures.[157] The sharia admitted these partnership practices on the grounds of traditional practice, the consensus of the community *(ijmā')* and its practical application for the well-being of the Muslim community.

Commercial requirements also found their way into other common practices. For example, a labour partnership between a stall owner and an artisan illustrates a contract of widespread commercial importance throughout the classical period. In a partnership described by al-Sarakhsī, a stall owner allows an artisan to utilise his stall, whereupon all profits were to be split equally amongst the parties; the same would apply to loss in the event of misfortune.[158] Such a partnership would be rendered void on account of the artisan's intangible investment, at least in monetary terms; and the stall owner's provision of his stall is equally difficult to value and is thus prohibited as a means of investment in a partnership. Likewise, the terms of the contract do not satisfy the conditions inherent in the contracts of hire or lease (*ijārah*) as the terms of the agreement have not been specified prior to the conclusion of the contract.

[155] Abraham L. Udovitch (n 138) 77.

[156] *Ibid.*, 251. [157] *Ibid.*, 175.

[158] Abraham L. Udovitch (n 134) 118.

Al-Sarakhsī offers his insight into why this sort of arrangement was permitted: 'By exercising juristic preference (*istiḥsān*), he [i.e. Shaybānī] permitted this arrangement because of its continuous use in the affairs of men without any disapproving voice being raised against it. Objecting to transactions which are in common use among the people is in itself a type of offence. In order to avoid this offence, this contract is permissible. For there is no explicit text nullifying it, and the people have a need for this contract'.[159] This is a more evident example of the differentiation between the adoption and subsequent Islamisation of customary usages of clear economic relevance, on the one hand, and the ideal theory of the sharia, on the other. But the adoption of customary practices is not merely a reasoned abandonment of the *uṣūl al-fiqh* in favour of a more practical and flexible approach to the law. On the contrary, it depicts a pliant and willing belief system, which in bestowing its grace and permission upon a set of not incompatible acts, enhances the strength and vibrancy of the Muslim community, and by extension, the Muslim faith.

The Cairo Geniza papers are not always clear with respect to which law, Jewish or Islamic, governed a contract. There is considerable circumstantial evidence, however, that indicates that local custom (the so-called merchant's law) and the contractual terms and conditions as agreed by the contracting parties established the guidelines regulating a contract.[160] Most of the Geniza documents available with respect to the governing law are court records. There are a number of records which deal with the termination of a partnership, known as a release. These releases were statements confirming that the parties to a business association had relinquished their claims against one another. As examined earlier, many settlements were made out of court, or before Muslim notaries. It is likely on account of the common usage of the Muslim *qirāḍ* that these settlements were made in the presence of Muslim notaries.[161] The following section analyses the use of interest in classical transactions.

3.8.2 The use of interest in commercial transactions

It is evident that Islamic ideals reinforced already strongly entrenched beliefs concerning the immorality of the practice of levying and paying interest. For instance, evidence from the Cairo Geniza shows that lending on interest was not only shunned religiously but was of little economic

[159] *Ibid.*, 117. [160] S. D. Goitein (n 99) 171.
[161] S. D. Goitein (n 146) 328.

importance throughout the fourth/tenth and fifth/eleventh centuries. It is thought that people at the time felt as though the acceptance of interest, or, perhaps unusually, employment, was to denigrate one's person as 'the borrower is a slave to the lender' (Proverbs 22:7) – a dependent relationship lacking dignity.[162] This mentality is highlighted by the then current notion of giving loans (*qarḍ ḥasan*) as an act of charity, which accords with the requirements of the sharia that loans bear no interest, and, in fact, are to be given as an act of charity without recompense in this life. Such loans were commonly advanced amongst relatives connected by common commercial undertakings.[163]

In the sixth/twelfth century, the Geniza shows that the mood shifts so that fixed interest, *ribā* (*ribbith* in Hebrew), is evidenced in documents which openly flaunt the prohibition. In this period it becomes unlikely that large amounts of money, such as 300 or even 180 dinars, which were lent for a period of six years, would not have been compensated without fixed interest or 'service'. Overall, however, scanty documentary evidence highlighting the use of interest is likely to be an indication that appearances were kept up, so to speak, and thus the open use of interest was still perceived as a social and religious anathema. Indeed, it seems that the creditors' objective was to arrange for an increase for themselves without publicly stipulating such profit in a signed and notarised contract.[164]

A telling sign of the times is evidenced in both Muslim and Jewish willingness to lend on interest to members of the opposing religion, whether it was for commercial or simply consumptive reasons. For instance, the terrible wars of the 1020s witnessed the decimation of the Jews of Jerusalem who were subsequently forced to borrow from Muslim usurers to pay the poll tax. In one Cairo Geniza letter signed by ten residents of the Holy City and posted to Old Cairo around 1040, it is written: 'In the current year we took a loan of 40 dinars for the poll tax alone from the usurer known to you'.[165] While the taint of interest has had a genuine social impact over centuries of religious practice, at least to the extent that it was clearly a sin according to all of the monotheistic religions, its usage has nonetheless waxed and waned over centuries of commercial practice.

162 S. D. Goitein (n 99) 254. 163 *Ibid.*

164 Robert S. Lopez and Irving W. Raymond (n 118) 159–61. Sobhi Labib, 'Geld Und Kredit: Studien zur Wirtschaftsgeschichte Aegyptens im Mittelalter' (1959) 2 *J.Econ.& Soc.Hist. Orient*, 225, 238.

165 S. D. Goitein (n 99) 257.

During the reign of the Ottoman Empire, for instance, lending at interest was a condoned practice. In fact, *ribā* or *fā'idah* (interest) at relatively low rates was perceived as different from the usurious form condemned in the Quran. An interest rate of 15 per cent was legally sanctioned. The clergy stood squarely behind the ruling and had those who denied its validity persecuted according to the Ottoman understanding of the sharia.[166]

Classical commercial practices indicate that customary business practices were adopted within the Islamic fold when their benefits were obvious, despite the fact that some of these practices exceeded doctrinal limits. The flexibility and pragmatism with which the sharia treated such practices provides a strong indication of jurists' willingness to adapt and extend the law to commercial requirements.

3.9 Concluding remarks

The system of Islamic nominate contracts, although premised upon the divine covenant, represents a disparate group of contracts in which each contains its own rules and particular legal effects. These rules restrict contracting parties' freedom to contract, as understood in the traditional sense, but many exceptions were made for customary practices of great importance to the community. These include the contracts of *istiṣnā'* and *salam*, both of which transgress basic sharia rules without this type of accommodation.

Likewise the complex rules concerning *ribā* and *gharar* may restrain contractual activity. The meaning of both prohibitions became more comprehensive and complex as a result of jurists' interpretive efforts. Yet historical records indicate that *ribā* was understood as simple interest in classical times while the meaning of *gharar* has been revisited in the modern period. Both prohibitions affect the structure and content of Islamic contracts by circumscribing what parties can contractually undertake.

Superficially the laws of Islamic nominate contracts appear fairly rigid yet school doctrines nuanced this rigidity considerably by accommodating

[166] See Neş'et Çağatay, 'Riba and Interest Concept and Banking in the Ottoman Empire' (1970) 32 *Stud.Islam.* 53, 65. Lending at interest, according to Çağatay, was a generally accepted practice from the tenth/sixteenth century onwards. See also Sami Zubaida, *Law and Power in the Islamic World* (London: I.B. Tauris, 2003), 110; and Ronald C. Jennings, 'Loans and Credit in Early 17th Century Ottoman Judicial Records: The Sharia Court of Anatolian Kayseri' (1973) 16 *J.Econ.& Soc.Hist.Orient* 168, 168–216.

customary business practices. Records of classical transactions underscore this aspect of the law; as do the legal writings of jurists whose understanding of the commercial needs of traders and merchants figured prominently. The ability of the sharia to envelop all sorts of practices – some of which clearly transgressed a conservative interpretation of school doctrine – testifies to the law's historical ability to adapt to changing commercial imperatives.

4

Global financial markets and legal transformation

International economic integration is not a new process. Largely due to advances in transportation and communication technologies, the dissemination of economic knowledge across national borders has been taking place for several centuries now.[1] Globalisation, on the other hand, entails the development of global formations that are partially or completely novel institutions. These include global formations as diverse as the international human rights regime and the emergence of global capital markets.[2]

While several factors, including growing interdependence, rapid advances in technology, or the power and influence of transnational corporations and global financial markets, represent important aspects of globalisation, the processes of producing, reproducing and servicing globalisation are what distinguish it as a global legal phenomenon. These processes, which involve state and non-state actors whose specialised functions facilitate the global economy, are at work in the transformation of Islamic law. Global actors – transnational corporations, lawyers, sharia scholars and international organisations – contribute to a highly specialised process of legal creation on the micro-level; at the macro-level these legal inputs interact with municipal legal systems to generate new, cross-pollinating structures of global normativity. The emergence of global financial centres connecting markets across the globe from Kuala Lumpur to Bahrain, Dubai and London offers strategic sites for the production of these specialised functions as well as the infrastructure to market and disseminate Islamic financial products.[3]

From an Islamic perspective, however, the transformation of Islamic commercial law challenges traditional assumptions concerning the

[1] Peter Isard, *Globalization and the International Financial System* (Cambridge University Press, 2005), 5.

[2] Saskia Sassen, *A Sociology of Globalization* (New York: W. W. Norton & Co., 2007), 12.

[3] *Ibid.*, 73.

articulation and ethical substance of the sharia. The actors, processes and formats involved in the modern articulation of the law, including its regulatory assimilation in municipal legal systems, are unparalleled. The legal hybrid that results from transformational processes such as legal standardisation cannot be adequately explained in terms of classical doctrine (*fiqh*). The modern financial environment and its actors are the primary contributors to the law's articulation and implementation. Islamic financial law is a globalised variant of Islamic law. It depends on the sharia for its legitimacy but not as a source of its legal development.

This chapter analyses the globalisation of financial markets, its embedded liberal values and relations to legal innovation. The activities of transnational corporations (TNCs) are examined, since TNCs generate much of the financial innovation taking place in Islamic finance. A particular example is dealt with in sub-section 4.11. It concerns a *wa'd* derivatives structure produced by a large transnational bank in conjunction with an Islamic finance consultancy. Furthermore, the chapter is concerned with the responses of Islamic non-governmental organisations to market pressures for standardised Islamic contracts, including these organisations' efforts to standardise sharia rules for accounting, auditing and sharia purposes. The ethical, religious and legal challenges associated with standardisation efforts are closely examined. Moreover, the role of transnational law firms in formulating IFL is examined, followed by the legal responses of sharia scholars to the transformation of Islamic law.

4.1 The globalisation of financial services

The increasing interconnection between peoples and countries, coupled with state policies directed at deregulating capital markets, have brought about a sea change in the global financial system.[4] Set off by the larger process of globalisation, one of the most important aspects of this change concerns the rapid rise in international capital flows from industrial to developing countries over the past few decades. The short-term nature of these capital flows, as well as the unprecedented level of cross-border lending, clearly distinguishes the modern period from the early 1900s, or indeed, earlier centuries in which international links were rooted in long-term investment.[5]

[4] Peter Isard (n 1) 4.

[5] *Ibid.*, 57. Some authors contest the utility of the term 'globalisation', since capital flows were also significant in previous centuries. However, globalisation entails more than increased investment flows. It concerns the use of technologies in the modern world and

Over the past thirty years a dramatic increase in international capital flows underscores the globalisation of financial markets. Gross capital flows between industrialised countries, the sum of the absolute value of capital inflows and outflows, increased by 300 per cent from 1991 to 2000.[6] A large share of this increase is attributable to enormous growth in foreign direct investment (FDI) and portfolio equity flows with each rising by roughly 600 per cent. By contrast, increases in the flow of gross bond issuances were more moderate at 130 per cent. Increases in these global flows substantially outpace the growth of the real economy or the growth in international trade.[7] In the same time period real GDP in industrialised countries increased by 26 per cent, while international trade increased by 63 per cent.[8]

An important marker of this new highly interconnected era began with the Bretton Woods agreement in 1946, which established an international system of gold–dollar exchange rate convertibility in the post-war period. In 1973 the growth and agility of internationally mobile capital led leading industrial countries to abandon the Bretton Woods framework and to adopt a regime of floating exchange rates.[9] This development paved the way for a sharp increase in financial arbitrage opportunities. By the end of the 1970s, partly as a result of market practitioners' ability to circumvent financial market restrictions, the leading economic powers, in particular the United States and the United Kingdom, initiated a wave of market deregulation. Thereafter nearly every industrialised nation state undertook a concerted campaign to liberalise their domestic financial systems, stock markets and international capital transactions.[10] The main objective was to create a hospitable environment for transnational firms and

the processes in which a multitude of global actors, including states, come together to produce, reproduce and service the global financial economy. For an alternative viewpoint, see Frederick Cooper, 'What Is the Concept of Globalization Good For? An African Historian's Perspective' (2001) 100 *Afr.Aff.*, 189, 189–213. In fact, international banking transactions in Europe occurred with high frequency as early as the third/ninth century. See James R. Lothian, 'The Internationalization of Money and Finance and the Globalization of Financial Markets' (2002) 21 *J.I.M.F.*, 699, 702. It seems likely that these types of link occurred even earlier in the Muslim world.

6 Martin D. D. Evans and Viktoria Hnatkovska, 'International Capital Flows Returns and World Financial Integration' (National Bureau of Economic Research, Working Paper 11701, October 2005), 4.

7 *Ibid.*, 5.

8 *Ibid.*, 5. Trade volume includes exports and imports. The statistics were compiled by the authors (see above, n 6) from the international finance statistics database, IMF. GDP figures were taken from the world development indicators database, World Bank.

9 Peter Isard (n 1) 29–35.

10 *Ibid.*, 60.

markets by instituting favourable competition policies, accounting and financial reporting standards and other market-oriented policies.[11]

Globalisation is driven by a still dominant power structure in which the rules and regulations of international finance are articulated and reproduced. In particular, the United States' predominant role in global financial markets acts as a driver of globalisation by influencing other states to adopt its economic vision of institutional structures, regulations and best practices.[12] The predominance of US corporations, the undisputed role of the US dollar as the world's reserve currency[13] and its great influence over the institutional structures of globalisation including the Basel process, the IMF and the World Bank underscore the country's economic power dimensions.

A central component of US strategy has been the promotion of financial liberalisation, which has opened countries to FDI. United States domestic markets have gained investment access to these economies in the process.[14] No place in the world has attracted more US FDI than the EU in past decades. From 2000 to 2009 the EU received 56 per cent of all US FDI, which in 2012 alone totalled US$206 billion. The top three destinations were the United Kingdom (US$36 billion), the Netherlands (US$35.3 billion) and Ireland ($US22.5 billion).[15] Likewise, EU investment in the United States comprised 71 per cent of all FDI in the United States. These extremely deep investment ties underscore the importance of the economic relationship of the most deeply integrated commercial artery in the world.[16] In recent years, the EU and its member states have taken an increasingly active role in the North Atlantic power nexus.[17] The EU's promulgation of

[11] *Ibid.*, 181.

[12] This view is almost undisputed. See Hans-Juergen Bieling and Johannes Jäger, 'Global Finance and the European Economy: The Struggle over Banking Regulation' in Bastiaan van Apeldoorn, Jan Drahokoupil and Laura Horn (eds.) *Contradictions and Limits of Neoliberal European Governance: From Lisbon to Lisbon* (New York: Palgrave Macmillan, 2009), 87–8.

[13] Despite the Global Financial Crisis (2008–09), US government paralysis and the emergence of competitors (China, the EU) Eswar Prasad makes an interesting case that the dollar's reserve currency status is stronger than ever. See Eswar S. Prasad, *The Dollar Trap: How the U.S. Dollar Tightened its Grip on Global Finance* (Princeton University Press, 2014).

[14] *Ibid.*, 87.

[15] Daniel S. Hamilton and Joseph P. Quinlan, *The Transatlantic Economy 2013*, vol. I (Washington, DC: Paul H. Nitze School of Advanced International Studies, 2013), vi.

[16] *Ibid.*, viii.

[17] I refer to this region as the 'North Atlantic', following Saskia Sassen's usage. The North Atlantic is a more accurate way of referring to the 'transatlantic' economies of the United States, Canada and the European Union.

global regulation, while said to differ in style from its US partners, is substantively similar.[18] The EU's single European Market is the largest market in the world; the largest exporting entity; the largest trading bloc in goods and services; the leading supplier of goods to developing countries including Brazil, Russia, India and China (BRIC); and the leading provider and recipient of FDI of all regions in the world.[19] Consequently, it has developed considerable bargaining power in the leading international forums including the G7, the G20, the Basel Committee, the Financial Stability Forum and the World Trade Organisation (WTO).[20]

Many economists argue that the North Atlantic's promotion of liberalisation policies has led to a structural shift in the global economy in which finance is prioritised over production.[21] Financialisation describes the increasingly speculative nature of economic activity and hence the de-linking of active production from the elastic creation of credit through the financial system.[22] This structural shift is evident in leading economic indicators. In 2011 the North Atlantic region dominated investment flows: it accounted for 57 per cent of the inward stock of all FDI and 71 per cent of the outward stock of FDI. Yet its share of international trade was less dominant: together it accounted for only 25 per cent of global exports and 31 per cent of global imports, the majority of which was invested in each other's economies.[23]

In the United States, in the years from 1950 until 2001, an increasingly higher share of revenues from non-financial companies was derived from financial sources of income relative to non-financial sources. During the 1970s this trend accelerated, peaking in the late 1980s 'at a level that is approximately five times the levels typical of the immediate post-war decades'.[24] The ratio retreated somewhat in the first half of the 1990s before recovering by the end of the second half.[25] The trajectory of the US economy over the past few decades shows a definitive trend toward the process of financialisation.[26]

[18] Hans-Juergen Bieling and Johannes Jäger (n 12) 87–8.
[19] Daniel S. Hamilton and Joseph P. Quinlan (n 15) v.
[20] Hans-Juergen Bieling and Johannes Jäger (n 12) 91.
[21] William K. Tabb, 'Financialization in the Contemporary Social Structure of Accumulation' in Terrence McDonough, Michael Reich and David M. Kotz (eds.), *Contemporary Capitalism and Its Crises: Social Structure of Accumulation Theory for the 21st Century* (Cambridge University Press, 2010), 149.
[22] *Ibid.*, 151. [23] Daniel S. Hamilton and Joseph P. Quinlan (n 15) v.
[24] Greta R. Krippner, 'The Financialization of the American Economy' (2005) 3 *Socio Econ. Rev.* 173, 175.
[25] *Ibid.*, 184–5. [26] Ibid., 199.

The globalisation of financial markets is also attributable to the widespread application of new communications and computer technology.[27] Rapid and cost-efficient advancements in information-processing and communication technologies have played a key role in the growth and dispersion of global financial markets and products.[28] These technologies allow financial institutions and other economic actors to manage their affairs on a global basis with minimal costs.[29] They have generated the innovation of new products and services, modes of distribution, pricing techniques and methods of risk management.[30] Furthermore, financial institutions can establish linkages with households, no matter how far flung, creating global connections where once the context of such interaction was on a strictly local basis.[31] People's use of these technologies within and outside their country of origin continues to evolve at an astonishing speed.[32] In many ways, the virtualisation of trade and the digitisation of finance have established the 'precondition for the broadening and deepening of the financial markets'.[33]

The globalisation of financial markets has led to a trend where major banks are represented in financial centres across the globe.[34] In fact, the globalisation of financial activity was mostly bank-led through the use of branches or consortia rather than wholly owned subsidiaries. This process of overseas expansion has gradually extended to all forms of business structure as well as the cross-border provision of services in banking and other financial services.[35]

Furthermore, leading financial centres such as London and New York are involved in financial operations for firms and governments from nearly every country, while newly established 'gateway' cities function as

[27] BIS, *Recent Innovations in International Banking* (Basel: Bank for International Settlements, April 1986), 7–9.

[28] Engelen E, Ertürk I, Leaver A, Froud J, Williams K, 'Reconceptualizing Financial Innovation: Frame, Conjuncture and Bricolage' (2010) 39 *Econ. Soc.*, 33, 48.

[29] Peter Isard (n 1) 60.

[30] Engelen E, Ertürk I, Leaver A, Froud J, Williams K, (n 28) 48.

[31] Saskia Sassen (n 2) 21.

[32] The Arab Spring of 2012, in which protestors communicated by Twitter and Facebook, demonstrates the novel uses of modern technologies in connecting people across entire regions, countries and continents.

[33] Engelen E, Ertürk I, Leaver A, Froud J, Williams K, (n 28) 48.

[34] Charles Goodhart, Philipp Hartmann, David T. Llewellyn *et al.*, *Financial Regulation: Why, How and Where Now?* (London: Routledge, 1998), 39. See also Saskia Sassen, 'Global Financial Centers' (Jan/Feb 1999) 78 *Foreign Aff.*, 75, 77.

[35] George Alexander Walker, *International Banking Regulation: Law, Policy and Practice* (The Hague: Kluwer Law International, 2001), 8.

conduits for the circulation of national and foreign capital. Gateway cities are the nexus between the country's wealth and global investment opportunities, on one hand, and between foreign investors and a country's investment opportunities, on the other. The result is an increased number of investment opportunities for internationally active banks.[36] Leading global investment, accounting and legal services tend to execute the most complex and innovative operations in gateway financial centres through the use of their affiliates and branches or through direct import.[37] For example, firms operating in the United Kingdom export more financial services than any other country in the world.[38] London utilises gateway financial centres such as those in the Gulf Cooperation Council (GCC) states to access global investment opportunities;[39] and as a way of acting as the world's largest creditor to emerging economies.[40] Gateway financial centres function within countries as the 'main mechanism for integration into the global financial market'.[41]

Statistics indicate that financial market integration is well under way. Although financial activity in emerging economies in total only accounts for a minority share of total financial activity, their combined share has risen across a range of markets in recent years. From 2005 until 2011 double digit growth rates were recorded in: equity markets capitalisation; new equity issues; derivatives exchange trading; global banking assets; and life and non-life insurance.[42]

As developing countries have continued to deregulate their economies the number of gateway financial centres has continued to grow, while financial centres within countries have been consolidated.[43] For example, Sao Paulo and Mumbai are now active in international capital markets

[36] Saskia Sassen, *Cities in a World Economy* (Thousand Oaks, CA: Pine Forge Press, 2006), 136.

[37] *Ibid.*

[38] TheCityUK, 'Key Facts About UK Financial and Professional Services' (2012), www.thecityuk.com/research/our-work/reports-list/key-facts-about-uk-financial-and-related-professional-services/. Accessed 21 March 2014.

[39] TheCityUK, 'Gulf Cooperation Council (GCC) Working Group, Annual Report' (2011), www.thecityuk.com/uk-financial-services-overseas/geographical-markets/gulf-cooperation-council-states/. Accessed 21 March 2014.

[40] TheCityUK (n 38) 2.

[41] Saskia Sassen (n 36) 136.

[42] TheCityUK, 'Financial Services in Emerging Economies' *TheCityUK*, London, July 2012, www.thecityuk.com/research/our-work/reports-list/financial-services-in-emerging-economies-2012/. Accessed 15 August 2014.

[43] Saskia Sassen (n 36) 138.

while Dubai, Bahrain, Doha and Kuala Lumpur have all become international players and increasingly important Islamic financial centres.[44]

4.2 Liberal values in the global economy

International political regimes, such as the Basel process, the Washington Consensus or the Bretton Woods agreements, represent instances of political authority that embody 'principles about fact, causation, and rectitude, as well as political rights and obligations that are regarded as legitimate'.[45] The creation and continued modification of these regimes underscore the internationalisation of political authority, but their factual existence does not explain the effects they have on economic transactions. The inventory of such regimes says little about their 'generative grammar'– the principles that underlie their order and meaning.[46] To understand the way in which regulatory structures help determine the nature of economic transactions the deeper roots and meanings of such regimes must be examined.

Taking the first case study of this book by way of example, the UK government's facilitation and regulatory approach to Islamic finance is premised on the principle of equality, which holds that 'like cases should be treated alike and different cases differently'.[47] Equality belongs to the set of values that engenders a modern politics of universalism, emphasising the equal dignity of all citizens, and substantively geared towards the equalisation of rights, entitlements and obligations.[48] In the United Kingdom and the EU in general legal intervention is not aimed at defining a substantive equality, which in practice is accepted as impossible. Rather it is directed at minimising inequality to the greatest extent possible in the areas of education, housing, employment and the acquisition of goods and services.[49] A politics of universalism strives for the creation of a society without 'first-class' and 'second-class' citizens; it seeks to create a procedural form of non-discrimination, blind to the differences of

[44] Duncan McKenzie, 'Islamic Finance' (London: TheCityUK, May 2011), 3, www.thecityuk.com/assets/Uploads/Islamic-finance-2011.pdf. Accessed 23 March 2014.

[45] John Gerard Ruggie, 'International Regimes, Transactions, and Change: Embedded Liberalism in the Postwar Economic Order' (1982) 36 *Int'l Org.*, 379, 380.

[46] *Ibid.* See also John Gerard Ruggie, 'Continuity and Transformation in the World Polity: Toward a Neorealist Synthesis' (1983) 35 *Wld.Pol.*, 261, 261–85.

[47] David Feldman, *Civil Liberties and Human Rights in England and Wales*, 2nd edn (Oxford University Press, 2002), 133.

[48] Charles Taylor, 'Multiculturalism and the Politics of Recognition' in Amy Gutmann (ed.), *Multiculturalism and the Politics of Recognition* (Princeton University Press, 1992), 44.

[49] David Feldman (n 47) 135.

its citizens, whether they are Christian, Muslim, Jewish, atheist, female, male, homosexual or heterosexual, and so on. Implicit in this approach is the assumption that its principles are based on neutral, difference-blind principles when, in fact, it is the political expression of a certain social understanding;[50] it is dependent on a moral judgment concerning the unacceptability of inequality with respect to these types of criteria.[51]

In other words, states cannot help but give partial establishment to the norms and values of a culture and these usually reflect those of the majority population.[52] Such predominant forms of being tend to 'define the meaning and identity of the individual, and the patterns of "appropriate" economic, political and cultural activity engaged in by those individuals'.[53] Moreover, institutions embody the purposes and legitimacy of states, organisations, professions and interest groups while demarcating the boundaries of activity appropriate to each.[54] Here institution is defined 'as a broad patterning of social structure and activity around general rules', although uncertainty surrounds the specific nature of such rules. The institutionalisation of a society's values is the process whereby a given set of units and patterns of activity come to be normatively and cognitively held in place, and in practice, taken for granted as lawful, although these may be customs and cultural knowledge. Viewing societal institutions in this manner exposes the myth that the capitalist environment of actors including states, regulatory bodies and conventional financial institutions are a priori, neutral elements of modern social processes. Instead, societal institutions should be seen as socially constructed and highly problematic. Their actions reflect an enactment of broad institutional patterns rather than autonomous, intrinsic choice, motivation and purpose; a finding very much opposed to an autopoietic view of the law or social systems, in general.[55]

[50] Charles Taylor (n 48) 44. [51] David Feldman (n 47) 135.

[52] Ayelet Shachar, *Multicultural Jurisdictions: Cultural Differences and Women's Rights* (Cambridge University Press, 2001), 23.

[53] John W. Meyer, John Boli and George M. Thomas, 'Ontology and Rationalization in the Western Cultural Account' in John W. Meyer, John Boli and George M. Thomas (eds.), *Institutional Structure: Constituting State, Society, and the Individual* (Newbury Park: Sage Publications, 1987), 13.

[54] *Ibid.*

[55] See Niklas Luhmann, *Soziologische Aufklaerung: Aufsaetze Zur Theorie Sozialer Systeme* (Koeln und Opladen: Westdeutscher Verlag GmbH, 1970); Niklas Luhmann, *Soziologische Aufklaerung 3* (Opladen: Westdeutscher Verlag GmbH, 1991); Gunther Teubner, *Law as an Autopoietic System* (Oxford: Blackwell Publishers, 1993); Niklas Luhmann, *Social Systems* (Stanford University Press, 1995).

Therefore, despite the multicultural makeup of the UK, the majority population's values and norms are deeply embedded within the institutions of the state. In particular, when the economy of the United Kingdom is examined – as well as other states' economies to varying degrees – a distinctive form of liberalism has emerged since Margaret Thatcher's terms of office as Prime Minister from 1979 until 1990. This liberalism holds that there are no better mechanisms, as general political institutions, to determine equal treatment than the two main institutions of our modernity: a free market to decide what goods shall be produced and how they shall be distributed; and representative democracy to determine what conduct shall be prohibited or regulated so that other conduct can be made possible and convenient.[56] The prototypical neoliberal believes that each of these institutions provides a more egalitarian settlement than any other general ordering of society.[57] If the market is made to function efficiently, it will determine a price for each product that reflects the cost in resources of material, labour and capital that might have been used to produce a different good for someone else (opportunity cost). A citizen's distribution of goods and services becomes a function of the personal preferences of others and his own. The sum of these personal preferences establishes the true cost to the community of meeting his or her own preferences for goods and services. The egalitarian distribution – that is, a perfectly free market – requires that 'the cost of satisfying one person's preferences should as far as possible be equal to the cost of satisfying another's'.[58] In other words, a free market does not impose value judgments concerning a citizen's preferences – at least within the spectrum of public policy. It does not attempt to decide for others what is good in life.

In contrast, religions necessarily attempt to impose certain moral visions and principles upon their adherents and the wider environment with which they come into contact. For instance, the sharia proscribes certain goods and services and requires parties to engage in types of transactions that reflect specific moral understandings of what is just,

[56] Ronald Dworkin, 'Liberalism' in Stuart Hampshire (ed.), *Public and Private Morality* (London: Cambridge University Press, 1978), 130.

[57] An example of these values in action is illustrated in the UK conservative government's decision, led by David Cameron, to sharply reduce state spending as a percentage of GDP, which has come to be known in financial circles as 'austerity'. The government believes that the market, in general, and the private sector, in particular, will be allowed to 'do what it does best' from increased confidence in the economy.

[58] Ronald Dworkin (n 56) 130–2.

equitable and fair in material affairs. Tensions necessarily arise between these divergent ideological and moral visions.[59]

From the Second World War a form of economic liberalism, coupled with multilateral arrangements, established a balance between free markets and national constraints designed to ensure domestic economic stability. Following liberalisation of the markets after the jarring oil embargoes of the 1970s, the ideology of neoliberalism came to dominate the leading economies, in particular those of the United States and the United Kingdom. These states, in particular, sought to deregulate markets, promote free trade and foster the creation of free and efficient markets. Globalisation and its effects on countries' economies have accelerated the process of deregulation. Policy makers continue to respond to these pressures, and the vicissitudes of the market economy, by enabling more flexible market processes.[60]

Neoliberalism represents a concerted effort to minimise the role of the state. A radical interpretation of the ideology sees the state as a provider of security from internal and external threats and nothing more. Citizens of a state should enjoy the right to non-intervention in their lives but not the right to goods. The state should take no responsibility for ensuring that people are able to exercise their liberties.[61]

Equally important to the creed is the idea that non-intervention of the state should be replaced with a conscious shift to viewing the market as the source of public good. The private sector should be privileged over the public via the displacement of public institutions and their substitution with private actors and entities. Optimal economic growth or the fulfilment of market potential then necessarily requires the implementation of a certain set of rules and practices and clear division of labour between the economic, the political or other non-economic sectors. 'Productive' and 'non-productive' tasks derive from this division.[62]

These distinctions allow neoliberal thinking to lend the market a natural, almost primal form in which the economy remains separate from the rest of social life. In a circular fashion the naturalness of the market

[59] For a very interesting and provocative illustration of these ideological differences see Shujaat A. Khan, 'Two Paths to Development: Capitalist vs. Islamic Approach' in Amer Al-Roubaie and Shafiq Alvi (eds.), *Islamic Banking and Finance* (London: Routledge, 2010), 22–35.

[60] Silvia Fazio, *The Harmonization of International Commercial Law* (Alphen aan den Rhine: Kluwer Law International, 2007), 148.

[61] David Feldman (n 47) 11.

[62] Kerry Rittich, *Recharacterizing Restructuring: Law, Distribution and Gender in Market Reform* (The Hague: Kluwer Law International, 2002), 49.

reinforces the need for pre-existing (natural) divisions of activities and responsibilities.[63]

Harking back to classical economic theory, neoliberalism proposes that 'human well-being can best be advanced by liberating individual entrepreneurial freedoms and skills within an institutional framework characterised by strong private property rights, free markets, and free trade'.[64] But beyond creating and preserving an institutional framework appropriate to such practices, the state should not intervene in the market. Market interventions distort market signals such as prices and interest rates, as these are the result of powerful interest groups whose self-serving interests interfere with the natural course of trade.[65] Hence, market forces are valued as an 'ethic in itself, capable of acting as a guide to all human action, and substituting for all previously held ethical beliefs'.[66] The regular use of descriptive guides such as 'level playing field' and the policy of 'neutrality' are key operating concepts in the neoliberal economic landscape as these principles reflect a devoted belief in an unfettered market. Indeed, the hegemony of neoliberalism is so pervasive that its incorporation into people's common sense manner of living, thinking and understanding the world goes almost unnoticed.[67]

The mental imagery of neoliberalism, the webs of social meaning and signification that derive from its ethos, strongly inform the institutional structures, regulations and practices of the global economy. The following section examines some ways in which this thinking informs financial practices.

4.3 Globalisation and financial innovation

The globalisation of financial markets has generated a sharp increase in financial innovation, resulting in a multitude of new investment vehicles comprising investments of high net-worth individuals and institutions on an informal, mostly unregulated basis.[68] The Schumpeterian tradition defines *invention* as an idea or 'a model for a new improved device, product process or system'.[69] *Innovation*, on the other hand, is the process

[63] *Ibid.*, 55.

[64] David Harvey, *A Brief History of Neoliberalism* (Oxford University Press, 2005), 2.

[65] *Ibid.* [66] *Ibid.*, 3. [67] *Ibid.*

[68] Howard Davies and David Green, *Global Financial Regulation* (Cambridge, UK and Malden, MA: Polity Press, 2008), 8.

[69] c.f. Paul Stoneman, *The Economic Analysis of Technological Change* (Oxford University Press, 1983), 8.

in which the idea or model is given effect in a commercial transaction.[70] This concept can be further refined to include 'a series of chains or sets of relations' in a commercial transaction rather than the creation of a 'specific technical item'.[71] Innovation, therefore, especially the financial sort, does not usually reflect absolute novelty or a rupture from earlier ideas. Instead, it is 'without exception a small variation on an established design ... The world of finance hails the invention of the wheel over and over again, often in a slightly more unstable version. All financial innovation involves, in one form or another, the creation of debt secured in greater or lesser adequacy by real assets'.[72]

The vast majority of financial instruments support this interpretation. Both conventional and Islamic structures are not revolutionary new instruments but merely combinations of older generation derivatives or standard money market contractual vehicles. A building block approach towards financial engineering is at the heart of finance; creativity is not about inventing products from scratch. Indeed, in the conventional financial industry four key financial instruments may be combined in various forms and guises to create all other financial products. These foundational products are the forward contract, the option contract, the deposit contract and the spot contract. A small number of highly exotic financial instruments are regarded as examples of 'accounting innovation' or 'ignorance innovation' and possess limited utility for end users. However, most utilised financial instruments can be broken down into one or other combination of the four mentioned products.[73]

Since the mid-1980s financial innovation has increasingly taken the form of market-ready securities comprising a series of complicated chains of risk that ultimately derive from underlying assets.[74] Because exchange rates, interest rates and commodity prices fluctuate, most financial institutions invest in hedging products to insure themselves against these risks. Consumers, on the other hand, have generally sought to free themselves from the financial constraints of their income by investing in hedging products such as pensions, mortgages, revolving loans and other

[70] *Ibid.*

[71] Engelen E, Ertürk I, Leaver A, Froud J, Williams K, (n28) 46.

[72] John Kenneth Galbraith, *A Short History of Financial Euphoria*, reprint edn (New York: Penguin Books Ltd, 1994), 19.

[73] Warren Edwardes, *Key Financial Instruments: Understanding and Innovating in the World of Derivatives* (London: Pearson Education Limited, 2000), 44.

[74] Zachary J. Gubler, 'The Financial Innovation Process: Theory and Application' (2011) 55 *Del.J.Corp.L.*, 72, 72.

financial products. The use of securitisation greatly extended the use of this product chain. By transforming illiquid income streams deriving from debt receivables such as car loans, credit card receivables and mortgages into tradable securities, financial institutions could generate huge fees. Eventually, securitisation transactions could be tiered, one on top of the other, resulting in an infinite number of further derivative contracts.[75] A pertinent example concerns a residential mortgage-backed collateralised debt obligation (CDO). A CDO is backed by cash flows deriving from residential mortgage-backed securities, which are also bond instruments backed by the pooled cash flows of residential mortgages.[76]

Although long heralded by industry practitioners and scholars alike as a means of diversifying risk,[77] these long chains of financial innovation obscure practitioners' ability to value the underlying assets. There are no economic models that can accurately assess the 'combination and diffusion of information resulting from such a structured financial product'.[78] For example, documentary information concerning a plain vanilla asset-backed CDO is numbered in the tens of thousands of pages while a more exotic variant can literally amount to millions of pages of securities disclosures.[79] The extremely high cost of navigating this information prohibits market practitioners from accurately assessing it, let alone retail customers whose skill-set and access to such information is limited. Consequently, economists generally agree that the complexity of these types of innovations generates enormous risks, particularly in interdependent world capital markets.[80] Not only do these structures entail numerous points of disruption, these types of risk interconnect in several ways. For example, the subprime mortgage crisis in 2008 involved the retail sale of sub-prime mortgages and the wholesale sale of mortgage-backed securities. Each type of contract was based on debt and any disruption in one would cause a problem with the other.[81] The new markets created by a long chain of innovation can fracture under stress as evidenced in the near financial meltdown of 2008, initially triggered by an increase in home mortgage foreclosures.

[75] Engelen E, Ertürk I, Leaver A, Froud J, Williams K, (n 28) 55.
[76] Zachary J. Gubler (n 74) 72.
[77] Howard Davies and David Green (n 68) 7–8.
[78] Zachary J Gubler (n 74) 72. [79] *Ibid.*, 78.
[80] Joseph E. Stiglitz, 'Capital-Market Liberalization, Globalization, and the IMF' (2004) 20 *Oxf. Rev. Econ. Policy*, 57, 62.
[81] Engelen E, Ertürk I, Leaver A, Froud J, Williams K, (n 28) 56.

Financial innovation has also changed the basic nature of financial intermediation in the past twenty years. This is due, in part, to capital adequacy requirements and internal credit limits, which limit the amount of risk banks can hold on their balance sheets.[82] The traditional role of financial intermediaries has shifted from taking and holding borrowers' loans on their own books to acting as facilitators of their clients' financial requirements on capital markets. Banks are increasingly securitising parts of their loan book, particularly their stock of mortgages, as a means of making room for more profitable risks. Market operations generally involve trading in derivative markets to achieve an optimal balance of risk and return. This, however, has spurred a dynamic expansion in market trading activities, particularly by banks in large, industrialised countries, which no longer see their primary role or optimal competitive position as one of pure financial intermediation.

A limited range of investment funds and derivatives that were traded in standardised exchanges has given way to creative financial instruments that enable investors to spread risk of all kinds on a much larger scale and in more complex ways. Today an almost unlimited variety of bespoke, over-the-counter transactions (derivatives) such as CDOs and synthetic CDOs are held by banks in off-balance sheet vehicles. These vehicles allow financial institutions to spread their risk to a much wider range of risk bearers and to make room for potentially more profitable assets. Some observers have argued that these structures tend to strengthen the economic system's soundness;[83] but they clearly obstruct regulators' ability to perceive systemic risks as they materialise.[84] Should serious risks arise, the network of these diffuse arrangements may well have an impact across the globe, again, as evidenced in the 2008 financial crisis.

These developments have several consequences with wide-ranging significance. First, traditional divisions between commercial and investment banks hardly exist any longer. Second, banking and insurance institutions now perform many of the same services, although the division remains clearer than between banks.[85] Extended group or conglomerate structures have been created that unify services from multiple areas of activity. The development has created an 'almost seamless collection

[82] Zachary J. Gubler (n 74) 74.

[83] Howard Davies and David Green (n 68) 7–8.

[84] See Gillian Tett, *Fool's Gold: How Unrestrained Greed Corrupted a Dream, Shattered Global Markets and Unleashed a Catastrophe* (London: Abacus, 2010).

[85] Charles Goodhart, Philipp Hartmann, David T. Llewellyn *et al.* (n 34) 39.

of essentially interchangeable or substitutable savings and investment media'.[86] Its implications are such that banks' range of allowable activities has been broadened in the absence of restrictive regulatory barriers. Today, the use of corporate conglomerate structures has become one of the most dominant business models in the industrial and commercial sectors of many leading financial markets.[87]

Financial conglomeration is a clear strategy for banks to compete both between themselves and with other financial sectors in providing the full range of retail financial services. The major British clearing banks, for example, which include Barclays, Lloyds, HSBC and NatWest, have all become financial conglomerates in both the wholesale and retail markets. Clearing banks now offer all major financial services with the exception of wholesale general insurance.[88]

Indeed, the entire structure of the UK financial system has shifted decisively in the direction of universal banking or the financial conglomerate corporate model. In the United Kingdom banks began to engage in securities trading in the mid-1980s and have since become involved in insurance manufacture. Even non-financial companies such as Marks and Spencer – a national retail store – have offered unit trusts or mutual funds, personal equity plans and consumer loans since 1988. Virgin Atlantic was authorised in the mid-1990s to market its own personal pension, life assurance and personal equity plans.[89]

Third, the legal and operational structure of banks has become much more complicated. For example, in universal banks or financial conglomerates there are no limits in cross-holdings of shares. Consequently, large numbers of diversified financial conglomerates are created since commercial banks, investment banks and insurance companies are permitted to own shares in each other (rules limit ownership in non-financial companies due to banks' capital adequacy requirements).[90] Fourth, the increased use of derivatives and off-balance-sheet positions has made the use of occasional or monthly balance sheets unreliable as a guide to a bank's soundness. As a result of these developments, external regulation

[86] George Alexander Walker (n 35) 8. [87] *Ibid.*

[88] David Llewellyn, 'Universal Banking and the Public Interest: A British Perspective' in Anthony Saunders and Ingo Walter (eds.), *Universal Banking: Financial System Design Reconsidered* (Chicago, IL: Irwin Professional Publishing, 1996), 180–4.

[89] *Ibid.*, 162.

[90] Carlos M. Pelaez and Carlos A. Pelaez, *Financial Regulation after the Global Recession* (Basingstoke: Palgrave Macmillan, 2009), 94.

of conventional financial institutions has become 'both less effective and less feasible'.[91]

Therefore, the effects of globalisation in financial markets, particularly in the last four decades, are profound. Yet the internationalisation of financial markets, the predecessor of financial globalisation, began many centuries ago. The following section is concerned with another offshoot of globalisation, namely the role of TNCs. In particular, the section deals with TNCs' involvement in Islamic finance.

4.4 Transnational corporations and Islamic financial law

The global expansion of Islamic finance has included some of the largest and most respected blue chip corporations. General Electric became the first western industrial company to issue *sukuk*, valued at US$500 million, as it sought to attract a new pool of investors.[92] The Islamic financial industry has also spread to some of the fastest growing economies. For example, China, which has a Muslim population of 80 million people, has begun to facilitate Islamic finance. South Korea and Thailand have expressed an interest in launching a sovereign *sukuk* issue.[93] Amongst Western countries, and those that have only recently begun to facilitate Islamic financial transactions, the United Kingdom's early steps to establish a legal and regulatory framework for Islamic finance have given the City of London an unrivalled competitive position.

Global expansion of the Islamic financial industry is directly connected to the way in which TNCs spearhead financial innovation. The introduction of sharia-compatible investments involves multiple jurisdictions and chains of market practitioners from a wide range of countries and religious, cultural and legal systems.[94] A number of conventional transnational investment banks, including BNP Paribas, Calyon, Citibank, HSBC, JP Morgan Chase, RBS and Standard Chartered, together with

[91] Charles Goodhart, Philipp Hartmann, David T. Llewellyn *et al.* (n 34) 39.

[92] Aline van Duyn, 'The US Holds Its Breath on Bonds' *Financial Times*, 7 December 2009, 4.

[93] Liau Y-Sing, 'Islamic Finance Set for Big China Leap' *Reuters* (2 October 2009), uk.mobile.reuters.com/article/fundsNews/idUKLNE59101I20091002. Accessed 28 April 2014; Kevin Brown, 'Wider Appeal Battles with Signs of Inefficiency' *Financial Times*, 7 December 2009, 5.

[94] Yusuf Talal DeLorenzo and Michael J. T. McMillen, 'Law and Islamic Finance: An Interactive Analysis' in Simon Archer and Rifaat Ahmed Abdel Karim (eds.), *Islamic Finance: The Regulatory Challenge* (Singapore: John Wiley & Sons (Asia), 2007), 160.

recent newcomers such as Barclays and Deutsche Bank, have come to dominate the Islamic finance industry. According to a survey conducted by *The Banker*, the balance sheets of conventional banks offering 'Islamic windows' rose from US$622 billion in 2007 to US$800 billion in 2008[95] – a clear indication of their competitive superiority relative to the industry's estimated size of US$1 trillion at the time. These conventional banks have chosen to adopt Islamic windows– conventional institutions that offer Islamic financial products and services – rather than developing dedicated Islamic subsidiaries, principally because windows leverage rather than dilute the financial strength of their respective institutions. Multinational financial wealth has enabled these institutions to offer far more resources to the industry than the fragmented Islamic finance sector, and as a result, much of the innovation stems from these banks.[96]

Transnational financial institutions, once wholly unfamiliar with the sharia, not to mention Islamic finance, are now developing their own Islamic finance programmes and playing to their native financial strengths, including innovations such as derivatives.[97] In many cases no suitable Islamic product exists on the market, yet market forces compel these institutions to seek the development of products that compete in both conventional and Islamic markets. The resulting pressure has led to a range of much more sophisticated financial instruments and products.[98]

The economic power of TNCs – a corporation that produces and/or delivers services in more than one country – may be so great that the legal environment itself is organised according to TNC operations. TNC market power directly influences the commercial customs of the relevant market, if not by enshrining recognised commercial customs into standard form contracts, then by persuading courts and legislatures to include them in court opinions and/or codify them into statutory law.[99] Indeed, the full extent of transnational corporate power is evidenced in

[95] IFSL, *Islamic Finance 2010* (International Financial Services London, 2010), 1.

[96] Simon Eedle, *A Global Bank's View of the Evolution of Islamic Finance* (London: Euromoney Yearbooks, 2009–2010).

[97] Deutsche Bank, 'Pioneering Innovative Shari'a Compliant Solutions' (Deutsche Bank Academic Paper, London, 2007), www.eurekahedge.com/news/07_mar_DB_Pioneering_Innovative_Sharia_Compliant_Solutions.pdf. Accessed 2 April 2014. Deutsche Bank, in partnership with a sharia consulting firm, developed a very interesting derivatives product, and provided an intriguing sharia legal analysis of its structure.

[98] Yusuf Talal DeLorenzo and Michael J. T. McMillen (n 94) 160.

[99] Peter T. Muchlinski, '"Global Bukowina" Examined: Viewing the Multinational Enterprise as a Transnational Law-Making Community' in Gunther Teubner (ed.), *Global Law without a State* (Aldershot: Dartmouth Publishing Company, 1997), 86.

those markets in which the market leader's standardised use of particular contracts becomes the industry norm.[100]

The origins of the most influential transnational actors determine the particular characteristics and nature of the law so as to reflect its native legal background and traditions. As examined, the United States and European states continue to dominate a large share of the world economy. The proliferation of TNCs from these countries' financial centres facilitates the dominance of American and European international standards and contractual methods.[101] From this perspective the deep involvement of nation states in the globalisation of financial markets becomes evident.[102] Moreover, the intensity of transactions between financial centres has risen markedly with a sharp growth in cross-border lending, mergers and acquisitions, and contracting for services.[103] These factors tend to encourage regulatory uniformity,[104] and exert pressures for IFL to be structured around TNC-designed rules and strategies.

An important characteristic of Islamic banking may be its ability to meet the financial needs of local populations and their particular understanding of the sharia. At the same time, transnational firms initiate a chain of innovation which eventually results in standardised contracts. In part, this reflects conventional trends in banking. Relationship banking is defined by the use of flexible contracts between the bank and the client. Such contracts are easily modified, if the circumstances, particularly macroeconomic conditions, warrant it.[105] However, conventional banking no longer follows this philosophy. Its mantra is that everyone in the world has similar banking requirements and these revolve around three core products: savings, payments and investments. In focusing on these foundational contracts, conventional institutions have striven to achieve economies of scale. Service delivery to the largest possible number of people is made more efficient with the creation of more rigid, standardised contracts and the development of a wide range of delivery channels and branches across the globe.[106]

[100] *Ibid.*

[101] Silvia Fazio (n 60) 9. See also Saskia Sassen (n 2) 69.

[102] Saskia Sassen (n 2) 35. [103] *Ibid.*, 28.

[104] Peter T. Muchlinski, *Multinational Enterprises & the Law* (Oxford University Press, 2007), 89.

[105] Zachary J. Gubler (n 74) 77.

[106] Joseph DiVanna and Antoine Sreih, *A New Financial Dawn: The Rise of Islamic Finance* (Cambridge: Leonardo and Francis Press, 2009), 106. See also *ibid.*, 77–8.

The large majority of new market entrants, including IFIs, consist of small and medium-sized firms that are not able to adopt this strategy. Instead, IFIs have focused on identifying market niches that exploit the different needs of a multitude of diverse ethnic groups. This strategy is seen as a competitive advantage for small and medium-sized IFIs in developing brand recognition and an ability to foster better customer service.[107] The challenge for these institutions, however, is to achieve a balance in which niche market product offerings are economically viable while complying with market forces, which demand the standardisation of the market.

4.5 Commercial pressures for standardised Islamic financial contracts

The terms standardisation, harmonisation and regulatory convergence are used in many different and sometimes conflicting ways throughout the disciplines of law, economics and political economy. The confusion centres on the legal and regulatory context that is the focus of analysis. Standardisation is often invoked when referring to the generation of rules and/or standards by non-state-based legal systems and/or non-governmental organisations. Harmonisation, on the other hand, is more often concerned with state-based legal systems where it is defined as 'the approximation of national legislations through the deliberate creation of international standards', such as Basel capital adequacy standards.[108] Finally, the term 'convergence' is often used to describe the processes underlying these terms, the narrowing of differences between legal rules, standards and/or codes, with little consideration whether there is indeed any difference between the terms. For the sake of analytical accuracy and ease this book will use these terms synonymously to refer to the approximation of rules, terms, standards and/or laws undertaken to further the financial integration of separate markets so that these markets can eventually enter into competition with one another. The synonymous usage of these terms reflects the empirical reality of the way in which law is created and develops in modern financial markets. Namely, law does not merely connote the rules, codes and/or regulations enacted and enforced by the

[107] Joseph DiVanna and Antoine Sreih (n 106) 106.

[108] Lucia Quaglia, 'The European Union in Regulating Global Finance', EUSA Conference Paper, Boston, 2011, 1–39, euce.org/eusa/2011/papers/12e_quaglia.pdf. Accessed 2 April 2014.

state. Rather, law can be seen from a much wider perspective, reflecting both state-based and non-national legal systems, which govern human behaviour irrespective of whether they are endowed with the authority of the nation state.

The globalisation of financial markets generates market pressure to standardise Islamic financial contracts. Commercial law, in general, tends towards convergence for commercial reasons, but some differences remain, nonetheless.[109] Legal standardisation is generally important for establishing market transparency, stability and predictability, all of which are essential components of a commercially viable and prosperous financial centre. Historically dominant centres of finance and industry such as the United States, England and France have been able to export their commercial and financial law as a result of their incorporation of these principles. Specifically, successful financial transactions establish clear parameters with respect to (1) the relative rights and remedies of the parties (2) the terms of many financial and commercial risk allocations and (3) the legal documentation.[110] Efforts aimed at standardising international commercial law are designed to produce these parameters.

Legal standardisation is also a means of alleviating the apprehension legal practitioners feel towards states' conflict of laws rules. Legal practitioners seek to minimise the risks and associated expenses of cross-border financial transactions because they may not be aware of certain applicable foreign laws and/or regulations. Standardisation also reflects leading states' ideological and political assumptions that convergence mitigates potential strife and encourages peaceful economic cooperation.[111] In specific jurisdictions legal documents are typically standardised as they are used for many years and have been the subject of extensive interpretive litigation. Thus 'there is great certainty and predictability as to how any particular provision will be interpreted and implemented with respect to the rights, obligations and remedies of all parties in a broad range of circumstances'.[112] The extensive track record of such standardised documentation has resulted in significant transaction cost efficiencies.

[109] See, in general, Nicholas H. D. Foster, 'Comparative Commercial Law: Rules or Context' in David Nelken and Esin Örücü (eds.), *Comparative Legal Studies: A Handbook* (Oxford: Hart Publishing, 2007), 263–85.

[110] Yusuf Talal DeLorenzo and Michael J. T. McMillen (n 94) 152.

[111] Roy Goode, Herbert Kronke and Ewan McKendrick, *Transnational Commercial Law* (Oxford University Press, 2007), 192.

[112] Yusuf Talal DeLorenzo and Michael J. T. McMillen (n 94) 152.

Yet to some extent the principles of stability, predictability and transparency are subjective. They refer to an individual's perception of the historical practices of market practitioners and their transactions. The fact that most market practitioners have little or no experience with Islamic financial transactions is an indication of the lack of certainty and predictability that these transactions incur. Moreover, the perceptions of most market actors will understandably be based on conventional structures and financing techniques that take no cognisance of the sharia and differences of risk allocation inherent in Islamic financial structures. These legal disadvantages underpin the commercial drive of Islamic market practitioners and Islamic financial institutions to develop standardised contractual vehicles for the industry.[113] Specifically, greater standardisation would benefit the industry in a number of ways by: (1) reducing transaction costs for firms and thereby lowering prices for consumers; (2) reducing the time necessary for marketing new products; (3) reducing the burden on sharia scholars of whom there is a shortage; (4) improving documentation standards and mitigating the risk of legal challenges; (5) and by improving consumer confidence in the authenticity of Islamic financial products and services.[114] Indeed, in the United Kingdom, surveys of potential Muslim investors indicate that the scant take-up of retail Islamic financial products is a direct consequence of consumers' uncertainty about the sharia-authenticity of Islamic financial products.[115]

Yet progress has been achieved since the 1990s in creating a general set of core products and services,[116] particularly in retail financial markets. Islamic capital markets are yet to benefit from standardisation, however, with *sukuk* providing a vivid example. AAOIFI has published sharia standard no. 17, which defines at least sixteen different types of investment *sukuk* but does not establish the risks and responsibilities of the parties with respect to the securitised asset.[117] The risks and responsibilities

[113] *Ibid.*, 153.

[114] Her Majesty's Treasury, *The Development of Islamic Finance in the UK: The Government's Perspective* (London: HM Treasury, 2008), 19.

[115] MCB, *Islamic Finance Transparency Standard: A Consultation* (London: The Muslim Council of Britain, 2008), 5.

[116] Mohamad Nadal Alchaar, Ahmed Al Khan, Afaq Khan *et al.*, 'Islamic Finance Debate: Prospects and Problems of Shari'ah-Compliant Finance', *Euromoney* (December 2008), www.euromoney.com/Article/2060693/Islamic-finance-debate-Prospects-and-problems-of-Shariah-compliant-finance.html. Accessed 23 March 2014.

[117] AAOIFI, *Shari'a Standards for Islamic Financial Institutions* (English Version) (Bahrain: The Accounting and Auditing Organization for Islamic Financial Institutions, 2010), 307.

of *sukuk* investment certificates do not depend merely on the type of underlying nominate structure. Rather, they depend on the assets used and the credit structure of the transaction.[118] Investors do not have access to standard form documentation or general guidelines for *sukuk* issuances, which would provide general disclosure requirements and otherwise provide guidance to the range of terms and conditions necessary for the issuance of a particular *sukuk* structure.

Islamic investment funds, on the other hand, are subject to greater regulation and supervision and thus tend to pose fewer standardisation requirements. Jurisdictions that permit the offer of investment funds require these to adhere to International Organization of Securities Commissions (IOSCO) guidelines so that certain regulatory criteria are consistently met.[119]

Although the industry has made some gains in standardisation, particularly in retail products, IFIs have not consistently adopted industry standards, with the result that Islamic finance continues to be practised differently between jurisdictions and even within the same jurisdiction.[120]

Yet the commercial benefits of standardisation are usually significant. In Malaysia,[121] a country where a centralised sharia supervisory board (Sharia Advisory Council) is part of the financial infrastructure, legal standardisation has resulted in *sukuk* becoming cheaper than their conventional counterparts by 5 to 10 basis points as inefficiency has been

[118] Sayd Farook, 'Do We Really Need Standardization in Islamic Finance? (Part 1 of 2)', *Islamic Finance News* (20 January 2010), www.Islamicfinancenews.com. Accessed 23 August 2013.

[119] Sayd Farook, 'Do We Really Need Standardization in Islamic Finance? (Part 2 of 2)', *Islamic Finance News* (27 January 2010), www.Islamicfinancenews.com. Accessed 23 August 2013.

[120] Some of the largest differences in practice exist between the two main centres of Islamic finance, Malaysia and the GCC states. Malaysian jurisprudence, largely based on the Shāfiʿī school, is viewed as considerably more liberal than the law of Islamic finance practised in the Gulf. The more conservative Ḥanbalī school is predominant in the Islamic financial jurisprudence of the Gulf, although the Hanafi and Malikī schools of law also play substantial roles.

[121] Malaysia and Bahrain are notable exceptions in that these states have created the institutional frameworks for Islamic finance to flourish. For example, Malaysia enacted the Islamic Banking Act in 1983 and the Takaful (Insurance) Act of 1984; and created a dual banking system that includes an Islamic inter-bank money market and an Islamic capital markets regulatory authority. While the country continues to be governed by the common law, it has constructed an Islamic legal and financial space that permits the industry to develop – more or less – on its own terms. See Maha-Hanaan Balala, *Islamic Finance and Law: Theory and Practice in a Globalized World* (London: I. B. Tauris, 2011), 162–3. Malaysia houses centralised sharia boards within its central bank and securities

reduced.[122] However, most analysts believe that the industry will continue to be plagued by differences of opinion on the finer points of the sharia. At present, Malaysian scholars are seen as more liberal than their Gulf peers. And intra-regionally there are just as many differences of opinion. In sum, the commercial benefits of standardisation are many but may not always be achievable. The next section focuses on the conceptual challenges that can impinge upon the industry's drive toward standardisation.

4.6 The religious and ethical aspects of standardisation

The standardisation of IFL has quite curiously not been the object of much discussion let alone debate in relation to the religious and ethical aspects of this effort. Legal standardisation, much like the process of codifying sharia that began in the late eighteenth century, raises important religious and ethical questions concerning the central function of contingency in the sharia – the mere probability that the Muslim jurist has interpreted the sources correctly. Contingency in the law legitimises normative pluralism within and between schools of *fiqh*; it has led to the peaceful co-existence of the various school doctrines and normative systems; and, most importantly, it underscores the primacy of God's law.[123] These attributes distinguish a religious law from a state-based legal system with central legal authority, wherein the state possesses the authority to determine the laws governing society in its sovereign territory.

From a traditional perspective Islamic law has been considered a method and a doctrine rather than a law code and codification has been said to distort its essential features.[124] Traditional *fiqhi* manuals have a discursive feel about them and do not offer final, definitive solutions to legal problems. Rather the *fiqh* is a jurists' law and as such contains scholarly discussions which are discursive and sometimes contradictory.[125]

commission. Bahrain has given statutory effect to AAOIFI sharia standards, effectively nationalising the standards and guidelines that this international Islamic organisation agrees.

122 Kevin Brown (n 93) 5.

123 Baber Johansen, *Contingency in a Sacred Law: Legal and Ethical Norms in the Muslim Fiqh*, vol. VII, *Studies in Islamic Law and Society*, edited by R. Peters and B Weiss (Leiden: Brill, 1999) 7, 38–9.

124 Joseph Schacht, 'Problems of Modern Islamic Legislation', (1960) 12 *Stud. Islam.* 99, 108.

125 Rudolph Peters, 'From Jurists' Law to Statute Law or What Happens When the Shari'a Is Codified' in B. A. Robertson (ed.), *Shaping the Current Islamic Reformation* (London: Frank Cass, 2003), 86.

Law codes, on the other hand, offer clear, unambiguous and final statements of the law. No room is made for contradictory opinions since to do so would be to undermine the state's authority and sovereign application of the law.

The idea of codification derives from the nineteenth-century continental European tradition of the civil law code, also the period in which the nation state became a dominant political and intellectual concept. In the nineteenth century the Ottomans were reeling from the military, political, scientific and economic domination of Europe. Some Ottoman elites felt that the reform of the 'chaotic and inaccessible' *fiqh* would help to reverse the Ottomans' fortunes. Codification became a concept that could help to restore the empire's strength and bring 'civilisation' to the domain of law.[126]

And yet the initial response was not to codify Islamic law but to abandon sharia and to adopt the legal systems of foreign states. Indeed, a leading scholar asserts that by the mid-twentieth century the sharia 'had been reduced to a fragment of itself at best and, at worst, structurally speaking, to a nonentity'.[127] This statement is largely confirmed by the historical facts.

In 1839, a series of major reforms known as the Tanzimat initiated the transformation process. The Ottomans promulgated a commercial code in 1850, a penal code in 1858, a code of commercial procedure in 1861, and a code of maritime commerce in 1863. All of these were almost entirely based on French law.[128] It was not until 1877 that the idea of codifying the sharia was put into practice in the Ottoman *Majallah* (gazette), which was, in general, a codified version of the Hanāfī treatises in all areas of private law except family law.[129] This curious reversal of fortune, preceded as it was by an almost complete secularisation of the law, nonetheless indicates that Western legal principles had found their way into God's law and Ottoman society at large. Furthermore, codification ushered in a period of law making in which the state and its actors realised that the state could make law when necessary, or even when merely convenient, and thus

[126] *Ibid.*, 88.

[127] Wael Hallaq, *Shari'a: Theory, Practice, Transformations* (Cambridge University Press, 2009), 284–85. See also James Norman Dalrymple Anderson, *Islamic Law in the Modern World* (London: Stevens & Sons Limited,1959), 1–2.

[128] Wael Hallaq (n 127) 385. And James Norman Dalrymple Anderson (n 127) 21–4.

[129] HaiderAla Hamoudi, 'The Death of Islamic Law' (Winter 2010) 38 *Ga.J.Int'l.& Comp.L.* 293, 306.

bypass the cumbersome aspects of the sharia as well as the traditional legal authority of jurists.[130]

In the following century the *Majallah* was gradually replaced. In the Arab world, a prominent marker of this change is the 1948 Egyptian Civil Code, which was drafted by the renowned Arab jurist, ʻAbd Razzāq al-Sanhūrī, and continues to govern in modified form throughout most Middle Eastern states. The almost complete secularisation of Middle Eastern legal systems other than in areas of personal status seems to confirm the notion that the state is now seen as the only viable source of central legal authority.[131] Furthermore, Muslim-majority states, and Islamist movements in particular, with the exception of Afghanistan under Taliban rule, have not shown any willingness to revert to a legal system based purely on the classical sharia.[132]

Despite this trend, there is, in fact, a long history of standardised contracts in Islamic law. Developed over the course of centuries, *shurūṭ* (formularies) were designed to facilitate commercial exchange. Individuals engaging in a transaction could simply agree to engage in an *ijārah*, *salam* or *istiṣnāʻ* and have a notary produce the relevant standardised contract. However, *shurūṭ* were drafted according to the doctrine of the respective school of law and could thus be arbitrated according to one's specific beliefs[133] and customary practices. The imposition of the market practitioners in sharia law-making practices changes this calculus to a great extent as examined below.

Standardised rules and regulations, while not law codes, are nonetheless similar to the extent that they are meant to function as authoritative and unambiguous expressions of the law on certain matters. Furthermore, such terms and conditions are designed for application in state-based legal systems. Courts and arbitration tribunals, as will be examined in subsequent chapters, will allow such standardised rules to govern the decision-making process.

The standardisation of IFL represents a historical continuation of the process of codification that began almost two centuries ago. The fact that very little discussion or debate has centred on this development suggests

[130] *Ibid.*, 308. [131] *Ibid.*, 334.

[132] Nicholas H. D. Foster, 'Using Comparative Commercial Law in the Study of Legal Transformation: Commercial Aspects of the Early Stages of Ottoman Legal Transition' in R. Shaham and A. Layish (eds.), *Islamic Law Facing the Challenges of the 21st Century* (The Van Leer Jerusalem Institute, 2011), 14–15, 32.

[133] Jeanette A. Wakin, *The Functions of Documents in Islamic Law* (Albany, NY: University of New York Press, 1972), 10–11, 13; Mahmoud A. El-Gamal, *An Introduction to Modern Islamic Economics and Finance* (Cambridge: Proceedings of the Fourth Harvard University Forum on Islamic Finance, Islamic Finance: The Task Ahead, 2000), 149.

that there is considerable Muslim support for the codification of sharia principles in the modern world or that Muslims are simply unaware that codification and/or standardisation may distort the traditional principles of Islamic law. It may be that the form of the law is no longer perceived as a distortion of sharia, so that standardisation can be used as an effective means of reinserting Islamic ethics and values into code-like statements of the sharia.

The next section examines the international methods by which legal standardisation is undertaken and how the efforts of Islamic standardisation organisations relate to these initiatives.

4.7 The methods and organisations of international legal convergence

In the globalised economy businesses and financial institutions increasingly do business across national borders. In cross-border transactions the reasons for standardising contract law include, in addition to those examined above, the additional concern that businesses and consumers may be less inclined to enter into a transaction when it is governed according to the law of another state. Reasons for this concern lawyers' uncertainty as to the law of the foreign jurisdiction as well as to their ability to minimise legal risks associated with their client's contractual interests. The development of an internationally recognised set of rules may give such transactions the appearance of neutrality, since they are not associated with a particular state. Consequently, such rules may reassure the parties that these rules can be adopted and used across jurisdictions.[134]

Lawyers involved in drafting cross-border contracts may be well informed about national rules but may lack knowledge of the applicability of particular terms and conditions in a foreign jurisdiction. The problem is less acute when internationally recognised rules are used, since lawyers will more readily be able to ascertain the consequences of their application in their contract. Take for example the United Nations Convention on Contracts for the International Sale of Goods (1980) (CISG)[135] (also

[134] Ewan McKendrick, 'Harmonisation of European Contract Law: The State We Are In' in S. Voguenauer and S. Weatherill (eds.), *The Harmonisation of European Contract Law: Implications for Private Laws, Business and Legal Practice* (Oxford: Hart Publishing, 2006), 14.

[135] UNCITRAL, 'United Nations Convention on Contracts for the International Sale of Goods' (United Nations Commission on International Trade Law, 1980), www.uncitral.org/pdf/english/texts/sales/cisg/V1056997-CISG-e-book.pdf. Accessed 15 August 2014.

known as the Vienna Convention), which is the leading document covering international sales.[136] Because the case law concerning its provisions is well developed and considerable academic commentary has been made upon the convention, lawyers should have little difficulty in determining the consequences of the application of CISG to their contract.[137]

International efforts aimed at standardising international commercial and financial law began early in the last century under the auspices of the old League of Nations. UNIDROIT, the International Institute for the Unification of Private Law, is one of the oldest organisations dedicated to the international convergence of commercial and financial law. It was re-established after the First World War as an independent organisation when it began to develop an International Sales of Goods Convention in 1928 at the initiative of Professor Ernst Rabel of Germany. These efforts later resulted in the Hague Conventions on Uniform Law in the International Sale of Goods, completed in 1951 and again in 1964.[138]

UNCITRAL, the United Nations Commission on International Trade Law, was created in 1966 and has been the more productive organisation. In the area of the international sale of goods, it took over the work formerly done by UNIDROIT, which resulted in the successor Vienna Convention of 1980. UNCITRAL operates in many areas of law and fosters convergence 'through conventions, model laws, legal guides and, in the area of arbitration, also rules and notes'.[139]

Another internationally active organisation is the Paris-based International Chamber of Commerce (ICC), which has compiled uniform rules, practices and trade terms (INCOTERMS) for application via contractual incorporation or on the basis of custom. In contrast to UNIDROIT and UNCITRAL these are not promulgated in any way but are nonetheless very important in the area of international trade.[140]

Finally, in the United States the American Law Institute (ALI) has developed Restatements of the Law for Conflict of Laws, Agency, Contracts, Property, Judgments, Restitution, Torts, Trusts and Security.[141] The basic objective of the Restatements is to address uncertainty in the law by restating the basic legal subjects and by clarifying their legal principles so that

[136] Jan H. Dalhuisen, *Dalhuisen on International Commercial, Financial, and Trade Law* (Oxford: Hart Publishing 2000), 212.
[137] Ewan McKendrick (n 134) 18.
[138] Jan H. Dalhuisen (n 136) 77–8. [139] *Ibid.*, 77.
[140] *Ibid.*, 78.
[141] ALI, 'ALI Overview' (The American Law Institute, 2012), www.ali.org/index.cfm?fuseaction=about.overview. Accessed 20 April 2014.

judges and lawyers have an unambiguous understanding of the law.[142] The Restatements depend on clarity for their effectiveness since they are not miniscule rules. Rather, they express legal principles that offer inspiration and guidance.[143] ALI has also collaborated with the National Conference of Commissioners on Uniform State Laws to develop and monitor the Uniform Commercial Code (UCC). The UCC addresses most aspects of commercial law and has been implemented with modifications in all fifty states of the union.[144]

These organisations and others such as the European Union represent the most important international organisations for the convergence or standardisation of international commercial and financial law. They provide instructive examples for the Islamic finance industry, which is also at work on the standardisation of IFL. In particular, the methods used by these organisations for standardising the law are useful examples of the ways in which organisations aim to standardise IFL. Such methods include the promulgation of model laws for adoption in international conventions as noted above. Other methods include the creation of uniform rules and principles of a general character, which are meant to apply to all types of transaction within a specific area of law. These, like model laws, can be promulgated by sovereign states, but are often adopted by parties for application in their contracts. Another important method of standardisation concerns commercial parties' use of standard contract forms relating to specific transactions. Finally, parties often incorporate general terms or conditions into their contracts, which are normally meant to apply to all transactions between the parties, unless expressly excluded.[145]

AAOIFI is one of the oldest and most respected international non-governmental organisations which promote standardisation in Islamic financial markets through the issuance of uniform rules and principles. Its objective is to create accounting, auditing and sharia standards with a view to creating more transparency in the industry.[146] Arguably, AAOIFI, like other IINGOs, has been created to develop ways in which the non-national legal infrastructure of Islamic finance could be developed in such a way that states are able to facilitate the industry within their municipal

142 *Ibid.* 143 Jan H. Dalhuisen (n 136) 80–1.
144 *Ibid.*, 78.
145 Carole Murray, *Schmitthoff's Export Trade: The Law and Practice of International Trade*, 11th edn (London: Sweet & Maxwell, 2004), 834.
146 AAOIFI (n 117) viii. Bjorn Sorenson, 'Ethical Money: Financial Growth in the Muslim World' (2008) 23 *Am.U.Int'l L.Rev.*, 647, 654.

legal systems. The *raison d'être* of IINGOs is directly connected with the unbundling, de-territorialising trends of the nation state. These organisations are undertaking work that nation states, due to the limits of sovereignty and territoriality which define the nation state, are unable to assume. Established in 1991 AAOIFI has issued up to seventy standards, many of which have been adopted and implemented in Islamic financial institutions across the globe.[147] Bahrain, Sudan, Jordan, Malaysia, Qatar and Saudi Arabia have made them either mandatory or recommended guidelines.[148] AAOIFI standards may be adopted by sovereign states and used as guidelines or they can be incorporated into the contracts of commercial parties. As such they play a clarifying role similar to that of the American Restatements, since their main objective is to provide a general framework of rules for specified Islamic nominate transactions and other commercial law aspects.

The sharia standards, of which there are now forty-one and several more under consideration, incorporate aspects of Islamic commercial law including rules for guarantees, assignment (*hāwalah*), possession (*qabḍ*), and the prohibition of *gharar.* Other rules deal with a range of topics including *zakah*, *waqf*, arbitration, the hiring of persons and the distribution of profit in *muḍārabah* profit- and loss-sharing investments.[149] The standards do not provide a comprehensive statement of the Islamic laws of contract, since the standards are not meant to deal with issues under the sovereign authority of national jurisdictions. Instead they provide guidelines for national regulators or general terms that parties may incorporate into their contracts. For instance, the standards do not deal with contract formation, factors that defeat contractual liability, (e.g. mistake, misrepresentation, illegality), remedies for breach of contract or other aspects of contract law.

For example, sharia standard no. 8 explains the Shari'a basis and rules for a '*Murabaha* to the purchase order' transaction. The standard deals with the stages of the transaction, and the sharia requirements that pertain to the structure.[150] The standard also provides related guidance on guarantees, security and the recovery of debt in relation to the transaction. Each standard includes an unusual section concerning the legal

[147] AAOIFI, 'AAOIFI Publishes New Standards' (The Accounting and Auditing Organization for Islamic Financial Institutions, 2011), www.aaoifi.com/AAOIFI%20-%20PR-Click%20Jordan%20-%20New%20Standards.pdf. Accessed 12 July 2013.

[148] Hossein Askari, Zamir Iqbal and Abbas Mirakhor, *New Issues in Islamic Finance and Economics: Progress and Challenges* (Singapore: John Wiley & Sons (Asia), 2009), 33.

[149] AAOIFI (n 117) ix. [150] *Ibid.*, 114.

basis of the sharia rulings for each contractual step. The relevance of the *fiqh* as an authoritative source of legitimacy for each standard is striking. Finally, each standard includes a table of definitions dealing with the general commercial concepts utilised.

A further method of standardisation concerns the use of standard form contracts, which are particularly useful for dominant and recurring transactions on which financial markets rely. The International Islamic Financial Market (IIFM) is another Islamic standard-setting body with the objective of harmonising Islamic capital and money markets. IIFM, in partnership with other standard-setting organisations, has produced several standard form contracts including: (1) a master agreement for treasury placement (MATP); (2) a *Mubadalatul Arbaah* profit rate swap; (3) and a *Tahawwut* master agreement (TMA).[151] The MATP is credited with gaining a critical mass in interbank *murābaḥah* transactions as several Islamic banks have adopted it as their standard document.[152] The *Mubadalatul Arbaah* profit rate swap and the *Tahawwut* master agreement (also intended for profit rate swaps) were created in partnership with the International Swaps and Derivatives Association (ISDA), which specialises in creating legal standards and documentation materials for over-the-counter derivatives.[153] ISDA's master agreement is said to be the master template for the derivatives market. The use of Islamic model contracts significantly reduces legal, sharia, operational and other costs by minimising negotiations between parties and sharia scholar involvement. Furthermore, variations between documentation and procedures are minimised with the result that these costs can be avoided.[154]

Over-the-counter derivatives, as examined earlier, are the types of private party derivative contracts that can disseminate enormous risk throughout the global financial system. Although these types of derivative have long been heralded as a way of spreading and thus reducing counterparty credit risk, the global financial crisis showed that they could also magnify the interconnected risks of the global economy. The Islamic finance industry's cooperation with ISDA indicates that it also wishes to appropriate the tools of ISDA. As such there is a general trend of convergence with the institutional, regulatory and legal practices of the

151 IIFM, 'Published Standards', www.iifm.net. Accessed 25 March 2014.

152 Sayd Farook (n 119).

153 ISDA, 'About ISDA' (2012), www2.isda.org/about-isda/. Accessed 6 April 2014.

154 Shafiq Alvi, 'Introduction to IIFM' (International Islamic Financial Market, 2009), www.iifm.net/media/PDF/presentation-paper/introduction%20to%20iifm%20by%20ijlal%20a.%20alvi%20-%206th%20dec%2009.pdf. Accessed 23 August 2013.

neoliberal global economy. Derivatives contracts are controversial under the sharia as several classical prohibitions and rules are in conflict with these modern structures. In particular, the transaction of these contracts is premised on unforeseen, future events in which parties agree to buy and sell a sometimes non-existent subject matter, which in almost all cases never changes hands. Some modern scholars have argued for the lawfulness of exchange traded derivatives by underscoring the ways in which a modern regulatory environment changes the meaning of classical sharia prohibitions.[155] A radically altered context changes the meaning of classically developed rules, since human subjectivities in understanding such rules are also very different.

In addition to debates concerning the lawfulness of derivatives contracts under the sharia, which is not the purpose of this examination, IIFM's collaboration with ISDA highlights the underdeveloped nature of Islamic commercial rules relative to the modern commercial environment. Modern scholars continue to search for classical legal bases to accommodate modern derivatives such as futures, options and swaps. In particular, the *salam*, *'urbun*, *wa'd* and *istisnā'* are mined for their similarity but, in fact, there is little correlation between these contracts and conventional derivative structures.[156] The reasoning behind some of these juristic efforts is often tenuous and quite strained.[157] Nonetheless, these substantive and legal differences have not stymied the efforts of financial institutions to develop sharia-compatible derivatives products with comparable returns and protection.[158] The gaps and conceptual difficulties that arise in developing these structures are simply ignored and western legal doctrines and commercial practices are used to surmount these challenges. As is the case in the municipal legal systems of Muslim-majority states, the practice of adopting secular, western-based notions of law is commonplace in the development of IFL. The following section deals with a further method of standardising IFL and some particular challenges that arise in relation to different understandings of language.

[155] The most authoritative work on the subject is Mohammad Hashim Kamali, *Islamic Commercial Law: An Analysis of Futures and Options* (Cambridge: Islamic Texts Society, 1990).

[156] See David M. Eisenberg, 'Derivatives and Islamic Finance' in Craig Nethercott and David Eisenberg (eds.) *Islamic Finance: Law and Practice* (Oxford University Press, 2012) 231.

[157] David M. Eisenberg (n 156) 232.

[158] A well-known case study of the difficulty of such efforts can be found in a Deutsche Bank academic paper, which is the subject of analysis in section 4.11. See Deutsche Bank (n 97).

4.8 Standard terms and conditions in cross-border financial transactions

Lawyers use standard terms and conditions known as 'boilerplate' clauses, which in the widest sense refer to clauses which are common to nearly all commercial contracts. Such terms have often been acquired from legal precedents and lawyers have a fairly good idea of how a court will construe such terms. Boilerplate clauses generally deal with the way in which a contract operates, rather than the substantive issues agreed by the parties themselves. However, in some cases, boilerplate clauses modify the substantive rights of parties to a contract as well as their operation and enforcement.[159] National courts will enforce standardised terms and conditions, particularly those developed under the auspices of trade and professional associations such as the ICC.[160]

Lawyers regularly incorporate boilerplate clauses into the contracts they draft on behalf of clients. Such clauses save valuable time and cover all the relevant issues, are usually known to counterparties and thus help to facilitate negotiations.[161] Examples include clauses relating to matters of jurisdiction, choice of law, arbitration, retention of title, *force majeure* and exclusion.[162] The importance of standard terms and conditions in commercial contracts is unquestionable. In fact, most rules of contract in municipal legal systems nowadays are default rules, which apply unless they are excluded by the terms of a contract. Yet, mandatory rules in a commercial context or between businesses are relatively few with the result that the terms of the contract play the most important role in regulating the relationship between the parties.[163]

Most major law firms and commercial parties develop their own standard terms of business, which they seek to apply in the transactions they conclude. The differences between such standard terms actually tend to be quite small. Many standard terms have an industry-wide presence so that most parties in a particular industry will use them, sometimes with regulatory approval. Standard terms differ from industry to industry but generally similar issues are dealt with in each.[164] Therefore, the use of

[159] Richard Christou, *Boilerplate: Practical Clauses*, 4th edn, Commercial Series (London: Sweet & Maxwell, 2005), 1.

[160] Peter Muchlinski (n 99) 87.

[161] Richard Christou (n 159) 3.

[162] Ewan McKendrick (n 134) 15. [163] *Ibid.*, 16.

[164] Ewan McKendrick, *The Creation of a European Law of Contracts: The Role of Standard Form Contracts and Principles of Interpretation* (Nijmegen: Kluwer-Deventer, 2004), 5.

standard terms in an industry or in an entire jurisdiction contributes significantly to the standardisation of contract law as a whole.

The increase in cross-border transactions has also increased pressure on lawyers to devise standard terms for cross-border applications. The importance of doing so concerns the fact that different jurisdictions may interpret terms in different ways. Contracting parties may have different understandings of the same terms with the result that parties will not arrive at a common understanding, with unforeseeable results.[165] In fact, most contractual disputes concern the proper interpretation of the terms of the contract concluded by the parties.[166] That this is so is evidenced in the well known case of *Investors Compensation Scheme* v. *West Bromwich Building Society*.[167] The most widely cited case in modern English contract law,[168] the case serves a useful purpose in elucidating the ways in which a jurisdiction, in this case that of England and Wales, applies specific interpretational guidelines for construing the terms of commercial contracts. It is also relevant for the reason that English law plays an important role in Islamic financial transactions and in financial transactions worldwide, so that the interpretational guidelines of English courts will often apply to transactions in which sharia principles are given expression.

Lord Hoffmann, in a decision given by the House of Lords, laid out the following principles:[169] First, the court will consider the meaning of a contractual document on the basis of the way in which a reasonable person with relevant background knowledge would have understood the meaning of that document. Furthermore, Lord Hoffmann allows for a broad and searching interpretation of that background: any circumstances that would have an effect on the way in which the contract's language would be understood by a reasonable person are admissible. Further, the range of admissible materials is narrowed by prohibiting pre-contractual negotiations or other subjective declarations as admissible evidence, as well as the conduct of the parties subsequent to the conclusion of the contract.[170]

Finally, Lord Hoffmann indicates a more liberal interpretational approach than has traditionally been the case in English courts by allowing a departure from the literal meaning of the words used by the parties in their contracts.[171] An example of this latter approach was illustrated in

[165] *Ibid.*, 27. [166] *Ibid.*

[167] [1998] 1 WLR 896, [1998] All ER 98.

[168] Ewan McKendrick (n 164) 27.

[169] [1998] All ER 98, 114–15.

[170] *Schuler AG* v. *Wickman Machine Tool Sales* [1974] AC 235.

[171] Ewan McKendrick (n 164) 38.

Kleinwort Benson Ltd v. *Malaysia Mining Corp Bhd* in which the Court of Appeal carefully examined the wording of a 'letter of comfort' to reach its verdict concerning its proper construction.[172] Two letters of comfort provided by the defendants, *Malaysia Mining Corp Bhd,* was part of an acceptance credit/multi-currency cash loan facility, which was granted by the plaintiffs, *Kleinwort Benson Ltd,* to the defendant's subsidiary known as MMC Metals in the amount of up to £10 million. In the letter, paragraph 3 stated that: 'It is our policy to ensure that the business of MMC Metals Limited is at all times in a position to meet its liabilities to you under the above arrangements.'[173] When in 1985 the tin market collapsed Metals, which traded on the London Metal Exchange, went into liquidation and the plaintiffs sought payment of the amount owing from the defendants. The court held that paragraph 3 of the letter of comfort was a statement of present fact and not 'a promise as to future conduct'. Moreover, the context in which the letters were written indicated that paragraph 3 was meant solely to convey a moral responsibility on the part of the defendants to meet Metal's debt.[174] Specifically, the defendants did not state that '*it is and will be* the defendants' policy to ensure that Metals is in a position to meet their liabilities'.[175]

The result of this latter interpretational strategy is likely to create uncertainty in that the role of the judge has been expanded from interpreting the meaning of words to the meaning of documents. This shift to the meaning of documents can lead courts to depart from 'the natural and ordinary meaning' of words in formal documents to an analysis of what may have gone wrong in relation to the use of words or syntax in the document. In *Antaios Cia Naviera SA* v. *Salen Rederierna AB* Lord Diplock strongly asserted this approach: 'if detailed semantic and syntactical analysis of words in a commercial contract is going to lead to a conclusion that flouts business common sense, it must be made to yield to business common sense'.[176] Lord Hoffmann did state that the court would 'not easily accept that people have made linguistic mistakes, particularly in formal documents' so courts' power to adjust and/or rewrite contracts would not be taken lightly. Nevertheless, the new approach introduces an element of uncertainty that makes it more difficult for parties to predict the outcome of litigation.[177]

172 [1989] 1 WLR 379. 173 *Ibid.*, 786. 174 *Ibid.*, 785.
175 *Ibid.*, 794. 176 [1984] 3 All ER 229, 233, [1985] AC 191, 201.
177 Ewan McKendrick(n 164) 39–40.

Lawyers involved in cross-border transactions will need to have an in-depth familiarity with the interpretational approach of the courts of the jurisdiction in which the counterparty is regularly domiciled and/or the transaction takes place according to the conflict of laws rules of the respective jurisdiction. This makes the development of a common set of standard terms for application in different jurisdictions a very difficult endeavour indeed.

Common law, civil law and sharia legal systems all possess different methodologies for the interpretation of contracts. The reader will recall the *madhaḥib's* different approaches to intention in a contract and the way in which the parties' intentions will or will not affect the validity of a contract. Civil law legal systems predominate in most Muslim-majority countries as these countries imported mostly French legal codes into their countries in the mid-nineteenth century.[178] Malaysia is a notable exception, since it inherited a common law legal system from Britain, which colonised the country in the early nineteenth century. Civil law legal systems each have particular approaches to the interpretation of contracts but some general trends can be ascertained. For example, in place of common law's more stringent focus on the language of the contract, the civil law approach is concerned with the context of the parties' consensus. Based on the normative or teleological interpretation method, this notion of consensus submerges individual desires and aims of the parties so that personal intent and declarations are detached from it. In doing so it resembles common law's expectations concerning what a reasonable person should understand in a particular situation, but unlike common law does not concern itself with what the other party intended or declared. Instead these are placed in the context of the circumstances of what is considered normal, usual, sensible, practical and justifiably or reasonably relied upon. In cases in which hardship or contractual imbalance concerns the court issues of fairness and morality may be taken into consideration on the basis of the social and economic context.[179] In practice, however, the two greatest differences between civil and common law legal systems concerns the way in which courts treat the parties' pre-contractual negotiations and post-contractual duties. In sum, the result of these differences is that parties cannot be certain that their boilerplate clauses will be interpreted in the same way in different jurisdictions.

[178] P. Nicholas Kourides, 'The Influence of Islamic Law on Contemporary Middle Eastern Legal Systems: The Formation and Binding Force of Contracts', (1970) 9 *Colum. J. Transnat'l L.*, 384, 385.

[179] Jan H. Dalhuisen, (n 136) 130.

Even in the European Union, where legal standardisation efforts are advanced, some terms and phrases that are in common use in commercial transactions such as '*force majeure*', 'indirect or consequential loss' and 'material breach' may be assigned different meanings in different European jurisdictions.[180] In July 2001 the European Commission launched a process designed to elicit suggestions for minimising the differences between national contract law and EU law.[181] One of its objectives concerned the elaboration of EU-wide general contract terms available for parties wishing to undertake cross-border transactions. In response to a set of Commission proposals a number of responses received indicated that problems in various jurisdictions prevent a standardised application of standard contract terms.[182] For example, in some jurisdictions it is sufficient to merely make reference to a standard set of terms. In others, e.g. Italy (Article 1341 of the *codice civile*), such terms must be attached and each signed separately. Furthermore, some jurisdictions will not admit certain terms while other jurisdictions, e.g. Germany and some Nordic countries, have strict standards concerning their fairness, even in business-to-business contracts.[183] Moreover, standard terms and rules are often defined in different ways with the result that basic terminology and rules such as 'contract' or 'damage' or rules concerning the non-performance of contracts are understood differently in different jurisdictions.

The Commission's response may highlight a useful way in which the standard terms used in Islamic financial contracts can be further developed and applied in cross-border jurisdictions. The Commission proposed the development of a 'common frame of reference',[184] which would establish common principles and terminology in European contract law. It would be designed to facilitate legal certainty in cross-border transactions within the common market. The Islamic finance industry does not yet have any similar tool at its disposal for the reason that it is an industry rather than a supranational legal authority. It depends on municipal legal systems for its facilitation, regulation and adjudication and these systems comprise diverse constellations of rules, procedures and legal cultures. Despite these differences, the EU's experience in developing a

[180] Ewan McKendrick(n 134) 44.

[181] Communication from the Commission to the Council and the European Parliament of 11 July 2001 on European Contract Law [2001] COM 398 final.

[182] Communication from the Commission to the European Parliament and the Council of 12 February 2003 on a more coherent European contract law: an action plan [2003] COM 68 final.

[183] *Ibid.*, 11. [184] [2003] COM 68 final.

'common frame of reference' may provide a useful example of the difficulties of standardisation and the possible ways that interested states can move forward.

The following section examines a standardised *murābaḥah* financing facility which is created by applying boilerplate contract terms and conditions. The analysis demonstrates the role and function of standard terms in sharia-based contracts, the resulting hybrid composition of these transactions, and the possible legal problems that can arise in cross-border transactions. The examination underscores the remarkable rupture with traditional notions of deriving and administering the sharia.

4.9 Standard terms in a syndicated *murābaḥah* facility

The Loan Market Association (LMA) is arguably the most important standard-setting organisation for international finance throughout Europe and the Middle East.[185] A syndicated *murābaḥah* facility, as provided in the 'LMA Users Guide to Islamic Finance Documents' (hereinafter 'Users Guide'), illustrates the extent to which conventional finance and its legal infrastructure have appropriated Islamic ethics within the conventional legal mould. Specifically, Islamic financing agreements are based on the standard LMA form or 'primary documents' for the syndicated lending market, which provides a standard form of syndicated facility agreement used widely in international finance.[186] The Users Guide was drafted by English law firms with no input from sharia scholars or IINGOs such as AAOIFI. This is also reflected in the conventional style of the standard, which, in fact, is applicable to most large-scale Islamic finance transactions globally.[187]

This particular type of legal transformation indicates that classical debates concerning freedom of contract, in particular the permissibility of creating novel contractual types[188] is completely irrelevant as IFL is the product of globalised finance and no longer the prerogative of jurists. The

185 Kilian Bälz, 'Sharia Risk? How Islamic Finance Has Transformed Islamic Contract Law' (Occasional Publications no. 9, Islamic Legal Studies Program, Harvard Law School, September 2008), 20, www.law.harvard.edu/programs/ilsp/publications/balz.pdf. Accessed 25 March 2014.

186 LMA, 'Users Guide to the Recommended Form of Primary Documents' (Loan Market Association, January 2012), 2.

187 Kilian Bälz (n 185) 20.

188 Susan E. Rayner, *The Theory of Contracts in Islamic Law* (London: Graham & Trotman 1991), 91.

entire structure of Islamic commercial law, including its most important principles, has undergone a very significant evolution.

The LMA's Users Guide is meant to assist lawyers in drafting sharia-compliant contracts by highlighting the legal fine-tuning such structures require to comply with sharia and to remain commercially effective.[189] The work of the LMA is important to the Islamic finance industry because it depends on the syndicated loan market to generate corporate financing via *murābaḥah* and *tawarruq* transactions, in particular those taking place on the London Metals Exchange. A syndicated loan facility provides a flexible and efficient source of funding to borrowers who require large, sophisticated and/or multiple types of facility. A syndicate is a group of lenders or group of banks, who, under a syndicated loan agreement, agree to lend using a single agreement between themselves for different types of facility. It avoids borrowers and lenders alike having to conclude multiple separate bilateral loans, each with their own terms and conditions.[190]

The Users Guide is designed to provide guidance on the ways in which terms located in the Primary Documents can be imported into a typical *murābaḥah* facility. The *murābaḥah*[191] is a sale-based contract used for financing and is particularly important to the Islamic finance industry. It comprises approximately 80 per cent of a typical IFI's balance sheet.[192] It is used to finance household items, cars or business equipment and/or supplies, and often used to replicate a conventional trade financing agreement. It is also used as a financing instrument via the purchase and sale of commodities in a so-called reverse *murābaḥah* or *tawarruq*.

The Users Guide differs from the Primary Documents in a very limited way. It provides guidance on: definitions specific to Islamic financing; the facilities available for a *murābaḥah* and the particular risks that arise;

[189] LMA, 'Users Guide to Islamic Finance Documents' (Loan Market Association, 20 February 2007).

[190] LMA, 'Guide to Syndicated Loans' (Loan Market Association, n.d.), 1, www.lma.eu.com/uploads/files/introductory_guides/guide_to_par_syndicated_loans.pdf. Accessed 12 August 2014.

[191] The classical *murābaḥah* was a spot sale of a good with a clearly disclosed profit margin. In that structure the initial price had to be known to the buyer as well as the profit margin. See Wahbah Al-Zuhayli, *Financial Transactions in Islamic Jurisprudence*, vol. I, trans. byMahmoud A. El-Gamal (Damascus: Dar al-Fikr, 2003), 355. It was a rather simple and straightforward means of avoiding the prohibition of *ribā*. See Muhammad Taqi Usmani, *An Introduction to Islamic Finance* (Alphen aan den Rijn: Kluwer Law International, 2002), 31–2, 37.

[192] Habib Ahmed, 'Islamic Law, Adaptability, and Financial Development' (2006) 13 *Islam. Econ. Stud.*, 79, 88–9; Yusuf Talal DeLorenzo, 'Shari'ah Compliance Risk' (2006–2007) 7 *Chi. J. Int'l L.*, 397, 406.

current practices in payment, prepayment and cancellation; the determination of profit and late payment; additional payment obligations; and sharia factors relevant to representations, undertakings, events of default and termination.[193] The scope of representations, undertakings, events of default and termination will be determined by the credit requirements of the financiers and the jurisdictional requirements of the purchaser.[194] This will be done through negotiations in which the drafting law firm distributes the first draft to the syndicate of banks and the borrowers.[195] Clauses not covered in the original Term Sheet for the facility are either taken from the firm's own precedents or drafted in a way that are as friendly to the client as possible. Once the borrower's counsel has reviewed and amended this draft, the parties will continue to exchange drafts in what is described as a 'battle of the forms' until a final draft has been agreed. The borrower's compliance with conditions precedent is monitored until the time of the first drawdown of the facility.[196] The process is similar for both conventional and Islamic finance transactions.

A syndicated Islamic facility innovatively combines a *murābaḥah* with a *muḍārabah* profit- and loss-sharing investment structure in which a financier acts as a fronting entity for other financiers, e.g. as a *muḍārib* (investment agent). Both types of agreement are referred to as 'funding agreements' and are governed by an investment agency agreement. Normally a single investment agency agreement is sufficient to govern a conventional facility but under the *murābaḥah* agency agreements must be entered into for each sale/purchase agreement so as to differentiate between each individual transaction.[197] Transactions must be executed independently of one another according to a majority of classical jurists so as to mitigate the possibility of *ribā* and *gharar*. As examined in Chapter 3, contracts must not comprise 'two sales in one'. In modern practice, however, the combination of nominate contracts via the binding promise (*wa'd*) to achieve a single economic objective is the single most important method of Islamic financial engineering. It demonstrates that jurists no longer see themselves bound to the conditions and effects of nominate contract structures. The premier law-making body of IFL, AAOIFI, has even issued a standard on the combination of contracts that affirms its basic legality (*jawāz*). According to that standard combined contracts may be formed for single or separate values and may even 'be

193 LMA (n 189) 14–23. 194 *Ibid.*, 23.
195 LMA (n 186) 5.
196 Kai Kreutzberger, 'Shari'a Compliant Finance'(Interview 7 June 2012).
197 LMA (n 189) 13.

stipulated as conditions in the other contracts'.[198] For instance, a contract in which one party offers the sale of his house on condition that the buyer rents the house to the seller for a specified period is now considered legal. This represents a substantial re-evaluation of classical principles, despite the efforts of the standard's authors to demonstrate otherwise.[199] It is clear that it makes contracts such as the *murābaḥah* viable in modern financial markets.

So, in light of this contractual synthesis, the *murābaḥah* and the 'funding agreement' are constructed so as to contain provisions that are analogous to those in one of the Primary Documents.[200]

A group of financial institutions (*ārbāb al-māl*) channels capital to the *muḍārib*, who, in turn, has a direct relationship with the customer for funding the *murābaḥah* aspect of the structure. In principle, under the *muḍārabah* side of the agreement investors (*ārbāb al-māl*) enter into the contract on the basis that they will earn a pre-agreed percentage share of the profits – if the venture is profitable – from the investment of their money with the *muḍārib*. In the event that the investment fails the investors should carry the total monetary loss, while the *muḍārib* only loses his time and effort in locating and contracting an appropriate investment. Furthermore, the *muḍārib* is not allowed to offer any collateral to the *ārbāb al-māl* for the reason that it is an investment partnership without consideration. A pre-determined guarantee of returns would amount to *ribā*.

The *muḍārabah* is more restrictive than an investment agency agreement for the reason that investors have limited means of monitoring the agent and/or his investment projects or in enforcing additional actions, again due to sharia.[201] For this reason the market prefers to use the investment agency structure as it is 'most similar' to the 'facility agent/bank' relationship of a conventional facility.[202] A syndicated transaction will contain all the provisions normally found in the documentation of a conventional facility, such as the funding mechanisms.[203]

The mechanics of the transaction will also be specified in a section of the agreement. Prior to entering into a *murābaḥah* transaction under the facility a notice of intent to purchase by the purchaser must be submitted

[198] AAOIFI (n 147) 445. [199] *Ibid.*, 451–7.

[200] LMA (n 189) 5.

[201] Mervyn K. Lewis and Latifa M. Algaoud, *Islamic Banking* (Cheltenham: Edward Elgar, 2001), 77.

[202] LMA (n 189) 9. [203] *Ibid.*, 12.

to the investment agent after a number of conditions have been met.[204] The investment agent may appoint the purchaser as his agent (*wakīl*) to source the commodity on his behalf. This scheme is controversial for the reason that it gives the appearance of creating a contract that is contingent upon the fulfilment of another. Modern jurists, however, while expressing reservations concerning the practice, deem it valid on the basis of necessity (*ḍarūrah*) and on condition that the steps are carried out separately and in consecutive fashion.[205]

Once the conditions have been met the investment agent purchases the commodity for a clearly specified profit and deferred payment price. The profit earned is the equivalent of interest in a conventional facility. It is calculated on the basis of the London Interbank Offered Rate (LIBOR) at the time at which the contract is entered into and is used to calculate the deferred payment price.[206] The investment agent takes possession and title to the commodity and thus assumes various ownership risks and tax liabilities, and must clarify whether any warranties regarding the commodities have been made.[207] Efforts to mitigate these risks may be undertaken, particularly those relating to ownership, by limiting the length of time the investment agent remains the owner. In practice, a 'time is of the essence' clause allows the investment agent to impose a time limit on the purchaser to accept the offer notice, which can otherwise take place, literally, in seconds. Failure to accept within a pre-agreed timeframe would allow the investment agent to dispose of the commodity to a third party.[208]

Ownership of the good ensures that the investment agent assumes risk in the commodity, including liability for potential damage, defects or outright loss. Any inherent defect in the article sold transfers an unconditional right of rescission of the contract according to sharia, a so-called option of fault (*khiyār al-ʿayb*) to the buyer.[209] According to classical law, such a stipulation cannot be waived by the buyer as it is an essential component of the contract of sale. The option of fault highlights the essence of certainty in the Islamic law of contracts; any exclusion of its provisions is, in itself, a nullity.[210] The prevalent industry practice, however, is similar to the conventional practice whereby the option of fault and the right

204 For details see ibid., 17.

205 Muhammad Taqi Usmani (n 191) 67.

206 LMA (n 189) 20.

207 *Ibid.*, 10.

208 *Ibid.*, 18.

209 Wahbah Al-Zuhayli (n 191) 200–1.

210 Noel Coulson, *Commercial Law in the Gulf States* (London: Graham & Trotman, 1984), 66.

to rescind the sale are excluded so that the investment agent is insulated from these commercial risks.[211]

Once the commodity has been procured the investment agent will send the purchaser an offer notice. The commodity is purchased upon receipt of an acceptance notice from the purchaser with a time normally specified in the agreement at which point title and risk to the commodity passes to the purchaser.[212] The profits from the transaction as well as the principal amounts are distributed to the syndicate (*ārbāb al-māl*) according to the terms specified in the agreement.

In sum, the use of conventional terms in a syndicated *murābaḥah* facility underscores the process of legal transformation in Islamic commercial law. In this case the combination of a *murābaḥah* with a *mudārabah* investment structure was structured in such a way as to replicate all the provisions which are normally present in a conventional facility structured under English law. The following section grapples with the ways in which sharia scholars approach these legal processes.

4.10 Islamic financial *ijtihād*

From the above analysis it is easy to discern that the central strategy for devising sharia-compatible financial contracts is undertaken by locating suitable commercial contracts from classical literature and adapting these to mimic conventional financial practices. There has been very little departure from the practices of conventional finance and the types of products and services it offers.[213]

One central reason lies behind the Islamic finance industry's conventional approximation: the industry seeks to be competitive with conventional finance. Muslim consumers/investors of Islamic financial products demand the same competitive returns that conventional financial institutions offer their clientele. IFIs seek competitive returns by focusing on 'the application of a new product or a technology to a specific market opportunity, such as a lifestyle'[214] while their efforts to address socio-economic

[211] Umar F. Moghul and Arshad A. Ahmed, 'Contractual Forms in Islamic Finance Law and Islamic Inv. Co. Of the Gulf (Bahamas) Ltd. v. Symphony Gems N.V. & Ors.: A First Impression of Islamic Finance' (2003–2004) 27 *Fordham Int'l L. J.*, 150, 181.

[212] LMA (n 189) 17.

[213] Charles Tripp, *Islam and the Moral Economy* (Cambridge University Press, 2006), 143–4.

[214] Joseph DiVanna and Antoine Sreih (n 106) 47.

problems such as directing capital towards small- and medium-sized businesses are less certain. In general, Islamic finance has innovated by developing products that cater to the niche demands of particular groups of customers.[215]

The free market is the force that determines this strategy. The low-cost ease of access through the internet has driven firms to innovate new financial products that meet the changing needs of the marketplace. Banks, in particular, usually adopt a needs-driven approach in seeking to provide their clients with better solutions to their problems. Firms that are not successful in creating novel structures to meet these needs generally fail.[216] For example, evidence suggests that IFIs that choose to offer less competitive, but perhaps more sharia-authentic contracts, i.e. those that are perceived to have a closer connection with classical commercial structures and other *fiqhi* rules, would probably see their clientele exit for more profitable investments.[217] As examined above, however, competitive financial transactions are those that have the lowest transaction costs. Lower transaction costs translate into higher rents. The origins of these costs and Islamic finance's particular disadvantages vis-à-vis conventional transactions push the industry to standardise Islamic financial products and services.

The legal tools used to achieve these economic objectives are represented in the practice of Islamic financial *ijtihād*. Islamic financial *ijtihād* is a modern form of collective *ijtihād*[218] used to adapt classical sharia contracts and rules to modern financial markets and regulatory requirements. Legal theory provides that any form of *ijtihād* should be exercised sparingly and then only in those instances in which novel legal problems arise.[219] Furthermore, it is only to be practised by a *mujtahid*, a Muslim jurist of the highest rank and erudition, which for centuries has not been considered to be possible.[220] Traditional scholars denied the right of *ijtihād* to subsequent generations of scholars following the imposition of *taqlīd* (juristic conformity) in the fourteenth century. Although, as previously discussed, the 'gates of *ijtihād*' could never have

[215] *Ibid.* [216] Warren Edwardes (n 73) 8–28.

[217] A recent survey indicates this fact. See Ernst & Young, 'The Islamic Funds & Investments Report' (Ernst & Young, 2008), www.ncusar.org/programs/09-02-17-materials/EY_Islamic_funds_investment_report_2008.pdf. Accessed 25 March 2014.

[218] See Aznan Hasan, 'An Introduction to Collective Ijtihad' (2003) 20 *AJISS*, 26.

[219] Imran Ahsan Khan Nyazee, *Islamic Jurisprudence: Uṣūl al-Fiqh* (Herndon, VA: International Institute of Islamic Thought, 2000), 266.

[220] *Ibid.*, 263.

been entirely sealed, the concept of *taqlīd* clearly gained purchase by a large majority of the juristic class (*fuqahā'*) and successive Muslim generations. Almost certainly, its impact on the development of the law must have been considerable. Therefore, the practice of *ijtihād* in Islamic finance and the seeming acceptance of doing so by traditional scholars indicate that traditional doctrine has lost quite a bit of ground in modern times.

In modern financial practice the concept has a much broader range of meaning and application. It includes those instances in which scholars choose from a range of past opinions (*takhayyur*), irrespective of the school of law to which the jurist belongs,[221] deemed to be of benefit (*maṣlaḥah*) for the Muslim community.[222] Further, it includes an unprecedented use of rationalising legal tools and *ḥiyal* to make transactions lawful that otherwise transgress classical sharia norms and rules.

Financial *ijtihād* does not represent an effort to conceive an independent legal theory. Indeed, for over a millennium Muslims have developed a very strong attachment to the traditional theory of sources and its central connection to the body of law.[223] It is therefore unlikely that traditional theory could be displaced. Rather it is an ad hoc legal practice designed to create an IFL that retains a legal, if not organic, connection to the legal doctrines and historical traditions of the classical sharia. It has never been the objective of Islamic financial theorisers to replace legal theory or even classical law. Instead, the strategy is conservative. It has tried to give effect to classical sharia after a lapse in the modern era in which Islamic civilisation is perceived to have declined.[224] There is a tacit, if not always explicit, understanding that the traditional edifice of the sharia is not only suitable for all times and places but the principal determinant in restoring the moral, financial and social successes of the Islamic world.[225] Therefore, Islamic financial theorisers[226] intentionally associate

[221] These may even be Shi'a school doctrines. See David L. Johnston, 'Maqasid Al-Shari'a: Epistemology and Hermeneutics of Muslim Theologies of Human Rights' (2007) 47 *Die Welt des Islams*, 149, 159.

[222] Frank E. Vogel and Samuel L. Hayes, *Islamic Law and Finance: Religion, Risk, and Return* (The Hague: Kluwer Law International,1998), 40–1.

[223] Ann Elizabeth Mayer, 'The Shari'ah: A Methodology or a Body of Substantive Rules?' in Nicholas Heer (ed.), *Islamic Law and Jurisprudence* (Seattle, WA: University of Washington Press 1990), 198.

[224] *Ibid.*, 26. [225] *Ibid.*

[226] This includes sharia scholars, Islamic finance practitioners and lawyers trained in Western-style law.

IFL with the 'rationalising discourse' of the *uṣūl al-fiqh,*[227] rationalising in the sense that the *uṣūl al-fiqh* was formulated several centuries after the genesis of Islamic law (*fiqh*). Therefore, it could not have played a significant role in formulating Islamic jurisprudence. Nevertheless, the hermeneutic, as examined in Chapter 2, exerts a powerful historical legacy and is endowed with religious and political legitimacy. Tightly bound to the holy sources, it offers a pathway for discerning God's intentions, which are not always evident. The historical and religious importance of the concept essentially means that 'any conception of the law [sharia], however ultimately defined, must rest on and presuppose a consciously formulated legal methodology'.[228] Despite IFL's tenuous adherence to this tradition, the theory remains extremely important for legitimising the emerging legal system.

IFL places a heavy emphasis on the use of legal tools that allow theorisers to adapt and extend the law in a legal and financial environment that overwhelms the structure and substance of classical commercial law. Such tools include *maṣlaḥah, takhayyur, ḍarūrah* and *ḥiyal.* However, it is uncertain whether these concepts are used more often or with greater scope than in the classical period. While evidence of their use historically is limited, available evidence indicates that these tools were probably used more frequently than would perhaps be assumed. However, given the radical changes that have taken place in the modern world, it seems likely that the use of such tools is both more frequent and of wider application than in the classical period.

In modern financial markets Islamic legal tools are the means of adapting and extending the law. *Maṣlaḥah*, in particular, is an underlying conceptual tool of IFL, but theorisers seem to apply it narrowly within the theoretical framework of the *uṣūl al-fiqh*. The standard approach of doing so resides in incorporating the concept in the procedure of *qiyās.*[229] Al-Ghazzālī provides the template for this method. He determined that *maṣlaḥah* had to be defined in order to be used in setting aside revealed laws. If *maṣlaḥah* could be determined with certainty to pertain to the essential elements of the law (*maqāṣid al-sharī'a*) – religion, life, intellect, offspring and property – then a scriptural ruling could be set aside. However, if *maṣlaḥah* concerned a need (*ḥājah*) or improvement (*taḥsin*)

[227] See Chapter 2 for a discussion of the *uṣūl al-fiqh*.
[228] Wael Hallaq (n 127) 502.
[229] Felicitas Opwis, 'Maslaha in Contemporary Legal Theory' (2005) 12 *I.L.& S.*, 182, 193.

with regard to the five elements of the law, then its application was unacceptable.[230]

This limited approach to *maṣlaḥah* provides a marked contrast to early fourteenth/nineteenth-century modern jurists, such as Muhammad Rashīd Riḍā and Jamāl al-Dīn al-Qāsimī (1866–1914), whose use of *maṣlaḥah* was premised on abandoning the classical Islamic tradition in favour of directly interpreting the textual sources, the Quran and Sunna. *Ijtihād* was to play the principal role in reviving Islamic law.[231] This essentially meant that *maṣlaḥah* was to form the basis of legislation for establishing truth and justice in society. *Maṣlaḥah* was viewed as an independent standard in its own right, separate from any particular textual indicant. As opposed to the *uṣūl's* strict methodologies and logically developed methods of extracting the law from the sources, modernists were less concerned with the manner in which the law was to be developed. A much greater emphasis was to be placed on the underlying ethical purpose of the law – however abstract a notion this may be – in order for a fatwa to be legally valid. Legal certainty or the ability to validly discern God's law was to be achieved by mapping the legal ruling to the law's underlying ethical purpose.[232] According to the modernists human intellect was capable of discerning this purpose as a concrete and objective criterion – a marked departure from the Aṣhari theological tradition.[233]

In IFL *maṣlaḥah* is used as a means of legitimating financial innovations that go well beyond any conception of law in the classical period. Yet the concept is not given the licence to change that modernists envisioned. It is applied more narrowly to alter, bypass or circumvent existing law without the modernists' concern for the ethical substance of the law. Al-Ghazzālī developed a similarly conservative procedure that he applied to *qiyās*. The use of *qiyās* in this respect is capable of producing contemporary transactions from classical nominate contracts that do not fulfil the condition of materiality required by the *uṣūl al-fiqh*.[234] Such is the case, for example, when jurists approve of the novel concepts of copyright and patents despite their immaterial attributes.[235] In cases when *qiyās* is not able to meet

[230] Abu Hamid Al-Ghazzālī, *al-Mustaṣfā* min 'Ilm al-Usūl (vol. II, 1904), 487, 489.

[231] Felicitas Opwis (n 229) 187. [232] *Ibid.*, 192.

[233] Felicitas Opwis, 'Islamic Law and Legal Change: The Concept of Maslaha in Classical and Contemporary Islamic Legal Theory' in A. Amanat and F. Griffel (eds.), *Shari'a: Islamic Law in the Contemporary Context* (Stanford University Press, 2007), 70.

[234] Habib Ahmed, *Product Development in Islamic Banks* (Edinburgh University Press, 2011), 48.

[235] *Ibid.*

the modern needs of the Muslim faithful, *ḍarūrah* is often invoked to circumvent a general prohibition.[236]

Furthermore, the application of diverse minority opinions (*takhayyur*) is probably unusual in the sense that the dominant opinions of the classical *madhāhib* became known as established, positive doctrine in the geographical area represented by the school.[237] Under the Ottomans, for example, *qadīs* were instructed to follow the most authoritative opinion of their school of law.[238] *Talfīq* (literally, patching) is a related principle which draws upon *takhayyur's* facility of eclectic choice, and is practised in the engineered products of Islamic finance. However, the principle of *talfīq* is of much more ancient origin. It is surmised to have first been debated after *taqlīd* became the juristic modus operandi. A widespread definition emphasises the scholar's role in bringing 'forward a fashion [rule of law] that no qualified legal interpreter teaches (*bi-kayfīyah la yaqūl bihā mujtahid*)'; in essence a number of opinions of different schools can be taken together to form a novel opinion.[239]

Takhayyur was first put to systematic use in the compilation of the *Majallah*,[240] but since then has expanded progressively in scope. It has proved to be the major expedient in the modernising legislative reforms throughout the Muslim world.[241] Whereas the *Majallah* included minority opinions from the Ḥanafī school, and at least one well-known Ḥanbalī opinion,[242] modernists extended the scope of this principle to include any opinion put forward from any Sunni school; or even to doctrines advocated by the early jurists prior to the formulation of the *madhāhib*; or to school doctrines which have since become extinct such as that of the Ẓāhirīs. On some occasions modernisers have even attempted to invoke Shi'i opinions, although these have seldom been expressly acknowledged in regard to legislation promulgated in a Sunni Muslim-majority country.[243]

236 *Ibid.*, 167.

237 Wael B. Hallaq, *Authority, Continuity, and Change in Islamic Law* (Cambridge University Press, 2001), 121.

238 Rudolph Peters (n 125) 87.

239 Birgit Krawietz, 'Cut and Paste in Legal Rules: Designing Islamic Norms with Talfiq' (2002) 42 *Die Welt des Islams* 3, 7.

240 See *ibid.*

241 Norman Anderson, *Law Reform in the Muslim World* (London: Athlone Press, 1976) 47–8.

242 Oussama Arabi, 'Contract Stipulations (Shurut) in Islamic Law: The Ottoman Majalla and Ibn Taymiyya' (1998) 30 *IJMES*, 29, 31.

243 Norman Anderson (n 241) 51.

The attempt to adhere to classical tradition in IFL represents a formalistic approach to the law which pays lip service to legal theory and diverges considerably from the ethical and religious substance of the sharia. Widely decried for its 'sharia arbitrage'[244] and religious formalistic attributes,[245] Islamic financial *ijtihād*, critics argue, is devoted 'to the creation of elaborate forms of potentially deceptive artifices in order to circumvent prohibitions derived under otherwise unworkable Islamic rules, most importantly those concerning interest on debt and forms of speculative risk'.[246] This line of reasoning argues that scholars should adopt a rationalist approach that emphasises experiential context and real-life human interaction, possibly aided by the legal tools that modernist reformers espouse.[247] A substantive rationalist approach[248] to the law would necessarily lead to a wholesale revision of Sunni Islamic jurisprudence, notwithstanding the financially relevant prohibitions of *ribā* and *gharar*.[249] However, the majority of Muslims across the globe would not readily agree to a re-interpretation of these historical doctrines, let alone the legal theory. A rationalist approach to financial *ijtihād* is unlikely to be perceived as a legitimate and authoritative interpretation of the holy sources.

The next section examines a case study of TNC involvement in the issuance of an online fatwa, which tested notions of sharia authenticity.

4.11 The limits of Islamic financial innovation

In February 2008 the sharia board of AAOIFI, headed by Justice Taqi Usmani, struck out at the current practice of *sukuk* issuance, which

[244] El-Gamal is a well-known proponent of this wholly valid criticism. See Mahmoud A. El-Gamal, *Islamic Finance: Law, Economics, and Practice* (Cambridge University Press, 2006).

[245] See Haider Ala Hamoudi, 'Jurisprudential Schizophrenia: On Form and Function in Islamic Finance' (2006–2007) 7 *Chi. J. Int'l L.*, 605; Haider Ala Hamoudi, 'Muhammad's Social Justice or Muslim Cant?: Langdellianism and the Failures of Islamic Finance' (2007) 89 *Cornell Int'l L. J.*, 89.

[246] Haider Ala Hamoudi, 'You Say You Want a Revolution: Interpretive Communities and the Origins of Islamic Finance' (2007–2008) 48 *Va.J. Int'l. L.* 249, 258.

[247] Haider Ala Hamoudi (n 245 'Schizophrenia'), 607.

[248] This is the term used by Opwis to describe a theoretical approach that emphasises ethical compatibility with a legal ruling. See Felicitas Opwis (n 229).

[249] Mahmoud A. El-Gamal argues that *ribā* should be seen in terms of efficiency rather than as a matter of exploitation by the strong of the weak and vulnerable. For his work on re-interpreting *gharar* see Mahmoud A. El-Gamal, *An Economic Explication of the*

shocked the market and slowed issuance considerably.[250] Sheikh Usmani asserted that the industry's practices in relation to *sukuk* issuances did not evidence a true sale of *sukuk* assets to investors, particularly in *sukuk* issuances structured around Islamic partnership concepts. The economic result of such structures was thus the Islamic equivalent of an interest-bearing bond, which, of course, is prohibited under sharia. Subsequently, the sharia board of AAOIFI issued several conditions that henceforth would be necessary for a *sukuk* to be considered sharia-compliant.[251]

According to the newly issued AAOIFI conditions, commentators concluded that around 80 per cent of *sukuk* structures were not Islamic. Sheikh Usmani's condemnation of *sukuk* issuances is thought to be based on his unwillingness to continue to condone a practice that was initially conceived as a stop-gap measure until the industry had attained a more secure institutional basis.[252] AAOIFI's statement reveals a well-known sentiment amongst many devout Muslims that Islamic finance has betrayed its Islamic roots. As such the statement represents a desire to strike a different course and thus provides signals to Muslim investors that the Islamic financial industry is striving for more 'authentic' means of financial intermediation.

The contestation for authentic financial structures is perhaps the most important issue for the long-term growth and development of the industry, since there is little reason for consumers to invest in products that do not offer a real alternative. It is a challenge that is made all the more difficult by the sheer number of actors, who are busily creating Islamic financial structures, each according to their own interests and interpretation of sharia. An illustrative case study concerns a major transnational financial institution (Deutsche Bank) and its sharia subsidiary (Dar Al-Istithmar), which developed the Islamic equivalent of a total return swap, a derivatives instrument. Deutsche Bank published a joint research

Prohibition of Gharar in Classical Islamic Jurisprudence (Houston, TX: Rice University, 2001), 1.

250 AAOIFI, *Sukuk Standard* (Manama: AAOIFI. 2008), http://islamicbankers.files.wordpress.com/2008/09/aaoifi_sb_sukuk_feb2008_eng.pdf. Accessed 15 August 2014. See Sheikh Usmani's statement on current *sukuk* practices: Muhammad Taqi Usmani, 'Sukuk and Their Contemporary Applications' (2008), www.iefpedia.com/english/wp-content/uploads/2009/11/Sukuk-and-their-Contemporary-Applications.pdf. Accessed on 15 August 2014.

251 See AAOIFI (n 250).

252 Davide Barzilai, *Syndicated Financing* (Islamic Project Financing: 2nd Annual One-Day Workshop. London: Institute for Islamic Banking and Insurance, 2010). This is a refrain often heard in Islamic finance.

paper that was to function as a fatwa, albeit presented in an unusual format and a discursive/analytical mode.[253] The paper, which was published online and sought to create transparency around the structure, presented an elaborate justification of its structural features from a sharia point of view. The jurisprudential arguments concerned its permissibility and were developed by Dar Al-Istithmar, an Islamic consultancy specialising in structuring Islamic transactions. The findings of the paper were subsequently approved by its sharia board. The nature of the paper, including its research format, indicates that it was not drafted by a sharia board.[254] The paper illustrates some fascinating arguments, all of which challenge classical *fiqhi* rules, which the authors clearly view as the source of Islamic law that must be reckoned with. The paper also uses arguments derived from Western moral philosophy as well as the liberal, free-market views of the famous Ḥanbalī jurist, Ibn Taymīyyah to justify its positions.

The structure allows Deutsche Bank (DB) to issue securities to investors upon receipt of their initial monies and these are used by DB (in its capacity as an investment manager or *muḍārib*) to purchase sharia-compliant assets, which are held in a so-called 'Islamic account'. However, investors receive a profit or loss on their investments in the securities based not on the performance of the securities but from a non-sharia-compliant reference index. The Islamic account, acting as a trustee on behalf of investors, gives a unilateral promise (*wa'd*) to DB (Promise 1) to sell a number of shares from a basket at a 'settlement' price whereas DB promises to buy the relevant shares from the Islamic account (Promise 2) at the settlement price.[255] These promises are known as outperformance put and call options whereby the outperformance of one asset such as the shares versus another asset (the index) entitles the relevant option/call holder to the profit of the outperformance.[256] For example, when the value of the shares increases more than the performance of the reference asset, DB can purchase the shares at a lower price (the relevant settlement price) than the market value of such shares and will call on the Islamic account to sell the relevant shares. On the other hand, when the value of the relevant shares decreases more than the performance of the reference asset, the Islamic account will call on DB to purchase the relevant shares at the relevant settlement price.[257] On settlement of the securities the cash amounts from the sale or purchase of the relevant shares are paid to investors. The economic effect is to allow the client to swap his return

[253] See Deutsche Bank (n 97). [254] Kilian Bälz (n 185) 17.
[255] Deutsche Bank (n 97) 2. [256] *Ibid.*, 5. [257] *Ibid.*, 3.

in sharia-compliant assets for another return which is benchmarked to a non-sharia compliant index.

The structure met with surprising controversy, although this was not due to the elaborate use of the *wa'd* so as to endow the structure with option-like features. Nor was it due to the indeterminacy of price (*thaman*) until the settlement date. The brunt of the backlash concerned the use of non-*halal* assets in the reference index.[258] Sheikh Yusuf Talal DeLorenzo, a prominent sharia scholar, famously described the fatwa as a 'doomsday fatwa' which 'seeks to make the *haram halal*' by equating the use of LIBOR as a benchmark (LIBOR is used as a benchmark in most, if not all, Islamic financial products) with the derivation of revenue from non-*ḥalāl* assets. According to DeLorenzo, the outcome of such a fatwa, if approved and used by the industry, would be to open the floodgates to investment in nearly anything, whether it was 'interest bearing bonds, debt-based derivatives, pork futures, bank, casino and brewery stocks'.[259] Arguably, however, the emergence of this type of structure was already in the works since at least 2004 when a prominent Saudi cleric allowed a 'small fee' to be charged for a *wa'd* on forex (a currency option) for the purpose of hedging.[260] Moreover, a minority of jurists elsewhere had equated any type of benefit or rights without obligation in the definition of *māl* (property), so that the jurisprudential groundwork had been laid.[261] The ability to trade an option for a price, independent from an existing contract of sale, challenged the traditional view that a promise is not a tangible or material good nor is it a usufruct, and hence cannot be the subject matter of a contract of sale.[262] Not too long ago this viewpoint was confirmed by the Islamic Fiqh Academy, Jeddah, which concluded that: 'Option contracts as currently applied in the world financial markets are a new type of contracts which do not come under any one of the shariah nominate contracts. Since the subject of the contract is neither a

[258] Chady C. Atallah and Wafica A. Ghoul, 'The Wa'd-Based Total Return Swap: Sharia Compliant or Not?' 19 (2011) *JOD*, 71, 71.

[259] Yusuf Talal DeLorenzo, 'The Total Return Swap and the "Shari'ah Conversion Technology" Stratagem' in Charles Beard (ed.), *Conventional? The Relationship Between Islamic Finance and the Financial Mainstream* (London: Arab Financial Forum, 2008), 8.

[260] Nikan Firoozye, 'Featured Structure: Wa'd and the Completeness of Islamic Markets', *Opalesque Islamic Finance Intelligence* (31 August 2009), www.opalesque.com/OIFI116/Featured_and_the_completeness_of_Islamic16.html. Accessed 6 May 2014.

[261] Mohammed Obaidullah, 'Financial Engineering with Islamic Options' (1998) 6 *IES*, 73, 76.

[262] *Ibid.*

sum of money nor a utility or a financial right which may be waived, the contract is not permissible in shariah.'[263] Yet Islamic banks preferred permissibility over prohibition and began to sell promises.

The total return swap structure marks a new level of innovation in that it extends the concept to non-compliant underlyings, which 'made the entire promise-for-sale concept truly extensible'.[264] In the end, criticism did not convince the parties involved to discontinue the total return swap. While the bank did reconsider using some types of underlying assets in the reference index, most continue to fall outside the *ḥalāl* category.[265]

The markets' response to the criticisms of sharia scholars indicates that scholars' views carry weight with regard to the financial claims IFIs are able to make. However, the extent to which the principal actors driving the development of the law ultimately adhere to such views is questionable. The trend is such that each market actor interprets the sharia differently and with a view to pursuing its own commercial interests.

4.12 Concluding remarks

The globalisation of financial markets represents a remarkable development of modernity. Financial markets linked through tightly knit networks of global cities, financial institutions and market players produce, reproduce and service globalisation through the exchange of information at lightning speed. At the apex of financial channels are the leading financial centres such as New York and London, which direct and re-circulate financial information to regional financial centres. Such is the case when the US Federal Reserve (the Fed), the central bank of the United States, decides – after a period of massive monetary expansion – to decrease its programme of 'quantitative easing'. The decision is interpreted almost immediately around the world as an indication that interest rates will rise, since the Fed's massive programme of securities purchasing injected up to US$2 trillion into the world economy. Global stock, bond and commodities markets respond with sharp decreases that reverberate into the real economy.[266]

[263] Islamic Fiqh Academy, 'Resolution No. 63/1/7 on Financial Markets' (Jeddah, Saudi Arabia: Council of the Islamic Fiqh Academy, 1992), 131.

[264] Nikan Firoozye (n 260).

[265] *Ibid.*

[266] Nathaniel Popper, 'Global Sell-off Shows Fed Reach Beyond the U.S.', *The New York Times*, 20 June 2013, www.nytimes.com/2013/06/21/business/economy/global-sell-off-shows-fed-reach-beyond-the-us.html. Accessed 1 August 2014.

Economic globalisation has dramatically altered the traditional manner of sharia law making and strictly delimited scholarly impact on the development of the law. The role of jurists has been replaced by market practitioners represented by TNCs, law firms, accountancies and sharia consultancies. The business interests of these actors, and their individual interpretations of sharia, are the driving factors behind the development of IFL. And yet IFL requires 'authenticity' so that it is viewed as a viable alternative to conventional finance. Scholars' legal opinions, despite their diminished role, still command a modicum of authority and prestige.

IFL represents a trend in global commercial law making. It is market-driven and hence articulated to a large extent by market practitioners with little understanding of Islamic law. This fundamental change in the articulation and administration of Islamic law is evidenced in the radical transformation of nominate structures, rules and classical principles. Will this emerging legal system continue to be regarded as Islamic, despite this radical transformation?

The answer may reside, partly, in jurists' intellectual treatment of the theoretical edifice of IFL. This chapter demonstrates beyond doubt that it is not the legal result of traditional Islamic legal theory. Moreover, the body of law that is emerging bears scant resemblance to the law as understood by classical jurists (*fiqh*). The current juristic strategy of adapting and extending the law with the aid of traditional legal tools can only go so far without making a mockery of Islamic legal tradition. Financial *ijtihād* of a much greater scope and depth is necessary; considered brainstorming about the substantive principles that are non-negotiable. The role of scholars in this process, whether academic or traditional, seems necessary for its revival.

5

Vehicular legal systems: the legislative implementation of sharia principles

The revolutionary idea of reviving classical Islamic commercial law in the modern world was first put into practice at an Islamic financial project in Mit Ghamr, Egypt in the 1960s. Thereafter, the first fully fledged Islamic commercial bank, Dubai Islamic Bank, was established in 1975.[1] Since then the industry's upward trajectory has taken observers by surprise with annual rates of asset growth ranging between 10 and 15 per cent. The global Islamic financial market, estimated at US$951 billion,[2] is now active in more than seventy jurisdictions across the globe.[3]

This chapter examines the law-creating processes involved in the UK government's legislative implementation of sharia principles. The accommodation of sharia principles in English law, mostly through the modification of tax measures in successive Finance Acts, demonstrates the legislative creation of IFL. The various ways in which UK municipal legal systems function as a vehicular legal system for IFL also underscore the type of accommodation given to the law. This type of accommodation is partly determinative of the type of law that results from the legislative process.

The chapter deals with the Islamic finance industry in the United Kingdom and the reasons for its existence there. In particular, the focus is directed to the debate concerning the accommodation of Islamic law or sharia principles in English law. The government's legislative and regulatory approach to Islamic finance is then scrutinised as well as various legislative measures undertaken to facilitate the industry within English and UK law. Finally, it deals with the legislative facilitation of *sukuk*, including regulatory modifications, and provides a specific case study of the way in which sharia-inspired structures are accommodated in law.

[1] Hossein Askari, Zamir Iqbal and Abbas Mirakhor, *New Issues in Islamic Finance and Economics: Progress and Challenges* (Singapore: John Wiley & Sons (Asia), 2009), 5.

[2] IFSL, *Islamic Finance 2010* (London: International Financial Services London, 2010), 1.

[3] Hossein Askari, Zamir Iqbal and Abbas Mirakhor (n 1) 5.

5.1 Islamic finance and the United Kingdom

The fact that the United Kingdom constitutes the ninth largest country in terms of the size of its Islamic assets, valued at US$19.4 billion in 2011, is an indication of the transnational reach of the Islamic finance industry.[4] In the United Kingdom, Islamic finance has benefited from the City of London's conventional financial prowess. The United Kingdom now houses five Islamic financial institutions which offer sharia-compliant financial products and services and the City of London has established itself as the third largest market for Islamic finance after the GCC states and Malaysia.[5] Seventeen conventional banks have established windows to offer Islamic financial products and services.[6]

Yet the history of Islamic finance in the United Kingdom is fairly recent. In the early 1980s a number of Middle Eastern Islamic banks established subsidiaries in the United Kingdom, conducting wholesale operations.[7] In 1982 the first retail Islamic financial operations were developed by the Jeddah-based Al Baraka Investment Company, which bought Hargrave Securities (a licensed deposit-taker), and transformed it into an Islamic bank.[8] Following Al Baraka's exit from the Islamic housing market, the United Bank of Kuwait, which had previously focused on Islamic trade financing for Gulf clients, began to offer home ownership plans based on the *murābaḥah* (cost mark-up) contract. These, however, incurred double stamp duty: in the first instance when the property was purchased by the bank and in the second when the property was sold to the client with a profit.[9]

Following the UK government's abolition of double stamp duty in the 2003 Finance Act, these transactions became more competitive with their conventional equivalents and ushered in new business activity.[10] In 2003 HSBC launched its *amānah* current account and home financing products and in 2005 Lloyds TSB also introduced a range of Islamic

[4] TheCityUK, 'The UK Retains Position as Key Western Centre for Islamic Finance', 4 May 2011, www.thecityuk.com/media/latest-news-from-thecityuk/the-uk-retains-position-as-key-western-centre-for-islamic-finance/. Accessed 7 April 2014.

[5] IFSL (n 2) 1.

[6] TheCityUK, 'Islamic Finance', May 2011, www.thecityuk.com/research/our-work/reports-list/islamic-finance-2013/. Accessed 26 March 2014.

[7] Rodney Wilson, 'Islamic Banking in the United Kingdom' in M. Fahim Khan and Mario Porzio (eds.), *Islamic Banking and Finance in the European Union* (Cheltenham: Edward Elgar, 2010), 212.

[8] *Ibid.*, 213. [9] *Ibid.*, 214–15. [10] *Ibid.*, 217–18.

retail banking products.[11] In 2004 the Financial Services Authority (FSA) licensed the Islamic Bank of Britain, the first wholly sharia-compliant retail bank in the United Kingdom.[12] Since then five other wholesale IFIs have been authorised, including the European Islamic Investment Bank, the Bank of London and the Middle East, Gatehouse Bank, Abu Dhabi Islamic Bank and, most recently, QIB UK. Moreover, at least nine Islamic fund managers, one sharia-compliant hedge fund manager, a *takaful* insurance provider and a growing number of advisory firms in the legal, accountancy and consultancy professions are active in the UK.[13]

Until 2009 the United Kingdom was the only country in the European Union to house stand-alone Islamic financial institutions[14] despite its small Muslim population relative to France's seven million and Germany's four million Muslims.[15] In large part this is due to the City of London's tradition of innovation and flexibility, its deep and highly liquid markets, and the fact that its exchanges are some of the most frequently used venues for listing and trading financial instruments globally.[16] Furthermore, commercial transactions under English law are protected so as to facilitate free trade and to mitigate the application of rules that would obstruct business activity.[17] The United Kingdom also maintains close linkages with Muslim states and their citizens as a result of its colonial history and subsequent immigration flows.[18]

[11] *Ibid.*

[12] NS&I, *Shari'a Compliant Savings Review* (London: National Savings & Investments 2008), 8.

[13] TheCityUK, 'UK, The Leading Western Centre for Islamic Finance', UK Islamic Finance Secretariat, October 2013, 5, www.londonstockexchange.com/specialist-issuers/islamic/downloads/islamic-finance-2013-f.pdf. Accessed 7 April 2014.

[14] HMRC, *Stamp Duty Land Tax: Commercial Sukuk: A Response to the Consultation* (London: HM Revenue & Customs, 2009), 3.

[15] In 2009 Germany issued a limited banking licence to an Islamic bank, Kuveyt Türk Beteiligungsbank. See Mushtak Parker, 'Islamic Bank Enters Germany', *Arab News*, 26 April 2010, www.arabnews.com/node/343397. Accessed 25 March 2014. In June 2011, Chaabi Bank Europe, a subsidiary of Banque Chaabi du Maroque, introduced the first Islamic retail products to the French market. See Antoine Saillon, 'Islamic Banking Finally Starting in France', *IFN Reports*, vol. 8, issue 27, 13 July 2011, 1, http://ddata.over-blog.com/4/08/16/46//IFN-report-July-2011.pdf. Accessed 25 March 2014.

[16] Michael Ainley, Ali Mashayekhi, Robert Hicks, Arshadur Rahman and Ali Ravalia, *Islamic Finance in the UK: Regulation and Challenges* (London: Financial Services Authority, 2007), 7.

[17] Roy Goode, *Goode on Commercial Law*, ed. by Ewan McKendrick, 4th edn (London: Penguin Books, 2010), 9.

[18] Jorgen S. Nielsen, 'Muslims in Western Europe' in Carole Hillenbrand (ed.), *The New Edinburgh Islamic Surveys Series* (Edinburgh University Press, 2004), 40–62.

London's Western pre-eminence is underpinned by multinational participation in the market as evidenced by the fact that Deutsche Bank and Barclays Capital are now among the world's top five issuers of *sukuk* (Islamic bonds).[19] Indeed, in July 2013 there were thirty-five *sukuk* issues listed on the London Stock Exchange, with total funds of over US$21 billion, an increase of US$7 billion since 2010.[20] Further, money flows through the UK capital via the commodity *murābaḥah* – used as inter-bank short-term lending and syndicated loans – are higher than any other financial centre.[21] In recent years, however, other jurisdictions have been catching up. Luxembourg has worked to amend some of its tax provisions to facilitate its development as an Islamic financial hub[22] and France, Germany and Ireland have begun to initiate tax changes to accommodate Islamic finance within their borders.[23]

5.2 The transmission of Islamic finance to the United Kingdom

Islamic financial transactions have been conducted in the United Kingdom since the early 1980s without any legal or regulatory accommodation. This fact underscores the government's policy of accommodating Islamic finance in response to the financial transactions that had long been taking place. This is not unusual. Law often develops in response to commercial and financial developments. Nonetheless, the government's policy to erect a tax and regulatory apparatus for Islamic financial transactions represents an important step in stimulating the growth and development of domestic and wholesale markets.

The government's primary objective in facilitating Islamic finance is to consolidate an Islamic financial centre in the City of London and thus maintain London's status as Europe's premier financial centre, and indeed, one of the leading financial centres in the world.[24] The sharp rise in oil prices since 2003 has resulted in enormous liquidity surpluses,

19 Paul Furneaux, Samer Hijazi, John Lee and Jamal Fakhro, *Cross-Border Development in Islamic Banking* (Islamic Finance Review, Euromoney Yearbooks, 2008/09), 45.

20 LSE, *Sukuk List*, July 2013. Pounds Sterling were converted at £1 to US$1.52.

21 David Oakley, 'London Leads in Race to Be Western Hub', *Financial Times*, 7 December 2009, 4.

22 Mushtak Parker, 'Islamic Finance Gaining Major Support in Britain', *Arab News*, 14 February 2010, www.arabnews.com/node/337075. Accessed 25 March 2014.

23 Farid Masmoudi and Tarik Belabed, *Islamic Finance in the Face of the Financial Turmoil: Opportunities and Challenges* (Paris: CAPmena, March 2010), 1–6.

24 City of London, 'Global Financial Centres 7' (2010), www.zyen.com/PDF/GFC%207.pdf. Accessed 7 April 2014.

primarily in GCC states. Yet the capacity of the region's financial markets has not been able to keep pace with the growth in liquid funds.[25] London's pre-eminent role as a leading financial centre, its strategic position in a global financial network and its historical ties to Middle Eastern states have enabled it to attract Middle Eastern capital in its bid to consolidate a leading international hub for Islamic finance.

The development of an Islamic financial hub in the City of London highlights the centrality of place against a policy-oriented and academic debate largely concerned with the neutralisation of the nation state by global communications, the hyper-mobility of capital, and the practices of transnational corporations.[26] According to this analysis, the sovereignty of nation states is being eroded by the liberalisation of world trade and global capital flows. As examined in Chapter 1, economic and financial globalisation has enabled the extension of the economy beyond the borders of the nation state. A number of leading economic sectors, especially international finance, are contingent upon global investor sentiment. Global financial markets operate within a regulatory framework that is primarily attuned to the demands of the market and the requirements of transnational corporations, rather than the bureaucracy of the state.[27] The world system is increasingly characterised by a highly interdependent and ambivalent relationship between the nation state and transnational capital.[28]

Yet the analysis of the UK government's facilitation of Islamic finance underscores the pre-eminent role of the nation state in creating a legal and regulatory framework, which enables a particular mode of finance to thrive. It strengthens the premise that global processes materialise, in part, in national territories through national institutional arrangements via legislation and the judicial process. The UK experience with Islamic

[25] Michael Ainley, Ali Mashayekhi, Robert Hicks, Arshadur Rahman and Ali Ravalia (n 16) 7.

[26] See Saskia Sassen, *Globalization and Its Discontents* (New York: New Press, 1998), xxi. See also Boaventura de Sousa Santos, *Toward a New Legal Common Sense: Law, Globalisation, and Emancipation* (London: LexisNexis Butterworths, 2002), 279; John Eatwell and Lance Taylor, *Global Finance at Risk* (Cambridge: Polity Press 2000), 96; and Peter Isard, *Globalization and the International Financial System* (Cambridge University Press, 2005), 65.

[27] Roger Cotterrell, *Law's Community: Legal Theory in Sociological Perspective* (Oxford: Clarendon Press 1995), 303; and Boaventura de Sousa Santos (n 26) 194.

[28] Avadhoot Nadkarni, 'World Trade Liberalisation: National Autonomy and Global Regulation' in Jonathan Mitchie and John Grieve Smith (eds.), *Global Instability* (London: Routledge 1999), 134. Nadkarni argues that national autonomy is being sacrificed to the liberalisation of world trade. Global structures should be erected to channel the destabilising process.

finance underscores the importance of the state in actively erecting fiscal and legal frameworks through which the global economy works and without whose instruments it simply could not function.[29]

Theoretically, the complexity of this accommodation of sharia principles in the state's regulatory systems could result in legal heterogeneity in state regulation, embodying diverse political and ideological assumptions as well as different types of law for different areas of state intervention. The emergence of multiple legal orders, constituting 'relatively unrelated and highly discrepant logics'[30] within a single state apparatus would unravel the coherence and uniformity of the state-based regulatory framework. Multiple microcosms within a single state, regulated by disparate regulatory logics and styles, would be the likely result.[31] Others argue that the overlap between legal systems creates inefficiency and legal uncertainty, as has been the case in legal pluralistic jurisdictions such as Malaysia and Egypt.[32] The United Kingdom's response to the emergence of Islamic finance undermines – to an extent – this premise. The United Kingdom has opted to assimilate Islamic finance into its regulatory system rather than to create a dual regulatory system that is likely to provide a more favourable and efficient regulatory structure for the industry, but which would undermine the coherence of the regulatory architecture. The state has subjected the flow of Islamic capital to national forces.

5.2.1 *Retail markets*

Another government objective for accommodating Islamic law concerns its desire to include a large domestic Muslim minority in the financial marketplace, which represents the government's principle of equality of access to financial markets. While discrimination on the grounds of religion or conscience has been unlawful since 2003,[33] the rationale in

[29] Jean Comaroff and John L. Comaroff, 'Millennium Capitalism: First Thoughts on a Second Coming' in Jean Comaroff and John L. Comaroff (eds.), *Millennial Capitalism and the Culture of Neoliberalism* (Durham, NC: Duke University Press, 2001), 38; and Robert O'Brien and Marc Williams, *Global Political Economy*, 3rd edn (Basingstoke: Palgrave MacMillan, 2010), 426.

[30] Boaventura de Sousa Santos (n 26) 281.

[31] *Ibid.*

[32] Ian Edge, 'Islamic Finance, Alternative Dispute Resolution and Family Law: Developments towards Legal Pluralism?' in R. Griffith-Jones (ed.), *Islam and English Law* (Cambridge University Press, 2013), 116–44.

[33] C.f. Mark Hill and Russell Sandberg, 'Is Nothing Sacred? Clashing Symbols in a Secular World' (Autumn 2007) *P.L.*, 488–507; and The Employment Equality (Religion or Belief) Regulations 2003, SI 2003/1660.

facilitating Islamic finance is not a political or legal response to incidences of unlawful discrimination. Rather, it is a pro-active, top-down and highly centralised series of measures rooted in a growing awareness that British Muslims have not been able to avail themselves of financial activities due to their Islamic beliefs. Hence, the government's decision sends a strong signal to the Muslim community that it understands their religious needs and seeks to create an environment in which Muslims are able to participate in financial activities in conformity with their beliefs, albeit within the conventional regulatory structure.

Despite the Islamic finance industry's international growth, particularly in wholesale markets, UK domestic demand for Islamic financial products and services has been limited. In 2013 HSBC Amanah, the largest provider of retail Islamic banking products and services, decided to close its operations in the United Kingdom along with several other states.[34] In fact, socio-economic data reveal that British Muslims are less economically active than the general population. Of a total of two million British Muslims, 1.4 million are 16 years of age and older. This age group does not actively engage in financial activities. While eight out of ten of most minority groups in the United Kingdom have accounts with financial institutions – compared with nine out of ten persons of the majority population – only two-thirds of those of Pakistani origin and just over half of those of Bangladeshi origin do.[35] Research has attributed these statistics to Muslims' beliefs in abstaining from interest-based financial transactions, even though British Muslim respondents occasionally argue that interest-based activities are permissible with respect to loans and non-essential consumption.[36] Recall that some modern Muslim thinkers argued that the prohibition of *ribā* applied solely to the essential commodities of daily life whereas loans with interest for purposes of production and wealth creation should escape the prohibition.[37]

[34] HSBC Amanah, 'Important Notice' (2013), www.hsbcamanah.com. Accessed 7 April 2014. Other states included the UAE, Bahrain, Bangladesh, Indonesia, Singapore and Mauritius. HSBC would continue to offer retail products and services in Saudi Arabia and Malaysia.

[35] Pamela Meadows, *Access to Financial Services* (London: National Institute of Economic and Social Research, 2000), 17.

[36] *Ibid.* Other, less often cited reasons for doing so relate to the classical differentiation between *dar al-ḥarb* (abode of war) and *dar al-islām* (abode of peace). Some classical jurists argued that interest could be accepted from infidels in the *dar al-harb*, i.e. non-Muslim territories.

[37] See, for example, Fazlur Rahman, 'Riba and Interest' (1964) 3 *Islam.Stud.*, 3, 3–4.

Research suggests that financially active British Muslims may be divided into three market segments. The first one includes those for whom Islamic financial products are the only financial products of which they would avail themselves. Only 4 per cent are considered under this 'staunch demand' category. The second category comprises those who might choose sharia-compliant products if they were widely available and competitive. This group constitutes a further 21 per cent of the population. Finally, those who will continue to use conventional products irrespective of whether Islamic products are widely available constitute 75 per cent of the British Muslim population.[38] Therefore, the short-term demand for retail sharia-compatible products looks to be relatively low, and indeed, their acquisition has thus far been limited.[39]

However, government consultations with industry practitioners and consultants on the development of Islamic financial products suggest that very significant medium- to long-term demand for such products exists in the domestic market,[40] particularly if the United Kingdom were to issue a sovereign *sukuk* (Islamic bond) and thus help to establish a secondary market and other key economic benchmarks that would facilitate the industry. In particular, it is believed that a *sukuk* issuance would help generate a wider range of retail financial products that thus far have remained quite limited.[41] In the short term the 'exchequer effect' – the inflow of tax revenues to the treasury – is negligible, while the government sees long-term inflows as potentially significant[42] as a result of the greater diversity and quality (authenticity) of Islamic products. In sum, the government foresees a thriving and competitive Islamic financial industry – both retail and wholesale – as benefiting London as a leading financial centre and generating 'further investment, jobs and tax revenues in the UK economy'.[43]

Furthermore, financial accommodation may help to incorporate unregulated Islamic financial activities the market participants of which

[38] NS&I (n 12) 3.

[39] MCB, *Islamic Finance Transparency Standard: A Consultation* (London: The Muslim Council of Britain, 2008), 5; and Mohammed Amin, 'Why Has Retail Islamic Banking Not Taken Off in the UK?', 21 June 2010, www.mohammedamin.com/Islamic_finance/Why_has_retail_Islamic_banking_not_taken_off_in_the_UK.html. Accessed 23 March 2014.

[40] HMRC, *Impact Assessment of Sukuk (Islamic Bonds) Legislation* (London: HM Revenue & Customs, 2008), 5.

[41] MCB (n 39) 5. [42] HMRC (n 40) 5. [43] *Ibid.*

are otherwise deprived of regulatory and consumer protections[44] and whose financial activities undermine the state's fiscal and monetary policies. Some minority groups have traditionally sought financial advice, borrowing and lending within the community on the basis of recommendations and kinship networks. In effect, informal credit unions have been established in many areas housing large minority communities.[45] For example, research concerning *ḥawālah*[46] money transfer systems highlights a complex web of global traders whose ability to transfer money to the far reaches of the globe undercuts the nation state's ability to keep tabs on its citizens' monetary activities.[47] *Ḥawālah* (transfer in Arabic) refers to informal value transfer systems, which facilitate informal, unregulated financial transfers with almost no paper trail or identification requirements. Operated from unlicensed and unregistered storefronts in Western Europe, North America and elsewhere, workers, in particular, use *ḥawālah* to transfer remittances to all manner of locations throughout Asia and the Middle East.[48] Such informal Islamic commercial transactions reflect the limits of state law as these are weakened by the allegiance of subjects to competing legal norms.[49] In co-opting informal Islamic financial practices Muslim minorities may feel that they should and can conform their behaviour to the requirements of state law. The government stands a greater likelihood of compelling compliance amongst minority Muslim populations by bringing previously informal transactions under legal auspices, into the regulatory light.

[44] HMRC, *Impact Assessment for Stamp Duty Land Tax, Capital Gains Tax & Capital Allowance Tax Reliefs for Alternative Finance Investment Bonds* (London: HM Revenue & Customs, 2009), 5.

[45] Pamela Meadows (n 35) 17.

[46] For an account of the classical sharia concerning *ḥawālah* see Nicholas Dylan Ray, 'The Medieval Islamic System of Credit and Banking: Legal and Historical Considerations' (1997) 12 *ALQ* 43, 61.

[47] See Roger Ballard, 'Coalitions of Reciprocity and the Maintenance of Financial Integrity within Informal Value Transmission Systems: The Operational Dynamics of Contemporary Hawala Networks' (2005) 6 *J.B.R.*, 319, 321. See also M. El Qorchi, S. M. Maimbo and J. F. Wilson, *Informal Funds Transfer Systems: An Analysis of the Informal Hawala System* (IMF/World Bank Occasional Paper 222, 2003), 1–71.

[48] *Ibid.*, 320–1.

[49] Antony Allot, *The Limits of Law* (London: Butterworths, 1980), 148; and Werner Menski, *Comparative Law in a Global Context: The Legal Systems of Asia and Africa* (Cambridge University Press 2006).

5.2.2 *The inclusion of the sharia in English Law*

There may be some public antipathy to the adoption of Islamic financial structures within the UK legal system. In a public response to a government consultation regarding the issuance of *sukuk* in June 2008 a number of respondents 'believed that it was inappropriate for the government to issue *sukuk* or to take any action which could result in the incorporation of the sharia law into English law'.[50] This may arise, in part, due to uncertainties surrounding the issue of sharia compliance. Respondents suggested that disclaimers might be required so as to shield the government from claims that it engaged in marketing non-sharia-compliant products. Furthermore, respondents observed that the government's facilitation of Islamic financial structures within English law forced it to adopt 'valid' interpretations of sharia-compatible structures. The government concedes that 'it has not yet decided its preferred way to ensure the sharia compliance of *sukuk* issuance',[51] which indicates that the legal ramifications resulting from its policies towards the industry are not yet known.

More generally, the facilitation of the sharia within English law adds oil to the fire of a raging debate in Europe concerning the public role of Islam and the compatibility of Islamic principles and values within a largely secular social environment. In February 2008 the former Archbishop of Canterbury, Dr Rowan Williams, delivered a speech in which he addressed the existence of minority communities within the United Kingdom, which subscribe to normative systems other than the English legal system alone.[52] The Archbishop examined whether space could be allowed alongside the secular law of the state for the legal norms and rules of faith groups, which did not trespass against society's commitment to human dignity. The most frequently raised objection to the recognition of supplementary jurisdiction in particular areas of the law, especially family law, concerns whether it may have the effect of reinforcing retrograde or regressive practices within ethnic minority communities. The treatment of women is a particular concern. The Archbishop acknowledged this concern by laying out a general framework of how faith-based

[50] Her Majesty's Treasury, *Government Sterling Sukuk Issuance: A Response to the Consultation* (London: HM Treasury, 2008), 39.

[51] *Ibid.*

[52] Rowan Williams, 'Archbishop's Lecture – Civil and Religious Law in England: A Religious Perspective' (2008), 262, www.archbishopofcanterbury.org/articles.php/1137/archbishops-lecture-civil-and-religious-law-in-england-a-religious-perspective. Accessed 25 March 2014.

legal practices could be accommodated. He stated that were 'any kind of plural jurisdiction … recognised, it would presumably have to be under the rubric that no "supplementary" jurisdiction could have the power to deny access to the rights granted to other citizens [regardless of faith affiliation], or to punish its members for claiming those rights'.[53] He stressed the importance of working to overcome the ultimatum that ethnic minorities have to choose between their culture and their rights.[54] The role and rule of law in a pluralistic society must be reconsidered. A society that is ethnically, culturally and religiously diverse and in which identity is formed within different 'contexts of belonging' must not be subject to a 'universal/abstract dimension of social existence'.[55] Indeed, as human beings our social identities are not comprised alone of a single set of relations or a mode of belonging.[56] That is why the role and rule of law should establish a space for 'everyone in which it is possible to affirm and defend a commitment to human dignity'.[57] It may be possible to accommodate 'certain carefully specified matters' such as Islamic finance or aspects of law that achieve this objective.[58]

The Archbishop stressed that manifold anxieties had arisen in the context of the discussion; an analysis that was confirmed in the vociferous response by the tabloid media to the Archbishop's presentation. He noted that social anxiety had arisen, in part, as a result of sensational reporting on particular Muslim communities who wish to live according to the sharia. He highlighted the fact that most people perceive the sharia as repressive towards women and archaic and brutal in its physical punishments for crimes that no longer exist in the modern world.[59] The Muslim scholar, Tariq Ramadan, voiced the unspoken when he wrote: 'In the West the idea of sharia calls up all the darkest images of Islam … It has reached the extent that many Muslim intellectuals do not dare even to refer to the concept for fear of frightening people or arousing suspicion of all their work by the mere mention of the word'.[60] Moreover, the sharia's fourteen-hundred-year history has suffered from the actions of global jihadists who invoke Islamic texts as a justification for terrorist attacks, notably in the attacks

[53] *Ibid.*, 268. [54] *Ibid.*, 270. [55] *Ibid.*, 271.

[56] See Rowan Williams, 'Civil and Religious Law in England: A Religious Perspective' in Griffith-Jones R. (ed.), *Islam and English Law* (Cambridge University Press, 2013), 23.

[57] Rowan Williams (n 52) 272. [58] *Ibid.*, 274.

[59] *Ibid.*, 263.

[60] Tariq Ramadan, *Western Muslims and the Future of Islam* (Oxford University Press, 2004), 31; and c.f. Rowan Williams (n 52) 263.

of 11 September 2001 and the London underground and bus attacks of 7 July 2005. Sectarian killings in the wars of Iraq and Afghanistan have repeated this trend and strengthened the perception that Islam is hostile to the democratic values of the West. A general wariness toward Islam pervades the Western social consciousness, and increasingly morphs into outright Islamophobic denunciations.[61] The ongoing debate concerning the multicultural society in the United Kingdom is also a debate about the role of Islam in public life.

The world of finance has generally been viewed as a much less delicate terrain in which to address issues of multicultural accommodation. Finance, in general, is seldom discussed in social or even intellectual circles. Indeed, commercial law is seen as less impermeable to outside influences and transplants. The national ethos of commercial law is less important and plays only a marginal role in shaping a country's legal culture.[62] This perception of commercial law is deeply engrained in both popular and academic cultures, as confirmed in a recent follow-up lecture by the now Dr Rowan Williams, preceding the launch of an edited book entitled *Islam and English Law.* Only one essay of the book deals with IFL and English law and even then it is dealt with only very briefly, while family law issues are the principal concern.[63]

This perception of commercial law is strengthened by the general emphasis on the importance of the economic substance of transactions – the so-called 'real' activity that can be objectively observed, whereas other areas of law are normatively conceived with respect to a society's values and culture. Culture apparently plays only a small role in this 'extra-cultural' analysis of commercial law.[64]

[61] The examples are numerous. Consider legislation across Europe to forbid the wearing of the *niqab* or head covering that conceals the face. France is the most prominent example. See Loi No. 2010-1192 du 11 Octobre 2010 interdisant la dissimulation du visage dans l'espace public (1). In the United States the Qur'an has been publicly burned and the building of mosques unduly criticised.

[62] Boaventura de Sousa Santos, *Toward a New Common Sense* (New York: Routledge, 1995), 213.

[63] Ian Edge (n 32) 116–44.

[64] Arthur Allen Leff, 'Economic Analysis of the Law: Some Realism About Nominalism' (1974) 60 *Va.L.Rev.* 451, 464. For a slightly different perspective see Richard A. Posner and Francesco Parisi, 'Wealth Maximization Revisited' in Richard A. Posner and Francesco Parisi (eds.), *Law and Economics* (Cheltenham: Edward Elgar Publishing, 1997); Eric A. Posner, *Law and Economics* (Aldershot: Ashgate/Dartmouth 2001); Richard A. Posner, 'The Law and Economics Movement' in Richard A. Posner and Francesco Parisi (eds.), *Law and Economics.*

It is also worth noting that globalisation assumes that commercial activity and law, in particular, converge towards cultural homogeneity and thus culture is regarded as superfluous. However, business and financial activities are, to an extent, just as much a reflection of local and national culture as any other area of human endeavour.[65] This is an overlooked fact, which is confirmed by this book's analysis of IFL.

The larger objective of furthering the development of an Islamic financial hub could be very profitable. The commercial benefits of continuing to lure Middle Eastern capital to the United Kingdom are potentially very significant and the social advantages of creating an inclusive financial system are many.[66] Even better, relatively few legislative amendments are necessary for facilitating the industry and these are neither overly burdensome nor expensive.[67] A series of regulatory impact statements regarding proposed tax amendments to facilitate the issuance of commercial *sukuk* reveal that the associated costs are negligible.[68] Furthermore, despite the recession of 2008 and the ensuing Eurozone crisis, finance remains a rather technical specialisation the complexities of which are not easily understood and do not command the attention of the general populace.[69] Perhaps unsurprisingly, the general public is still largely unaware of the government's role in facilitating Islamic finance in the UK.[70]

The cultural and values-dominated debate concerning the inclusion of sharia in English law has not featured prominently in the facilitation of Islamic finance. This has freed the hands of the government to undertake a number of legislative and regulatory measures to facilitate and develop the industry in the UK.

[65] Nicholas H. D. Foster, 'Comparative Commercial Law: Rules or Context' in David Nelken and Esin Örücü (eds.), *Comparative Legal Studies: A Handbook* (Oxford: Hart Publishing 2007), 263, *in passim*.

[66] Islamic financing was central to the Clifford Chance-assisted £1.25 billion acquisition and funding of the Chelsea Barracks site. It also plays a role in the construction of commercial real estate projects such as the Shard – at 308 metres, the second tallest free-standing structure in the UK. Furthermore, real estate buyers from the Arab world continue to invest in London properties – particularly after the Arab Spring of 2011 – and Islamic finance is considered a suitable vehicle for doing so. See Ed Hammond, 'Construction: Investors Transform UK Horizon' *Financial Times*, 11 May 2011, www.ft.com/cms/s/0/3dbd26fe-7aa1-11e0-8762-00144feabdc0.html#axzz1WKYWWLm7. Accessed 25 March 2014.

[67] HMRC (n 44) 2. [68] HMRC (n 40) 2–5.

[69] John Lanchester, *Whoops: Why Everyone Owes Everyone And No One Can Pay* (London: Allen Lane, 2010), xv.

[70] Her Majesty's Treasury, *The Development of Islamic Finance in the UK: The Government's Perspective* (London: HM Treasury, 2008), 21.

The following section examines these measures and the UK government's general approach towards accommodating Islamic finance.

5.3 The legislative and regulatory approach to Islamic financial transactions

The UK government characterises its uniform legislative and regulatory approach to Islamic finance as fair and consistent, rooted in the belief that no financial system deserves special treatment to the detriment of others. It states unequivocally that 'all financial institutions authorised by the FSA and operating in the UK, or seeking to do so, are subject to the same standards. This is true regardless of their country of origin, the sectors in which they wish to specialise, or their religious principles'.[71] In essence, the government espouses a religiously neutral position predicated on the establishment of a level playing field for Islamic finance that is not distorted by tax and regulatory law originally conceived for the conventional, interest-based system.[72] As a result, since 2003 all legislative amendments to acts of parliament including both finance and regulatory provisions refer to Islamic financial services as 'alternative financial instruments' and 'alternative investment bonds' in the case of Islamic bonds. The religiously descriptive 'Islamic investments' is replaced with the ideologically neutral 'alternative financial instruments'. These usages are in line with a universalistic approach to the law, which emphasises the equal dignity of citizens and refrains from taking legislative positions on particular religious, cultural or value-embedded norms of minority populations.

The government states unequivocally that 'legislation will not be tied to the Quran or the Islamic faith, but rather uses intrinsic features of the underlying contracts under UK law to define transactions to which the rules will apply'.[73] However, as this section demonstrates, sharia principles and rules have been accommodated within English law. In fact, English common law is renowned for its flexibility and openness towards the accommodation of parties' contractual interests. So while the state does not take responsibility for the religious interpretation of the transactions it facilitates, statutory law necessarily does have a connection to the Quran and Islamic law. Furthermore, the state, in opting to facilitate

[71] Michael Ainley, Ali Mashayekhi, Robert Hicks, Arshadur Rahman and Ali Ravalia (n 16) 11.

[72] Her Majesty's Treasury (n 70) 13.

[73] Her Majesty's Treasury, *Alternative Finance Products, Regulatory Impact Assessment* (London: HM Treasury, 2007), 6.

the industry, has accepted and given validity to certain Islamic financial contracts, which reflect a market-driven interpretation of Islamic commercial law. The state has not taken any direct action in determining the religious meaning of these structures, but it has willingly accepted others' interpretation of what the sharia constitutes in financial dealings. But the government insists that it is able to retain neutrality, since it sees its role as a mere facilitator of these transactions. According to its universal understanding of the law, it is prevented by the terms that underlie its legitimacy and existence from dictating the preferences or wants of its citizens.

The following section examines how the government's approach directs the legislative implementation of Islamic financial transactions. The treatment of tax issues in this book is limited to the most important principles as a detailed treatment of such issues is not suitable for the purpose of this work.

5.4 The legislative implementation of Islamic financial transactions

The government highlights several critical barriers to industry development in which it aims to focus its attention: namely, (1) taxation and regulation; (2) standardisation; (3) industry awareness; and (4) the development of industry-related skills.[74] In practice, the government's focus has principally centred on amending tax measures so as to accommodate Islamic financial structures within the UK's complex tax regime. It has enacted very few regulatory measures as such an approach would require differential regulatory treatment. The government's efforts in pursuit of legal standardisation have been relatively limited insofar as it does not assume a role in determining valid sharia structures. Finally, the government has expended some effort in establishing industry awareness and related training programmes.[75]

In terms of taxation and regulation, the government, quite crucially, has adopted the principle that treatment should follow the economic substance of transactions rather than their legal form.[76] This is particularly important since it enables Islamic financial products to be implemented competitively within the conventional tax regime. If Islamic financial transactions were taxed according to legal structure in such a regime, they would be given less favourable tax treatment as a result of their multi-

[74] Her Majesty's Treasury (n 70) 15.
[75] TheCityUK (n 6).
[76] Her Majesty's Treasury (n 70) 15.

tiered architectures. The economic substance approach results in Islamic financial products being treated on the same basis as equivalent interest-bearing financial products; ordinary tax rules should apply where possible; and rules that foster undesirable or unpredictable results should be amended.[77]

For tax purposes, Islamic financial products are categorised in two types of return, namely: alternative finance returns and profit share returns. Both types are treated equally for corporation tax purposes in that they describe 'amounts paid or received' that are, in substance, equivalent to interest.[78]

In light of these objectives the government, in conjunction with industry and through the joint HM Treasury and HM Revenue & Customs Tax Technical Group, initially set out to deal with alternative property financing, known in the industry as Islamic home mortgage purchase plans (HPPs). To this effect, stamp duty land tax (SDLT) was amended for alternative finance arrangements in the Finance Act 2003.[79] Stamp duty land tax is a real estate transfer tax that falls due on real estate purchases at varying rates. After the March 2010 Budget a maximum rate of 5 per cent can be levied.[80] A purchaser of real estate pays SDLT on the entire purchase price of the property. No further payment of SDLT is required with repayment of the loan.[81] Popular nominate contracts used in real estate financing such as the *murābaḥah* and the diminishing *mushārakah* entail the transfer of property in at least two steps: once when the IFI purchases the asset and again, when the IFI sells the asset to the client buyer. In each transaction SDLT would be payable, making such transactions considerably more expensive than conventional ones.

The law was amended so that contracting parties' acquisition of a chargeable interest or property acquisition would not be taxed multiple times.[82] By removing this obstacle Islamic financial institutions were able to offer the *murābaḥah* or the *tawarruq*. These contracts, whose returns

[77] *Ibid.*

[78] HMRC, *Stamp Duty Land Tax: Commercial Sukuk* (London: HM Revenue & Customs, 2008), 22.

[79] Finance Act 2003, ss 72–3.

[80] DirectGov, 'Budget March 2010 – Tax Changes', The National Archives, 25 June 2010, webarchive.nationalarchives.gov.uk/20121015000000/http://www.direct.gov.uk/en/Nl1/Newsroom/Budget/Budget2010/DG_186638. Accessed 22 March 2014.

[81] Mohammed Amin, 'British Government Policy on Islamic Finance', 3 April 2010, www.mohammedamin.com/Islamic_finance/British_Government_Policy_on_Islamic_finance.html. Accessed 23 March 2014.

[82] Finance Act 2003, ss 72, 73.

equate in economic substance with an interest-bearing loan, would be taxed as if they were loans.[83]

SDLT provisions were extended in 2005 to equity sharing arrangements such as the *muḍārabah*. Alternative finance returns resulting from the transaction were treated as interest payable on a loan.[84] Thus Islamic financial institutions could introduce deposit arrangements based on the *muḍārabah* contract that had previously treated *muḍārabah* profits as dividends.[85]

As previously explained, the *muḍārabah* is an investment partnership, which, if successful, generates a profit from the investment. The Income and Corporations Taxes Act 1988 (ICTA) had long prevented companies from disguising equity finance in the form of debt so as 'to obtain tax relief for payments that are economically equivalent to dividends to risk bearing shareholders'.[86] The Income and Corporations Taxes Act 1988 s 209 (2)(e)(iii) defines a distribution as: '(e) any interest or other distribution out of assets of the company in respect of securities of the company (except so much, if any, of any such distribution as represents the principal thereby secured and except so much of any distribution as falls within paragraph (d) above), where the securities are – … (iii) securities under which the consideration given by the company for the use of the principal secured is to any extent dependent on the results of the company's business or any part of it'. Under section 209 (2)(e)(iii) any profits generated from the transaction would be treated as a distribution and subjected to corporation taxes. The profit share would not be tax deductible by the IFI,[87] which would make these transactions uncompetitive. The government solved this problem by amending Finance Act 2005, section 54, which excluded the *muḍārabah* from 1988 s 209 (2)(e)(iii):[88] Profit share return is not to be treated by virtue of section 209(2)(e)(iii) of ICTA as being a distribution for the purposes of the Corporation Tax Acts.

Therefore, for the purposes of the Finance Act 2005, the *muḍārabah* is treated as a loan relationship.[89] Of course, the theoretical *muḍārabah* should not be transacted as a loan relationship as this implies a fixed

[83] Her Majesty's Treasury (n 70) 16.

[84] Finance Act 2005, pt 2, ch 5.

[85] Her Majesty's Treasury (n 70) 16. However, the *muḍārabah*-like contract IFIs offer on the deposit-taking, liabilities side of their balance sheet differs considerably from the classical principles of the contract.

[86] ICTA, s 209 (2)(e)(iii); Mohammed Amin (n 81).

[87] *Ibid.* [88] Finance Act 2005.

[89] Colin Hargreaves, Paul Davidson and Sarah Perfect, Freshfields Bruckhaus Deringer, 'Accidentally Alternative? Scope of the Alternative Finance Arrangements Provisions,

interest return. Yet if the contract is to be practised as set out in classical texts its profits should be treated as dividends and taxed accordingly. Otherwise, conventional equity investments would not benefit from the same exclusions. The fact is, however, that the industry does not practise the *muḍārabah* in conformity with the sharia, and hence the Finance Act 2005 has carved out an alternative loan relationship[90] that treats its dividends as interest. Chapter 6 examines the regulatory rationales for treating it in this manner.

Further relief was carved out for shared ownership products such as the diminishing *mushārakah* (a form of progressively diminishing shared ownership in which the borrower gradually acquires the lender's share in the asset), by giving it SDLT relief. Moreover, the existing *ijārah wa iqtinā'* (lease-based mortgage) received relief, effective in Scotland. Finally, in 2005, sharia-compliant child trust funds were regulated so that providers could enter the market competitively.[91]

The Finance Act 2006 enabled the introduction of the *wakālah* or profit share agency whereby an investor appoints an agent to manage an invested sum of money and is entitled to a return that is equated, in substance, to interest.[92] Further modifications in 2006 included the introduction of legislation enabling the use of *ijārah wa iqtinā'* in asset finance; HM Revenues & Customs allowed the use of diminishing *mushārakah* as a standard loan; SDLT relief was extended to companies, trusts, charities and partnerships seeking Islamic products (it was previously only available to individuals); and secondary legislation empowered the FSA to regulate Islamic HPPs.[93]

Alternative property finance relief is available only where the 'first transaction' is one in which any of the reliefs under schedule 7, paras. 1–13 of the Finance Act 2003 apply, e.g. group, reconstruction and acquisition reliefs. This requirement ensures that only one relief can be claimed in an effort to stem tax avoidance.[94]

The following sections deal with the UK's work on *sukuk* issuances, which is particularly important to the industry in the country. The case

Part II', *Tax Journal*, 2008, www.taxjournal.com/tj/articles/accidentally-alternative-20916. Accessed 23 March 2014.

[90] Finance Act 2005, s 50(2)(b).

[91] HMRC (n 78) 7; Finance Act 2005, ch 5.

[92] Her Majesty's Treasury (n 70) 16; Finance Act 2006, ss 95–8.

[93] Financial Services and Markets Act 2000 (Regulated Activities) (Amendment) (No. 2) Order 2006, SI 2006/2383. HMRC (n 78) 7.

[94] Natalie Schoon, *Islamic Banking and Finance* (London: Spiramus Press, 2009), 157.

study also provides some important insights into the UK's treatment of Islamic finance as a whole.

5.5 IFIs and the benefits of sovereign *sukuk* issuance

This section is primarily concerned with wholesale markets. In particular, it examines some of the issues concerning a UK sovereign *sukuk* issuance. The objective of the section is to examine the economic issues concerning the UK government's legislative facilitation of *sukuk* issuances.

The London Stock Exchange has emerged as a global centre for the issuance of *sukuk*. By 2013 the exchange had listed fifty-three *sukuk* issues with a value over US$38 billion, more than any other global exchange.[95] However, the government would like to develop the market further inasmuch as it sees the potential benefits of *sukuk* issuance flowing to the City of London and to the wider community. In particular, sovereign *sukuk* issuance would enhance the City of London's ability to attract further commercial *sukuk* structuring activity and, more generally, business activity related to the Islamic financial industry.

In April 2007, the government launched a feasibility study on the issuance of sovereign *sukuk* to examine the benefits and costs of its issuing wholesale sterling Islamic financial instruments, and to consider the legal implications of doing so.[96] It is thought that a UK sovereign *sukuk* issuance could potentially facilitate the development of a greater range of sharia-compliant retail financial products such as Islamic individual savings accounts (ISAs), other savings accounts and capital guaranteed investment products. This has the potential of including those in financial markets who would otherwise refrain from investing in the conventional financial system.[97]

Market participants are concerned about liquidity risks as several sharia prohibitions, such as the prohibition of trading in debts (*bay' al-dayn*), restricts banks' ability to generate liquidity rapidly.[98] Most conventional

95 LSE, 'Islamic Factsheet', 2013, www.londonstockexchange.com/specialist-issuers/islamic/downloads/london-a-global-hub-for-islamic-finance.pdf. Accessed 23 August 2013.

96 See Her Majesty's Treasury, *Government Sterling Sukuk Issuance: A Consultation* (London: HM Treasury, 2007).

97 *Ibid.*, 8. For the general reasons behind sovereign bond issuances, see Maxwell J. Fry, *Emancipating the Banking System and Developing Markets for Government Debt* (New York: Routledge, 1997).

98 Daud Vicary Abdullah, 'Liquidity Management in Institutions Offering Islamic Financial Services', Paper Presented at Second Islamic Financial Stability Forum, Jeddah, 2010) 1–26, www.ifsb.org/docs/David_Vicary_IFSF_paper_FINAL.pdf. Accessed 25 March 2014.

institutions repackage and sell off their loans and thus retain relatively accessible deposits of liquidity. This process – known as the negotiability of claims – enables parties to trade loans and other contingent claims. Negotiability is not only the defining characteristic of a capital market, it dramatically enhances the power of financial technology.[99] Islamic law's prohibition of the sale of debts means that this financial innovation is largely outside its reach. The resulting dearth of Islamic financial instruments has prevented Islamic banks from quickly raising funds from money markets.

The underdevelopment of cross-border Islamic inter-bank money markets or lender of last resort (LLR) facilities – to which IFIs could turn for short-term loans that do not engage in interest-based financing – compounds this problem.[100] The inter-bank market is a wholesale market in which banks lend surplus funds or borrow from each other when their reserves are low. Loans are normally for very short periods (from overnight to fourteen days) although some institutions lend for three-month, six-month and one-year terms.[101] The current inadequacy of cross-border Islamic liquidity markets negatively affects IFIs' ability to manage their liquidity and risk management requirements.[102] Instead Islamic inter-bank lending arrangements generally originate from bespoke financing rather than capital market structures, although some central banks including those of Malaysia, the UAE and Indonesia have established Islamic inter-bank platforms.[103] For example, in February 2002 the governments of Bahrain, the UAE, Saudi Arabia and Kuwait established the Liquidity Management Centre (LMC) in an effort to establish an active and geographically expansive Islamic inter-bank market. Each country's 25 per cent equity stake is designed to help financial institutions address liquidity mismatches through the issuance of short- and medium-term liquid investments.[104] Further, the central bank of Malaysia, Bank Negara

[99] William N. Goetzmann and K. Geert Rouwenhorst, 'Financial Innovations in History' in William N. Goetzmann and K. Geert Rouwenhorst (eds.), *The Origins of Value: The Financial Innovations That Created Modern Capital Markets* (Oxford University Press, 2005), 7.

[100] M. Umer Chapra and Tariqullah Khan, *Regulation and Supervision of Islamic Banks*, Occasional Paper no. 3 (Jeddah: Islamic Development Bank, Islamic Research and Training Institute, 2000), 32.

[101] In London the rate of interest paid on inter-bank loans is known the London InterBank Offer Rate or LIBOR. It is an important reference for banks since it indicates the cost of raising immediate surplus funds. See Peter Howells and Keith Bain, *Financial Markets and Institutions*, 5th edn (Harlow: Pearson Education Limited, 2007), 129–30.

[102] Daud Vicary Abdullah (n 98) 1–26.

[103] *Ibid.*, 8.

[104] LMC, 'Vision & Role', Liquidity Management Centre, 2011, www.lmcbahrain.com/role.asp. Accessed 25 March 2014.

Malaysia, operates a commodity *murābaḥah* programme based in large part on the *bay' al-'inah* contract. The *bay' al-'inah* is repudiated by most schools of law, particularly those which predominate in the Arab Middle East. This difference of interpretation highlights the challenge in creating globally accepted and standardised products that have an appreciable effect on markets outside of Malaysia.[105]

These problems have resulted in cumbersome settlement and operational procedures as well as a limited supply of short-term money market instruments.[106] A number of institutions offer overnight *murābaḥah* structures on an accommodation basis, but there is no Islamic institutional arrangement equivalent to the conventional inter-bank market.[107] Another difficulty in creating a sharia-compliant overnight product consists in developing the right risk/yield profile. A number of products have been launched but subsequently withdrawn despite a huge demand for the facility.[108] Thus the potential market for overnight products is large and will likely prove to be a watershed in the development of the industry.

The dependence on bilateral arrangements for the deployment of inter-bank liquidity has empowered the institutions able to accommodate such instruments. The small cadre of institutions which dominates overnight lending has slowed the development of standardised products and systems that otherwise remain ad hoc and variable across regions. Despite the fact that the Islamic financial industry needs a centralised inter-bank liquidity programme, the difficulty resides in locating sufficient numbers of founder participants who are willing to invest in and support its development – a task that has not been easy.[109]

As a result, the commodity *murābaḥah* is the preferred structure for inter-bank lending across most jurisdictions.[110] Known in practitioner circles as the '*murābaḥah* syndrome', the allocation of liquidity across all Islamic finance markets has been dominated by the *murābaḥah*. Reviews of audited financial statements reveal that more than 65 per cent – 80 per

[105] Asyraf Wajdi Dusuki, 'Commodity Murabahah Programme (CMP): An Innovative Approach to Liquidity Management' in Mohd Daud Bakar and Engku Adawiah Engku Ali (eds.), *Essential Readings in Islamic Finance* (Kuala Lumpur: CERT, Centre for Research and Training, 2008), 179.

[106] Daud Vicary Abdullah (n 98) 1–26.

[107] Stella Cox, 'The Role of Capital Markets in Ensuring Islamic Financial Liquidity' in Simon Archer and Rifaat Ahmed Abdel Karim (eds.), *Islamic Finance: The Regulatory Challenge* (Singapore: John Wiley & Sons (Asia), 2007), 274.

[108] Stella Cox (n 107) 274. [109] *Ibid.*, 275–6.

[110] Daud Vicary Abdullah (n 98) 1–26.

cent according to many estimates – of banks' balance sheets is allocated to this type of investment.[111] Yet a number of fixed costs associated with transacting in *murābaḥah* make short-term investment in these instruments expensive.

On the other hand, UK market observers argue that a 'bill-like' *sukuk* – a *sukuk* with a shorter maturity – would lower transaction costs so that Islamic banks could address their liquidity and reserve requirements more cost-effectively.[112] Most issuances offer maturities of three, five and ten years and thus do not solve IFIs' requirements for alternative money market-like instruments with considerably shorter maturities.[113]

5.6 UK sovereign *sukuk* issuance

In the United Kingdom there are no institutionalised inter-bank lending arrangements that do not involve interest. The issuance of short-dated sovereign *sukuk* similar to Treasury bills would help alleviate short-term liquidity pressures.[114] The characteristic mismatch between the long-term maturities of originated loans (via partnership or other investment contracts), and short-term financing derived from retail bank deposits, which are available on demand, has limited IFIs' long-term investments. The result is a situation characterised by either a surplus of cash in need of investment or a shortage of cash to meet liabilities.[115] Long-term investments are generally less liquid, but more profitable; whereas short-term investments are less profitable, but more liquid. Banks have generally shied away from making investments in partnerships, in part, due to short-term liquidity concerns, but primarily due to an aversion to commercial risk in preference for less risky modes of short- and medium-term structures such as the *ijārah* and *murābaḥah*.[116] Short-term *sukuk* would provide Islamic banks with an essential tool to manage their liquidity and investment requirements.[117]

[111] Stella Cox (n 107) 272.

[112] Her Majesty's Treasury (n 50) 17.

[113] Joseph DiVanna and Antoine Sreih, *A New Financial Dawn: The Rise of Islamic Finance* (Cambridge: Leonardo and Francis Press 2009), 57.

[114] Mohammed Amin, 'Liquidity Management at UK Islamic Banks' (2011), www.mohammedamin.com/Islamic_finance/Liquidity-management-at-UK-Islamic-banks.html. Accessed 25 March 2014.

[115] Dahlia El-Hawary, Wafik Grais and Zamir Iqbal, *Regulating Islamic Financial Institutions: The Nature of the Regulated*, World Bank Policy Research Working Paper (Washington, DC: The World Bank, 2004), 23.

[116] *Ibid.*, 17. [117] Joseph DiVanna and Antoine Sreih (n 113) 58.

UK sovereign *sukuk* issuance would also encourage other Western sovereign and corporate issuers to access Islamic financial markets due to the framework it would establish. It could act as a risk-free benchmark to facilitate the pricing of other issues in the Islamic financial market. Indeed, a liquid benchmark reference may provide a pricing reference for other *sukuk* issuances, and thereby avoid the need for benchmarking against an interest-based product, as is the case with the frequent use of LIBOR. Importantly, it would increase secondary market liquidity in the *sukuk* market[118] with important results for the types of financial instrument Islamic financial institutions must necessarily offer so as to remain commercially viable. Finally, sovereign *sukuk* issuance may provide a catalyst for the development of Islamic pensions and insurance (*takāful*) due to the degree of certainty with respect to a bank's cash flows that issuance may provide.

Sovereign *sukuk* issuance would also assist IFIs in meeting their capital reserve requirements by generating liquid structures, which are tradable in secondary markets. Thus issuance would also help to strengthen the balance sheet of UK IFIs by providing AAA-rated sterling-denominated assets for investment, which qualify as a claim on a central government according to the 2004 Basel II recommendations.[119] Basel capital adequacy requirements will be examined in depth in Chapter 6.

Basel II leads banks to use instruments with a nil or low regulatory capital, which highly rated liquid investments such as 'bill-like' *sukuk* would offer as opposed to less highly rated (riskier), less liquid *murābaḥah*.[120] The ability to invest reserve requirements in government *sukuk* would provide IFIs with a much needed liquidity instrument and simultaneously reduce capital costs.

Islamic investors would also benefit from the diversification of investment opportunities that sovereign issuance would afford. The UK government's consultations concerning the proposed legislation and its subsequent implementation are designed to create a legal path towards plain vanilla *sukuk al ijārah*[121] offerings, whereas other *sukuk* structures could be introduced over time. Past *sukuk* issuances have been relatively limited in structural diversity. *Murābaḥah sukuk* have generally been issued in Malaysia while GCC states have preferred *mushārakah sukuk*.

[118] Her Majesty's Treasury (n 50) 15.

[119] *Ibid.* [120] Her Majesty's Treasury (n 50) 17.

[121] Plain 'vanilla' financial products are the most basic and standard versions of financial instruments. They are not exotic or customised to any great extent.

The expansion of *sukuk* issuance beyond these regional centres would improve the asset risk exposure of investors. Furthermore, the lion's share of *sukuk* issuances are denominated in US dollars or in local currencies, so an issuance in sterling would diversify the existing currency spectrum and provide opportunities for implicit foreign exchange hedges, enabling financial institutions to manage exchange rate risk more efficiently.[122]

In June 2008 the government issued a report entitled, 'Government Sterling *Sukuk* Issuance: A Response to the Consultation' which described several negative factors affecting the decision to issue sovereign *sukuk*.[123] A number of points were made, including concerns whether issuance could be more costly than conventional issuance, either as a result of up-front structuring costs, or because investors could charge a premium to invest in *sukuk*. Demand for AAA-rated sterling denominated *sukuk* issuance is completely untested and may prove to be limited as a result of currency preferences and/or the relatively low yield investors could extract from such investments. The potential for differential pricing between bond-like *sukuk* and gilts is likely to be due to the lower liquidity in bond-like *sukuk* secondary markets. *Sukuk* holders tend to buy and hold their investment certificate, thus minimising their liquid enhancing quality.[124] And the issuance of bond-like *sukuk* rather than bill-like *sukuk* (with considerably shorter maturities) creates a price risk due to the importance placed on liquidity of longer-dated instruments.[125] Finally, the success of a *sukuk* issuance is usually measured by the pricing and distribution achieved. Issuances priced at substantially higher levels than conventional equivalents of similar credit quality are generally unattractive to investors.[126]

Some respondents argued that bond-like *sukuk* issuance could fragment sovereign debt issuance to the detriment of the gilt market and lead to overall increased costs. Interestingly, a large number of respondents felt that Middle Eastern investors would not be interested in bond-like *sukuk*, as Islamic banks in the region have relatively high funding costs, which may make UK sovereign issuance priced at, or close to, gilts less attractive. However, existing gilt investors, as well as UK-based Islamic banks

[122] Andreas Jobst, Peter Kunzel, Paul Mills and Amadou Sy, *Islamic Bond Issuance – What Sovereign Debt Managers Need to Know*, IMF Policy Discussion Paper (Washington, DC: International Monetary Fund, 2008), 18.

[123] Her Majesty's Treasury (n 50) 11–20.

[124] Joseph DiVanna and Antoine Sreih (n 113) 58.

[125] Her Majesty's Treasury (n 50) 20.

[126] Robert Gray and Arshad Ismail, 'Regulating Islamic Capital Markets' in Simon Archer and Rifaat Ahmed (eds.), *Islamic Finance: The Regulatory Challenge*, (Singapore: John Wiley & Sons (Asia), 2007), 285.

and overseas central banks, were thought likely to take an interest in a bond-like issuance.[127] In addition to pricing risks, respondents noted that the sharia risk associated with the structuring of *sukuk* issuance could potentially affect whether *sukuk* issuance is acceptable to a broad range of investors due to the lack of standardisation in the market. Moreover, the emerging standardisation of sharia-compliant products raises questions as to whether a *sukuk* issuance, once deemed sharia-compliant, may subsequently be found to fall outside the standard,[128] a critical issue that resurfaces across the range of Islamic financial contracts.

In November 2008 the government announced that sovereign issuance of *sukuk* would not offer value for money.[129] The decision coincided with a global financial crisis of historic proportions, which reinforced the importance of UK sovereign gilt issuance. As an as-of-yet untested product with an uncertain investor base the government was clearly concerned about the long-term costs of debt issuance confronted by a weak economy and increased borrowing projections.[130] Nevertheless, the government proceeded with implementing regulatory changes on the basis of the above-discussed industry consultations.[131]

After years of government inaction, in October 2013, the Chancellor of the Exchequer, George Osborne, announced the government's intention to become the 'unrivalled western centre for Islamic finance'. In support of that intention the government is preparing a UK sovereign *sukuk* issuance worth about £200 million, which would be the first sovereign issuance outside Muslim-majority states.[132] A sovereign *sukuk* issuance has the potential to kick-start the industry. The next section examines UK legislative and regulatory measures designed to facilitate *sukuk* issuance.

[127] Her Majesty's Treasury (n 50) 20. [128] *Ibid.*

[129] Christina Fincher, 'British Gilt Issuance to Hold Broadly Steady in 08/09', *Reuters*, 7 March 2008, uk.reuters.com/article/2008/03/07/britain-budget-gilts-idUKL0776505020080307. Accessed 25 March 2014.

[130] *Ibid.*

[131] At a Norton Rose event Sarah McCarthy Fry MP, Exchequer Secretary to the Treasury, made the announcement. See Norton Rose, 'MPs Confirm UK Commitment to Islamic Finance at Norton Rose Event', 27 January 2010, 1–2, www.nortonrosefulbright.com/news/26132/mps-confirm-uk-commitment-to-islamic-finance-at-norton-rose-event. Accessed 25 March 2014.

[132] George Osborne, 'London Can Lead the World as an Islamic Finance Hub' *Financial Times*, 28 October 2013.

5.7 The implementation of *sukuk*

In 2007 the government's policy of developing the Islamic finance industry was extended to commercial *sukuk* issuance. The target market for commercial *sukuk* is directed towards high net-worth individuals, largely from the Muslim world, as well as corporate investors. The government felt that some interest could be generated amongst sovereign wealth funds and Western investors as these entities may require relatively secure investments as part of their portfolio management.[133] Further, because IFIs are unable to raise finance via traditional securities markets, the ability to issue *sukuk* in the United Kingdom would assure them of much-needed wholesale funding. Reports indicate that up to 26.2 per cent of global issuance is undertaken by IFIs.[134] Therefore, the Treasury and HMRC set out to establish a transparent tax structure for commercial *sukuk* in the 2007 Finance Act, which would provide tax certainty for all interested parties.

Before 2007, *sukuk* received a more onerous tax treatment than conventional debt securities. *Sukuk* were taxed according to the underlying legal form of the transaction, which had to be assessed on a case-by-case basis. The ad hoc nature of these arrangements placed issuers and thus investors at a competitive disadvantage relative to conventional debt issuances. The absence of commercial *sukuk* issuance in the UK restricted the funding available to IFIs and accordingly affected Muslim consumers and businesses from accessing *sukuk* funds.[135] Uncertainty concerning the tax treatment of *sukuk* undermined the UK's objective of creating a leading Islamic financial centre.

The government announced a specific tax regime for *sukuk* in the 2007 Budget. The Finance Act 2007 retrospectively introduces an alternative finance investment bond (AFIB) in sections 48(A) and 48(B) of the Finance Act 2005.[136] Section 48 introduces a number of conditions to be satisfied for an investment product to be treated as an AFIB and any 'interest-like' payments made or received from the bonds are treated as an alternative finance return. Section 48(A)(1)(d) requires the bond-issuer:[137]

[133] HMRC (n 78) 14.

[134] FSA & Her Majesty's Treasury, *Consultation on the Legislative Framework for the Regulation of Alternative Finance Investment Bonds (Sukuk)* (London: Financial Services Authority, 2008), 22.

[135] Her Majesty's Treasury (n 73) 4.

[136] Finance Act 2007, s 53.

[137] *Ibid.*

(ii) to make a repayment of the capital ('the redemption payment') to the bond-holder during or at the end of the bond-term (whether or not in instalments), and
(iii) to pay to the bond-holder other payments on one or more occasions during or at the end of the bond term ('additional payments').

In s 48(A)(2)(d)(ii) the Act requires some sort of purchase undertaking in the agreement, with the attendant implications for true sale criteria of the assets,[138] but there is no requirement that assets must be repurchased at par value.

Section 48(A)(2)(h) provides that:

(h) the amount of the redemption payment may (but need not) be subject to reduction in the event of a fall in the value of the bond assets or in the rate of income generated by them.

Furthermore, with reference to section 48(A)(1)(d)(iii), section 48(A)(2)(f) provides that additional payments may be:

(i) fixed at the beginning of the bond term,
(ii) determined wholly or partly by reference to the value of or income generated by the bond assets, or
(iii) determined in some other way.

The legislation takes into account the asset-based nature of *sukuk* and allows dividends to be generated from bond assets, while providing for the return of bondholders' principal.

A further set of conditions demonstrates that the government treats *sukuk* as debt instruments for tax purposes, similar to the way in which conventional bonds are treated, providing that:[139]

[138] The key determinant of a true sale resides in whether the risks inherent in the assets have been retained by the originator or have been transferred to the issuer and through the issuer to the note holders. If the risks of the assets have transferred to the SPV – in other words, a true sale has occurred – the originator's creditworthiness is not taken into account as its continued financial health is of no further significance to the transaction. However, in a secured lending structure such as a mortgage – a structure wherein the debtor has the right to receive the charged collateral upon payment of the secured debt as well as any surplus monies in the case that the creditor enforces payment and sells off the collateral – the originator is the borrower and its financial health plays a significant role in any rating of the transaction. A *sukuk* structure with sale and/or purchase undertakings may not meet true sale criteria. For more see Patrick Clancy, 'Legal Structure of Cash and Synthetic Transactions' in Rick Watson and Jeremy Carter (eds.), *Asset Securitisation and Synthetic Structures: Innovations in the European Credit Markets* (London: Euromoney, 2006), 41.

[139] Finance Act 2005, s 48(B)(2).

(a) a bond-holder shall not be treated as having a legal or beneficial interest in the bond assets,
(b) the bond-issuer shall not be treated as a trustee of the bond assets,
(c) profits and gains accruing to the bond-issuer in connection with the bond assets are profits and gains of the bond-issuer and not of the bond-holder (and do not arise to the bond-issuer in a fiduciary or representative capacity),
(d) payments made by the bond-issuer by way of redemption payment or additional payment are not made in a fiduciary or representative capacity, and
(e) a bond-holder shall not be entitled to relief for capital expenditure in connection with bond assets.

The tax treatment of AFIBs is designed for structures that differ markedly from classical sharia principles that reward profit via the assumption of ownership risks. In (a) the bond holder is not treated as having a legal or beneficial interest in the underlying assets; the certificate holders do not own pro-rata shares in the assets. In (b) the bond issuer (usually a special purpose vehicle (SPV)) is not to be treated as a trustee so as to differentiate the structure from collective investment schemes where different tax and regulatory rules apply; and in (c) profits are not to be attributed to bond holders, which would otherwise indicate their proportionate legal ownership of the assets (requiring taxation). In (d) any payments made to bond holders are not done in a fiduciary capacity, thus preventing an ownership scenario from arising; and in (e) bond holders as non-owners of the asset(s) are not entitled to capital expenditure relief. The structure is therefore designed to ensure a guaranteed return for the investor with a fixed or variable payment equivalent to the rate of interest. From a sharia perspective the structure transgresses the fundamental rules concerning *ribā* and its prohibition of a guaranteed or unjustified return.

From the originator's perspective, *sukuk* are treated as a loan or debt-relationship and tax rules for corporate debt apply. Despite the *sukuk*'s equity-like features – or underlying assets – the government's tax treatment of the structure is premised upon an interest-generating debt instrument.[140] For purposes of corporation tax, *sukuk* are taxed according to the rules on loan relationships; for income tax purposes, *sukuk* returns are treated as if they were interest; and for purposes of capital gains tax, *sukuk*

[140] Mohammed Amin, 'The New UK Tax Law on Sukuk', *New Horizon* (Jan–March 2008), 3, www.kantakji.com/media/8018/m173.pdf. Accessed 23 March 2014.

are taxed as qualifying corporate bonds and are exempt from tax if they meet equivalent conditions.[141] This potentially makes *sukuk* tax-deductible and issuers (not bond holders) are taxed as if they beneficially owned the assets. This entitles issuers to any capital allowances or tax depreciations for which the assets qualify.[142] With these measures AFIBs were given tax certainty with respect to income and corporation taxes, capital allowances, inheritance tax and capital gains.[143] However, SDLT was not covered in the legislation so that tax inequalities remained.

Moreover, because *sukuk* often involve the creation of a trust and are thus treated as a collective investment scheme (CIS) under the Financial Services and Markets Act (FSMA) 2000,[144] the legislation excludes AFIBs from tax provisions relevant to trusts or CISs.[145] In particular, Finance Act 2005 section 48(B)(5) 'ensures that alternative finance investment bonds are not treated as a unit trust scheme either for the purposes of the Income and Corporation Tax Act 1988/s 469 or the Income Tax Act 2007/s 1007 or the Taxation of Chargeable Gains Act 1992'. Nor are they treated as an offshore fund. Further, with respect to companies, they are not classified as a 'relevant holding in a unit trust or offshore fund for loan relationships purposes'.[146]

The government issued a consultation document with the objective of resolving SDLT issues relating to commercial *sukuk* issuance in June 2008.[147] *Sukuk* structures, in general, are often backed by underlying interests in property or land – tangible assets that are compatible with an Islamic view of the creation of wealth and value. Conventional bonds do not convey ownership interests to bond holders; bond holders merely have a right to the payment of interest and repayment of principal. Because SDLT is levied on the acquisition of a 'chargeable interest', a plain vanilla *ijārah sukuk* might have been taxable in at least three instances. First, the acquisition of an asset by the SPV from the originator would require SDLT to be payable by the purchaser at a rate of 4 per cent on an asset valued at more than £500,000. Second, the re-purchase of the asset at the end of the *sukuk*'s maturity would again invoke SDLT at the same

141 Her Majesty's Treasury (n 50) 35.
142 Mohammed Amin (n 140) 3.
143 Her Majesty's Treasury (n 73) 10.
144 Financial Services and Markets Act 2000, pt XVII.
145 Finance Act 2007, s 53, in Finance Act 2005, s 48(B)(5)(a), (b) and (d). Her Majesty's Treasury (n 73) 36.
146 Finance Act 2007, s 53, in Finance Act 2005, s 48(B)(5)(a), (b) and (d)..
147 HMRC (n 78) 1–24.

rate. Furthermore, *sukuk* holders might be liable to SDLT as owners of the beneficial interest of an underlying asset.[148] Together, these additional SDLT charges would make the issuance of commercial *sukuk* unfeasible.

The Finance Act 2009 created a legislative framework that extended relief to: (1) the transfer of the asset from the originator to the *sukuk* issuer or SPV; (2) the repurchase by the originator from the *sukuk* issuer (SPV); and (3) to the issue and resale of *sukuk* in secondary markets.[149] A series of conditions must be satisfied with respect to each specific stage of relief. In particular, stage one requires that the *sukuk* issuers in England and Wales 'enter a legal charge over the asset in favour of HMRC'[150] for the duration in which the asset is held by the issuer. The charge should be equivalent in value to the SDLT on the market value of the underlying asset at the time of the transaction.[151] The charge gives HMRC an interest in a charged property so that 'in the event of avoidance or default HMRC are able to collect any SDLT and related interest and penalties that become due'.[152] In 2010 HMRC amended the Finance Act 2003 to ensure that SDLT relief was available for *ijārah sukuk* issuance as was originally intended in the Finance Act 2009.[153]

However, competitive disadvantages still remain in the area of value-added tax as *sukuk* investors may be subject to a VAT charge of approximately 17.5 per cent on any rental payments received from the SPV and on their purchase of *sukuk*.[154] The government is working with industry practitioners to resolve these additional liabilities. However, the government may be constrained by its EU obligations, in particular the Sixth VAT Directive, which clarifies the operation of the VAT system throughout the European Union.[155] The Directive was first promulgated in 1977,[156]

[148] *Ibid.*, 12.

[149] Finance Act 2009, sch 61; pt III, ss 6–9; HMRC (n 14) 11.

[150] Finance Act 2009, sch 61; pt III, s 6(a).

[151] HMRC (n 14) 11. [152] Finance Act 2009, sch 61; pt III, s 5(6).

[153] Financial Services and Markets Act 2000 (Regulated Activities) (Amendment) Order 2010, SI 2010/86, s 3. HMRC, Stamp Duty Land Tax (Alternative Finance Investment Bonds) Regulations 2010, SI 2010/184.

[154] Her Majesty's Treasury (n 50) 38. Different VAT rates apply to different goods and services. These must be assessed on a case-by-case basis.

[155] Council Directive 2006/112/EC of 28 November 2006 on the common system of value added tax [2006] OJ L347/1. See also Abu Umar Faruq Ahmad, *Theory and Practice of Modern Islamic Finance: The Case Analysis from Australia* (Boca Raton, FL: Brown Walker Press, 2010), 261.

[156] Council Directive 77/388/EEC of 13/6/1977 on the harmonisation of the laws of Member States relating to turnover taxes – common system of value added tax: uniform basis of assessment [1977] OJ L 145.

but has since been updated to allow exemptions to certain transactions. Different rates of VAT are permissible as long as these are not less than 15 per cent.[157]

The government has pursued a rigorous legislative agenda so as to accommodate *sukuk* and to develop the Islamic finance industry. Legally mandated consultations with the public, from which much of the above information derives, highlight the willingness of the government to approach the regulation of the industry in a flexible manner and in line with industry standards and practices. For instance, several early requirements were dropped in response to practitioners' concerns that such requirements would render the industry uncompetitive.[158]

The scale of tax modifications necessary to eliminate disadvantageous tax treatment underscores pivotal differences between the legal structures of Islamic and conventional structures. The government's approach is intended to categorise Islamic structures according to the conventional tax system. Importantly, however, such structures represent industry norms and standards so that the UK government's particular treatment of Islamic finance cannot be attributed to its own institutional biases and/or preferences. While alternative regulatory structures for the industry were never contemplated, the UK's approach is sensible with regard to the existing regulatory structure. From an institutional, political and social perspective the UK government sees its role in safeguarding the application of a uniform approach to all financial markets as the fairest and most efficient manner of regulating financial markets.

5.8 Concluding remarks

The UK government's facilitation of Islamic financial transactions such as the *sukuk* is a strategy designed to attract Islamic capital to the City of London. The government's experience with Islamic finance indicates that economic globalisation, which relies on the legal and regulatory frameworks of nation states, influences the creation of law at the state level and the legal inputs which feed into the state-based law-creating process. These inputs, in the form of sharia principles, industry norms and inter-

[157] Council Directive 2010/88/EU of 7 December 2010 amending Directive 2006/112/EC on the common system of value added tax, with regard to the duration of the obligation to respect a minimum standard rate [2010] OJ L326/1, art 1.

[158] In particular, see HMRC (n 42). And HMRC (n 14) 11.

national standards, interact with municipal legal systems to create novel legal structures, and, indeed, 'alternative' categories of legislation.

Can we consider the results of this law-creating process an independent legal system? If 'independent' signifies a legal system not subject to the jurisdiction or authority of a nation state, then clearly IFL does not meet these requirements. The role of municipal legal systems in providing a fiscal and regulatory framework for Islamic financial transactions is indisputable. More important, however, is the jurisprudential insight that IFL does not depend on municipal legal systems alone for its creation, dispersion or enforcement. It is created in a process that requires the interaction of both municipal legal systems and non-national legal inputs. Such inputs are generally the legal material, which states examine and carefully select for use in modifying legal and regulatory frameworks.

The examination of the UK's legislative implementation of *sukuk* demonstrated that the mode of accommodating IFL affects both the economic substance and legal aspects of the law. While the UK study indicates that the government preferred an assimilative strategy, other states have pursued different strategies. Moreover, once legislated and made part of a state's legal framework, the law-making process continues ad infinitum via the cross-pollination of ideas and legal inputs in global financial markets.

This globalised law-making process is not just significant in commercial terms. On the contrary, it indicates ways in which global processes affect municipal legal changes as well as social and political considerations and thereby affect the quality of people's lives. Again, the case study of the United Kingdom is indicative of this trend. The former Archbishop of Canterbury's now famous 2008 speech was essentially a plea to consider this important aspect of belonging in a globalised legal environment. That Islamic finance and thus sharia principles have been willingly accommodated in English law, without much public debate, demonstrates the liberality and commercial prerogatives of the English legal system. It has had the positive knock-on effect of allowing people to practise their faith in the course of their financial dealings.

6

The regulation of Islamic financial institutions in the United Kingdom

The regulation of financial institutions including IFIs is a complex topic that requires the analysis of multiple layers of law or legal systems and the ways in which they interact and influence one another in the production of rules and regulations. This chapter is concerned with the regulation of IFIs in the United Kingdom, in particular, but more broadly with global regulatory dynamics and their impact on municipal legal systems across the globe. The standards and best practices originating from global organisations as well as others articulated domestically interact to produce regulatory outcomes that condition the types of financial services on offer. The complex of regulatory law that is applicable to IFIs is no different in this regard. Islamic financial services on offer in the United Kingdom, as in other municipal legal systems, are influenced to a great extent by layers of regulatory requirements as well as consumer preferences, which drive the market.

This chapter explores financial market regulation, starting with a country-specific (UK) context, moving onto regional structures and finally focusing on global regulatory standards. An examination of the enforcement of Islamic financial transactions in English courts rounds up the analysis.

The chapter examines the particular type of financial intermediation that Islamic banking espouses in theoretical terms and then looks closely at the practice of Islamic banking. With this knowledge and context in mind, the chapter addresses the FSA/PRA approach to regulating Islamic finance, dealing first with the classification of representative products and then with the way in which the government regulates sharia supervisory boards (SSBs). Following the examination of UK regulatory law, the chapter deals with EU law, its growing regulatory importance and its applicability in all member states of the EU including the United Kingdom. Next, global regulatory law, its nature, origins and problems of representativeness are explored. Finally, the last mode of regulation, litigation, is examined in relation to Islamic financial agreements.

6.1 The regulation of financial markets

Ways in which classical sharia principles are modified for application in financial markets become evident by examining the economic imperatives of financial services regulation. Most important is the fact that regulation is designed to shore up confidence or trust in the financial system and thus mitigate systemic risk. In this important respect, the regulation of Islamic financial institutions proceeds from the same substantive economic premise as is the case for conventional institutions.[1] The following discussion is focused, in particular, on the regulation of banks in the financial system.

6.2 The objectives of financial services regulation

Financial services regulation is principally concerned with maintaining financial system stability in light of banks' important role as financial intermediaries and linchpins of the payments system. Deposit-taking institutions act as lenders and through the origination of loans transform risks into different maturities. Banks usually create long-term, illiquid assets, which are financed by accepting short-term deposits. This results in an asset-liability mismatch in retail deposit-taking institutions; it differs from the securities business, for example, which accepts investments that are not guaranteed, so that market risk is effectively transferred to the investor. Furthermore, banks operate as agents within a network of other institutions as facilitators or clearing houses of market transactions based on a variety of mediums of exchange. The failure of one single agent in the payments system poses dangers for the entire system.[2]

Other pertinent reasons include the need to maintain consumer confidence and a consumer demand for regulation that offers the investor a degree of assurance and overall lower transaction costs. Generally, the case for the regulation of retail financial services is considered to be stronger than the case for regulating the wholesale market. This is due to greater information asymmetry in retail transactions than in wholesale

[1] Michael Ainley, Ali Mashayekhi, Robert Hicks, Arshadur Rahman and Ali Ravalia, '*Islamic Finance in the UK: Regulation and Challenges*' (Financial Services Authority, 2007), 13.

[2] Johannes Koendgen, 'Regulation of Banking Services in the European Union: A Comparative View' in Juergen Basedow, Harald Baum, Klaus J. Hopt, Hideki Kanda and Toshiyuki Kono (eds.), *Economic Regulation and Competition* (The Hague: Kluwer Law International 2002), 29.

ones. However, this assumption has proved to be rather tenuous in the aftermath of the 2008 global financial crisis in which wholesale transactions were the primary cause of instability. One reason for this may be the fact that retail markets are easier to regulate than wholesale services as wholesale business tends to 'disappear' to less constraining regulatory environments.[3]

Three core regulatory objectives are pursued in devising financial regulation: (1) sustaining systemic stability; (2) maintaining the safety and soundness of financial institutions; and (3) protecting the consumer.[4] These objectives give rise to two general types of regulation: prudential regulation, which focuses on the solvency, safety and soundness of financial institutions; and conduct of business regulation, which largely focuses on how financial firms conduct business with their customers.

Regulators have several instruments at their disposal to fulfil their regulatory objectives. These are generally classified according to the level of market intervention. Accordingly, low intervention is associated with the regulation of information. It forces suppliers to disclose details concerning the quality of their goods and services. Further, it can be carried out in the form of private regulation, which imposes obligations but can only be enforced by those for whom the benefits of regulation have been devised. Economic incentives may also induce information disclosure by market participants. Second, a medium-level degree of intervention is often referred to as command-and-control in which standards are supported by criminal sanctions on non-compliant businesses. Third and finally, the highest degree of intervention characterises the instrument of prior approval, which prohibits an enterprise from undertaking an activity without a licence or express permission to do so from a government agency.[5] The PRA, formerly the FSA, the financial services regulator in the United Kingdom, employs a combination of all three methods in regulating Islamic financial institutions.

The greater part of statutory regulation in the financial field relates to consumer protection. Conduct of business regulation's remit is to

[3] John Kay, 'The Forms of Regulation' in A. Seldon (ed.), *Regulation or over-Regulation?* (London: Institute of Economic Affairs, 1988), 41.

[4] Charles Goodhart, Philipp Hartmann, David T. Llewellyn *et al.*, *Financial Regulation: Why, How and Where Now?* (Routledge 1998), 4; and David Llewellyn, *The Economic Rationale for Financial Regulation*, FSA Occasional Papers in Financial Regulation (London: Financial Services Authority, 1999), 9–10.

[5] Anthony I. Ogus, *Regulation: Legal Form and Economic Theory* (Hart Publishing 2004), 4–5.

safeguard consumers in their dealings with financial institutions. This includes mandatory information disclosures, ensuring the honesty and integrity of firms and their employees, standardising the level of competence of firms providing financial services and products, ensuring fair business practices, and maintaining fair, transparent and honest marketing practices.[6] The risks of consumers' adverse selections are mitigated by capital requirements, which ensure that financial institutions have at least some minimal provision of resources available to honour their commitments to consumers. Capital requirements are intended to mitigate moral hazard by requiring owners of a financial institution to ensure that the firm conforms to conduct of business rules and does not engage in fraud – if merely to avoid fines and/or loss of equity value.[7]

Problems of customer protection within the financial services field tend to be more severe than in other professions.[8] Money is at risk and the opportunity for fraud and principal–agent conflicts of interest requires a strong regulatory regime.[9] In general, the confidentiality or secrecy typically associated with financial services transactions contributes to a greater likelihood of fraud.[10] This is also a problem in Islamic financial intermediation particularly with respect to principal–agent conflicts in various forms of partnership investments.

Many factors shape consumer behaviour but the known existence of asymmetric information can reduce consumer demand for goods and services. Consumers know that good and bad products and firms exist on the market but they lack credible information to distinguish them at the point of purchase. For example, Muslim consumers of financial products take a particular interest in the sharia-compliance of the investment products they wish to purchase. A growing body of evidence supports this conclusion and further suggests that particular groups of Muslim consumers are not convinced that some Islamic financial product offerings have achieved this standard. Hence, the issue of confidence and trust in the authenticity of these products plays a significant role in how the industry will fare. Generally, the price that buyers will pay reflects the average quality of products in the market. Sellers of high-quality products, who

[6] David Llewellyn (n 4) 11.

[7] Richard Herring and Till Schuermann, 'Capital Regulation for Position Risk in Banks, Securities Firms, and Insurance Companies' in H. S. Scott (ed.), *Capital Adequacy Beyond Basel: Banking, Securities, and Insurance* (New York: Oxford University Press, 2005), 19.

[8] Charles Goodhart, Philipp Hartmann, David T. Llewellyn *et al.* (n 4) 7.

[9] David Llewellyn, 'Regulation of Retail Investment Services' (1995) 15 *Ec.Aff.*, 1–12.

[10] Charles Goodhart, Philipp Hartmann, David T. Llewellyn *et al.* (n 4) 7.

know that their products are good, may refuse to sell their products at a lower value. Sellers of low-quality products, on the other hand, will be satisfied to accept a price reflecting an average value since they are aware that their products are of poor quality.[11] For their part, some consumers may respond to poor-quality products by decreasing spending or exiting the market altogether. In the most extreme scenario the market may break down completely. Known in economic theory as the *adverse selection* problem, the case exemplifies the importance of transparency and disclosure in markets. Consumers may decide to forgo purchases of high-quality products simply because of their aversion to the high risk and high cost of purchasing a poor product. Thus an additional role of conduct of business regulation consists in setting minimum standards to prevent or remove low-quality producers from the market. In fact, good-quality businesses tend to support these standards so that poor-quality producers are not in the position to tarnish their reputation and economic performance.[12] The subsequent analysis of the UK government's strategy toward SSBs examines whether conventional conduct of business regulation provides adequate protection to Muslim investors.

Prudential regulation is designed to ensure a stable financial system. A stable financial system is necessary to provide a favourable environment for efficient resource allocation and the promotion of economic growth. Prudential regulation is therefore directed against systemic risks. It is designed to address banks' special position in the financial system – their role in providing liquidity and their management of the payments system.[13]

Bank lending has the function of augmenting or constraining the money supply, as the recent credit crunch and economic situation illustrate. In this important sense, banks act as extensions of the government's monetary policy.[14] A major function of banks as financial intermediaries is their role as delegated monitors in a world of asymmetric information between those seeking funds and those who supply them. In some cases, outsiders cannot easily obtain information, which may require a significant outlay in funds or an extensive and continuous relationship with a firm. Important savings can be achieved in these circumstances

[11] Frederic S. Mishkin, *The Economics of Money, Banking, and Financial Markets* (Boston: Pearson, Addison Wesley, 2004), 176.

[12] David Llewellyn (n 4) 25–6.

[13] *Ibid.*, 13; and Howard Davies and David Green, *Global Financial Regulation* (Cambridge, UK and Malden, MA: Polity Press, 2008), 16.

[14] Johannes Koendgen (n 2) 32.

by delegating certain functions to financial intermediaries. A financial intermediary's costs are reduced by avoiding duplication of these functions. These consist of gathering relevant information prior to securing a funding decision and monitoring borrowers' actions once they have committed to their investment projects.[15]

Therefore, banks occupy a pivotal role at the centre of the financial payments network. A large, systemically important bank's failure may result in contagion across the financial sector. The failure of one insolvent bank can cause depositors of other banks – though they might be solvent – to withdraw their deposits. A solvent institution can become insolvent because the vast majority of bank assets are not easily marketable or liquid. On the one hand, this scenario is indicative of the importance of consumer confidence in the market and, on the other, it reflects the pivotal role of market players' perception of the viability of specific financial institutions in a bear market.[16] The degree of confidence or lack of it permeates nearly every institution to some extent.

A recent example provides a terrifying depiction of the reality of this market characteristic. Bear Stearns, the global investment bank, had nearly US$18 billion in cash reserves. It was brought to near ruin in a run that was not the result of a criminal indictment or some mammoth quarterly loss, but of rumour and innuendo – a dramatic and erosive loss of confidence in the institution's liquidity.[17] It required the unusual assistance of the US Treasury Department to fashion a deal in which Citigroup acquired Bear Stearns for a paltry US$2 per share – an enormous loss of equity in one of the world's largest investment banks.

A lesson from Bear Stearns is that banks' marketable assets may dramatically decline in value due to panic. If a bank run does occur, banks are forced to dispose of assets, which cannot be sold off at par value as potential buyers impose high risk premiums on the purchase price.[18] Commonly referred to as *asset liquidity risk*, this scenario represents 'the risk that an entity will be unable to unwind a position in a particular

[15] Joao Cabral dos Santos, 'Bank Capital Regulation in Contemporary Banking Theory: A Review of the Literature' (2001) 10 (2) *Financial Markets, Institutions & Instruments*, 4–5.

[16] A bear market is an extended period of time over the course of which the stock market has declined significantly.

[17] Bryan Burrough, 'Bringing Down Bear Stearns', *Vanity Fair*, 1 August 2008, 1–2.

[18] David Llewellyn (n 4) 13–14.

financial instrument at or near its market value because of a lack of depth or disruption in the market for that instrument'.[19]

Two factors underpin this dynamic. First, a critical problem lies in conventional banks' solicitation of debt contracts for liquid deposits. These liquid deposits finance the acquisition of illiquid assets of uncertain value while the redemption value of the deposit is independent of the performance of the bank or the value of its assets. Second, the value of a bank's assets cannot be traded with confidence in a secondary market or to another financial institution. The value of such assets on a going-concern basis is linked to insider information within the bank that is based on a borrower's payment history and long-term relationship with the bank. Thus an asymmetric information problem exists where outsiders are unsure of banks' underlying assets. A liquidation or break-up of the bank would cause the banks' assets to be valued significantly lower than on a going-concern basis, hence US$2 per share in the equity of Bear Stearns. Moreover, the failure or even significant losses of one bank may then cause outsiders to wholly revise their view of the value of other banks' assets.[20] A substantial spill-over effect may ensue on the 'real' economy.

Further, the aggregate capabilities of bank employees may be lost if banks are liquidated, resulting in fewer specialists able to distinguish between good and bad assets. The result is a sharp decrease in the amount of lending, and severe recession in the overall economy.[21] This theoretical description of the loss of confidence in a financial institution and its subsequent consequences provides a remarkably accurate portrayal of the steps leading to the global financial crisis of 2008 – the most severe financial crisis since the Great Depression. In practice, these considerations are also applicable to IFIs. Yet IFIs may also be susceptible to a set of different risks including sharia-compliance risk and regulators must assess the nature of such risks so as to ensure consumer confidence. The next section examines the way in which Islamic finance intermediates between depositors and borrowers and what particular risks may arise.

[19] The Joint Forum, *Risk Management Practices and Regulatory Capital: Cross Sectoral Comparison* (Basel Committee Joint Publication, 2001), 23.

[20] Dirk Schoenmaker, 'Contagion Risk in Banking', LSE Financial Markets Group Discussion Paper (London School of Economics, 1996), 87, www.imes.boj.or.jp/cbrc/cbrc-03.pdf. Accessed 25 March 2014; and Diane Scott Dockey, Mark Herschey and Elaine Jones, 'Information and Contagion Effects of Bank Loan-Loss Reserve Announcements' (1997) 43 *JFE*, 219.

[21] Richard Herring and Till Schuermann (n 7) 20.

6.3 Islamic financial intermediation

Regulators must understand a financial institution's risks in order to regulate effectively. Islamic financial institutions and the products they offer comprise a unique cocktail of risks that distinguish the industry from its conventional peer. Islamic financial contracts are asset-based and so are based on the sale and purchase of sharia-compatible assets and/or usufructs. Such products include the *murābaḥah, salam, istisnā‘* and *ijārah*. Partnership products such as *muḍāraba, mushārakah* or securities such as *sukuk* as well as investment portfolios and funds are also generally based on such assets. The asset-based aspect of such products means that an IFI's gross return is the difference between the cost of the asset and the amount that can be earned from selling or leasing it. As a result, asset-based contracts are exposed to price risk with respect to the asset (which is a type of market risk) and credit risk with respect to the counterparty. Profit- and loss-sharing investments, *mushārakah* and *muḍārabah*, are exposed to risk in the nature of an 'equity position not held for trading' along the lines of an 'equity position in the banking book', according to the Basel Capital Accord (Basel II). Such investments are subject to credit risk except in the case of investments in assets for the purpose of trading, which are subject to market risk.[22] A number of other risks involving the legal, governance and liquidity infrastructure of IFIs are also particular to the industry.[23]

Both IFIs and regulators are concerned with designing effective risk management systems that recognise and effectively manage the specific risks in Islamic financial products. In particular, financial institutions must concern themselves with risk measurement and disclosure as a means of fulfilling Basel II and the implementation of new liquidity standards.[24] Basel II and the recent strengthening of liquidity systems and

[22] IFSB, 'IFSB-15: Revised Capital Adequacy Standard for Institutions Offering Islamic Financial Services (Excluding Islamic Insurance [Takāful] Institutions and Islamic Collective Investment Schemes)', December 2013, para 1.5, www.ifsb.org/standard/2014-01-28_eng_IFSB15%20Revised%20Capital%20Adequacy_(Jan%202014).pdf. Accessed 25 March 2014.

[23] Vasudevan Sundararajan, 'Risk Characteristics of Islamic Products: Implications for Risk Measurement and Supervision' in Simon Archer and Rifaat Ahmed Abdel Karim (eds.), *Islamic Finance: The Regulatory Challenge* (Singapore: John Wiley & Sons (Asia), 2007), 41.

[24] See FSA, *Strengthening Liquidity Standards* (London: Financial Services Authority, 2008), 1–166.

Table 6.1: *Generalised balance sheet of an Islamic bank*

Assets	Liabilities
Cash balances	Demand deposits (*amānah*)
Financing assets (*murābaḥah, salam, ijārah, istiṣnāʿ*)	Investment accounts (*muḍārabah*)
Investment assets (*muḍārabah, mushārakah*)	Special investment accounts (*muḍārabah, mushārakah*)
Fee-based services (e.g. *juʿālah, kafālah*)	Reserves
Non-banking assets (property)	Equity capital

Source: Author's own.

controls require an appropriate capital buffer depending on the level of these risk measurements.

It is helpful to examine an IFI's balance sheet so as to conceptualise the unique nature of Islamic financial intermediation (see Table 6.1). On the liabilities side, IFIs often accept deposits on the basis of *muḍārabah* and *wakālah* contracts. Deposit accounts are usually offered in current, savings, investment and special investment accounts. Savings and investment accounts are available on a restricted and unrestricted basis. Unrestricted accounts entitle banks to invest depositors' investments according to the bank's discretion. They do not permit depositors to issue instructions with respect to the object, time period or jurisdiction of the investment. By contrast, restricted accounts designate a specific portfolio of investments that are pre-agreed between the depositor and the bank.[25] As *muḍārib* (agent), the bank accepts the deposit from the customer, which it considers an investor (*rabb al-māl*) in terms of the objective of the *muḍārabah* contract. The bank and the agent will agree that the agent is entitled to retain a pre-specified percentage share of the profits – if the venture is profitable – from his investment of the bank's money. If a loss arises the *muḍārib* does not share in any monetary loss attributable to the investment but does lose his time and effort in locating and contracting an appropriate investment. Since no collateral may be offered to the bank according to the sharia, the risk of the investment is relatively high. This risk is compounded by the bank's inability to monitor the entrepreneur or enforce additional actions by legal devices.[26] Deposits can be made

[25] Salman Syed Ali, *Islamic Banking in the MENA Region* (Jeddah: Islamic Development Bank – Islamic Research and Training Institute, 2011), 7–8.

[26] Mervyn K. Lewis and Latifa M. Algaoud, *Islamic Banking* (Cheltenham: Edward Elgar, 2001), 77.

in a multitude of pre-agreed maturities, which range from one month upwards and may be withdrawn either immediately or upon advance notice. Distributions between the bank and depositors are allocated – according to a pre-determined ratio or expected profit ratio – usually with 80 per cent channelled to investors and 20 per cent to depositors.[27]

Theoretically, Islamic investment deposits would not constitute a liability for the bank. Rather they would take the form of an equity investment. According to the model, an IFI's portfolio of well-diversified assets, including profit- and loss-sharing (PLS) modes on the assets side, and equity investment-like PLS structures on the other, would create a more efficient and stable mode of financial intermediation. The model is often referred to as a pass-through method of financial intermediation on the basis that IFIs do not carry risk on their banking books associated with investors' deposits, as all risks are carried by depositors, save for misconduct or negligence.[28]

In most jurisdictions where Islamic banking is practised, IFIs' actual utilisation of funds deviates starkly from the theoretical model. Islamic banks' investment of depositors' funds should undertake to screen potential investment projects on behalf of depositors and thus engage in partnership-like contracts (*sharikah*). Yet the typical balance sheet of an IFI shows a clear preference on the assets side for less risky trade-finance assets of considerably shorter maturities such as *murābaḥah*, *istiṣnā'*, *ijārah* and *salam* (see Figure 6.1).[29] Trade-based instruments backed by assets and leasing (*ijārah*) products dominate the assets portfolio of IFIs. Together these can constitute 80 per cent and upwards of total assets with the remainder devoted to profit- and loss-sharing investments.[30] The use of short-term trade financing structures backed by real assets minimises the risks of verification, moral hazard and adverse selection, which are all inherent in PLS modes of investment.[31] Furthermore, vulnerability to liquidity problems on the liabilities side of the balance sheet encourages the use of short-term liquid contracts so as to avoid a typical asset–liability mismatch.[32]

[27] Dahlia El-Hawary, Wafik Grais and Zamir Iqbal, *Regulating Islamic Financial Institutions: The Nature of the Regulated* (World Bank Policy Research Working Paper 2004), 12.

[28] Hennie van Greuning and Zamir Iqbal, 'Banking and the Risk Environment' in Simon Archer and Rifaat Ahmed Abdel Karim (eds.), *Islamic Finance: The Regulatory Challenge* (Singapore: John Wiley & Sons (Asia), 2007), 19.

[29] *Ibid.*, 17. [30] Dahlia El-Hawary, Wafik Grais and Zamir Iqbal (n 27) 18.

[31] Mervyn K. Lewis and Latifa M. Algaoud (n 26) 72.

[32] Dahlia El-Hawary, Wafik Grais and Zamir Iqbal (n 27) 18.

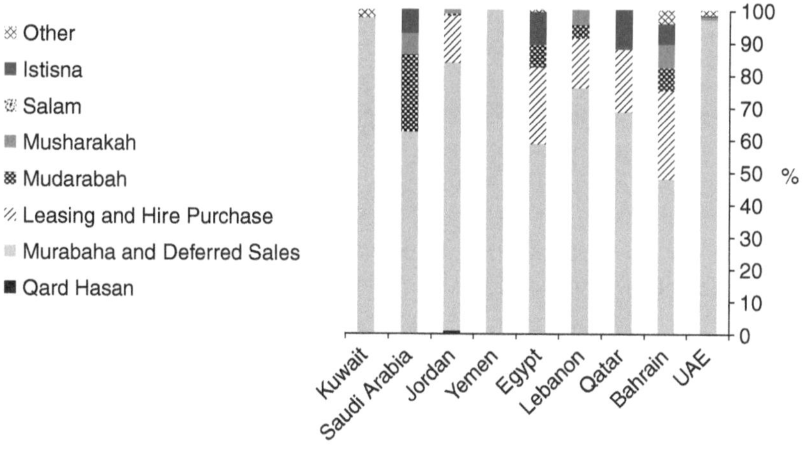

Figure 6.1: Percentage composition of Islamic financial structures across a range of Islamic banks in MENA countries in 2008

Source: Salman Syed Ali, *Islamic Banking in the Mena Region* (Jeddah: Islamic Development Bank, Islamic Research and Training Institute, 2011), 18.

Figure 6.1 depicts asset compositions from a sample of thirty Islamic banks in 2008 located in countries of the Middle East and North Africa (MENA). The *murābaḥah* is by far the dominant mode of financing used by Islamic banks in all MENA countries, accounting for more than 90 per cent in some countries. In others it figures less prominently, comprising less than 50 per cent. However, the average proportion of *murābaḥah* financing across the MENA region is high, about 75 per cent. The *ijārah* contract is the second most utilised structure in Bahrain, Kuwait, Jordan and Qatar. *Istiṣnā'* is the third most popular structure. Only in Saudi Arabia was the *muḍārabah* the second largest mode of financing.[33] From a substantive point of view, therefore, the risk profile of Islamic financial products is similar to conventional financial practices. Islamic financial investments display similar risk preferences and offer financial institutions greater means of control and hedging opportunities.[34]

The high concentration of asset-backed trade financing structures limits IFIs' capacity to achieve maximum profitability from their portfolios by narrowing investment options to short-term and less profitable investments. Further, asset-backed instruments may expose IFIs to heightened

[33] Salman Syed Ali (n 25) 18.

[34] Mervyn K. Lewis and Latifa M. Algaoud (n 26) 72.

levels of credit, operational, market and exchange rate risks, which pose important questions for regulatory authorities. These types of investment are considered risky from a capital adequacy perspective. IFIs may also possess a limited capacity for risk mitigation due to sharia restrictions concerning the use of guarantees and derivatives products.[35]

From a regulatory perspective, PLS modes of finance may increase the overall level of risk on the asset side of a bank's balance sheet. In particular, the degree of operational risk is an important consideration for regulatory authorities. The management of PLS modes of financing requires investment activities that are not normally undertaken by conventional banks. These include the determination of PLS ratios from assorted investments as well as the ongoing auditing of investment projects to ensure that projects are properly managed and appropriately valued. As mentioned earlier, IFIs have no legal recourse to control the investment activities of agents/entrepreneurs as per sharia law. Agents are entitled to direct the investment activities to the best of their ability. Unlike trade-financing transactions, PLS modes cannot be hedged with collateral or third-party guarantees to reduce counterparty credit risk since the sharia prohibits these.[36]

Known as the principal–agent problem in conventional finance, the separation of management and ownership entails moral hazard, because managers may not possess the right incentives to maximise profit as owners would have them do. The principal–agent problem arises because of the asymmetric information between the manager and the owner. The owners/equity holders of a firm do not possess complete information about the manager's activities and the monitoring process is costly in terms of time and money.[37] The equity contract is a less attractive contract in conventional finance, which presents a clear indication of why PLS modes of financing are similarly underused.

On the liabilities side of the balance sheet, PLS modes of financing pose fiduciary risks in the case of misconduct or negligence on the part of the *muḍārib*. In the case of misconduct or negligence a PLS investment

[35] Simon Archer and Rifaat Ahmed Abdel Karim, 'Measuring Risk for Capital Adequacy: The Issue of Profit-Sharing Investment Accounts', in Simon Archer and Rifaat Ahmed Abdel Karim (eds.), *Islamic Finance: The New Regulatory Challenge* (Singapore: John Wiley & Sons (Asia), 2013), 289.

[36] Vasudevan Sundararajan and Luco Errico, *Islamic Financial Institutions and Products in the Global Financial System: Key Issues in Risk Management and Challenges Ahead* (Washington, DC: International Monetary Fund, 2002), 5–6.

[37] Frederic S. Mishkin (n 11) 181–2.

account would lose its equity features and become a liability of the bank, giving rise to prudential concerns.[38] AAOIFI defines fiduciary risk as the act of becoming legally liable for a breach of the investment contract either for non-compliance with sharia rules or for mismanagement of investors' funds.[39] If an IFI was found to be liable for breach of its fiduciary responsibilities towards depositors, it could lead to both direct and indirect losses. Indirect losses resulting from damage to its reputation would lead to a decrease in the price of its listed shares. A loss of confidence in the financial institution could lead to a bank run, exposing shareholders and investment account holders (IAHs) to substantial economic losses.[40]

The *muḍārabah* requires that IAHs bear the risk of loss in the case that the bank's investment loses money. This primary feature, coupled with information asymmetry via unrestricted account holders, engenders significant moral hazard since banks' incentives are directed towards risk-taking and maintaining low levels of capital.[41] The bank, after all, is not investing its own money and earns a profit in proportion to the success of the venture. The greater the profit earned, the larger the amount of profit the bank is able to retain. Moreover, the *muḍārabah* generally offers a bank's management significant freedom in fund management decisions. Yet there is a general lack of transparency with respect to management's investment choices; with regard to management's ability to alter profit shares as a reward due to the *muḍārib*; in the allocation of liquidity costs between shareholders and IAHs; and, finally, in the management's choice of whether losses should be absorbed by internal reserves or whether these costs should be passed on to IAHs and/or shareholders.[42]

Islamic banks, in order to offer investment yields that are competitive with conventional financial institutions, establish profit and investment risk reserves to smooth any potential losses from depositors' investments. This effectively negates market risk on the part of the investor but may weaken the IFI's equity reserves, since the funds of IAHs and shareholders

[38] Hari Bhambra, 'Supervisory Implications of Islamic Finance in the Current Regulatory Environment' in Simon Archer and Rifaat Ahmed Abdel Karim (eds.), *Islamic Finance: The Regulatory Challenge* (Singapore: John Wiley & Sons (Asia), 2007), 207.

[39] AAOIFI, *Shari'a Standards* (Manama: The Accounting and Auditing Organization for Islamic Financial Institutions, 2004–2005).

[40] Dahlia El-Hawary, Wafik Grais and Zamir Iqbal (n 27) 21.

[41] Vasudevan Sundararajan and Luco Errico (n 36) 7.

[42] Elisabetta Montanaro, 'Islamic Banking: A Challenge for the Basel Capital Accord' in M. Fahim Khan and Mario Porzio (eds.), *Islamic Banking and Finance in the European Union* (Cheltenham: Edward Elgar, 2010), 116.

are typically commingled.[43] In practice, PLS investments, which theoretically do not guarantee the value of the deposit, seldom pass on a loss to depositors.[44] As a result, IFIs' own capital is exposed to investment losses on the assets managed for investors.[45] They may even forgo all or part of their share of the profits to be able to make these transfers. Known as displaced commercial risk (DCR) this practice varies between countries as some regulators require IFIs to carry virtually all of the risk, while in some jurisdictions depositors may incur a loss.[46] Displaced commercial risk generates market uncertainty and regulatory authorities are keen to address its particular risks and capital requirements.[47]

On an international basis some banking supervisors basically view this as the modus operandi of transacting in PLS accounts, so that IFIs have a constructive obligation to carry on with the practice. Instead of remaining a voluntary practice, PLS accounts become capital certain accounts and take on an institutional character. In the event that this becomes the supervisory perspective, capital adequacy requirements must mirror the practice.[48]

In addition to accepting deposits on the basis of PLS investment contracts, IFIs differentiate themselves from conventional institutions by combining different functions of banking under a single roof. Brokerage, investment banking and commercial banking form the activities of IFIs, similar to that of the universal bank model.[49] However, universal banks offering conventional products separate fund management and investment operations from commercial banking operations according to function. They also erect firewalls to separate investment and commercial financial activities legally, financially and managerially.[50] In practice conventional banks' segregation of banking functions may not protect institutions from systemic shocks such as that of the 2008 financial crisis, but it does minimise inherent conflicts of interest and provides a buffer between banking activities. Islamic financial institutions conduct the

[43] Vasudevan Sundararajan (n 23) 41–2.
[44] Rodney Wilson, 'Regulatory Challenges Posed by Islamic Capital Market Products and Services' in Amer Al-Roubaie and Shafiq Alvi (eds.), *Islamic Banking and Finance* (London: Routledge 2010), 379.
[45] Mansur Noibi, 'Prudential Regulation of Islamic Banks' in Amer Al-Roubaie and Shafiq Alvi (eds.), *Islamic Banking and Finance* (London: Routledge 2010), 184.
[46] Vasudevan Sundararajan (n 23) 41–2.
[47] Hari Bhambra (n 38) 207.
[48] Simon Archer and Rifaat Ahmed Abdel Karim (n 35) 292.
[49] Hennie van Greuning and Zamir Iqbal (n 28) 19.
[50] Dahlia El-Hawary, Wafik Grais and Zamir Iqbal (n 27) 16.

same activities without any such separation, which may lead to greater instances of conflict of interest or insider dealing within firms.[51]

Current Islamic financial practice pools funds mobilised on the basis of *muḍārabah* with equity holders' capital. Barriers between different types of accounts are 'treated as one large bucket'.[52] According to the theoretical model, a clear separation of risks and performance associated with individual investment projects clarifies the rights and responsibilities of all involved stakeholders. In practice, the proceeds of all investments, including demand deposits, are divided amongst shareholders and IAHs relative to their share of the capital. An IAH's return equals the total revenue minus the percentage due to the *muḍārib* or bank's shareholders. Therefore, shareholders and IAHs must bear the credit and market risks in proportion to their investment. Yet only the shareholders must countenance operating risks associated with illegal and negligible behaviour by the bank's management.[53] From a regulatory perspective, the fact that different stakeholders carry different risks and thus require different safeguards may strengthen the argument that uniform regulatory treatment is insufficient or overly restrictive.[54]

While most Islamic banks report these funds on the balance sheet, many banks have placed them off-balance sheet. The latter clearly regard these as fiduciary investments, since risk is borne by the investor. On a global basis regulatory authorities have required different accounting treatments of investment accounts that render financial comparability extremely difficult, if not impossible. The variability of this accounting treatment directly impacts capital adequacy requirements, liquidity or treasury management as well as fiduciary issues with respect to the evaluation of funds transfers between IAHs' funds and those of equity holders or the bank's own funds.[55] In the United Kingdom, financial institutions' annual report and financial statements are undertaken according to International Financial Reporting Standards (IFRS), as adopted by the European Union and implemented in the UK Companies Act 2006.[56] The certainty and consistency of accounting treatment in the United Kingdom

[51] Michael Clode, 'Regulatory Issues in Islamic Finance' in Simon Archer and Rifaat Ahmed Abdel Karim (eds.), *Islamic Finance: Innovation and Growth* (London: Euromoney Books 2002), 69.

[52] Dahlia El-Hawary, Wafik Grais and Zamir Iqbal (n 27) 16.

[53] Elisabetta Montanaro (n 42) 116. [54] *Ibid.*

[55] Taha Eltayeb Ahmed, 'Accounting Issues for Islamic Banks' in Simon Archer and Rifaat Ahmed Abdel Karim (eds.), *Islamic Finance: Innovation and Growth* (London: Euromoney Books, AAOIFI, 2002), 116.

[56] George J. Benston, Michael Bromwich, Robert E. Litan and Alfred Wagenhofer, *Worldwide Financial Reporting: The Development and Future of Accounting Standards*

removes the disadvantages of incomparability and greatly facilitates the regulator's task. Questions remain, however, regarding the appropriateness of conventional accounting treatments of Islamic financial products in jurisdictions in which accounting standards vary. Guidelines determining ratios for capital adequacy, other reserves and provisions as well as overall liquidity may be more meaningfully expressed under AAOIFI accounting standards than IFRS.[57]

The theoretical model of Islamic banking is a useful starting point to conceptualise the practice of Islamic banking and possible reasons for any divergence. The following section examines the way in which the PRA deals with the practice of Islamic banking.

6.4 The FSA/PRA regulatory approach to Islamic finance

With the election of a conservative government in May 2010, the Chancellor of the Exchequer, George Osborne, announced the abolition of the FSA. Osborne blamed the FSA for not foreseeing the credit crisis, including the weakness of banks such as Northern Rock. He claimed that the 'FSA became a narrow regulator, almost entirely focused on rules-based regulation'.[58]

The new system of regulation replaces the universal regulatory authority with a 'twin peaks' regulatory structure in which two separate institutions are given responsibility for different regulatory objectives. On 1 April 2013 the FSA became the Financial Conduct Authority (FCA) and is responsible for promoting effective competition and conduct of business regulation, i.e. the manner in which financial institutions treat their customers. Prudential regulation and supervision is now the responsibility of the Prudential Regulatory Authority (PRA), a part of the Bank of England. The PRA is concerned with the safety and soundness of the financial system and the 'securing of an appropriate degree of protection for policyholders'.[59] The PRA was created by the Financial Services Act 2012, which amends the Bank of England Act 1998, the FSMA 2000 and

(Oxford University Press, 2006), 93; IBB, *Annual Report and Financial Statements* (London: Islamic Bank of Britain, 2009), 10. See Companies Act 2006, s 474(1).

[57] Taha Eltayeb Ahmed (n 55) 122.

[58] George Parker and Brooke Masters, 'FSA to Be Abolished in Osborne Shake-Up' *Financial Times*, 17 June 2010, 1.

[59] PRA, 'Prudential Regulation Authority', Bank of England (2013), www.bankofengland.co.uk/PRA. Accessed 27 July 2013.

the Banking Act 2009.[60] On issues in which the regulatory bodies have joint responsibility, the PRA's decision will have greater weight.[61]

There is no legislative or other indication of government policy to suggest that the PRA will approach Islamic finance any differently than the FSA. However, after a number of years in which the conservative government has been inactive towards the industry, it recently launched an Islamic Finance Task Force with the objective of promoting the United Kingdom as an investment destination and to raise the profile of Islamic finance in the City of London.[62] The continued rapid growth of the industry, as well as several high-profile infrastructure projects in London in which Islamic finance backed part of or the entire project, are the principal reasons behind the development. In particular, the government would like to encourage private investors and sovereign wealth fund investment in the United Kingdom.[63] It would also like its professional services in accounting, finance and law to continue to play a dominant role in the development of the industry.[64]

The following section discusses the ways in which the UK regulatory authority classifies Islamic financial contracts. The section sheds light on the institutional rules for dealing with financial services in general.

6.5 The regulatory classification of Islamic financial products

Two central provisions regulate financial services and their promotion under FSMA 2000. The first, known as the 'general prohibition' in section 19 of the FSMA 2000, restricts anyone other than an 'authorised person' or 'exempt person' from undertaking a 'regulated activity' in the United Kingdom. The second, known as the 'financial promotion restriction' and set out in section 21, restricts the promotion of 'investment activity'.[65] The

[60] Financial Services Act 2012, 'Introduction', c 21.

[61] Brooke Masters, 'Stability Priority in Finance Rules Shake-up', *Financial Times*, 26 July 2010, www.ft.com/cms/s/0/e22d16ce-98be-11df-a0b7-00144feab49a.html?siteedition=intl#axzz3AjOVrmpS. Accessed 17 August 2014.

[62] Her Majesty's Treasury and Foreign & Commonwealth Office, 'Government Launches First Islamic Finance Task Force', 11 March 2013, www.gov.uk/government/news/government-launches-first-islamic-finance-task-force. Accessed 7 April 2014.

[63] *Ibid.*

[64] Sayeeda Warsi, Baroness Warsi, 'The Future of Islamic Finance in a Global Economy', Foreign & Commonwealth Office, 7 June 2013, www.gov.uk/government/speeches/the-future-of-islamic-finance-in-a-global-economy. Accessed 7 April 2014.

[65] Eva Lomnicka, 'Collective Investment Schemes' in Michael Blair, George Walker and Robert Purves (eds.), *Financial Services Law*, 2nd edn (Oxford University Press, 2009), 916.

scope of the terms 'regulated activity' and 'investment activity' found in these sections is specified by Treasury Order: the Regulated Activities Order;[66] and the Financial Promotion Order.[67] A person or firm wishing to undertake a 'regulated activity' must gain permission under Part IV of the FSMA 2000.[68]

The importance of the definition of these terms becomes apparent with regard to the way in which regulators classify particular financial products and services. Classification affects how a regulator will treat a particular product including its marketing. Arguably, classification is even more important with regard to Islamic financial products and services due to their different legal structures, which often have no conventional parallel. Product classification illustrates 'the nature and scope of the business of an IFI' as well as the way in which regulators deal with IFIs in the UK.[69] Moreover, it may have an impact on the way in which the regulator will approach an IFI's conduct of business.[70] The following section deals with the regulatory classification of *sukuk*, a contract of particular importance to wholesale Islamic financial markets.

6.5.1 *The regulatory classification of* sukuk

The *sukuk*, although commonly known as an Islamic bond, is perhaps more appropriately described as an Islamic investment certificate.[71] *Sukuk* certificates represent a holder's proportionate ownership interest in an underlying asset and thus share characteristics of asset-backed securities and equity investment. However, *sukuk* also share characteristics with

66 FSMA 2000 (Regulated Activities) Order 2001, SI 2001/544.

67 FSMA 2000 (Financial Promotion) Order 2005, SI 2005/1529.

68 The Financial Services Act 2012 amends the Bank of England Act 1998, the FSMA 2000 and the Banking Act 2009. The Act amends FSMA 2000 in order to create the PRA and FCA. An IFI seeking permission to carry out a regulated activity as described in section 19 of the Act would now require permission from the PRA under the authority of the Financial Services and Markets Act 2000 (PRA-Regulated Activities) Order 2013, No. 556. Existing permissions granted prior to the creation of the new regulators remain valid.

69 Andrew Henderson, 'Islamic Financial Institutions' in Craig Nethercott and David Eisenberg (eds.), *Islamic Finance: Law and Practice* (Oxford University Press, 2012), 66.

70 *Ibid.*

71 Rodney Wilson, 'Overview of the Sukuk Market' in Nathif J. Adam and Abdulkader Thomas (eds.), *Islamic Bonds: Your Guide to Issuing, Structuring and Investing in Sukuk* (London: Euromoney Books 2004), 3.

unsecured debt securities, which makes it difficult to classify them in any of these categories.[72]

Sukuk[73] are a modern innovation borrowed from the conventional concept of the asset-backed securitisation and designed to replicate the payment profile of conventional bonds. Conventional bonds are mid- to long-term debt instruments in which an investor lends money for a defined period of time and receives a fixed or floating amount of interest income. Bonds have a set maturity date at which time the issuer agrees to pay the holder his principal investment.[74] Bonds bear interest and accordingly are not permissible under the sharia. Funds generated from bond issuances are not screened according to sharia criteria and thus could possibly be used for *ḥarām* purposes including alcohol, pornography or highly leveraged corporations.[75]

A conventional asset-backed securitisation, on the other hand, is a structure that generates profit from the performance of an underlying tangible asset(s), transaction(s) and/or venture(s) and thus meets general sharia requirements concerning the generation of wealth.

Under FSMA 2000 the regulatory classification of *sukuk* and other Islamic financial transactions has not been straightforward. Although producing similar economic results, a *sukuk*'s legal structure and associated risk characteristics are markedly different from a conventional bond.[76] For example, consider the asset-based aspect of the *sukuk*. While a conventional bond is a simple debt instrument, a *sukuk* securitisation involves the sale and re-purchase of tangible assets via an SPV. Issues related to ownership in the underlying assets create legal risks for

[72] Edana Richardson, *The Integration of Islamic Finance into the Irish Legal System* (Dublin: Trinity College, 2011), 8.

[73] The modern *sukuk*, sg. *ṣakk* (the plural form is almost always used) originated from the classical *ṣakk*, an ancient monetary instrument first described in Malik's famous treatise, *al-Muwatta*. In the first Islamic century the Umayyad caliphate would pay soldiers and public servants in cash and in kind. Payment in kind was known as *sukuk al-badāʿiʿ*, something akin to commodity coupons or grain permits. *Ṣakk* holders would produce their certificate upon its maturity date at the treasury and receive a fixed amount of commodity, usually grains. See Mohammed Rafe Md. Haneef, 'Recent Trends and Innovations in Islamic Debt Securities: Prospects for Islamic Profit and Loss Sharing Securities' (Paper presented at Harvard University Forum on Islamic Finance, 'Islamic Finance: Current Legal and Regulatory Challenges', Cambridge, MA, 2005), 29.

[74] Peter S. Rose and Milton H. Marquis, *Money and Capital Markets: Financial Institutions and Instruments in a Global Marketplace*, 10th edn (New York: McGraw-Hill Irwin, 2008), 68.

[75] Rodney Wilson (n 71) 5. [76] *Ibid.*

investors. As a result of these characteristics, Islamic securities may not be captured under the existing regulatory framework.

The challenge is exacerbated by the fact that each *sukuk* issuance may have differing risk, legal and economic characteristics despite belonging to a particular nominate heading. The *sukuk al-ijārah* (lease-based *sukuk*) is the most popular form of *sukuk* in today's capital markets, although AAOIFI lists fourteen other forms of permissible *sukuk* modelled on the nominate contract scheme. For example, *sukuk* proceeds are routinely invested in *muḍārabah*, *mushārakah* equity partnerships and *istiṣnā'* (hire or construction) projects.[77] Thus the contracts of *mushārakah*, *muḍārabah* and *murābaḥah* are generic terms that describe particular types of transaction but do not describe the products themselves. The same generic contract or conglomeration of contracts may entail fundamentally different financial products in terms of their risk profiles and economic substance.[78] Hence the government employs a strategy of reviewing the economic substance of alternative financial investments in order to accurately assess the risk profile of *sukuk* issuances.

The FSA, after studying the *muḍārabah sukuk*, concluded that the instrument could be treated in two possible ways: as an unregulated CIS or listed as a debt instrument.[79] Some Islamic financial transactions appear to fall within the definition of a CIS as defined by the FSMA 2000. In fact, CIS regulation should be given consideration with regard to its impact on a broad range of sharia-compliant structures for two reasons. First, the definition of a CIS is all-inclusive so that any arrangement for collective investment could be regarded as a CIS. The definition covers almost all types of investment funds with two exceptions: schemes that assume a corporate form other than the 'open-ended investment company', also defined in FSMA;[80] and those

[77] Richard T. de Belder, *Shari'ah-Compliant Project Financing Securitisation Structures*, Islamic Project Financing: 2nd Annual One-Day Workshop (London: Institute of Islamic Banking and Insurance, 2010); Farmida Bi, *Islamic Project Finance: Project Finance Sukuk*, Islamic Project Financing: 2nd Annual One-Day Workshop (London: Institute of Islamic Banking and Insurance, 2010).

[78] IOSCO, *Analysis of the Application of IOSCO's Objectives and Principles of Securities Regulation for Islamic Securities Products* (Executive Committee of the International Organization of Securities Commissions, 2008), 48.

[79] Michael Ainley, Ali Mashayekhi, Robert Hicks, Arshadur Rahman and Ali Ravalia (n 1) 1–33.

[80] FSMA 2000, s 236.

of a limited liability partnership.[81] And second, Islamic structures are premised on the sharing of risks and returns and may thus be captured within the definition.[82]

Section 235(1) of the FSMA 2000 describes a CIS as 'any arrangement with respect to property of any description, including money, the purpose or effect of which is to enable persons taking part in the arrangements (whether by becoming owners of the property or any part of it or otherwise) to participate in or receive profits of income arising from the acquisition, holding, management or disposal of the property'.[83] It is also provided that such schemes must not be arranged so that participants have day-to-day control over the management of the property. At least one or both of the following characteristics must also apply:

(1) Arrangements must pool participants' contributions as well as profits or income;
(2) The property is managed on behalf of, or in whole by, the operator of the scheme.[84]

Schemes that do not fulfil these requirements would be treated as an unregulated CIS, which has the effect of prohibiting their promotion to the general public.[85] Unregulated schemes are created to undertake collective investment, unconstrained by PRA regulation with regard to the structure and operation of the arrangement. Examples of unregulated CISs are private equity or venture capital, which provide funds for start-up businesses.[86] Some originators of *sukuk* may want to avoid Part IV FSMA 2000 authorisation but the issue is one that affects any entity offering Islamic financial transactions, particularly those premised on PLS arrangements, capital market arrangements or other miscellaneous contracts.[87]

[81] For a general analysis see Eva Lomnicka (n 65) 873. Despite the all-inclusiveness of the definition, not all schemes require the regulatory treatment accorded to CISs and thus the Treasury has been given the power to adjust the definition by excluding various types of arrangements in specified circumstances. It does this by Order via the Financial Services and Markets Act 2000 (Collective Investment Schemes) Order 2001 (the Treasury CIS Order), SI 2001/1062.

[82] Andrew Henderson (n 69) 67. [83] *Ibid.*

[84] FSMA 2000, s 235 (2)–(3).

[85] FSMA 2000 (Financial Promotion) Order 2005, SI 2005/1529, s 238.

[86] Andrew Henderson, 'Islamic Financial Services' in Michael Blair, George Walker and Robert Purves (eds.), *Financial Services Law*, 2nd edn (Oxford University Press, 2009), 915.

[87] Andrew Henderson (n 69) 68.

The regulatory regime for CISs is more comprehensive than is the case for conventional debt securities as they are the only product that is specifically regulated under FSMA 2000. CISs are subject to a wider range of controls and may require authorisation for marketing purposes. Authorisation would limit the range of eligible assets for investment as well as gearing and marketing capabilities.[88] Therefore, *sukuk* issuers would be disadvantaged compared to issuers of conventional debt instruments were they regulated according to CIS rules.

The FSA decided to proceed with a regulatory policy towards AFIBs designed to introduce legislative changes to align the regulatory treatment of *sukuk* with conventional bonds. A unique regulatory definition for the purpose was created,[89] underscoring the distinctive legal attributes of *sukuk*. Further, the government included AFIBs as a specified investment under the Financial Services and Markets Act 2000 (Regulated Activities Order (RAO) 2001). Recall that the RAO specifies the scope of regulated activities under FSMA 2000. The range of instruments subject to the new definition is highly circumscribed so that only those instruments that grant debt-like returns are captured.[90]

Notably, the government stipulated that AFIBs should be subject to a mandatory listing requirement on a recognised stock exchange. This requirement again attempts to stem regulatory arbitrage by creating a high level of transparency and oversight of AFIBs. The government is concerned that various investments will exploit the legislative loophole and be excluded from CIS regulation. The government cites consumer protections for retail investors, in particular, but the loss of tax revenues is also a concern. It is not considered to be unduly burdensome as public listing is a pre-requisite of preferential tax treatment.[91] However, conventional bond issuance is not subject to any such requirement. The policy underscores the difficulty of placing *sukuk* within the uniform regulatory framework.

AFIBs are subject to a reasonable commercial rate of return clause, which stipulates that the amount of additional payments must not exceed an amount deemed to be a reasonable return on a loan of the capital.[92]

[88] *Ibid.*, 15.

[89] See SI 2001/544, art 77a. FSA & Her Majesty's Treasury, *Consultation on the Legislative Framework for the Regulation of Alternative Finance Investment Bonds (Sukuk)* (London: Financial Services Authority, 2008), 14. The Financial Services and Markets Act 2000 (Collective Investment Scheme) Order 2001, SI 2001/1062 was also amended so as to exclude AFIBs from the definition of a CIS.

[90] PRA & FCA, 'Handbook' (Prudential Regulation Authority & Financial Conduct Authority, n.d.), http://fshandbook.info/FS/html/handbook. Accessed 7 April 2014.

[91] *Ibid.*, 23. [92] *Ibid.*, 15.

This measure is designed to help prevent equity-like instruments from benefiting from this exclusion, thus preventing regulatory arbitrage, which would also disadvantage conventional equity investments. The measure highlights the government's determination to align the regulatory treatment of *sukuk* with conventional debt instruments. There is no such requirement for conventional bonds.

The following section deals with the *muḍārabah*, the central contract in the theoretical model of Islamic banking. The regulatory authority's treatment of the contract provides a further illustration of the United Kingdom's general approach to Islamic finance.

6.5.2 *The regulatory classification of* muḍārabah

The Islamic Bank of Britain (IBB), the first Islamic retail bank in the United Kingdom, upon applying for authorisation under FSMA 2000, applied to use the *muḍārabah* as a deposit-based contract. Section 5(2) of the FSMA 2000 RAO defines a deposit as a sum of money paid on terms 'under which it will be repaid, with or without interest or premium, and either on demand or at a time or in circumstances agreed by or on behalf of the person making the payment and the person receiving it'.[93] Therefore, UK statutory law requires 'capital certainty' for all bank deposits. Unless a bank is insolvent, it is required to return a depositor's principal plus any interest earned, if applicable. A *muḍārabah* has all the characteristics of a CIS and would likely be classified as a CIS were it not able to be excluded from the definition under paragraph 3 of the CIS order. That order treats it as a pure deposit-based scheme.[94] The FSA's classification of the contract as a deposit effectively allowed the authorisation of the IFI. The FSA noted, however, that the classification of *muḍārabah* as a deposit contract may not be appropriate in other contexts,[95] suggesting that it may not always treat PLS modes as deposits.

In order to meet the demands of the sharia with regard to the *muḍārabah* contract the IBB adopted an innovative solution. Islamic finance institutions may offer an account in which a customer's money is invested into a pool from which returns are paid and the capital is guaranteed. In the case of loss, the bank is required, in accordance with the law, to provide funds from its own resources to ensure that customers are repaid in full. Customers have the right to decide whether they wish to receive full

[93] SI 2001/544. [94] SI 2001/1062.

[95] Michael Ainley, Ali Mashayekhi, Robert Hicks, Arshadur Rahman and Ali Ravalia (n 1) 14.

repayment in the case of losses arising and are advised that they will be acting contrary to the sharia if they choose to accept full repayment.[96]

The UK deposit guarantee scheme is a further impediment to the application of sharia-authentic modes of PLS investment. Deposits are guaranteed in the United Kingdom by the Financial Services Compensation Scheme up to £85,000 per person per firm against firms declared in default,[97] as required by the Deposit Guarantee Scheme directive.[98] The directive was implemented in Part XV of FSMA 2000, which covers all regulated activities.[99]

The deposit guarantee scheme would guarantee a return to the investor despite any losses that may accrue. This runs contrary to the principle of profit- and loss-sharing. Furthermore, the scheme invests its funds in interest-bearing accounts and is not structured to segregate Islamic funds from conventional banks' interest-bearing funds. Some states have found solutions to these problems. Turkey has taken pains to engineer a solution by establishing a sharia-compatible deposit *takāful* in which Islamic funds are pooled. Malaysia has also launched a deposit insurance scheme that segregates Islamic deposits.[100] This particular problem has not been addressed in the United Kingdom.

The implication for IFIs in the United Kingdom is that by law they are not permitted to offer PLS accounts on the liabilities side of their balance sheets. IFIs are still able to offer PLS modes on the asset side but in practice these investments have been much less attractive than sales-based contracts.

The PRA avoids a whole host of principal–agent risks, including consumer protection issues, by treating the *muḍārabah* as a deposit. Further, income recognition policy and the funding structure of ventures, i.e. an IFI's profit distribution between IAHs and shareholders, do not need to be regulated. As long as returns on IAH funds and shareholder funds are properly disclosed, market discipline should ensure that appropriate distributions are made. If the IFI, acting as an agent, appropriates too

[96] *Ibid.*

[97] FSCS, 'Compensation Limits', Financial Services Compensation Scheme, 2010, www.fscs.org.uk/what-we-cover/eligibility-rules/compensation-limits/. Accessed 24 March 2014.

[98] Council Directive 94/19/EC of the European Parliament of the Council of 30 May 1994 on deposit-guarantee schemes [1994] OJ L135; amended by Directive 2009/14/EC.

[99] E. P. Ellinger, Eva Lomnicka and Richard Hooley, *Ellinger's Modern Banking Law* (Oxford University Press, 2006), 49.

[100] Juan Sole, 'Introducing Islamic Banks into Conventional Banking' in Amer Al-Roubaie and Shafiq Alvi (eds.), *Islamic Banking and Finance* (London: Routledge 2010), 122.

large a share of the profit, its competitors will seek to attract its investors/depositors.[101] Finally, problems related to corporate governance and capital adequacy requirements are avoided. In particular, IAHs rightly do not have an interest in shareholder-type rights as long as they are assured of their principal investment. The issue continues to bedevil jurisdictions in which IAHs' equity-like holdings are not allowed participation in the governance of the IFI.[102]

In April 2008 the IBB introduced a deposit-taking investment account known as *wakālah* in response to the particular requirements of British Muslim consumers. A *wakālah* is a traditional Islamic contract, the equivalent of agency. The *wakālah* investment account enables depositors' funds to be managed individually on a PLS basis; funds are not pooled with the monies of other investors and the bank offers customers an expected rate of return. If, for any reason, there are doubts that the expected rate of return will not be achieved, the deposit plus any accrued monies are returned to the customer.[103] The *wakālah* offers Muslim investors a compromise in the modern economy. Depositors are able to invest their monies with the assurance that their principal investments will be safeguarded while employing a traditional Islamic structure to facilitate their requirements. Contracts resembling the *wakālah* such as *wadī'ah yad ḍamānah* (guaranteed safekeeping) or *al-qard* (loan) are used as guaranteed principal contracts throughout the Islamic finance industry.[104]

The concept of PLS as a means of fund mobilisation – which represents the theoretical foundation of Islamic finance – has proven to be inadequate in meeting the requirements of modern Muslim investors. While it is legally prevented from being applied in the United Kingdom as well as many other jurisdictions worldwide, there is little evidence to suggest its popularity in the absence of legal restrictions. The result is that IFIs accept deposits in an almost identical manner as conventional banks do. Therefore, UK financial services law affects the manner of fund mobilisation undertaken by IFIs but this is in no way the only or

[101] Michael Clode (n 51) 73.

[102] Hennie van Greuning and Zamir Iqbal, *Risk Analysis for Islamic Banks* (Washington, DC: The World Bank, 2008), 193.

[103] Joseph DiVanna and Antoine Sreih, *A New Financial Dawn: The Rise of Islamic Finance* (Cambridge: Leonardo and Francis Press, 2009), 45.

[104] Asyraf Wajdi Dusuki, 'Commodity Murabahah Programme (CMP): An Innovative Approach to Liquidity Management' in Mohd Daud Bakar and Engku Adawiah Engku Ali (eds.), *Essential Readings in Islamic Finance* (Kuala Lumpur: CERT, Centre for Research and Training, 2008), 175.

even primary reason why PLS is an inadequate instrument of mobilising depositors' funds. In terms of investor choices and product uptake empirical evidence suggests that a Muslim investor's preference for religiously authentic products does not supplant their need for the stability and predictability of modern financial practices or for returns that approximate conventional earnings. For example, it has been documented that the religious element of Islamic financial products represents the most important factor in British Muslims' uptake of such products. Yet in practice the higher cost of Islamic financial products such as Islamic home mortgages has prevented a vigorous uptake.[105]

British Muslim consumers are not likely to forgo the high and stable returns offered by conventional banks.[106] In this sense, Muslim investor preferences are not intrinsically different than conventional preferences,[107] suggesting that the globalisation of Muslim consumer values may also be contributing to the transformation of classical notions of Islamic commercial law.

The next section underscores the importance of the SSB to the concept of Islamic financial services. The section deals with the responsibilities, processes and risks regulators encounter when dealing with SSBs. Some difficult questions are then posed.

6.6 The sharia audit process

The sharia audit process is an integral part of the corporate governance of IFIs. The SSB is the primary organ responsible for ensuring the integrity and credibility of the IFI by issuing fatwas and auditing the sharia compliance in all aspects of the products, operations and activities of the financial institution.[108] This includes both the *ex ante* and *ex post* aspects of all Islamic finance transactions, which indicates that both the legal composition of contracts and the way in which an Islamic financial product

[105] Mohammed Elkhatim Mamoun Tameme, *Demand and Supply Conditions of Islamic Housing Finance in the UK: Perceptions of Muslim Clients* (University of Durham, Ph.D. Thesis, 2009), 199–201.

[106] However, some populations of Muslim-majority states do favour Islamic financial services even if forced to sacrifice profits. See Ernst & Young, 'The Islamic Funds & Investments Report' (2008), 40, www.ncusar.org/programs/09-02-17-materials/EY_Islamic_funds_investment_report_2008.pdf. Accessed 25 March 2014; Elisabetta Montanaro (n 42) 119.

[107] Theodore Karasik, Frederic Wehrey and Steven Strom, 'Islamic Finance in a Global Context: Opportunities and Challenges' (2007) 7 *Chicag.Journ.Int'l.Law* 379, 390.

[108] IFSB, 'Guiding Principles on Corporate Governance for Institutions Offering Only Islamic Financial Services (Excluding Islamic Insurance [Takaful] Institutions and

is transacted must be reviewed for their sharia compliance.[109] The audit process involves the review of investment policies, the disposal of non-sharia-compliant income, the monitoring of charitable activities, as well as the calculation and payment of *zakāh*.[110] Finally, an SSB should certify in an annual report that an IFI has complied with the sharia in all of the tasks outlined above.[111]

In practice, the internal sharia audit systems of IFIs differ according to provisions stipulated in firms' articles of association or, in some jurisdictions, according to national regulatory requirements. Yet, according to a survey of thirteen IFIs, all firms were responsible for their own *ex ante* monitoring of sharia compliance. Only infrequently did national or international regulators stipulate SSB-rules that detailed specific competencies, decision-making authority and the composition of such bodies.[112] Regulators who do oversee IFIs' internal sharia auditing processes delegate responsibility for the design and functioning of such systems to IFIs, which allows secular regulators the freedom to regulate these processes indirectly.[113]

For example, the articles of association of IBB describe its sharia-related supervision accordingly: 'It is intended that the business affairs of the company shall be conducted in accordance with Sharia'a. Activities of the Company will at all times be supervised by the Sharia'a supervisory committee. The Directors of the Company are obliged to ensure that the business of the Company is at all times Sharia'a compliant'.[114] This disclosure does not clarify SSB procedures for ensuring these objectives, nor does it offer indications of how the SSB arrives at fatwas, which sanction the products and services the bank offers.

Sharia scholars should perform regular audits of new products or transactions and issue fatwas if they are satisfied that the product meets sharia guidelines.[115] Straightforward products such as *murābaḥah*, *ijārah* and *wakālah* usually involve minimal oversight due to their relatively

Islamic Mutual Funds)' (2006), para. 47, www.ifsb.org/standard/ifsb3.pdf. Accessed 25 March 2014.

109 *Ibid*., para 48(i). 110 *Ibid*., para 48(ii).

111 Wafik Grais and Matteo Pelligrini, *Corporate Governance and Sharia Compliance in Institutions Offering Islamic Financial Services*, World Bank Policy Research Working Paper 4054 (Washington, DC: The World Bank, 2006), 7.

112 Hennie van Greuning and Zamir Iqbal (n 102) 189.

113 Hari Bhambra (n 38) 202.

114 IBB, *Articles of Association of the Islamic Bank of Britain* (London: Islamic Bank of Britain, 2008), 9–10.

115 Wafik Grais and Matteo Pelligrini (n 111) 7.

standardised forms. More innovative and complex products such as *sukuk*, *wa'd*-based instruments (derivatives-based hedging instruments) and hybrid sharia structures, however, require direct and prolonged involvement in the development process.[116] According to the industry, many complex products are channelled through a long development process only to be rejected as *ḥarām*, which clearly impacts the competitiveness of IFIs.[117]

Despite these safeguards, IFIs' sharia audit systems raise serious concerns regarding a conventional regulator's ability to deal with them effectively. In particular, conflicts of interest often surround the appointment of members of the sharia board. The AAOIFI standard for this stipulates that members should be appointed by the Board of Trustees for a four-year term[118] so that SSB members are not subject to any undue influence by the executive management, which should not have the authority to appoint or to dismiss them.[119] While the application of this standard varies from country to country, according to one survey conducted by the International Institute in Islamic Thought, almost 80 per cent of sharia board member appointments were made directly by management. Another survey conducted by Hasan Yusuf Dawud in 1996 found that only 39 per cent of appointments were made by shareholders.[120] Returning to the example of the IBB, SSB members there are appointed and suspended directly by directors, so sharia scholars are, in effect, dependent on the firm's management for their continued employment.[121] Sharia scholars therefore have an economic stake in the firm and cannot be said to carry out their roles independently.

In practice conflicts of interest may be mitigated to some extent by sharia scholars' ethical standards and the high cost that would be inflicted upon their reputation and career prospects should their services be deemed to have denigrated the sharia.[122] However, the risk raises

[116] Muhammad Nurullah Shikder, 'Placing Faith in Islamic Finance', *New Horizon*, January–March 2009, 30, www.islamic-banking.com/resources/7/NewHorizon%20Previouse%20Issues/NewHorizon_JanMar09.pdf. Accessed 25 March 2014.

[117] Michael Ainley, Ali Mashayekhi, Robert Hicks, Arshadur Rahman and Ali Ravalia (n 1) 15.

[118] AAOIFI (n 39) xii.

[119] Mohammed Daud Bakar, 'The Shari'a Supervisory Board and Issues of Shari'a Rulings and Their Harmonisation in Islamic Banking and Finance' in Simon Archer and Rifaat Ahmed Abdel Karim (eds.), *Islamic Finance: Innovation and Growth* (London: Euromoney Books, 2002), 78.

[120] *Ibid.* [121] IBB (n 114) 9–10.

[122] Hennie van Greuning and Zamir Iqbal (n102) 189.

important questions about whether SSBs are in a position to credibly perform their duties to the best of their ability and in accordance with the body's religious aspirations. In assuming the role of vetting Islamic financial products and services for their sharia compatibility, the SSB takes responsibility for the religious interests of the Muslim consumer or investor. The responsibility of sharia scholars to assess independently the substance of Islamic financial products for their compatibility with sharia principles is a serious one.

Another survey conducted by the International Institute of Islamic Thought brought an equally serious problem to attention. The survey sought to uncover the methods by which sharia scholars came to know of a sharia-relevant problem or issue, which required their expertise. SSBs that had established permanent offices in IFIs and whose duty it was to vet all products and related documentation totalled 10.8 per cent of all respondents. SSBs that conducted periodic meetings to address issues brought forth by the management, totalled a staggering 48.5 per cent. Only 6.2 per cent of respondents addressed sharia issues by way of regular audit. Finally, 27.3 per cent described having employed alternative methodologies to undertake sharia-related tasks.[123] The implication of this survey, if it is to be taken as a general trend, is troubling. The disproportionate percentage of SSB respondents who come to address issues of sharia relevance via their firm's management reveals a strong level of dependence upon the availability, amount and quality of information supplied by the management. While there are a number of reasons why a firm's management could fail to disclose sharia-relevant information to its SSB, the circumstances demonstrate the pitfalls of moral hazard that threaten the credibility of the sharia internal audit system.

A related issue concerns the qualifications and skills of SSB members and hence the quality and consistency of judgment employed in making sharia-related decisions. Sharia scholars are expected to be knowledgeable in Islamic law as well as financial and accounting practices. Yet, in practice, very few scholars, on a global basis, are considered to possess expertise in all these disciplines.[124] Moreover, no formalised system of accreditation or professional association has been established so as to provide regulators with the knowledge and confidence that sharia scholars

[123] Mohammed Daud Bakar (n 119) 81.

[124] Wafik Grais and Matteo Pellegrini, *Corporate Governance in Institutions Offering Islamic Financial Services: Issues and Options*, World Bank Policy Research Working Paper (Washington, DC: The World Bank, 2006), 20.

are competent and capable of fulfilling their auditing and advisory roles, despite IFSB recommendations.[125] While Malaysia has taken steps to remedy this problem by creating a national sharia advisory council, other countries such as the United Kingdom have been very reluctant to do so for reasons that have been examined.[126] However, the rather low percentage of sharia scholars who are able to combine knowledge of the sharia with financial theory is gradually improving with the introduction of many educational programmes in Islamic finance, as well as state-based law and conventional finance.[127] In addition, many IFIs have established in-house sharia training programmes in which young scholars are paired up with senior scholars on a mentoring basis.[128] The recruitment and training of additional staff with sharia knowledge and financial expertise will contribute significantly to the quality of sharia supervision and will help to dispel conflict of interest issues associated with multiple SSB memberships.

The issue of consistency of sharia legal opinions across IFIs and jurisdictions continues to bedevil the industry, as noted in Chapter 4 concerning the issue of sharia standardisation. Besides limiting the growth prospects of the industry, however, a lack of consistency undermines consumer confidence in the types of product that have been allowed and in the industry as a whole.[129]

Another issue concerns the disclosure of all information relating to an IFI's sharia supervisory process. In general, investors are faced with an absence of information relating to the activities of the SSB. Ideally, an IFI would disclose the duties, competence, composition and decision making of the SSB, including the publication of all fatwas.[130] In practice, the irregular conduct of the internal sharia audit and the non-existent provision of information concerning the SSB's decision making disadvantages the consumer from making optimal investment decisions. Finally, the fatwa concerning the financial product provides no indication of the legal reasoning employed to approve a product. This lack of disclosure discourages confidence in the industry and prevents a larger role for market discipline from taking effect.

125 IFSB (n 108) para. 52.
126 Rodney Wilson (n 44) 385. Reasons include the UK government's unwillingness to involve itself in the process of religious interpretation.
127 Mohd Daud Bakar (n 119) 78.
128 Muhammad Nurullah Shikder (n 116) 31
129 Wafik Grais and Matteo Pellegrini (n 124) 20–1.
130 Hennie van Greuning and Zamir Iqbal (n 28) 36.

Once a product has been approved and formally launched, 'sharia supervision may take the form of ongoing monitoring through periodic audits. Such audits may be undertaken by means of site visits, document reviews, or consultation with management at regular intervals'.[131] In practice, however, the *ex post* verification of transactions has received much less attention from SSBs. Most IFIs, in fact, do not undertake an *ex post* verification of transactions for their sharia-compliance.[132] This was recently highlighted in the 2008 AAOIFI statement concerning the failure of IFIs to properly monitor the transaction of Islamic financial products and services – in this case, the manner of *sukuk* issuance. AAOIFI admonished SSBs for limiting their work solely to the *ex ante* review of products and services. Its SSB stated that:

> Shari'ah Supervisory Boards should not limit their role to the issuance of fatwa on the permissibility of the structure of sukuk. All relevant contracts and documents related to the actual transaction must be carefully reviewed [by them], and then they should oversee the actual means of implementation, and then make sure that the operation complies, at every stage, with Shari'ah guidelines and requirements as specified in the Shari'ah Standards.[133]

The next section deals with the particular approach of the FSA/PRA to regulating SSBs.

6.7 The risks of sharia non-compliance

As mentioned in Chapter 5, the UK government utilises neutral language when referring to Islamic financial transactions in the United Kingdom. This approach reflects the government's unease in transgressing the social boundaries regarding the appropriate role of religion in the United Kingdom. In line with this approach the government takes no responsibility for problems of choice of evaluative criteria such as whether an Islamic financial product or service complies with the sharia as it states

[131] Yusuf Talal DeLorenzo, 'Shari'a Supervision in Modern Islamic Finance' (2009), www.guidanceresidential.com/wp-content/uploads/2013/10/shariah_supervision_in_modern_islamic_finance.pdf. Accessed 3 May 2014.

[132] Habhajan Singh, 'Absence of Shariah Audit a "Serious Loophole"' *Malaysian Reserve*, 29 June 2009, 2.bp.blogspot.com/_PGH0ddCyO7U/Skrsjw4GpsI/AAAAAAAAAZw/q-ro7fBbfi4/s1600-h/090629-TMR-ShariahAudit-MASB-IssamRasameel-p32.JPG. Accessed 25 March 2014.

[133] AAOIFI, 'AAOIFI Statement on Sukuk' (The Accounting and Auditing Organization for Islamic Financial Institutions, February 2008), islamicbankers.files.wordpress.com/2008/09/aaoifi_sb_sukuk_feb2008_eng.pdf. Accessed 8 April 2014.

that this would be 'inappropriate' as a 'secular' regulator.[134] Individual financial institutions are wholly responsible for determining the sharia compliance of the products and services they offer. In accordance with AAOIFI standards, most IFIs in the United Kingdom opt to form an SSB comprising three sharia scholars trained in classical Islamic commercial law, although others have chosen to use sharia consultancy services or have merely hired a single sharia scholar. The state does not stipulate any requirement regarding sharia compliance or enforcement with respect to the many functions of Islamic financial intermediation. The FSA stated that 'it would not be appropriate, even if it were possible, for the FSA to judge between different interpretations of sharia law'.[135] Hence the FSA believed that neutrality could be achieved by avoiding any subjectivity or bias and by focusing on concrete data that can be understood in absolute terms and free of context. Moreover, a neutral position can be claimed between and vis-à-vis faith-based arguments.[136]

The accommodation of the unique role of sharia scholars within IFIs is acknowledged by the FSA as having potential implications for their solvency. In particular, the market's response to a breach of sharia rules could dispel confidence in IFIs, as compromised assets would automatically be seen as liabilities and a bank's solvency could be thrown into question.[137] As IFIs become more systemically important and more closely connected with conventional banks, this risk increases,[138] particularly for large, wholesale institutions.

While such a scenario is unlikely to take place in the United Kingdom in the foreseeable future, the risks are more acute in regions such as the GCC, where Islamic finance and banking continues to increase its market share. In the United Kingdom anecdotal evidence suggests that British Muslims' low take-up of retail Islamic financial products is related to their highly sceptical opinion concerning the sharia-authenticity of Islamic financial products or the basic difference between them and conventional

[134] Her Majesty's Treasury, *The Development of Islamic Finance in the UK: The Government's Perspective* (London: HM Treasury, 2008), 19.

[135] Michael Ainley, Ali Mashayekhi, Robert Hicks, Arshadur Rahman and Ali Ravalia (n 1) 13.

[136] Maleiha Malik, 'Faith and the State of Jurisprudence' in Peter Oliver, Sionaidh Douglas Scott and Victor Tadors (eds.), *Faith in Law: Essays in Legal Theory* (Oxford: Hart Publishing, 2000), 138–9.

[137] Michael Ainley, Ali Mashayekhi, Robert Hicks, Arshadur Rahman and Ali Ravalia (n 1) 18–19.

[138] Juan Sole (n 100) 126.

products.[139] Overseas investments from Gulf state investors are even more dependent upon the industry gaining the trust and confidence of clients in the sharia authenticity of their products. The British investment bank, Kleinwort Benson, in its first stab at creating an Islamic unit trust in 1986, was not very successful, in part as a result of not employing a sharia supervisory board or even a single sharia advisor to monitor the fund. It had not established the necessary credibility with Gulf investors.[140] Yet the FSA's and now the PRA's approach to regulating IFIs places all its emphasis upon evaluating and mitigating the financial risk that institutions may present. It ignores the 'religious risk' associated with the development of the industry since it is not quantifiable.

The FSA acknowledged the unique role of SSBs in IFIs since these entities are responsible for approving and legitimating the 'Islamic' products and services that originate from such institutions. Yet the state stops short of developing criteria and procedures to address the qualitative nature of the boards other than those employed to examine corporate governance as applied to conventional financial institutions. The FSA's emphasis centred on the role of the SSB in each authorised firm with particular emphasis on the SSB's impact on the direction or operation of the firm. This is partly undertaken by reviewing the terms and conditions of sharia scholars' contracts.[141] The FSA (now PRA) must determine whether sharia scholars are assigned an executive role or whether they merely provide advisory services to the institution.

According to the FSA Approved Persons rules,[142] the suitability of anyone acting as a director is assessed according to fit and proper criteria. For example, these criteria relate to the competence and capability of the candidate, so a prospective director would be expected to have relevant experience and education. If a sharia scholar's role does resemble that of an executive director, multiple memberships of different financial institutions' SSBs would be problematic due to significant conflicts of interest. On an international basis the practice of sharia scholars sitting on multiple

139 MCB, *Islamic Finance Transparency Standard: A Consultation* (London: The Muslim Council of Britain, 2008), 5.

140 Rodney Wilson, 'Challenges and Opportunities for Islamic Banking and Finance in the West: The United Kingdom Experience' in Amer Al-Roubaie and Shafiq Alvi (eds.), *Islamic Banking and Finance* (New York: Routledge, 2010), 370.

141 Michael Ainley, Ali Mashayekhi, Robert Hicks, Arshadur Rahman and Ali Ravalia (n 1) 14.

142 FSA, 'The Fit and Proper Test for Approved Persons (FIT)' in *FSA Handbook* (London: Financial Services Authority, 2011), fshandbook.info/FS/html/handbook/FIT. Accessed 24 March 2014.

supervisory boards is a common, if not regular, occurrence. However, the FSA/PRA has determined to date that authorised IFIs employ sharia scholars in advisory roles only so that their responsibilities do not interfere in the management of the firm.[143] This finding is unconvincing as the SSB's objective to ensure the 'sharia compliance in all an entity's products and transactions'[144] plays a pivotal role in the organisation. Arguably, the SSB's existence legitimises the Islamic label and constitutes an important motivation for Muslim consumers' demand for Islamic financial products and services. It seems unlikely that those individuals who decide whether a product can be brought to market under the Islamic brand do not materially impact the management and overall direction of the firm.

The FSA justified its position by highlighting consumer protection requirements for IFIs to 'pay due regard to the interests of its customers and treat them fairly'.[145] The FSA's Treating Customers Fairly programme lays emphasis on the provision of clear information, suitable advice and an acceptable level of service.[146] However, these requirements do not oblige the FSA/PRA or the IFI to provide information on whether particular products are sharia-compliant. The FSA/PRA does require IFIs to provide an explanation of Islamic financial products and their associated risks,[147] but this information concerns the economic risks of products; it takes no notice of any qualitative attributes. For example, the government has made an effort to distribute factsheets on Islamic home mortgage purchase plans (known as HPPs), which provide a 'step-by-step guide to each product and the associated risks and benefits'.[148] Yet this information is not sufficient to determine whether such products comply with Islamic law.

Finally, issues concerning financial malfeasance and false advertising are applicable concerns. In particular, the Consumer Protection from Unfair Trading Regulations 2008[149] reinforces other consumer protection Acts including those covering trade descriptions[150] and fraud.[151] In general, this legislation makes illegal misleading actions based upon false information as to the nature or main characteristics of the product or service. Such actions are those which cause or are 'likely to cause the average consumer to take a transactional decision he would not have taken

[143] *Ibid.* [144] *Ibid.*, 15. [145] *Ibid.*, 24.
[146] *Ibid.* [147] *Ibid.*, 25. [148] *Ibid.*
[149] 'Consumer Protection', SI 2008/1277.
[150] Trade Descriptions Act 1968.
[151] Fraud Act 2006.

otherwise'.[152] Yet an offence can only be established under the regulations if it can be proven that the service provider knowingly or recklessly engaged in a misleading action.[153] Since there is no agreed standard on what constitutes sharia compliance other than the non-binding standard-setting efforts of international organisations such as AAOIFI, claims of false advertising are generally non-justiciable.

The following section addresses a higher level of law, EU law, and its impact on financial institutions operating in the United Kingdom and elsewhere. European Union regulatory law is an increasingly important source of law for EU member states and for global financial markets in general. It also provides an important demonstration of legal harmonisation and the ways in which such efforts affect financial market players.

6.8 The impact of EU regulatory harmonisation

Nation-state regulatory frameworks are increasingly subject to regional and international standard-setting initiatives designed to minimise the inefficiencies and distortions of global financial markets. These initiatives are conceived and designed by the leading global powers whose conception of the market economy is rooted in their national commercial interests. As a supranational authority the European Union increasingly wields considerable economic and regulatory rule-making power as the largest single market in the world and as an unrivalled supranational authority comprised of twenty-eight member states.[154] The EU occupies a position at the forefront of globalisation, premised on the transnationalisation of capital accumulation, regulation and the development of civil society.[155] Greater financial integration, fuelled by the creation of the Euro currency, has strengthened its rule-setting capacity on a global level.[156] An example is the EU's influence in the Basel process, which will be dealt with below.

152 'Consumer Protection', pt 2, s 5(2)(b).

153 MCB (n 139) 11–12.

154 Leading scholars argue that market size matters. See, for example, Daniel Drezner, *All Politics is Global: Explaining International Regulatory Regimes* (Princeton University Press, 2007), 32–3.

155 Hans-Juergen Bieling and Johannes Jaeger, 'Global Finance and the European Economy: the Struggle over Banking Regulation' in Bastiaan van Apeldoorn, Jan Drahokoupil and Laura Horn (eds.) *Contradictions and Limits of Neoliberal European Governance: From Lisbon to Lisbon* (New York: Palgrave Macmillan, 2009), 92.

156 *Ibid.* The Euro has provided a powerful impetus because it has eliminated exchange rate risk for a vast number of transactions, particularly in cross-border retail business. Full enjoyment of the potential benefits of currency union depends on efficient financial

Although the United Kingdom, along with the United States, has long dominated international financial issues on the basis of market size, the international composition of markets and the efficiency/sophistication of regulatory systems,[157] its role within the European Union has taken on added importance. This is due, on the one hand, to its long tradition of regulatory expertise and financial know-how. As a result the United Kingdom and the United States are globally known for the best practices their regulatory and supervisory systems establish.[158] On the other hand, the United Kingdom's membership of the European Union adds considerable regulatory weight to the global impact of the supranational authority, which is now considered to rival that of the long-time regulatory hegemon and largest economy in the world, the United States.[159]

In its bid to consolidate the single market and shore up the European currency, the EU produces legislation and regulatory rules designed to harmonise the financial markets of EU member states, albeit with international impact. Financial institutions operating in the United Kingdom or elsewhere in the European Union are subject to a growing body of EU banking and investment law, which requires member state implementation and enforcement. The development of the single market, legally enshrined in the 1986 Single European Act, underscores the objectives and scope of the European project. Article 13 states that: 'The internal market shall comprise an area without internal frontiers in which the free movement of goods, persons, services and capital is ensured in accordance with the provisions of this Treaty.'[160]

The creation of the internal market, although initially a project protective of the interests of neo-mercantilist and European capital classes, spurned the further integration of national economies and strengthened

institutions, deep and liquid capital markets, and sound, reliable and cheap infrastructure. See Howard Davies and David Green (n 13) 130–1.

[157] Beth A Simmons, 'The International Politics of Harmonization: The Case of Capital Market Regulation' in David Vogel and Robert A. Kagan (eds.), *Dynamics of Regulatory Change: How Globalization Affects National Regulatory Policies* (Berkeley, CA: University of California Press, 2004), 46.

[158] *Ibid.*, 47–8.

[159] Elliot Posner, 'Changing Transatlantic Financial Regulatory Relations' in Geoffrey Underhill, Jasper Blom and Daniel Mügge (eds.), *Global Financial Integration Thirty Years On: From Reform to Crisis* (Cambridge University Press, 2010), 224. See also Daniel Drezner (n 154) 38.

[160] Single European Act [1986] OJ L169/23.

the impact of mostly US-centred globalising forces.[161] Market integration, while neutralising antagonisms between competing visions of Europe, allowed the neoliberal policy agenda to gain primacy. Since the 1990s the EU has increasingly taken on the role of promoting competition-oriented reforms of domestic labour policies and welfare systems.[162] The overriding objective of competitiveness often subsumes national concerns such as those of the labour movement and social democratic policy agendas.[163]

Initially, the single market was cobbled together on the basis of achieving a minimum level of harmonisation amongst member states' legal systems. The concepts of mutual recognition and home country control assisted in achieving this objective. In practical terms, this was largely undertaken via the implementation of directives. Conversely, the use of regulations creates a greater degree of harmonisation since regulations do not allow member states room for national transposition.[164] All EU directives and regulations are legally binding with the European Commission responsible for monitoring member states' implementation, while the European Court of Justice is empowered to enforce compliance.[165] Although supervision and enforcement capacities remain the prerogative of member states, market participants are increasingly governed by a single set of rules across the continent.[166]

EU regulatory harmonisation has evolved from the early practice of mutual regulatory recognition, which left a double-regulatory burden for a foreign entity attempting to establish itself in the host country.[167] This problem was solved by creating a single licence for an EU member state-authorised institution so that it may offer financial products and services throughout the European Union without the need for separate

[161] Bastiaan van Apeldoorn, 'The Contradictions of "Embedded Neoliberalism" and Europe's Multi-Level Legitimacy Crisis: The European Project and its Limits' in Bastiaan van Apeldoorn, Jan Drahokoupil and Laura Horn (eds.) *Contradictions and Limits of Neoliberal European Governance: From Lisbon to Lisbon* (New York: Palgrave Macmillan, 2009) 24.

[162] Hans-Juergen Bieling and Johannes Jaeger (n 155) 92.

[163] Bastiaan van Apeldoorn (n 161) 25–6.

[164] Rosa Lastra, 'The Governance Structure for Financial Supervision and Regulation in Europe' (Fall 2003) 10 *Colum.J.Eur.L.*, 49.

[165] Lucia Quaglia, 'The European Union in Regulating Global Finance', EUSA Conference Paper (Boston, 2011) 3, euce.org/eusa/2011/papers/12e_quaglia.pdf. Accessed 2 April 2014.

[166] Elliot Posner (n 159) 226.

[167] Howard Davies and David Green (n 13) 130.

authorisation in each member country.[168] Investment companies are also able to offer their products and services on the basis of this Council Directive.[169] Furthermore, the single licence provision of the directive establishes that the banking activities undertaken by a foreign bank in a host country are not limited by that state's banking model. The Banking Consolidation Directive, for example, is based on the German universal bank model in which a whole host of non-traditional banking activities such as securities trading, mergers and acquisitions, and portfolio management are conducted.[170] Islamic financial institutions authorised in the United Kingdom are therefore able to offer Islamic financial products and services to member state financial markets, which comprises approximately 20 million European Muslims. The Bank of London and the Middle East is the first UK-based Islamic bank to have taken advantage of this opportunity.[171]

By formally binding EU member states to legislation under EU treaties and devoting considerable effort to the creation of a single financial market, the European Union has achieved an advanced level of regulatory capacity that is both legally binding in member states and increasingly influential on the global stage.[172] This capacity looks set to increase as the trend toward greater integration of EU member states has taken on added significance in the wake of the 2008 global financial crisis. The crisis affecting highly indebted Eurozone countries exposed a critical lack of common European governance and decision-making authority, which led some states to act unilaterally in ways prejudicial to the long-term stability of the Eurozone.[173] But the crisis has served a useful purpose in galvanising member states to develop common economic institutions. Market pressures continue to demand regulatory and supervisory convergence

[168] Directive 2013/36 of the European Parliament and of the Council of 26 June 2013 on access to the activity of credit institutions and the prudential supervision of credit institutions and investment firms OJ L176/338.

[169] Silvia Fazio, *The Harmonization of International Commercial Law* (Alphen aan den Rijn: Kluwer Law International 2007), 156. Council Directive 93/22/EEC of 10 May 1993 on investment services in the securities field [1993] OJ L141 was repealed by Council Directive 2004/39/EC of 21 April 2004 on markets in financial instruments OJ L145/1.

[170] E. P. Ellinger, Eva Lomnicka and Richard Hooley (n 99) 57.

[171] Michael Ainley, Ali Mashayekhi, Robert Hicks, Arshadur Rahman and Ali Ravalia (n 1) 30.

[172] Elliot Posner, 'Making Rules for Global Finance: Transatlantic Regulatory Cooperation at the Turn of the Millennium' (Fall 2009) 63 *Int'l Org.*, 665, 668.

[173] For example, Germany's move to ban naked short-selling or Ireland's unilateral decision – in the midst of the global economic crisis – to ensure the full value of banking deposits. See Alan Crawford, 'Germany to Temporarily Ban Naked Short Selling, Some

within Eurozone countries. These forces are likely to lead to a more coherent institutional framework and eventually affect all financial services institutions operating within EU member states and internationally.[174]

The historical trend justifies these projections. In 2012, in the context of poorly functioning interbank markets, the tight provision of liquidity and continuing uncertainty concerning banks' exposure to sovereign debt, the European Council announced the establishment of a single supervisory mechanism (SSM) for credit institutions. An SSM is thought to be a first step in establishing a banking union, as its function would address EU-wide prudential supervision, an area that historically has been left to individual member states. The establishment of a single rulebook for financial services and supervision applied in the same manner to all credit institutions operating in member states will help to break the link between member states' sovereign debt and their financial institutions.[175]

6.9 Global regulatory initiatives

Prior to the abandonment of the Bretton Woods agreements and leading economies' transition to free-floating exchange rates, national regulators felt that the safety and soundness of their financial systems could be monitored unilaterally without the cooperation of foreign regulatory authorities. By the 1970s that perception had changed markedly.

Swaps of Euro Bonds', *Bloomberg*, May 2011, www.bloomberg.com/news/2010-05-18/germany-to-start-temporary-ban-on-naked-short-selling-of-euro-bonds-banks.html. Accessed 21 March 2014; and John Murray-Brown and Neil Dennis, 'Ireland Guarantees Six Banks' Deposits', *Financial Times*, 30 September 2008, www.ft.com/cms/s/0/2124f8f4-8eb9-11dd-946c-0000779fd18c.html3#axzz1XkWOA76T. Accessed 25 March 2014.

[174] The alternative is for the Eurozone to fail as a monetary union. Efforts towards regulatory and supervisory standardisation have accelerated in the past year with the establishment of a European Systemic Risk Board (ESRB) and the European System of Financial Supervisors (ESFS) in 2009. While the ESRB's recommendations will be non-binding, the three committees operating under the ESFS – the European Banking Authority, the European Securities and Markets Authority and the European Insurance and Occupational Pensions Authority – will have the power to issue binding technical standards; the power to adopt emergency decisions in periods of crisis (such as prohibiting short selling); and the power to authorise and supervise some cross-border European groups such as credit rating agencies and EU central counterparty clearing houses. European Commission, *Commission Staff Working Document* (Brussels: European Union, 2010); Freshfield Bruckhaus Deringer, *The New Regulatory Architecture: The Changing Role of the FSA* (Freshfields Bruckhaus Deringer, 2009), 2.

[175] European Commission, *European Financial Stability and Integration Report 2012*, Commission Staff Working Document, Brussels, April 2013), 17–18.

Regulators perceived the growing interdependence of banks as well as the diminishing effectiveness of national rules.[176] Moreover, growing interbank relations meant that weak financial institutions potentially could transmit externalities to other financial institutions in the global banking system.[177] The absence of international agreements concerning the sharing of information and the establishment of common regulatory standards for preserving the safety and soundness of global markets increased the danger that national banking problems could be rapidly transmitted anywhere within the banking network.[178]

In response to the 1980s savings and loan crisis in the United States and a growing trend toward capital deterioration the two largest and most influential financial centres, the United States and the United Kingdom, concluded a bilateral agreement that provided for a common definition of capital, a risk-weighting system for each class of assets and a formula for calculating capital requirements according to the risk-weighted asset profile of individual financial institutions. The agreement set off intense negotiations amongst G10 countries concerning a common approach to capital requirements.[179]

By 1987 G10 countries had adopted guidelines for evaluating their financial institutions' capital requirements and had agreed to require a minimum level of capital by 1992. By the end of 1993 all internationally active financial institutions had attained capital levels well in excess of the required minimum.[180] By the mid-1990s the European Union, not yet the global rule maker it would eventually become, had also transposed G10 guidelines into its first Capital Adequacy Directive.[181]

The Basel Committee on Banking Supervision (BCBS), a committee of the Bank for International Settlements (BIS) headquartered in Basel, Switzerland, represents the formalised body that grew out of this process. It has been described as the herald of international regulatory cooperation across the globe by a non-state administrative actor, which seeks to form a response to the dramatic globalisation of the economy.[182] Basel's

[176] Ethan B. Kapstein, 'Resolving the Regulator's Dilemma: International Coordination of Banking Regulations' (1989) 43 *Int'l Org* 323, 328–9.

[177] Beth A. Simmons (n 157) 601.

[178] Ethan B. Kapstein (n 176) 326.

[179] Beth A. Simmons (n 157) 602–3. [180] *Ibid.*, 603–4.

[181] See Council Directive 93/6/EEC on the Capital Adequacy of Investment Firms and Credit Institutions [1993] OJ L204/13.

[182] David Zaring, 'International Law by Other Means: The Twilight Existence of International Financial Regulatory Organizations' (1998) 33 *Tex Int'l LJ* 282, 285.

chief objective, to strengthen the 'resilience of the banking sector',[183] is sought by creating international regulatory standards that can be applied to all banks operating internationally or on a cross-border basis. Capital adequacy requirements, in particular, are designed to protect the safety and stability of the global financial system from the activities of under-capitalised institutions. Now comprised of senior banking supervisors from the central banks and regulatory authorities of leading world economies, the Basel Committee managed to compel its members to fully implement the 1988 Basel Accord (Basel I).[184]

Basel capital adequacy standards have left a lasting imprint on the international financial system as evidenced by the intention of at least 100 countries to implement the Basel II agreement at varying dates. The process is widely acknowledged for its contribution to the widespread use of risk-based capital outlays both as a measure of banks' soundness and as a trigger for regulatory intervention.[185] The accord has become a signpost of a country's commitment to sound and competitive financial markets, albeit with adjustments to local conditions. Members are said to value the non-binding informality of Basel agreements in that these provide flexibility in local implementation – thus enhancing the democratic legitimacy of the agreements. Members cannot be threatened with judicial action in the case of non-compliance. Instead the organisation's extra-legal status employs a type of international soft law that induces members to comply by 'naming and shaming' or extracting reputational costs associated with non-compliance.[186]

The global adoption of Basel capital adequacy standards is incentivised by the disciplining forces of the free market, including the leading positions of Western financial institutions in the global economy. Information asymmetries, which characterise financial markets in general, can be tempered by rules requiring capital adequacy as these convey information

[183] Basel Committee on Banking Supervision, *Basel II and Revisions to the Capital Requirements Directive*, remarks by Stefan Walter, Secretary General, Basel Committee on Banking Supervision, to the European Parliament Committee on Economic and Monetary Affairs on the BCBS's reform programme (Basel Committee on Banking Supervision May 2010).

[184] David Zaring (n 182) 290. The Committee consists of representatives from supervisory authorities and central banks from Argentina, Australia, Belgium, Brazil, Canada, China, France, Germany, Hong Kong, India, Indonesia, Italy, Japan, Korea, Luxembourg, Mexico, the Netherlands, Russia, Saudi Arabia, Singapore, South Africa, Spain, Sweden, Switzerland, Turkey, the United Kingdom and the United States.

[185] Joao Cabral dos Santos (n 15) 42.

[186] David Zaring (n 182) 304.

concerning the quality of a financial institution and its potential as counter-party to an agreement. Financial institutions are not likely to neglect such standards and to opt for price alone as their international reputation would suffer as a result.[187] Moreover, jurisdictions will freely choose to adopt Basel standards so as to signal their competitiveness with leading financial centres. Failure to emulate the regulatory innovations of leading financial centres could make doing business in the home jurisdiction costly or unduly risky. Powerful market forces incentivise the adoption of Basel standards.[188]

For example, Gulf banks are highly dependent on global capital markets as investment outlets, though – unusually – not as sources of capital. Indeed, more than 70 per cent of their holdings are invested in North American and European markets. These same financial institutions rely on Western banks for their financial expertise and international networks, including their facilitation of short-term liquidity management. These banks must comply with Basel standards so as to obtain regulatory legitimacy and approval. Their ability to effectively operate in the global economy would be impaired if not prevented outright were they not willing or able to do so.[189]

Gulf Cooperation Council states have implemented Basel proposals extensively, particularly those concerning capital adequacy, large exposures, derivatives and markets risks, accounting standards and loan provisioning. Moreover, the states have worked towards the potential integration of payments systems, which would create solid regional linkages in an important area of the world. This development marks a significant adoption and implementation of the Basel Committee's regulatory and supervisory recommendations on a global basis.[190]

The founding countries of the Basel Committee did not include any developing countries, let alone those in which Islamic finance is prevalent. None of these countries were included in either Basel I or Basel II negotiations.[191] The premise that great powers, which oversee large internal markets, are the primary actors involved in the creation of rules that govern the global economy finds strong support in the Basel process.

[187] Beth A. Simmons (n 157). [188] *Ibid.*, 49.

[189] Kristin Smith, *Islamic Banking and the Politics of International Financial Harmonization*, Paper presented at Harvard University Forum on Islamic Finance, 'Isḷamic Finance: Current Legal and Regulatory Issues', Cambridge, 2005), 170–1.

[190] George Alexander Walker, *International Banking Regulation: Law, Policy and Practice* (The Hague: Kluwer Law International 2001), 63.

[191] Elisabetta Montanaro (n 42) 113.

The global application of Basel standards belies the relatively few actors involved in their formulation, with the foreseeable result that the preferences embodied in such standards reflect a narrow set of private and autonomous state interests.[192] Basel rules are largely seen as promoting an Anglo-Saxon model of capitalism, since they help to consolidate the dominance of global finance. For instance, the role of ratings agencies, investment firms and analysts are strengthened.[193]

The rising importance of the G20 has done little to change this calculus. Despite a larger number of states given membership on the Basel Committee, the regulatory power structure established by developed countries and their dominant financial institutions remains intact and advantageous to their relative financial strengths.[194] A pattern in which market size translates into regulatory power in the era of globalisation is consistently observable.[195]

Basel II received European-wide compliance.[196] In accordance with the Second Council Directive of the European Union of 15 December 1989, the United Kingdom implemented the EU Capital Accord within the framework of the FSMA 2000.[197] An Individual Capital Guidance (ICG) scheme applies to all banks operating in the United Kingdom whereby recommendations are made based on Basel II requirements.[198]

In the following sub-sections Basel capital adequacy requirements, including the most recent Basel III standards, are analysed with a view to their function and impact on IFIs.

[192] Geoffrey Underhill, Jasper Blom and Daniel Mügge, 'Introduction: the Challenges and Prospects of Global Financial Integration' in Geoffrey Underhill, Jasper Blom and Daniel Mügge (eds), *Global Financial Integration Thirty Years On: From Reform to Crisis* (Cambridge University Press 2010), 13. See also Stijn Claessens and Geoffrey Underhill, 'The Political Economy of Basel II in the International Financial Architecture' in *ibid.*, 118.

[193] Hans-Juergen Bieling and Johannes Jaeger (n 155) 88.

[194] *Ibid.*, 14.

[195] Daniel Drezner (n 154) 32. See also Beth A. Simmons (n 157) 589–620.

[196] Council Directive 2006/48/EC of the European Parliament and of the Council of 14 June 2006 relating to the taking up and pursuit of the business of credit institutions (recast) [2006] OJ L177; Council Directive 2006/49/EC of the European Parliament and of the Council of 14 June 2006 on the capital adequacy of investment firms and credit institutions (recast) OJ L 177.

[197] FSA, *UK Implementation of the New Basel and EU Capital Adequacy Standards* (London: Financial Services Authority, 2002), 10. Second Council Directive 89/646/EEC of 15 December 1989 on the coordination of laws, regulations and administrative provisions relating to the taking up and pursuit of the business of credit institutions and amending Directive 77/780/EEC [1989] OJ L311.

[198] IBB (n 56) 27.

6.9.1 *The impact of Basel II*

Basel II was agreed in 2004 and relies on three complementary elements or pillars. Pillar I establishes minimum capital requirements based on the application of risk weights to a bank's assets. In addition to requiring capital reserves for market risk, operational risks are now capital-charged, and emphasis has been placed on the measurement of credit risk.[199] Adequate capitalisation is viewed as a first line of defence in protecting a bank from insolvency and thereby insulating the financial system from contagion. Further, mandating minimum capital adequacy requirements is a means to reduce competitive inequality due to differential regulatory treatment amongst international banks. While increased capital adequacy reserves reduce profits by forcing banks to retain more of their capital, they are also believed to increase the safety and soundness of financial institutions.[200] Most banks have been shown to reduce the scale of investment to incorporate larger capital buffers. In turbulent economic periods banks tend to hold capital above the minimum capital requirements. Yet despite increased reserves in bad times, bank failure is not necessarily lower relative to periods of market upswing. Unsurprisingly, with the exception of very small banks, banks have been shown to fail less in economic upswings, suggesting that capital reserve requirements play 'a powerful disciplinary role in containing excessive risk-taking during economic upswings'.[201]

Pillar II mandates supervisory reviews, including an assessment of a bank's internal systems and controls, and risk management procedures. This assessment may result in an adjustment of pillar I capital levels. Finally, pillar III calls for more stringent market discipline, including detailed rules on disclosure and transparency.[202]

The Accord has retained the basic requirement of banks to hold total capital equivalent to 8 per cent of risk-weighted assets. Its chief innovation consists in allowing banks' own internal systems to assess risks as part of the input to capital calculation. A detailed set of minimum requirements provides a framework to ensure the integrity of internal risk assessments. Supervisors are left to judge a bank's readiness to apply

[199] Natalie Schoon, *Islamic Banking and Finance* (London: Spiramus Press, 2009), 167.

[200] Kristin Smith (n 189) 178.

[201] Haibin Zhu, *Capital Regulation and Banks' Financial Decisions*, BIS Working Papers (Basel: Bank for International Settlements, 2007), 18–20.

[202] Howard Davies and David Green (n 13) 43.

its own internal systems as part of the regulatory process. A number of options exist for banks and supervisors in how they deliver the capital requirement for credit and operational risk. Banks may choose the most appropriate approach for their particular operations and financial market infrastructure. These approaches consist of: the standardised approach, which is viewed as appropriate for banks lacking sophisticated risk models (and geared towards financial institutions in the developing world); or one of two approaches based on the application of internal ratings known as the foundation or advanced internal ratings-based (IRB) approaches. This flexible set of strategies does not deviate from the establishment of minimum capital requirements for internationally active banks, while national authorities may adopt arrangements that set higher levels of minimum capital or other supplementary capital measures.[203]

This is the approach taken by the United Kingdom in its recent push to strengthen the liquidity standards of FSA/PRA-authorised financial institutions in the aftermath of near financial meltdown. The regime requires firms to increase their liquidity buffers with highly liquid, high-quality government debt instruments such as gilts, highly rated bonds from countries of the European Economic Area (EEA), Canada, Japan, Switzerland and the United States. Further, increased buffers may consist of reserves held with the Bank of England or with the central banks of the countries listed above.[204] These added requirements present an additional challenge to IFIs as bonds and central bank reserve facilities are interest bearing.

Basel differentiates capital into two categories: tier 1 and tier 2 with requirements based on their relative size and relation to assets. Capital, from the perspective of a bank, can be defined as share capital, reserves (equity) and non-deposit liabilities. Thus a distinction is made between internal capital (shares, reserves) and external capital (non-deposit liabilities).[205] Assets receive different risk-weighting treatment according to a standardised risk-grid that assigns greater weight for a bank's business with the private sector, as opposed to central governments, and for non-OECD states versus those of the OECD.[206] Risk weighting according to the type of counterparty is designed to differentiate between low- and

[203] *Ibid.*, 44–5.

[204] FSA (n 24) 54.

[205] John Board and Hatim el-Tahrir, 'Risk and the Need for Capital' in Simon Archer and Rifaat Ahmed Abdel Karim (eds.), *Islamic Finance: The New Regulatory Challenge* (Singapore: John Wiley & Sons (Asia), 2013), 277.

[206] Kristin Smith (n 189) 179.

high-quality borrowers. Regulatory capital is determined by aggregating all risk-weighted assets and multiplying these by 8 per cent.[207] The scheme potentially restricts Islamic banks from investing in asset classes such as government bonds, which appear prominently in banks' balance sheets, particularly in more volatile markets in developing countries. Observers have also noted that IFI's preferred mode of trade financing, the *murābaḥah*, may be less competitive since these contracts are geared towards private industry and thus attract a higher capital charge. According to the Basel framework, these instruments would require a risk weight of 100 per cent or more, resulting in a relatively higher risk weighting for non-OECD private sector assets.[208] Non-financial, tangible assets such as copper, houses and automobiles – the preferred assets of *murābaḥah* trades – generally require banks to retain more capital reserves.[209] *Ijārah*-based structures such as those used in UK home mortgage plans are subject to a 50 per cent higher capital risk weighting than a conventional home mortgage, in accordance with Basel II's provisions for mortgage loans on residential properties.[210] The prevalence of *murābaḥah* and *ijārah*-based contracts in IFIs' balance sheets exposes them to a competitive vulnerability that conventional institutions do not countenance.

Furthermore, Basel II differentiates significant equity positions from debt-based financing. Preferred modes of mobilising funds via the *muḍārabah* PLS contract can be characterised as equity positions in the banking book when unrestricted IAHs are liable for any losses. However, as examined above, the more prevalent scenario is that a part of the bank's risk-bearing capital derives from PLS accounts by virtue of a bank guaranteeing the capital funds. That part is risk weighted and included in the denominator of the CAR formula. As a result, an Islamic bank would have to retain regulatory capital in proportion to the risks of the assets. Banking supervisors are responsible for determining the proportion.[211]

Basel II introduces counterparty grading (or a risk-sensitive capital regime) so as to distinguish between low- and high-quality borrowers. This disadvantages small financial institutions, which are forced to maintain higher capital charges in good times to reduce the level of bank

[207] Natalie Schoon (n 199) 168.

[208] Kristin Smith (n 189) 179.

[209] Dalila Abu Bakr, *Basel II Enhances Islamic Banks* (Islamic Finance Asia, 2008), 26, www.iefpedia.com/english/wp-content/uploads/2009/11/Basel-II-Enhances-Islamic-Banks.pdf. Accessed 17 August 2014.

[210] Mansur Noibi (n 45) 185.

[211] Simon Archer and Rifaat Ahmed Abdel Karim (n 35) 292.

lending under the standardised approach. Development and compliance costs may exclude smaller banks from utilising the foundation and IRB approaches provided under the regime, which have resulted in capital reductions for large institutions.[212] Smaller banks are assumed to be riskier; they are not able to diversify their asset portfolios to the same extent as large institutions. A larger capital buffer relative to their assets effectively mitigates the build-up of excessive risk taking. Large banks enjoy a 50 per cent reduction in capital charges, unlike the flat rate required by the Basel I Accord. On the other hand, small banks must increase their capital by 50 to 60 per cent under the risk-weighted capital regime.[213] Basel II does not account, however, for smaller banks' advantages with regards to the information they obtain from close, relationship-based banking practices. These may help to offset some of the risks normally associated with their weaker control systems and relatively concentrated asset exposures.[214]

Stand-alone IFIs tend to be very small relative to their conventional counterparts.[215] Basel II may incentivise their consolidation as some observers have remarked that Basel II fosters the consolidation of banks in their efforts to achieve economies of scale. Regulators in several countries, including Turkey, Pakistan, Indonesia and Sudan, have either required institutions to strengthen their capital reserves or merge to help buttress banks against counterparty risks.[216] However, this tendency is lamented in that consolidated giants may harbour systemic threats as these may become too big to fail without unleashing systemic ripples. Moreover, big conventional banks operating Islamic windows will enjoy a large advantage over smaller, indigenous Islamic banks[217] and thus be able to dictate the terms of the industry including its legal development.

In sum, however, the risk-weight capital regime is credited with restoring market efficiency by establishing a mechanism in which asset quality is linked to capital requirements. The flat-rate model did not impose sufficient capital charges on high-risk loans while effectively penalising high-quality investments as these were charged at the same rate as low-

212 Stijn Claessens and Geoffrey Underhill (n 192) 121.
213 Haibin Zhu (n 201) 20–1.
214 Stijn Claessens and Geoffrey Underhill (n 192) 122.
215 M. Umer Chapra and Tariqullah Khan, *Regulation and Supervision of Islamic Banks*, Occasional Paper no. 3 (Jeddah: Islamic Development Bank, Islamic Research and Training Institute, 2000), 57.
216 *Ibid.*; Mansoor Shakil, 'The Impact of Basel II on the Future of Islamic Banking' in Nizam Ali (ed.), *Islamic Finance: Current Legal and Regulatory Issues* (Cambridge, MA: Islamic Finance Project, Harvard Law School, 2005), 162.
217 *Ibid.*

quality assets.[218] Nevertheless, the Islamic financial industry has sought differential treatment on the basis that the types of transaction it practises are less risky. Therefore, in 2002 the IFSB, a financial standard-setting organisation based in Kuala Lumpur, was established to promulgate prudential standards for the supervision of Islamic banks. In 2005 the IFSB released two prudential standards; one on capital adequacy and the other on corporate governance.[219] Its most recent standard on capital adequacy will be analysed in relation to the jurisdiction of Bahrain, which applies IFSB prudential standards, in the following chapter.

6.9.2 Basel III capital and liquidity reforms

Basel III is likely to have a very significant impact upon IFIs.[220] The package of reforms represents the Committee's response to the global financial crisis. Implicit in the reforms is the realisation that the capital reserves of banks were of an insufficient quality to withstand the credit losses of the crisis. Thus the importance of increasing both the level and quality of capital and liquidity requirements has become the most important consideration.[221] Moreover, the definition of capital across jurisdictions has varied widely on a historical basis. Compounded by a lack of disclosure, market participants were unable to assess and compare banks' quality of capital.[222] Basel III builds on the three pillars of Basel II by increasing the quality and quantity of banks' capital, by introducing a leverage ratio designed to constrain excess leverage in the banking system and by introducing global liquidity standards.[223] In particular, the agreement calls for core tier 1 capital to increase from Basel II's requirement of 2 per cent to 7 per cent.[224] A new capital conservation buffer comprises 2.5 per cent of

[218] Haibin Zhu (n 201) 21.

[219] Simon Archer and Rifaat Ahmed Abdel Karim, 'Supervision of Islamic Banks and Basel II: The Regulatory Challenge' in Simon Archer and Rifaat Ahmed Abdel Karim (eds.), *Islamic Finance: The Regulatory Challenge* (Singapore: John Wiley & Sons (Asia), 2007), 3.

[220] Philipp Härle, Matthias Heuser, Sonja Pfetsch and Thomas Poppensieker, *Basel III: What the Draft Proposals Might Mean for European Banking* (Munich: McKinsey & Company, 2010), 5.

[221] John Board and Hatim el-Tahrir (n 205) 276.

[222] BCBS, 'Basel III: A Global Regulatory Framework for More Resilient Banks and Banking Systems' (Bank for International Settlements, June 2011), 20, www.bis.org/publ/bcbs189.pdf. Accessed 22 March 2014.

[223] BCBS (n 222) 2.

[224] Jaime Caruana, *Basel III: Towards a Safer Financial System*, Paper presented at the 3rd Santander International Banking Conference (Madrid, 2010), annex.

the increase. The buffer will be composed of common equity – after the application of deductions such as deferred taxes – and will force banks whose capital ratio dips below the buffer to progressively restrict payouts on dividends, share buybacks and bonuses.[225] The agreement raises the total tier 1 capital ratio to 6 per cent from its current level of 4 per cent whereby total capital (tier 1 and tier 2 capital) must comprise 8 per cent of total risk-weighted assets at all times. Core tier 1 capital must comprise at least 4.5 per cent of risk-weighted assets at all times, which includes top quality capital such as retained earnings and common equity.[226] Total tier 1 capital may include so-called additional tier 1 capital. The agreement also calls for a countercyclical buffer comprised of common equity in the range of 0 to 2.5 per cent, depending on authorities' judgment concerning the build-up of an unacceptable level of systemic risk in the banking system. The reform package will be phased in from January 2013 through January 2019.[227]

Due to the types of asset IFIs carry, as well as systemic reasons, the implementation of the world's first set of minimum liquidity requirements under the agreement is particularly important. These requirements would ensure that banks have sufficient liquidity so that they would be able to withstand very severe short-term financial shocks.[228] The goal of the new standards is to encourage financial institutions to maintain both a prudent thirty-day liquidity profile as well as a minimum amount of stable sources of funding over a one-year horizon, able to meet contingent liquidity needs and off-balance sheet commitments.[229] Liquid assets would be comprised mostly of sovereign debt but may also include high-quality corporate debt. Sovereign and corporate debt instruments are interest-based assets, so IFIs will need to make alternative arrangements for fulfilling enhanced liquidity standards. The IFSB, aware of the growing emphasis on managing liquidity risk, issued a standard enti-

[225] Steve Slater, Huw Jones, Mark Felsenthal *et al.*, 'Factbox: Basel III Banking Agreement', *Reuters*, London, 12 September 2010), www.reuters.com/article/2010/09/12/us-basel-banks-fb-idUSTRE68B1ZG20100912. Accessed 25 March 2014.

[226] Jaime Caruana (n 224) annex.

[227] BCBS, 'Basel Committee on Banking Supervision Reforms – Basel III', www.bis.org/bcbs/basel3/b3summarytable.pdf. Accessed 8 April 2014.

[228] BIS, *The Group of Governors and Heads of Supervision Reach Broad Agreement on Basel Committee Capital and Liquidity Reform Package* (Basel: Bank for International Settlements, 2010), annex.

[229] BCBS (n 222) 17.

tled 'Guiding Principles on Liquidity Risk Management for Institutions Offering Islamic Financial Services' in March 2012.[230]

Higher capital and liquidity requirements increase the cost of lending incurred by banks without accounting for lending restrictions such as credit rationing. For example, each percentage point increase in the capital ratio increases the cost of credit by 13 basis points. The additional costs of meeting new liquidity standards amount to a 25 basis point increase in lending spreads – assuming risk- weighted assets remain stable. Lower regulatory capital is required as a direct result of banks' holding of low-risk assets, thus resulting in a lending spread of 14 basis points.[231] Some of the costs are likely to be met by increased productivity. Despite these added costs and considerable uncertainty as to the magnitude of the effect, evidence suggests that higher capital and liquidity requirements may significantly minimise the likelihood of banking crises.[232] Some observers argue, however, that increased capital requirements encourage heightened competitive pressures, i.e. banks are forced to carry the same amount of tier 1 capital and thus the rents they offer embody similar cost structures. As a result, banks may be encouraged to take greater risks on more profitable parts of their portfolios.[233] Although initially intended for implementation in January 2015, banks managed to secure the concession that liquidity standards will be phased in over four years by 2019.[234]

The following section rounds up this examination by underscoring how the private enforcement of contracts plays an indispensable and ultimate role in the regulation of Islamic finance. A particular focus on the enforcement of Islamic financial transactions in English courts demonstrates the challenges in enforcing non-national legal systems such as the sharia.

[230] IFSB, 'Guiding Principles on Liquidity Risk Management for Institutions Offering Islamic Financial Services', March 2012, www.ifsb.org/standard/eng_IFSB-12%20Guiding%20Principles%20on%20Liquidity%20Risk%20Mgmt%20(Mar2012).pdf. Accessed 25 March 2014.

[231] BCBS, *An Assessment of the Long-Term Economic Impact of Stronger Capital and Liquidity Requirements* (Basel Committee on Banking Supervision, 2010), 10.

[232] *Ibid.*, 9.

[233] Jacques de Larosiere, 'Basel Rules Risk Punishing the Wrong Banks', *Financial Times*, 26 October 2010, 13.

[234] Dan Milmo, 'Banks Win Concessions and Time on Liquidity Rules', *The Guardian*, 7 January 2013.

6.10 Islamic financial transactions in English courts

Parties to international commercial and financial transactions often adopt English law as the governing law of their contract due to its 'well-known and well-developed jurisprudence ... which is not open to doubt or disputation on the basis of religious or philosophical principle'.[235] In particular, freedom of contract in English law has proved pivotal to English law's international predominance. It represents a laissez-faire approach that views the 'courts' role as that of enforcing parties' bargains' so long as they do not transgress acceptable norms of behaviour.[236] Freedom of contract in English law has helped to create some of the most efficient and flexible financial markets in the world and has allowed the development of a regime for security interests 'which is unrivalled for its informality and its willingness to allow the parties to define their own rights and remedies and to organise their relationships in whatever way they consider best suited to their needs'.[237] English courts have a strong reputation for impartiality and competence, and the English legal profession has a high reputation for its specialist international commercial expertise. Both domestic and international traders have come to associate English law with the stability and predictability that is necessary for international commerce to flourish.[238] It is not surprising that Islamic financial transactions are often governed by English law.

Only a handful of published court decisions involving Islamic financial transactions have been reported worldwide. Malaysia is one jurisdiction in which some published case law exists. Many Middle Eastern jurisdictions, however, do not report their case law and private law firms are not disposed to report cases in which they have acted as counsel. Kilian Bälz indicates that plain vanilla financial transactions have generally become non-litigious. Financial institutions are wary of creating innovative structures that expose them to lawsuits.[239] In fact, most financial transactions are settled out of court. All of these factors may have contributed to a scarcity of case law. The section below analyses the few English law cases on public record.

[235] *Shamil Bank* v. *Beximco Pharmaceuticals Ltd* [2004] EWCA Civ 19 [54].

[236] Royston Miles Goode, *Commercial Law in the Next Millennium* (London: Sweet & Maxwell, 1998), 31.

[237] *Ibid.* [238] *Ibid.*

[239] Kilian Bälz, 'A Murabaha Transaction in an English Court' (2004) 11 *I.L.& S.* 117, 118–19.

6.10.1 *The* Symphony Gems *case*

Islamic Investment Co Ltd v. *Symphony Gems NV*[240] (Symphony Gems case) is reportedly the first Islamic financial transaction decided in a Western court.[241] The case involved a *murābaḥah* financing agreement made between the parties 'in accordance with the Islamic Shariah' that was nonetheless governed by and construed according to English law.[242] The case is not authoritative but it offers an illustration of the way in which English courts uphold parties' contractual agreements where these are not constrained by the rules of mandatory legal provisions or public policy. It also demonstrates pluralistic legal interaction in the enforcement of Islamic financial transactions. Specifically, it shows the interaction of the sharia, English law and the law of the Bahamas, together with internationally recognised commercial principles, when these are enforced in an English court of law.

The Islamic Investment Company (IIC), the claimant, and Symphony Gems (SG), the first defendant (the second and third defendants served as guarantors) made an agreement involving a revolving sale and purchase facility. The seller (IIC) granted the purchaser (SG) the facility. IIC agreed to purchase rough diamonds from a supplier and immediately sell these to SG on deferred payment terms pursuant to purchase agreements. Two purchase agreements were made, each to equal US$7,500,000 in rough diamonds. According to the purchase agreements, IIC transferred US$15 million to the account of Precious Ltd, based in Hong Kong and was to receive US$7,917,450 in payment for each advance. However, IIC did not receive payment and sought to retrieve these monies, accrued interest and damages, minus US$7.5 million recovered pursuant to a bank guarantee.[243]

The case turned on the defence's claim that the outstanding balance required delivery of the rough diamonds to the purchaser, or whether the sale price is due in the absence of delivery. Tomlinson J took note of the fact that the defendants did not raise the issue of absence of delivery to the claimants prior to the proceedings, a fact that assisted him in reaching his conclusion.[244] A purchase agreement, per Tomlinson J, 'means an

[240] [2002] ALL ER (D) 171 Transcript.

[241] Umar F. Moghul and Arshad A. Ahmed, 'Contractual Forms in Islamic Finance Law and Islamic Inv. Co. of the Gulf (Bahamas) Ltd. v. Symphony Gems N.V. & Ors.: A First Impression of Islamic Finance' (2003–2004) 27 *Fordham Int'l L.J.* 150, 155.

[242] *Symphony Gems* (n 240) (A). [243] *Ibid.*

[244] *Ibid.*

agreement made between the Purchaser and the Seller for the purchase of Supplies by the Seller from the relevant Supplier and for the sale of those Supplies by the Seller to the Purchaser'.[245] Pursuant to clause 4.3, those purchase agreements required the purchaser 'to enter into arrangements with the supplier to the effect that the seller will purchase the supplies from the supplier', or else the agreement would be automatically terminated.[246] On this basis, Tomlinson J concluded that 'all of the arrangements concerning the acquisition of goods by the seller from the supplier fall to be made by the purchaser, for the very good reason that this is a financing agreement facilitating or apparently facilitating the purchase of supplies by the purchaser'.[247] Furthermore, 'if therefore there has been no delivery of goods from the supplier to the seller and thus from the seller to the purchaser, that can only be because the purchaser has not made the necessary arrangements'.[248]

Payment was to be made unconditional of any event. Clause 4.4 provides that 'the instalments are payable whether or not the seller is in breach of any of its obligations under the relevant purchase agreement' and this would certainly include failure to deliver.[249] Nowhere in the agreements was a delivery date specified nor were any procedures provided for the logistics of such arrangements. Hence, Tomlinson J ruled that the delivery of goods was 'not a prerequisite to recovery by the sellers of the relevant instalments of the sale price from the purchaser'.[250]

In *Symphony Gems* the legal issue concerning the Islamic legal definition of a *murābaḥah* contract[251] was not a concern of the court, because the issues on which the court was to decide were strictly matters of English contract law. Clause 25 of the agreement clearly stated: 'This Agreement and each Purchase Agreement shall be governed by, and shall be construed in accordance with, English law.'[252] Morrison J concluded that he 'must simply construe it [the agreement] according to its terms as an English law contract'.[253]

The defence also claimed that the contract was illegal, a claim dependent on the court's construction of the contract being found unlawful in

[245] *Ibid.*, cl 3. [246] *Ibid.*, cl 4.3.

[247] *Ibid.*, cll 4.4, 5.1, 5.2, 5.6. [248] *Ibid.*

[249] *Ibid.*, cl 4.4. [250] *Ibid.*

[251] Expert evidence provided by Dr Yahya Al-Samaan, partner of the law firm Salah Al-Hejailan in Saudi Arabia and Dr Martin Lau, then Lecturer in South Asian law at the School of Oriental and African Studies, indicated that the transaction did not meet the requirements of the classical *murābaḥah*.

[252] *Ibid.*, cl 25. [253] *Ibid.*

the place of performance. The defence claimed that the contract envisaged performance in Saudi Arabia. In that case the sharia would be applicable to the transaction and its terms and conditions would likely be void. Tomlinson J did not find that the contract called for performance in Saudi Arabia and therefore ruled that the principle of illegality was irrelevant.[254]

The next argument relied upon by the defence was an *ultra vires* argument. *Ultra vires* is a nineteenth-century doctrine that limited a company's legal capacity to the objects stated in its memorandum of association. Any action which transgressed those limits was in principle void.[255] With respect to this particular contract the defendant claimed that the 'contract is outwith the objects stated in the Claimant's Memorandum of Association, which includes the limitation to carry out in a manner which is consistent with Islamic laws, rules, principles and traditions the following objects'.[256] Referring to expert testimony, Tomlinson J agreed that the essential characteristics of the *murābaḥah* had not been met in this transaction. Yet the application of the *ultra vires* doctrine depended on the law of the Bahamas, the jurisdiction in which IIC was incorporated, because the capacity of corporate entities is determined by the place of incorporation rather than the governing law of the contract. Tomlinson J ruled that Bahamian law did not prevent the IIC from acting outwith its objects, so *ultra vires* could not be relied upon by the defence.

In *Symphomy Gems* Tomlinson J's judgment for the claimant highlights an English tradition of freeing the hands of commercial parties and thus upholding the bedrock doctrine of party autonomy. The court's primary concern was in upholding a properly agreed contract and thus safeguarding commercial interests. This represents a historical continuity of English courts upholding reasonable business practices where these are not otherwise constrained by the rules of mandatory legal provisions or public policy. As a result, the business community is granted wide discretion to agree the terms of contracts.[257]

The following section analyses an authoritative case concerning municipal legal systems' treatment of non-national systems of law.

[254] *Ibid.*

[255] Paul L. Davies, *Gower and Davies' Principles of Modern Company Law*, 8th edn (London: Sweet & Maxwell, 2008), 153.

[256] *Symphony Gems* (n 240).

[257] Kilian Bälz (n 239) 126.

6.10.2 *The* Beximco *case and the Rome Convention*

Shamil Bank v. *Beximco Pharmaceuticals Ltd* (the *Beximco* case) was an appeal from the High Court, in which Morrison J found in favour of the respondent, Shamil Bank of Bahrain, and made an award of US$49.7 million. Appeal to the Court of Appeal was granted on a single point 'in relation to the construction and effect of the form of the governing law clause contained in the financing agreements'.[258] The clause in question reads: 'Subject to the principles of the Glorious *Sharia'a*, this Agreement shall be governed by and construed in accordance with the laws of England'.[259]

The Court of Appeal's ruling illustrates two key principles. The first pertains to the use of the Rome Convention on the Law Applicable to Contractual Obligations[260] – an EU treaty whose provisions, in general, established the law governing contractual relations in the United Kingdom at the time the case was heard. In this case, the convention made clear that a contract could only be governed by the law of a country so that a contract seeking to incorporate a non-state law or body of principles such as the *lex mercatoria* or the sharia would not be recognised as the applicable law of a contract.[261]

Second, the judgment demonstrates the relevant application of the English doctrine of incorporation, in which parties may incorporate specific 'black letter' terms of a foreign law or general legal principles or non-state law into an English contract, but they can only serve as a source of law from which the governing law may draw. 'Incorporation' is a shorthand method of including a limited set of terms so as to avoid laying out the articles of a foreign law in full. The court would construe an English contract, 'reading into it as if they were written into it the words' of the foreign law.[262] In a case in which ambiguity existed or doubt as to the effect of such rules, the court would rely upon the testimony of experts in

258 *Shamil Bank* v. *Beximco Pharmaceuticals Ltd* [2004] EWCA Civ 19 [1].

259 *Ibid.*

260 European Convention 80/934/ECC on the Law Applicable to Contractual Obligations (Rome Convention) [1980] OJ L266/1.

261 *Ibid.*, [48]; Lawrence Collins, *Dicey, Morris and Collins on the Conflicts of Laws*, vol. II (London: Sweet & Maxwell, 2006), 1568. A subsequent EU Regulation on the law applicable to contractual obligations, known as Rome I, now supersedes the Rome Convention in all EU member states. See Regulation (EC) No 593/2008 of the European Parliament and of the Council of 17 June 2008 on the law applicable to contractual obligations (Rome I) [2008] OJ L177/6.

262 Lawrence Collins (n 261) 1571.

foreign law.[263] However, the courts are not bound to the expert evidence on foreign law inasmuch as they are 'interpreting the terms of an English contract and not applying foreign law,' as established under the authority of *Stafford Allen & Sons Ltd* v. *Pacific Steam Navigation Co.*[264]

The background of the case centred on the Beximco Group's efforts to seek working capital from the respondent, Shamil Bank – an IFI – whereby monies were advanced via two '*morabaha* financing agreements'.[265] A principal *murābaḥah* financing agreement was entered into between the first defendant, the second defendants and the bank, under which the bank agreed to purchase, with the second defendant acting as its agent, certain goods to be sold to the first defendant.[266] Pursuant to the initial 1995 *murābaḥah* agreement, Shamil Bank advanced the second defendant US$15 million. In 1996 a second *murābaḥah* agreement was agreed and another US$15 million was advanced for the purchase of specified goods. By December 1999 the defendants had defaulted on the agreements.

Subsequent negotiations led the bank and the first and second defendants to enter into two Exchange in Satisfaction and User Agreements (ESUA) modelled on an *ijārah* contract, with the third, fourth and fifth defendants acting as guarantors. The ESUAs provided that the bank would discharge the amounts outstanding under the 1995 and 1996 *Morabaha* agreements in exchange for unencumbered title to certain assets. The defendants were entitled to use those assets in the normal course of their business 'in consideration for payment by instalments of a user fee' as well as other 'payments of accrued compensation'.[267] Subsequently, termination and default events occurred and Shamil initiated proceedings in the English court.[268]

Article 1.1 of the Rome Convention requires the parties to choose the law of a country to govern their contract.[269] It stipulates that 'the rules of this Convention shall apply to contractual obligation in any situation involving a choice between the laws of different countries'.[270] On the face of it Article 1.1 is not 'applicable to a choice between the law of a country and a non-national system of law, such as the *lex mercatoria*, or "general

263 *Halpern* v. *Halpern* [2007] EWCA Civ 291 [31].
264 [1956] 2 All ER 716. Lawrence Collins (n 261) 1572.
265 *Beximco* (n 258) [12]. 266 *Ibid.*, [14].
267 *Ibid.*, [19]–[20]. 268 *Ibid.*, [20]–[21].
269 Rome Convention [1980]. Article 3.1 of the Rome Convention was implemented in the United Kingdom under Article 3, para 1 of the Contracts (Applicable Law) Act 1990 and applied to all contracts made after 1 April 1991.
270 Rome Convention [1980], art. 1.1.

principles of law", or as in this case, the law of *Sharia*'.[271] Article 3.1 of the Rome Convention, which provides that 'a contract shall be governed by the law chosen by the parties' and, with reference to choice of a 'foreign law' in conjunction with Article 3.3, 'make it clear that the Convention as a whole only contemplates and sanctions the choice of the law of a country'.[272]

Yet the appellants contended that the financing agreements were only enforceable in the event of compliance with both the sharia and English law.[273] The principles of the sharia should be given legal effect.[274] It was argued that the construction of the governing law 'produces a result no different from the incorporation by reference of a codified system of rules, such as the Hague Rules or the Warsaw Convention into a contract governed by English law'.[275] For example, the Court of Appeal in *Nea Agrex SA* v. *Baltic Shipping Co Ltd*[276] rejected a lower court's conclusion that a 'paramount clause provision was to be treated as ineffective to incorporate the Hague Rules into a charterparty'.[277] In that case the Court of Appeal held that the court should strive to give meaning to an incorporated clause if at all possible, rather than rendering it meaningless.[278] On these grounds the defence argued that the rules relating to interest and the nature of the *murābaḥah* and *ijārah* agreements should be read into the agreement in accordance with the 'principles of the Glorious *Sharia*' governing clause.[279]

Nonetheless, the court ruled that the doctrine of incorporation can only function where the parties have identified the terms of their contract in 'specific "black letter" provisions of a foreign law', international code, or set of other rules such as the Hague Rules, which are amenable to incorporation as terms of the relevant contract. The doctrine enables

[271] *Ibid.*

[272] *Beximco* (n 258) [48]. For analysis of this case see Kilian Bälz, 'Islamic Law as Governing Law under the Rome Convention' (2001) 6 *Unif.L.Rev.*, 45; Jason C. T. Chuah, 'Islamic Principles Governing International Trade Financing Instruments: A Study of the Morabaha in English Law' (2006–2007) *Nw.J.Int'l L.& Bus.*, 137, 168; Yusuf Talal DeLorenzo and Michael J. T. McMillen 'Law and Islamic Finance: An Interactive Analysis' in Simon Archer and Rifaat Ahmed Abdel Karim (eds.), *Islamic Finance: The Regulatory Challenge* (Singapore: John Wiley & Sons (Asia), 2007), 162; and Andreas Junius, 'Islamic Finance: Issues Surrounding Islamic Law as a Choice of Law under German Conflict of Laws Principles' (2007) 7 *Chicag.Journ.Int'l.Law*, 537.

[273] *Beximco* (n 258) [27], [42]; [2003] EWHC 2118 [15].

[274] *Beximco* (n 258) [42]. [275] *Ibid.*, [43].

[276] *Nea Agrex SA* v. *Baltic Shipping Co. Ltd* [1974 N. No. 2011] – [1976] QB 933.

[277] *Beximco* (n 258) [43]. [278] *Nea Agrex* (n 276), 935.

[279] *Beximco* (n 258) [49].

parties to an English contract to agree a contract which is construed in accordance with the relevant articles of a foreign law or non-state law. The effect of such would not make a non-state or foreign law the governing law of the contract, rather the specific articles of such a law would be incorporated as contractual terms into an English contract.[280]

Unlike *Nea Agrex*, in the present case, 'the general reference to the principles of the sharia … affords no reference to, or identification of, those aspects of sharia law which are intended to be incorporated into the contract, let alone the terms in which they are framed'.[281] Thus the court agreed with the general consensus amongst experts that the reference to the sharia does not afford the court with a direct reference to specific terms or other legal rules intended to be incorporated into the contract.[282] This prevented the court – even if it was able to do so – from determining the dispute according to such religious principles.[283] If specific provisions of the sharia had been included in the parties' agreements with respect to *ribā* and the contractual essentials of the *murābaḥah* and *ijārah*, the 'defendants would have been likely to succeed'.[284]

The UK government's decision to opt into the Rome I Regulation[285] has allowed the successor to the Rome Convention to be applied to contracts concluded after 17 December 2009.[286] Like the Rome Convention, the principle of party autonomy in relation to parties' choice of law is 'substantively the same' as in Rome I.[287] Like the convention the regulation does not foresee parties' choice of a non-state body of law as the choice of law despite an early draft resolution which might have permitted parties to choose public international law.[288] The final session of regulation does offer parties the means to incorporate non-state law or international standards by reference into their contract.[289] Recital 13 of the preamble to Rome I provides that the regulation 'does not preclude parties from incorporating by reference into their contract a non-state body of law or an international convention'.[290] This leaves unresolved the problems of

280 Lawrence Collins (n 261) 1571.
281 *Beximco* (n 258) [52].
282 *Ibid.*, [55].
283 Jason C. T. Chuah (n 272) 151; *Beximco* (n 258) [40].
284 *Ibid.*, [55].
285 Note that Rome I is a regulation and is thus directly effective in English law.
286 Out-Law News, 'UK Signs up to Rome I Rules on Cross-Border Contract Disputes' (2008), www.out-law.com/page-9337. Accessed 8 April 2014.
287 Ministry of Justice, *Rome 1 – Should the UK Opt In?* (London: Ministry of Justice, 2008), para. 45.
288 Philip R. Wood, *Conflict of Laws and International Finance* (London: Sweet & Maxwell, 2007), 62.
289 Ministry of Justice (n 287) para. 13.
290 *Ibid.*

convincing an English court, in the light of the *Beximco* decision, that the sharia is a body of law that can be incorporated.[291]

Some observers have perceived this as a slight to Islamic jurisprudence and a relegation of the legal system to second-class status.[292] Some Muslims have taken offence at Morrison J's comments in *Beximco* to the effect that the sharia was unfit to govern modern commercial or banking transactions on the basis that its provisions are difficult to specify or ascertain. They view this as a '*capitis deminutio*', a diminution of the sharia and contextualise the court's findings in the light of early arbitration awards such as *Sheikh Abu Dhabi* v. *Petroleum Ltd*,[293] *Ruler of Qatar* v. *International Marine Oil Company Ltd*,[294] and the well known 1958 *Aramco* v. *Government of Saudi Arabia*[295] award. In each of these cases, British judges held that the sharia could not 'reasonably be said to exist', or it 'contains no precise rule' concerning a particular contract, so that Islamic law could not 'reasonably' be used as the governing law.[296] Furthermore, they assert that many legal systems entail similar difficulties, and that the law of the land in Saudi Arabia is the sharia. Still, the sharia is an internationally recognised body of law. The International Court of Justice recognises the sharia as belonging to the general principles of law recognised by civilised states.[297] Why then should the problem of ascertaining the law arise, when, in fact, it is applied, recognised and enforced in international commercial arbitrations?[298]

An important consequence of the *Beximco* case concerns the religious risks that arise from non-compliance with the sharia. Potter LJ remarked that neither party 'was under any illusion' as to the true nature of the transactions that provided long-term working capital and that both parties 'were content to dress the loan transactions up as *morabaha* sales (or *ijārah* leases), whilst taking no interest in whether the proper formalities of such a sale or lease were actually complied with'.[299] Accordingly, Potter LJ felt that the dispute should be approached in accordance with the actual

[291] Following discussions with Nicholas Foster, Senior Lecturer, SOAS/University of London.

[292] Jason C. T. Chuah (n 272) 168.

[293] [1952] 1 Int Comp LQ 247.

[294] [1953] 20 Int LR 534.

[295] [1958] 27 Int LR 117.

[296] Ibrahim Fadlallah, 'Arbitration Facing Conflicts of Culture: The 2008 Annual School of International Arbitration Lecture Sponsored by Freshfields Bruckhaus Deringer LLP' (2009) 25 *Arb Intl*, 303, 307–8.

[297] William Ballantyne, *The Shari'a: The Use of Money* (London: Serle Court, 2010), 11.

[298] Examples of arbitration in which parties have chosen the sharia as the substantive law of their agreement are considered in the following section.

[299] *Beximco* (n 258) [47].

substance of the agreement rather than construing the wording in a manner which would be irreconcilable with the authors' intentions.[300] The effect of the *Beximco* judgment in City law firms and financial institutions has been to reduce the sharia aspect of deals to a matter of compliance and not law.[301] The court indirectly determined that the types of *murābaḥah* and *ijārah* transactions performed in the case at hand did not comply with a strict interpretation of the sharia. As a result, the court intimated that a genuine link between the subject matter and the financing must be made for these contracts to fulfil their Islamic criteria. The Court of Appeal has indirectly defined the 'authentic' version of these transactions as sale-based transactions. In doing so, issues of liability and mandatory policy as discussed above could limit the flexibility and use of these types of instruments in the mid- to long-term.[302]

Beximco also illustrates the importance of the industry's standardisation efforts. Specifically, the sharia will not be applied in an English court of law unless it can be convinced that a black letter interpretation of the sharia can be determined. AAOIFI standardisation efforts are an important step in this process and yet the willingness of financial institutions and affected countries to implement these rules has been ad hoc and varied. The lack of convergence around such standards or of another set of authoritative standards prevents parties from making a more general contractual reference to the agreed standards of Islamic commercial law, but it may enable parties to incorporate specific AAOIFI rules as long as these are clearly indicated. Second, the judgment must necessarily refocus the industry's attention on the important work of sharia supervisory boards' audit and assessment of IFI's products and transactions. English courts have made it very clear that they will not play the role of SSBs in determining the sharia compliance of financial transactions. The judgment is a very important marker for IFIs in terms of their legal expectations. The burden of ascertaining the Islamicity of products lies in the preparation of contracts and internal sharia audit systems and controls,[303] all of which are the responsibility of the SSB under English law.

300 *Ibid.* 301 Personal communication from Nicholas H. D. Foster.

302 Jason C. T. Chuah (n 272) 149.

303 Andreas Junius (n 272) 542. Some arguments have been advanced that *Uddin* v. *Choudhury* [2009] EWCA Civ 1205 has overturned the persuasive precedent set by the Court of Appeal in *Beximco*. However, from this author's standpoint, *Uddin* v. *Choudhury*, a matrimonial dispute, is not relevant to the *Beximco decision*. This is supported by the absence of any mention of Rome I or the *Beximco* judgment. An unpersua-

6.10.3 *The* Investment Dar *case*

The *Investment Dar* case[304] would be unimportant if not for the reason that it illustrates the risks of sharia non-compliance. It provides an illustration of the types of lawsuits and legal issues that may arise as the Islamic finance industry gains steam. The Investment Dar Company KSCC (incorporated in Kuwait – TID) and Blom Developments Bank SAL (Blom) entered into a *wakālah* (agency) agreement pursuant to which Blom made several deposits. Blom's principal investments as well as an anticipated profit return were guaranteed, equivalent to a loan-bearing investment with interest.[305] TID's SSB approved the sharia compliance of the agreement in October 2007.[306]

Blom claimed sums allegedly due under the agreement and applied for summary judgment. Summary judgment, a legal device to expeditiously dispose of a case without a trial, is used when there is no dispute concerning the material facts of the case, and a party is entitled to judgment as a matter of law. Blom claimed in both contract and trust.

TID's memorandum of association required that all transactions were sharia-compliant.[307] Paradoxically, TID argued that the agreement was not sharia-compliant, and therefore ultra vires its memo and void under Kuwaiti law. A court's ruling that a contract had been undertaken ultra vires its articles of association would be deemed void despite any recitals, contractual representations and promises not to challenge the sharia-compliance of the agreement, which was provided in the master *wakālah* agreement.[308]

At the summary judgment hearing, Master Bragge found that this was a triable issue but found for Blom with respect to its trust claim.[309] However,

sive argument was made in John R. Bowen, 'How English Courts Recognize Shariah?' (2010) 7 *Univ. St. Thomas L.J.* 411.

304 *The Investment Dar Company KSCC* v. *Blom Developments Bank SAL* [2009] EWHC 3545(Ch) [12].

305 *Ibid.*, [2].

306 *Ibid.*, [10]. See also Andrew Cunningham, 'Role of Sharia Boards Needs Modernisation', *Financial Times*, 21 April 2010, www.ft.com/cms/s/0/a5a6e474-4d54-11df-baf3-00144feab49a.html#axzz1WK1rhXTO. Accessed 12 April 2014.

307 *Investment Dar* (n 304) [3], [4].

308 Norton Rose, 'The Implications for the Islamic Finance Market of the Investment Dar Company KSCC v Blom Developments Bank SAL [2009] EWHC 3545 (Ch)', March 2010, www.nortonrose.com/knowledge/publications/27334/the-implications-for-the-islamic-finance-market-of-the-investment-dar-company-kscc-v-blom-developments-bank-sal-ewhc-3545-ch. Accessed 12 April 2014.

309 *Ibid.*, [18].

Purle J ruled that the trust claim 'was sufficiently arguable … that there is no trust claim', and so decided it was a triable issue.[310] Purle J agreed with Master Bragge, that the ultra vires claim was also a triable issue.[311]

The Investment Dar caused much consternation in Islamic financial markets as a result of the sharia compliance risks the case highlights.[312] Yet the case has no precedential value. It is merely an appeal from summary judgment. There is nothing out of the ordinary about the court's decision – it was simply that the ultra vires issue was triable. The case has not been to trial and the issue has not been argued, so we do not know what the result would have been (e.g. there might not have been a problem under Kuwaiti law). Furthermore, ultra vires is a well-known issue and the possibility of its occurrence is a matter of standard due diligence. It is disquieting that an IFI should have produced such an argument, but it remains highly unusual.

6.11 Concluding remarks

The regulatory context in which financial markets are conceived and engineered determines in large part the types of financial products and services that are available for investment. In the United Kingdom the liberal values that underlie the construction and function of financial markets are evident both in the types and predominance of particular modes of investment as well as the regulatory authority's regulatory objectives and manner of supervision.

The regulatory context in which multi-layered legal systems interact in the United Kingdom is applied to the Islamic finance industry according to the same regulatory approach as the conventional industry. Economic substance over form is the *leitmotif* by which regulators address the particular risks of Islamic banks including the classification of Islamic products. Otherwise, the economic risks arising from such products would not be adequately supervised. The SSB, although a unique organ particular to IFIs, is treated according to UK financial services law in much the same way as conventional financial institutions are. However, there are clear limitations to this approach in qualitative terms, allowing so-called sharia risks with destabilising effects to emerge. Yet the conventional risks associated with financial institutions' corporate governance systems are

310 *Ibid.*, [19]–[20]. 311 *Ibid.*, [20].

312 TheCityUK, 'Islamic Finance', May 2011, www.thecityuk.com/research/our-work/reports-list/islamic-finance-2013/. Accessed 26 March 2014.

addressed to the extent that the risks arising from the SSB and its functions can be likened to such risks. Whether the government should consider a different manner of addressing the sharia compliance function of IFIs, perhaps in an effort to attract a greater volume of business to UK shores, may be better ascertained from other jurisdictions' supervisory approaches. The following chapters provide insights into some alternative approaches to regulating SSBs.

The UK regulatory authority has faced several difficulties as a result of the hybrid legal structure associated with Islamic financial contracts. These include questions of how to categorise Islamic financial contracts according to the FSMA 2000 RAO. Another challenge concerns the statutory definition of a deposit and its capital guarantee requirement. The law prevents Islamic banks from using the *muḍārabah* on the liabilities side of the balance sheet. The result is that the PLS model – the cornerstone of Islamic finance – is not a lawful mode of retail deposit taking in the United Kingdom. There is reason to believe that British Muslims, and indeed most Muslim investors who have availed themselves of Islamic financial products, have not shown a definite preference for PLS modes of finance. Evidently, Muslim consumers/investors enjoy the certainty and predictability that capital-guaranteed investment accounts afford.

European Union law plays an increasingly important role in UK financial markets as EU directives and regulations require implementation in all EU member states. The United Kindgom's traditional strength as one of the world's largest financial centres contributes significantly to the growing regulatory weight of the EU and strengthens the regulatory reach of UK law. Many Gulf state jurisdictions are significantly affected by the regulatory influence of EU law and English/UK law. This interplay of normative influences illustrates a dynamic in which regulatory systems are conceived, created and adapted. As the world's most powerful supranational authority the EU's neoliberal influence on the legal processes and best practices of jurisdictions across the globe is an increasingly important factor in the creation of global commercial law.

An example of the EU's enhanced regulatory capacities is evident in its implementation of Basel capital and liquidity standards. Conceived by the leading economies of the world, many of which belong to the EU, Basel standards advance the interests of these states' financial institutions and regulatory structures. The transposition of global regulatory standards to supranational authority and further onward to municipal legal systems demonstrates an important chain of global commercial law creation.

Beximco, in particular, underscores the prerogative of municipal legal systems to determine the authority of the legal systems that come into play before its courts. Nation states will jealously guard against any diminution of their authority and jurisdiction. The relatively stateless condition of the sharia results in its non-recognition in the global system. Chapter 10, however, examines an alternative mode of dispute resolution – arbitration – which itself is a product of globalisation. Arbitration provides IFL with a coveted means of legal enforcement, which is a necessary mechanism of an efficient legal system.

7

The regulation of Islamic financial institutions in Bahrain

Bahrain is one of the early pioneers of Islamic finance and remains one of the largest Islamic financial centres in the world, despite growing competition from its Gulf peers and recent internal political upheaval threatening its political stability. Since the establishment of the first Islamic bank in 1975 Bahrain has undertaken the construction of an industry-specific financial system for Islamic finance, within its offshore banking centre, that would be comparable to the best international practices.[1] Bahrain's particular approach to Islamic finance has resulted in the country hosting a large number of IFIs as well as a substantial share of the international Islamic non-governmental organisations (IINGOs). The presence of numerous IINGOs in Bahrain is a competitive advantage as it adds weight to the country's claim to be the largest and most competitive Islamic financial centre in the world. It is also a reflection of Bahrain's dual regulatory system, which accords a large role to these organisations' promulgation of a wide range of Islamic financial, accounting and sharia standards. Bahrain, for example, mandates the use of AAOIFI financial, accounting and sharia standards, which makes such standards an important aspect of Bahraini financial services law. Therefore, Bahrain is not only an important centre of Islamic finance; it is a critical centre for the promulgation of IFL as well as a conduit for the dissemination of Islamic financial standards to jurisdictions across the region.

This chapter examines Bahrain's complex regulatory framework for Islamic finance. It focuses on the role of IINGO standards in the Bahraini legal system and the extent to which they impact Bahraini financial services law. The interaction of multiple legal systems in Bahrain provides an unequivocal demonstration that IFL is a process-driven legal composite, which cannot be viewed in jurisdictional isolation or as a classical sharia

[1] Ahmed Bin Mohammed Al-Khalifa, *The Progress of Islamic Banking and Finance in Bahrain*, Proceedings of the Fifth Harvard University Forum on Islamic Finance, 'Islamic Finance: Dynamics and Development' (Cambridge, 2000), 1.

transplant. The use of IINGO standards as well as other international best practices to facilitate and regulate the industry is increasingly the norm in GCC states.

Within this context, this chapter examines Bahrain's position with respect to other GCC states and the legal trends that define those relations. Second, the legal system of Bahrain including the role of the sharia within that system is analysed. Third, an analysis of Bahrain as an international Islamic financial centre reveals its strength in terms of the capacity of its financial and legal infrastructure. The remainder of the chapter addresses the ways in which Bahrain regulates Islamic finance. In particular, it is concerned with understanding the types of legal interaction that take place and their results.

7.1 Islamic finance and GCC financial centres

The GCC was established in 1981 as a supranational authority, similar to the European Union, comprising six founding member states: Bahrain, Kuwait, Qatar, Oman, the United Arab Emirates (UAE) and Saudi Arabia. The objectives of the GCC are to strengthen the integration, coordination and interconnection between the peoples of its member states. In practical terms this involves the harmonisation of legislation in the following areas: economic and financial affairs; commerce, customs and communications; education and culture; social and health affairs; information and tourism; and legislative and administrative affairs.[2] All member states comprise a heterogeneous set of independent jurisdictions and financial centres, despite a sense of common purpose and destiny as Arab Gulf states.

Legal convergence between jurisdictions is a principal objective of the GCC project as it is felt to be the key to unlocking the economic and social benefits of union. An important aspect of convergence concerns the financial services law of GCC states, which is the focus of the next three chapters. Legal convergence is mandated by the GCC pursuant to a revised economic agreement of 2001, which set out a number of conditions member states agreed to fulfil with the objective of achieving monetary and economic union. Legal convergence between GCC member states is underpinned by a customs union and a common market that, although

[2] GCC, 'Foundations and Objectives' (Cooperation Council for the Arab States of the Gulf n.d.), www.gcc-sg.org/eng/index895b.html?action=Sec-Show&ID=3. Accessed 1 May 2014.

not as tightly integrated as the EU, display a similar developmental trend.[3] The GCC project also includes the eventual creation of a currency union. Member states, for the purpose of achieving 'a high level of harmonisation between member states' agreed to: (1) unify investment-related laws and regulations; (2) accord national treatment to investments owned by GCC citizens; (3) integrate financial markets in member states, which includes harmonising all related legislation; and (4) adopt harmonised standards and specifications for products.[4]

Legal convergence in the GCC is an outgrowth of the rapid development of modern financial centres throughout the Gulf region as well as the rising importance of Islamic finance as a share of financial market assets. Financial centres, which comprise a high concentration of activity in the international trade of capital and financial services, are built on their reputation for stability, integrity, impartiality and confidentiality. Political stability and a transparent, impartial and flexible legal framework are essential prerequisites of a financial centre. The reputation, accessibility and ability to function as a haven for foreign enterprise are also important factors in the emergence of financial centres.[5] The aforementioned is largely the result of deliberate government action or action by private elites. Competitive advantages also concern a financial centre's location, its transportation network and the economic characteristics of the goods and services in which a particular economic area specialises.[6]

Nearly every Gulf state has aspired to develop its financial markets over the past decade. Many jurisdictions such as Dubai, Qatar and Bahrain have aimed at creating not just regional financial hubs in the MENA region but at developing international financial centres with global ambitions. Developing modern financial centres has been viewed as a means of diversifying economies heavily reliant on oil and gas production and

[3] Chatham House, *The Gulf as a Global Financial Centre: Growing Opportunities and International Influence* (London: Royal Institute for International Affairs, June 2008), 8.

[4] GCC, *Economic Agreement Between the Gulf Cooperation Council States* (Oman: The Cooperation Council for the Arab States of the Gulf, December 2001), Art 5., ss 1–4.

[5] Geoffrey Jones, 'International Financial Centres in Asia, the Middle East and Australia: A Historical Perspective' in Richard Roberts (ed.), *International Financial Centres: Concepts, Development and Dynamics*, vol. 1 (Cheltenham: Edward Elgar, 1994), 311, 317.

[6] Charles P. Kindleberger, 'The Formation of Financial Centers: A Study in Comparative Economic History' in Richard Roberts (ed.) *International Financial Centres: Concepts, Development and Dynamics*, vol. I (Cheltenham: Edward Elgar, 1994), 198.

as a way of generating attractive employment opportunities for Gulf nationals.[7]

The development of modern financial centres in the GCC is closely connected to soaring energy prices and the channelling of surplus funds to domestic economies. Beginning in 2003 significant increases in the price of oil, from under US$30 per barrel to near US$100 at the end of 2007, fuelled a market boom across the GCC region with real GDP growth of 6–7 per cent. Although almost all GCC states experienced a severe economic downturn during the 2008 financial crisis, the region's GDP has more than quadrupled since 2002. In 2013 the region's GDP totalled US$1.37 trillion.[8] Increased GDP has also meant increased savings as well as trade and current account surpluses, which have partly been channelled into the region's financial centres.

Financial centres can be organised according to the following general typology: (1) sub-regional financial centres in which international financial activities are clustered but which are focused on bilateral trade between the host economy of the centre and other economies; (2) regional financial centres, which provide financial services to an entire region; and (3) global financial centres, which provide a broad range of financial services across the globe.[9] Bahrain and the financial centres of the UAE and Dubai are considered to rank in the second category, i.e. regional financial centres. In particular, these financial centres are considered to function as collection centres in which intermediation is directed outwards as opposed to inwards to its host economy. The market area surrounding a collection centre attracts surplus savings due to the low absorptive capacity of the region's economies. International banking institutions are positioned to invest the money on an international scale and in a more sophisticated manner than what is generally considered feasible for local financial intermediaries. Therefore, collection centres provide the efficient management of global investment funds.[10]

The high concentration of financial centres in GCC states leads to positive externalities and economies of scale. Firms, including their branches and subsidiaries, become interconnected in markets in which liquidity and efficiency gains can be won with an increased number of participants.

[7] Steffen Kern, *Current Issues: Global Financial Markets* (Frankfurt am Main: Deutsche Bank, 2012), 3.

[8] GCC, 'Economic Indicators' (n.d.), www.gcc-sg.org/eng/. Accessed 1 May 2014.

[9] Geoffrey Jones (n 5) 302.

[10] Y. S. Park, 'The Economics of Offshore Financial Centers' in Richard Roberts (ed.), *Offshore Financial Centres*, vol. I (Cheltenham: Edward Elgar, 1994), 6.

Regularised business flows are conducive to price stability. Other advantages include the development of specialised ancillary services and the pooling of professional skills. In addition to bankers and investors, lawyers, accountants and consultancies establish professional networks in financial centres, which results in forward momentum towards further growth. Generally, after having established dense business networks professionals have shown a reticence to leave.[11]

The Islamic finance sector has been a beneficiary of the emergence of these financial centres. Islamic financial asset volumes increased annually by 11 per cent in Saudi Arabia, 14 per cent in the UAE and 31 per cent in Qatar from 2008 to 2012. The annual growth rate in Saudi Arabia was 3.6 times faster than that for conventional assets. In the UAE it was 3 times faster and in Qatar 1.8 times faster than conventional assets growth.[12] With more than 130 financial institutions active in Islamic finance in the GCC region and a share of 42 per cent of industry assets worldwide, the GCC has become the epicentre of Islamic finance. Relative to conventional financial assets in the region, Islamic finance comprises 18 per cent of total assets, underscoring the industry's growing importance to GCC economies.[13]

Increased foreign participation in GCC stock markets, private equity activity and international investment by GCC-based corporations has resulted in greater exposure to international standards and market expectations that international best practices will be adopted. International standards as well as the regulatory lessons learnt from the 2008 global financial crisis, almost all of which are derived from the United States and the European Union, are important determinants of the ways in which GCC financial centres are reformed and further developed.[14] The increasingly global nature of banking regulation is evident in subsequent analyses of its adoption and application in multiple GCC financial centres.

Before turning to the regulatory analysis of Islamic finance in Bahrain the next section examines the pluralistic Bahraini legal system and the ways in which sharia is applied in practice.

[11] Geoffrey Jones (n 5) 317.

[12] Ernst & Young, 'World Islamic Banking Competitiveness Report' (2013–14), 15, www.ey.com/Publication/vwLUAssets/EY_-_World_Islamic_Banking_Competitiveness_Report_2013-14/$File/EY-World-Islamic-Banking-Competitiveness-Report-2013-14.pdf. Accessed 18 August 2014.

[13] Steffen Kern (n 7) 17.

[14] Chatham House (n 3) 50.

7.2 The role of the sharia in the legal system of Bahrain

The legal system of Bahrain is a pluralistic legal system influenced by a number of normative traditions including English common law, sharia, civil law and customary law.[15] The influence of English common law originates from the United Kingdom's colonisation of Bahrain and other Gulf states in the late eighteenth century. Britain became heavily involved in the legal and political affairs of Bahrain beginning in 1798, when France occupied Egypt. Britain's earlier focus on its commercial interests in the region was recalibrated to include an interest in establishing British jurisdiction over all non-Bahrainis in the territory. In July 1909, Sheikh Isa, the ruler of Bahrain, was forced to grant Britain this jurisdiction.[16] British extra-territorial jurisdiction also extended to Kuwait, Qatar and the Emirates. Kuwait was the first state to terminate this jurisdiction in 1961 while Bahrain, Qatar and the Emirates did so in 1971. As a result, Kuwait's 1962 constitution formed the basic template for these other states, whose constitutions were promulgated in 1973, 1972 and 1971, respectively.[17]

As a result of Britain's jurisdiction in Bahrain, common law, until recently, has played a significant role in the country's legal system. In fact, Bahrain's general law of obligations (contract and torts) was based on common law until the promulgation in 2001 of the new Civil Code.[18] Since then the role of common law has diminished, although common law doctrines such as the requirement of adequate consideration in contract remain in force in the new code.[19]

As was the trend throughout the Middle East, from the late nineteenth century the sharia was gradually replaced in Bahrain in favour of European law codes, mainly from France. Although there have been restatements of the sharia such as the codification of Hanāfī law as per the *Mejelle* (1877), Islamic procedural and commercial law were almost entirely abandoned in favour of the adoption of the French Civil Code.[20] Specifically, the

[15] CIA World Factbook, 'Bahrain', www.cia.gov/library/publications/the-world-factbook/geos/ba.html. Accessed 1 May 2014.

[16] Hassan Ali Radhi, *Judiciary and Arbitration in Bahrain: A Historical and Analytical Study* (Boston: Kluwer Law International, 2003), 26–7.

[17] William Ballantyne, 'Note on the New Commercial Code of Bahrain (Decree Law 7/1987)' (1987) 2 *ALQ* 3, 27.

[18] The Bahrain Contract Law of 1961 and the Bahrain Civil Wrongs Ordinance of 1970 dealt with those topics respectively.

[19] Legislative Decree No. 19 of the year 2001 with respect to Promulgating the Civil Code, Arts 111–112.

[20] David Suratgar, 'The Development of the Legal Systems of the Middle East; Islamic Law and the Importance of Civil Law to the Process of Modernisation' in Brian Russell

civil codes and commercial laws of Bahrain are derived from other Arab jurisdictions, most notably Egypt and Kuwait, but behind these codes are European civil law influences, primarily the French Civil Code.[21]

In the modern period, after promulgation of its constitution in 1973, Bahrain sought membership in the Arab League whereupon it adopted a policy of arabising the law. This was a policy that meant the country would gradually adopt legislation similar to other Arab countries. In general, the civil codes of Arab countries are influenced by Egyptian legislation and, specifically, by one of Egypt's most famous jurists, 'Abd al-Razzaq al-Sanhūrī (d. 1971). Al-Sanhūrī led the commission entrusted with drafting the Egyptian Civil Code of 1948 and subsequently participated in drafting many Arab states' civil codes and constitutions.[22] In addition to borrowing from the French Civil Code Al-Sanhūrī utilised two earlier civil codes as well as a codification of Egyptian case law. Moreover, he included comparative legal aspects as well as some general principles of sharia in drafting the Egyptian Civil Code.[23]

Like other Arab countries, Bahrain adopted a largely secular civil law legal system and delegated jurisdiction to the sharia only in personal status matters arising from marriage and inheritance. However, the constitution of Bahrain, like those of other Arab states, declares in Article 2 that 'Islam shall be the religion of the State' and that 'Islamic Sharia (Islamic Law)' shall be 'a main source of legislation'.[24] Although a considerable amount of confusion centres on this provision, in practice, the role of the sharia in the legal systems of Middle Eastern states has not been determined by the particular wording of the respective constitution.[25]

Devout Muslims believe that it is their divine duty to apply the sharia in all aspects of their lives. On the other hand, however, there is a deep desire to embrace modernity in the Muslim world, which generally includes the adoption of influences originating in the West. A chasm between the pull of modernity and traditionalism has thus ensued, which is a consistent

(ed.), *An Introduction to Business Law in the Middle East* (New York: Drake Publishers, 1975), 9.

21 William Ballantyne (n 17) 32–3.

22 Hassan Ali Radhi (n 16) 77.

23 David Suratgar (n 20) 11–12.

24 Constitution of the State of Bahrain, Art 2.

25 Ann Elizabeth Mayer, 'Law and Religion in the Muslim Middle East' (1987) 35 *Am.J.Comp.L.*, 127, 138. See also William Ballantyne, *Commercial Law in the Arab Middle East: The Gulf States* (London: Lloyd's of London Press, 1986), 50. However, in those states in which the role of the sharia is changed from being 'a' source of legislation to 'the' source, the amendment, particularly of the constitutional variety, must surely have been made to produce some effect.

driving force behind the development of IFL. It has resulted in the somewhat awkward inclusion of the sharia in the otherwise secular constitutions of many Muslim Middle Eastern states.[26]

This development derives from the impact of colonial regimes on the customary legal systems of Arab polities. Contemporary Arab jurisprudence generally classifies sources of law into primary and material sources.[27] Primary sources consist of legislation, which is applied in the first instance to a legal problem. Material sources are used to fill a lacuna in the primary sources. They do not consist of binding legal rules per se, rather they refer to the background material, 'the remote sources of law', from which the primary law ultimately derives.[28] Until recently the dearth of law in the commercial field made the constitution's designation of the sharia as a main source of legislation important, since it was conceptualised as a means of filling legislative lacunae if secular law was silent on the matter.[29]

The particular phrasing of the constitutional clause creates confusion. The designation of the sharia as a main source of legislation seems to indicate that the sharia, as a material, supplementary source, is not a binding source of law. Rather, it should be referred to by the legislature as a material source from which formal legislation can be derived and subsequently be given binding legal force. However, as examined below, legislation specifically requires that the judiciary interpret these sources in the event of a legislative lacuna. In effect, the material sources of law are given binding legal force via judicial interpretation of such sources.

For example, Article 3 of the 1971 law governing the judiciary stated that:[30]

> If the judge does not find a legislative paragraph that can be implemented, the bases of his verdict shall be derived from Islamic shari'ah law and its rulings. If no shari'ah ruling is found, rules of convention shall be applied. Special convention shall take precedence over general convention. If no convention is found, rules of natural law and justice and common sense are applied.

26 Butti Sultan Butti Ali Al-Muhairi, 'The Position of Sharia within the UAE Constitution and the Federal Supreme Court's Application of the Constitutional Clause Concerning Shari'a' (1996) 11 *ALQ*, 219, 225–6.

27 *Ibid.*, 224. 28 *Ibid.*, 223.

29 Saleh Majid, 'Application of Islamic Law in the Middle East' (2003) 20 *I.C.L.R.*, www.mondaq.com/x/52976/international+trade+investment/Application+Of+Islamic+Law+In+The+Middle+East. Accessed 1 May 2014.

30 Legislative Decree No. (13) of 1971 Governing the Judiciary.

So, in the event of a legislative lacuna, the judge is directed to consult the sharia. It is unclear whether this means that secular law is preferred to the sharia or it may conflict with the sharia. Secondly, if a ruling of the sharia is not found, custom applies, which indicates that the sharia may be deficient in supplying a legal solution to a problem. The question remains whether custom that runs contrary to the sharia would still be applicable. The same question applies to the rules of natural law and justice. If these do not accord with the sharia, are they still to be applied? These difficult questions raise the issue that is foremost on foreign investors' minds, namely whether many aspects of commerce and banking would be found to be illegal.[31]

The introduction of the Commercial Code in 1987 seems to have gone some way in resolving these questions, however, particularly with respect to its provisions for the use of interest in banking and commercial transactions. Article two provides that:[32]

(1) There shall apply to commercial matters that which the two contracting parties have agreed upon provided that such agreement does not conflict with mandatory legislative provisions.
(2) If there is no special agreement the principles of commercial custom shall apply insofar as there is no relevant provision in this or any other law relating to commercial matters. Special custom shall be preferred over general custom.
(3) If there is no commercial custom the laws relating to civil matters shall be applied in the absence of which the judge shall deduce the bases of his judgment from the principles of the Islamic Shari'a then the principles of natural law and justice.

Paragraph one indicates that legislators have adopted the western notion of freedom of contract. In the absence of an express agreement, however, the hierarchy of sources thus created appears to provide for:

(1) the Commercial Code
(2) any other laws relating to commercial matters
(3) specific commercial customs over general, unspecified customs.

In the absence of commercial custom, the civil code should be consulted,[33] followed by the sharia and the principles of natural law and justice. There

[31] William Ballantyne, 'The States of the GCC: Sources of Law, the Shari'a and the Extent to which it Applies' (1985) 1 *ALQ* 3, 11.
[32] Legislative Decree No. (7) of 1987 Promulgating the Commercial Code.
[33] Prior to the promulgation of the Civil Code of 2001 the Contracts Law and the Law of Civil Wrongs comprised Bahrain's Civil Code.

remains some confusion with regard to what is meant by mandatory public policy and whether it is commensurate with the sharia, so that the sharia trumps everything else. Generally speaking, the legal systems of the Middle East have treated sharia norms as part of the *ordre public*.[34] The provisions of this Commercial Code, however, as will be examined below, as well as the overall jurisprudential situation of Bahrain, indicate that this would not be the case. For example, the Commercial Code, in Articles 76 and 275, allow commercial loans and/or deposits with interest – provisions that would otherwise conflict with the sharia's prohibition of interest.

The new Civil Code, which in 2001 replaced the contracts law and law of civil wrongs, seems to confirm this interpretation of Bahraini law. The rank of the sharia has now been relegated to third position after custom. Moreover, the law makes the role of the sharia contingent on the country's circumstances. The judge, only in the absence of custom, will decide a case 'in accordance with the principles of Islamic Sharia that suit the conditions and circumstances of the country,'[35] allowing the judge flexibility in the application of the sharia.

Therefore, the role of the sharia in Bahrain is generally circumscribed to matters of personal status as articulated in Article 13 of the 2002 judicial authority law,[36] which provides that: 'The shariaa judiciary courts shall have jurisdiction to examine all personal status disputes for Muslims except for the disputes related to estate assets and liquidation thereof which shall be subject to the qualitative competence of the concerned civil court.'[37] The law divides sharia courts into a high sharia court of appeal, a mid-ranking high sharia court and, finally, a lower sharia court. Each instance consists of a Sunni court as well as a Jaafari court, which is the Shia sect of Bahrain's Shia majority. Jurisdiction with respect to personal status matters is determined on the basis of membership to one of the sects so that 'matters related to inheritance, gift, will and endowment shall be determined according to the sect of the testator, gift-maker, legator or dedicator of a *waqf*.'[38]

The judicial authority law provides for a civil court system comprised of a court of cassation, a civil higher appeals court, a greater civil court and a lesser court. The civil courts have jurisdiction in civil, commercial and administrative matters as well as in disputes concerning the

[34] Ann Elizabeth Mayer (n 25) 144.
[35] Legislative Decree No. (19) of 2001 Promulgating the Civil Code, Art 1, s (b).
[36] Legislative Decree No. (42) of the year 2002 with respect to promulgating the judicial authority.
[37] *Ibid.*, Art 13. [38] *Ibid.*, Art 14.

personal affairs of non-Muslims and criminal law.[39] Disputes involving commercial transactions in Bahrain are resolved in secular civil law courts. Theoretically, the principles of sharia or its legal rules should not be applied to commercial law cases in Bahraini courts. Still, the sharia has had an influence on the manner in which IFL is practised in the Bahrain financial centre.

7.3 Bahrain: an Islamic financial centre

Bahrain, an archipelago comprised of thirty-three small islands, has the highest concentration of IFIs amongst all international financial centres despite its relatively small population of just over 1 million. Bahrain first established its offshore banking centre in 1975 and soon thereafter pioneered the Islamic finance sector by laying the legal and regulatory foundation for the industry.[40] Since then Bahrain has become one of the leading financial centres in the Middle East. The Global Financial Centres Index rates Bahrain the fifty-second most competitive centre in the world. However, both Qatar and Dubai now outperform Bahrain and are considered the most competitive financial centres in the region.[41] Yet the creation of the Bahrain financial harbour in 2009, a purpose-built financial district, is a reminder that Bahrain remains competitive within the region.

Bahrain's first Islamic bank, Bahrain Islamic Bank, was established in 1978 as a retail financial institution. In September 2013 Bahrain hosted 407 financial institutions, with the financial sector contributing 16.8 per cent to GDP. Of a total of 111 banking institutions with US$193.5 billion in assets, 24 were Islamic with assets of US$26.2 billion. Furthermore, eight *takāful* and *retakāful* firms[42] were operative, as well as ninety-six Islamic funds with total assets of US$1.8 billion in Bahrain.[43] In much the same way as London is known as an international financial centre Bahrain is synonymous with Islamic finance.[44]

[39] Legislative Decree No. (42) of the year 2002 with respect to promulgating the judicial authority, Art 6.
[40] Steffen Kern (n 7) 3.
[41] Mark Yeandle, Nick Danev and Z/Yen Group, *The Global Financial Centres Index 14* (London: Z/Yen Group Limited, 2013), 21.
[42] Central Bank of Bahrain, 'CBB Factsheet 2013', www.cbb.gov.bh/page-p-financial_sector_fact_sheet.htm. Accessed 1 May 2014.
[43] Central Bank of Bahrain, 'CBB Welcomes Innovation by Financial Firms' (2013) June *Rev.* 1, 1.
[44] Ricardo Baba, 'Islamic Financial Centres' in M Kabir Hassan and Mervyn K Lewis (eds.), *Handbook of Islamic Banking* (Cheltenham: Edward Elgar, 2007), 384.

Moreover, much of the financial infrastructure of the global Islamic finance industry is based in Bahrain. The financial infrastructure, similar to the conventional sector, is comprised of public and private IINGOs. IINGOs serve as an important nexus between Islamic and conventional financial sectors and help to integrate Islamic finance into conventional global financial markets, which is a central part of their mission. Yet IINGOs also focus on developing uniquely Islamic solutions to financial markets that have the effect of formalising differences between financial sectors. Such differences are reinforced by the underlying sharia ethos of the industry.[45] IINGOs comprise SSBs, which approve and oversee the development and dissemination of industry standards and guidelines. Chapter 4 introduced the work of the Bahrain-based AAOIFI with a focus on the institution's promulgation of sharia standards. AAOIFI is an example of an IINGO engaged in the promulgation of accounting, auditing and sharia standards as a way of integrating and carving out a special niche for Islamic finance in financial markets. A number of other Islamic IINGOs with global missions are also based in Bahrain. These include the Liquidity Management Centre (LMC), the International Islamic Rating Agency, the General Council for Islamic Banks and Financial Institutions, the Bahrain Institute for Banking and Finance and the International Islamic Financial Market (IIFM). The reader may recall that the IIFM, in conjunction with ISDA, developed the *tahawwut* master agreement (a profit-rate derivative product) and other standard form contracts.

Bahrain is one of the few jurisdictions that created an industry-specific dual regulatory framework for the Islamic finance industry. A dual regulatory framework implies that Bahrain has carved out an alternative legislative and regulatory system for Islamic finance that captures the particular features and risks of its mode of financial intermediation. A dual, more centrally directed system can be usefully distinguished from a self-regulatory model in which the industry is largely assimilated in the legal and financial framework.[46] The United Kingdom's facilitation of Islamic finance, discussed in Chapters 5 and 6, is an example of that particular strategy.

The Central Bank of Bahrain (CBB) is the sole regulatory and monetary authority in the Kingdom of Bahrain. It was established by the Central Bank of Bahrain and Financial Institutions Law in September 2006,

[45] Heather McKeen-Edwards and Tony Porter, *Transnational Financial Associations and the Governance of Global Finance* (Abingdon: Routledge, 2013), 145.

[46] Ali Adnan Ibrahim, 'Regulation of Shari'ah Governance' (2012) 30 *Rev.*, 8, 8.

replacing the now defunct Bahrain Monetary Agency. This law is considered to be a significant modernisation of Bahrain's financial services law.[47] As the sole regulatory and supervisory authority for all financial institutions in Bahrain, the CBB is empowered to issue regulatory instruments with which all financial institutions must comply. These instruments are catalogued in the CBB rulebook, which is divided into seven volumes, each covering different areas of financial services. Volume two deals specifically with Islamic bank licensees and provides much of the source material from which the subsequent analysis draws.[48]

The CBB rulebook is organised according to two formal rule-making instruments, namely regulations and directives. Regulations have general application throughout Bahrain.[49] Directives, although binding, do not have general application but rather are addressed to specific licensees or categories of licensees, registered persons or approved persons. Directives, unlike regulations, do not require consultation or prior publication in the official gazette, though in practice the CBB consults with parties regarding directives. The rulebook itself is given the status of rules or guidance. The breach of a rule constitutes a breach of CBB law whereas a breach of guidance, while not binding, is generally considered an indication that the addressee may have also breached a rule.[50] All rulebook content is at least of the status of a directive while some content may also be that of a regulation. Therefore, all rulebook content is legally mandatory and must be complied with.[51]

The following section analyses the first and most fundamental requirement of financial services law. It addresses the way in which Bahrain authorises Islamic financial institutions.

7.4 The authorisation of Islamic banking services

In the Kingdom of Bahrain, as is the case in nearly every financial services framework, no person may carry out a regulated service unless it has been licensed by the Central Bank. Regulated services are those provided

[47] Central Bank of Bahrain, 'Profile', www.cbb.gov.bh/page-p-profile.htm. Accessed 1 May 2014.

[48] Volume 2 was published in January 2005. Central Bank of Bahrain, 'CBB Rulebook', cbb.complinet.com/cbb/microsite/cbb_rulebook.html. Accessed 1 May 2014.

[49] Regulations are made pursuant to Article 37 of the Legislative Decree No. (64) with respect to the Central Bank of Bahrain and Financial Institutions Law 2006 (hereinafter 'CBB Law').

[50] Central Bank of Bahrain (n 48) UG-11.4-1.2.3.

[51] *Ibid.*, UG-1.2.7.

by financial institutions including 'those governed by Islamic Sharia principles'.[52] One of the primary tasks of the Central Bank is to regulate and supervise any licensee that provides such services.[53] A person who wishes to undertake a regulated Islamic banking service is required to be licensed by the CBB as an Islamic bank licensee.[54] An application to provide a regulated service must be made to the Central Bank.[55]

7.4.1 Types of licensee

There are three general categories of Islamic banking services that can be carried on 'by way of business' and that are subject to licensing: (1) the acceptance of sharia money placements/deposits; (2) the management of PLS investment accounts; and (3) the offer of sharia financing contracts. A number of other services may also be undertaken.[56] These are considered the requisite activities necessary to receive an Islamic banking licence. Licensing requirements also provide that only 'operations in compliance with sharia economic principles' may be carried out and that only Islamic bank licensees may identify themselves as fully sharia-compliant institutions.[57] Generally, bank licensees cannot engage in any non-financial business. An exception is made for Islamic banks that engage in commercial activities arising from their financial business. Such business includes transacting in Islamic contracts such as the *murābaḥa*, *ijāra* and *mushāraka* in which the bank may have title to physical assets being financed or leased. Other activities not considered to detract from a bank's financial activities may also be allowed subject to regulatory approval.[58]

Islamic bank licensees consist of two categories: Islamic retail banks and Islamic wholesale banks. Each particular type of bank may be subject to specific regulatory requirements. For example, Islamic retail banks may undertake transactions in any currency and with regard to Bahraini or non-Bahraini residents or non-residents. Furthermore, to qualify as an Islamic retail bank an entity must be involved in the activity of accepting sharia money placements/deposits, and/or managing PLS investment accounts and offering sharia financing contracts.[59] In particular, an

[52] CBB Law (n 48) Arts 39–40. [53] *Ibid.*

[54] Central Bank of Bahrain (n 48) LR-A.1.3.

[55] CBB Law (n 49) Art 44(a).

[56] Central Bank of Bahrain (n 48) LR-1.3.4. See LR-1.3.1 for a list of other regulated Islamic banking services.

[57] *Ibid.*, LR-A.1.3. [58] *Ibid.*, LR-1.1.12.

[59] *Ibid.*, LR-1.2.5

Islamic retail bank must have at least 20 per cent of its assets in the form of sharia financing contracts, although other finance-related activities may also be taken into account.[60]

Wholesale Islamic banks may also undertake transactions without restriction as to the counterparty. However, transactions denominated in Bahraini Dinar (BD) and/or with a resident of Bahrain must be wholesale in nature. This means that the initial amount invested under one of the three categories of regulated services described above must be BD7 million (US$18,567,640) or more to be considered a wholesale transaction, i.e. those of large corporations and high net-worth individuals.[61] Other Islamic banking services may be undertaken with residents of Bahrain and/or in Bahraini Dinar, which are US$100,000 or more.[62] The effect of this rule is to limit the onshore Bahraini Dinar transactions of Islamic wholesale banks to larger transactions. In general, an entity must engage in the three regulated services of Islamic banking as mentioned above in order to qualify as an Islamic wholesale bank. In contrast to the requirements of Islamic retail banks there is no requirement that sharia financing contracts constitute a significant part of the bank's business. The regulator's intention is to provide wholesale banks with flexibility and to recognise that non-credit related risks arising from wholesale banks' client base do not require the same level of regulatory attention.[63] Finally, the CBB makes an exception for transactions with the government of Bahrain, any Bahraini public sector entity, CBB bank licensees and transactions in securities on the Bahrain stock exchange undertaken to fund regular operating expenses.[64]

7.4.2 The regulatory definition of Islamic financial services

The state's devising of a dual regulatory system provides a useful example of the way in which nation states contribute to the process of creating IFL. The state's intervention is not limited to its own legislative and regulatory promulgation. In a strategic manner Bahrain has harnessed the utility and market legitimacy of international standards originating from international Islamic standard setters such as AAOIFI and the IFSB. This section addresses this aspect of IFL law making by examining the areas of law in which the CBB requires Islamic bank licensees to utilise AAOIFI sharia and accounting standards. Unlike the UK regulatory authority, the

[60] *Ibid.*, LR-a.1.5, LR-a.1.6. [61] *Ibid.*, LR-1.2.14, LR-1.2.15.
[62] *Ibid.*, LR-a.1.7. [63] *Ibid.*, LR-1.2.12. [64] *Ibid.*, LR-1.2.20.

CBB makes such standards mandatory and thus endows them with sovereign authority.[65] A resulting nexus between the state and supranational organisations is created.

Unlike the FSA in the United Kingdom, which struggled to find an appropriate conventional classification for the types of contract used by Islamic banks, Bahrain's creation of an industry-specific regulatory system allows the Central Bank to classify such products according to their own risk profile and economic outcome. This allows the CBB to avoid making the regulatory tradeoffs that sometimes accompany attempts to fit an Islamic regulated service into the legal category of a conventional regulated service. It is also interesting to note that Bahrain, a Muslim-majority jurisdiction, uses Islamic legal terms to categorise and define regulated financial services, whereas the United Kingdom decided on the neutral moniker, 'alternative financial investments'. The role of Islam in Bahrain is clearly an accepted fact of public life.

The CBB defines sharia money placements/deposits 'as the acceptance of sums of money or safe-keeping (*al-wadia*', *qard*) in a sharia compliant framework, under which it will be repaid, either on demand or in circumstances agreed by the parties involved, and which is not referable to the giving of security.'[66] *Wadi'ah* literally means safekeeping or deposit in Arabic. In Islamic banking it refers to sums of money deposited in a sharia-compliant framework that will be repaid in full upon demand by the customer. The bank is deemed keeper and trustee of the funds and is wholly liable for the entire sum in its possession. *Qarḍ*, on the other hand, refers to a loan. However, it has the same basic function as the *wadi'ah* in Islamic banking, where it is used to accept deposits without interest and to repay these on demand. Both *wadi'ah* and *qarḍ* allow IFIs to guarantee the repayment of deposits in the same way that conventional financial institutions do.

The second general category of regulated services concerns the management of 'unrestricted shari'a profit sharing investment accounts.'[67] This regulated service involves the management of an 'account, portfolio or fund whereby a sum of money is placed with the service provider on terms that a return will be made according to an agreed Shari'a-compliant profit-sharing arrangement, such as a *mudaraba* or *musharaka*

[65] *Ibid.*, PB-1.1.10. [66] *Ibid.*, LR-1.3.16.

[67] In the interest of uniformity I have adopted the nomenclature of profit- and loss-sharing investment accounts (PLSIA). Different jurisdictions use different nomenclatures for essentially the same investment product.

partnership without the customer laying down any restrictions as to where, how and for what purpose the funds should be invested.'[68] The definition refers to AAOIFI financial accounting standard no. 6 for further guidance as to the way in which the equity of unrestricted investment account holders should be dealt with in the books of the bank.[69] Islamic finance institutions 'are not contractually obliged to make good losses arising from Islamic financing assets funded by the investment accounts, unless these losses arise from the negligence on the part of the Islamic bank as manager (*muḍārib*) or as agent (*wakīl*)'.[70] Therefore, the CBB's approach to unrestricted PLS accounts does not categorise them as deposit-taking accounts. The result of this approach is that the credit and market risks, which are financed by such accounts, can be treated for regulatory purposes as being borne by PLS account holders. In the unlikely event that profit smoothing could be excluded, IFIs would not be required to retain capital reserves for such accounts. The CBB's treatment of such accounts for capital adequacy purposes indicates that profit smoothing does in fact take place. This is examined in the section below dealing with CARS.

Furthermore, *muḍārabah* contracts, in particular, are subject to general disclosure rules that require banks to develop policy statements and procedures so as to safeguard PLSIA investors. Policies must deal with the following issues:[71]

> (1) the basis for allocation of profit or loss to the [PLSIA]; (2) policy for making provisions and reserves against assets and equity for [PLSIA] and to whom these provisions and reserves revert to in case of write-back or recovery; (3) policy on the priority for investment of own funds and those of unrestricted investment account holders; and (4) basis for allocating expenses to the [PLSIA].' AAOIFI financial accounting standard no. 11 must be consulted regarding the rules and/or procedures for making these determinations.

A 'restricted Shari'a profit sharing investment account', on the other hand, is defined as 'managing an account, portfolio or fund, whereby a sum of money is placed with the service provider on terms that a return will be made according to an agreed Shari'a compliant profit-sharing

[68] Central Bank of Bahrain (n 48) LR-1.3.17a.

[69] AAOIFI, *Accounting, Auditing and Governance Standards for Islamic Financial Institutions: Financial Accounting Standards* (Manama: The Accounting and Auditing Organization for Islamic Financial Institutions, 2010), no. 6.

[70] Central Bank of Bahrain (n 48) CA-A.3.7.

[71] Central Bank of Bahrain (n 48) BC-7.1.3.

arrangement, such as a *mudaraba* or *musharaka* partnership where the customer imposes certain restrictions as to where, how and for what purpose the funds should be invested'.[72] The assets and liabilities arising from such investments are to be treated separately from the bank's assets and liabilities according to AAOIFI financial standard 6.[73]

The third general category of regulated Islamic banking services includes sharia-financing contracts. These are broadly defined as 'entering into, or making arrangement for another person to enter into, a contract to provide finance in accordance with shari'a principles, such as *murabaha*, *bay muajjal*, *bay salam*, *ijara wa iktina* and *istisna'a* contracts'.[74] The rulebook explains in clear terms what dealing as principal or as agent means. It also provides definitions for managing, safeguarding and arranging deals in sharia-compliant financial instruments.[75]

Bahrain's approach differs from the UK approach by providing in a very transparent manner the types of regulated Islamic banking services that require authorisation. This approach helps to avoid problems of defining Islamic products according to conventional categories. It may also make room for more innovation in the industry, since it is allowed to compete on its own terms. Finally, it may help to mitigate sharia-compliance risks in IFIs, since financial products are not categorised conventionally.

The next section analyses CARs for IFIs, which, as has been noted, originate in the standard-setting initiatives of leading economies. It is particularly concerned with the influence of CARs on Bahrain's regulatory apparatus for Islamic finance.

7.5 Capital adequacy requirements for IFIs

The CBB rulebook provides specific rules for Islamic banks' CARs, which are designed to provide a buffer against unexpected losses and to ensure an orderly wind-down of operations without loss to depositors. Capital adequacy rules are applicable to locally incorporated stand-alone IFIs as well as consolidated groups including subsidiaries and other investments. As part of its prudential requirements for IFIs the CBB also mandates that banks maintain adequate liquidity and identify and control large exposures. Bahrain's prudential requirements are 'in all substantial respects' consistent 'with the approach recommended by the Basel Committee on Banking Supervision and Islamic Financial Services Board (IFSB) for

[72] Central Bank of Bahrain (n 48) LR-1.3.17b.
[73] *Ibid.* [74] *Ibid.*, LR-1.3.18. [75] *Ibid.*, LR-1.3.19-50.

capital adequacy', clearly indicating the incorporation of international standards, some Islamic, within Bahraini law.[76] However, the CBB recognises that Islamic products and services may possess specific characteristics that are not covered by Basel standards and thus the CBB employs a risk-based approach that tailors rules to the specific risk profile of Islamic banks.[77]

7.5.1 Minimum capital adequacy ratios

Historically, the CBB has applied a minimum capital adequacy ratio of 12 per cent on a consolidated basis for all banks incorporated locally. Locally incorporated banks operating on a solo basis (and consolidated basis where applicable) are required to maintain a minimum 'trigger' CAR of 8 per cent. Locally incorporated banks must also set 'target' CARs on both a solo and consolidated basis. An initial minimum target of 8.5 per cent is the rule while high-risk banks may be subject to 12.5 per cent target ratios.[78] Banks which breach CARs may be subject to a formal licensing reappraisal.[79]

A risk profile assessment by the CBB may replace predetermined ratios. The assessment is calculated in a formula whereby a bank's own regulatory capital applies to the numerator and the risk-weighted assets are placed in the denominator. Deductions for restricted and unrestricted PLSIAs from total risk-weighted assets are made[80] for the reason that investors are expected to assume any losses that arise. Thus the IFI would not need to make good on those losses. As examined in Chapter 6, the theoretical model of IFIs' financial intermediation allows losses to pass through to depositors/investors, making IFIs more stable than conventional institutions, which are beset by asset-liability mismatches. In practice, IFIs establish profit equalisation reserves (PER) and investment risk reserves (IRR) to smooth the income to PLS account holders so as to minimise displaced commercial risk and to buttress the safety and soundness of the financial institution. The CBB stipulates that a proportion of such reserves should be deducted from the risk-weighted assets, since they are legitimately passed on to customers. According to IFSB guidelines, however, the CBB requires that IFIs retain 30 per cent of the risk-weighted assets and liabilities financed by unrestricted PLS accounts so as to account for profit

[76] *Ibid.*, CA-A.2.8. [77] *Ibid.*, CA-A.2.9.
[78] *Ibid.*, CA-A.3.3–CA-A.3.4. [79] *Ibid.*, CA-1.4.6.
[80] See *ibid.*, CA-A.3.2 for the exact formula.

smoothing. The result is that the risk-weighted assets (the denominator of the formula) 'consist of the sum of risk-weighted assets financed by an IFI's own capital and liabilities' as well as 30 per cent of risk-weighted assets derived from unrestricted PLS accounts.[81]

The numerical value of the total risk-weighted assets is measured by applying Basel II methodologies with regard to the different types of risk, including credit risk, operational risks and market risks. Some methodologies require explicit approval from the CBB. So, for example, the measure of credit risk for capital adequacy purposes is obtained by applying the standardised approach whereby different categories of counterparties are assigned different risk weights according to a broad categorisation of relative risks.[82] For example, claims on corporates, including insurance companies, which are given the highest rating of AAA to AA- receive a 20 per cent risk while those with the lowest rating below BB- receive a 150 per cent risk weighting. Unrated entities receive a 100 per cent risk weighting.[83] Other categories of risk are subject to different risk weight methodologies.

The numerator of the CAR formula, on the other hand, comprises tier 1 core capital and tier 2 supplementary capital. Tier 1 capital should comprise at least half of all eligible capital while tier 2 capital is limited to 100 per cent of tier 1 capital.[84] Core capital supports credit risk-weighted assets as well as the calculation of operational and market risk. Supplementary capital supports credit risk, operation and market risks, subject to limitations.[85] The CBB has broadly adopted IFSB standards with regard to the definition of tier capital. It places some restrictions on the inclusion of investment risk and profit equalisation reserves as tier 2 capital.[86]

The CBB treats Islamic financing assets according to their unique risks and recognises that unlike conventional products, Islamic banks are exposed to price risk as well as credit and market risks in their banking book. Price risks are identified and measured for the purpose of capital adequacy. The following section addresses the capital adequacy risk weighting of a binding *murābaḥah* to the purchase orderer (MPO) on the assets side of the balance sheet. The analysis indicates that the CBB's approach to measuring the unique risks of Islamic financing assets results in the calculation of specific risk weights for each product. In addition to

[81] *Ibid.*, CA-A.3.7. [82] *Ibid.*, CA-A.3.8.
[83] *Ibid.*, CA-4.2.14. [84] *Ibid.*, CA-2.2.1.
[85] *Ibid.*, CA-A.3.5. [86] *Ibid.*, CA-2.1.3.

the MPO the CBB rulebook provides specific rules for the full range of Islamic financing assets.

7.5.2 *Minimum capital requirements for a* murābaḥah *to the purchase orderer*

A binding MPO refers to a contract in which a bank sells a specified asset to a customer at cost plus an agreed profit margin that it has acquired based upon the customer's promise to purchase the asset. The promise can be binding or non-binding. A binding MPO obliges the customer to take delivery of the asset at a pre-determined price. In the event that the customer does not honour his obligations under the promise to purchase, the bank will be forced to sell the asset to a third party at a price that may be lower than the acquisition price. This risk can be mitigated by securing a *hamish jiddiyyah* (HJ), which is a security deposit that is held as collateral by the bank.[87] A bank may also secure a pledge of the asset or underlying asset or another tangible asset, which must be documented in a separate security agreement. A third party guarantee is also permissible whereby the risk weighting of the guarantor can be substituted for that of the purchaser in the event that the guarantor has a better credit rating.[88]

The following application of risk weights applies to an asset that is available for sale and thus is on the balance sheet of an Islamic bank. The risk weight is determined by assessing a default event such as when a customer defaults on his promise to purchase. In this case the bank will dispose of the asset to a third party. In some instances a bank may have the legal right to recoup any loss after having disposed of the asset and having had recourse to the HJ. When that is the case the right constitutes a claim receivable and is exposed to credit risk. The exposure can be measured by subtracting the market value of the asset as collateral subject to any haircut as well as the amount of any HJ from the amount of the total acquisition cost. The risk weight is based on the credit rating of the obligor, which an external credit assessment institution (ECAI) may furnish. When an ECAI rating is not available a risk weight of 100 per cent applies.[89] Islamic financing assets are categorised according to claim categories as indicated above, which provide specific risk weights for different types of counterparty.[90]

87 *Ibid.*, CA-3.2.8. 88 *Ibid.*, CA-3.2.9.
89 *Ibid.*, CA-3.2.14. 90 *Ibid.*, CA-4.2.

The following application of risk weights also applies to an asset for sale, which means that the asset is on the balance sheet of the bank. It is calculated by envisioning a default event in which a bank does not possess a legal right to recoup any loss after having disposed of the asset. Such would be the case with a non-binding MPO in which a promise to purchase is not agreed. In that case the cost of the asset to the bank constitutes a market risk. Exposure to market risk can be reduced by the amount of HJ the bank has retained.[91] Market risk is expressed as price risk and is given a 15 per cent capital charge.[92]

When the asset is sold and delivered to a customer, the sale of the asset creates an accounts receivable amount, which should be assigned a risk weight net of the specific provisions (such as the sale of the asset to recoup the acquisition cost); any amount secured by eligible collateral and/or any amount that is more than 90 days past due.[93] The risk weight is based on the customer's rating by an ECAI or given a 100 per cent rating for unrated customers.

The following section examines a further aspect of Islamic finance that differs markedly from conventional finance and thus has required the Bahraini regulator to issue industry-specific standards and rules. The section concerns the manner in which Bahrain regulates and supervises the sharia compliance function of Islamic banks.

7.6 Governance standards for sharia supervisory boards

Unlike the United Kingdom, which does not regulate the risk of sharia non-compliance and thus depends on IFIs to self-regulate, Bahrain's CBB has created an extensive regulatory framework for the risk of sharia non-compliance. The CBB defines the risk as 'the risk that arises from Islamic bank licensees' failure to comply with the Shari'a rules and principles determined by the Shari'a board of the Islamic bank licensees and the CBB'.[94] It states that the risk may negatively affect the systems and controls of an Islamic bank, including 'the risk of loss resulting from inadequate or failed internal processes, people and systems or from external events'.[95] The CBB thus recognises that sharia compliance is 'critical to Islamic bank licensees' operations and such compliance requirements should permeate throughout the organisation and their products and

[91] *Ibid.*, CA-3.2.15. [92] *Ibid.*, CA-3.2.24.
[93] *Ibid.*, CA-3.2.17. [94] *Ibid.*, RM-7.2.3.
[95] *Ibid.*, RM-7.2.1.

activities.'[96] As argued in Chapter 6, the CBB recognises that consumers' uptake of Islamic financial products is in large part contingent on their perception of such products as complying with sharia and hence the sustainability of IFIs is directly connected to this perception.

7.6.1 A hands-on approach to sharia governance

The advantage of this approach is that the CBB involves itself directly in creating a regulatory and supervisory framework that assists IFIs in upholding the principles of sharia in their financial dealings. In addition to safeguarding consumer interests, it is evident that the CBB wishes to safeguard the value system that it associates with sharia, so that IFIs, which hold themselves out as 'Islamic', are regulated for their adherence to 'Islamic' principles as determined by the CBB.[97] To reinforce the protections of the sharia value system Bahrain requires IFIs to bear 'additional responsibilities to their stakeholders' including 'additional governance requirements and disclosures to provide assurance to stakeholders that they are following Shari'a principles'. An SSB should be established, comprising at least three sharia scholars, to ensure compliance with sharia principles.[98] The SSB of an IFI must comply with AAOIFI's governance standards no. 1 and no. 2[99] as well as standard no. 3.[100]

Bahrain's use of AAOIFI governance standards highlights the nation state's incorporation of IINGO standards in its legal system and thereby reflects an important way in which IFL is articulated, produced and maintained. AAOIFI governance standard no. 1 deals with the definition, appointment, composition and report of the SSB. The standard is critical for developing confidence, credibility and transparency in the formation, composition, selection, dismissal and reporting function of the SSB. Governance standard no. 2 provides standards and guidelines for the conduct of the sharia review so that compliance with sharia principles and rules can be adhered to. A sharia review examines 'the extent of an IFI's compliance, in all its activities, with the Shari'a,' which includes the examination of contracts, policies, products, transactions, memorandum and articles of association, reports and financial statements.[101] Standard

[96] *Ibid.*, RM-7.2.4. [97] *Ibid.*, HC-9.1.1.

[98] Bahrain, 'The Corporate Governance Code of the Kingdom of Bahrain' (Central Bank of Bahrain, 1 January 2011), prin. 9.1.

[99] Central Bank of Bahrain, (n 48) HC-9.2.1.

[100] *Ibid.*, HC-9.2.6. [101] AAOIFI (n 69) no. 2.

no. 3 establishes an internal sharia review in order to 'examine and evaluate the extent of compliance with Islamic Shari'a rules and principles, fatwas, guidelines, and instructions issued by the IFI's Shari'a supervisory board'.[102] The review, which is to be carried out by an independent department or division, should determine whether the management has carried out its responsibilities according to the sharia determinations of the SSB. The standard provides a number of criteria relating to the independence and objectivity of the review as well as its professional proficiency and the procedures/processes in which the review is conducted.

Recall that the CBB requires all IFIs to comply with AAOIFI sharia and accounting standards, so that any type of sharia review utilises AAOIFI standards as a comparative basis as to what the general rules and principles underlying permissible Islamic financing transactions are.[103]

Uniquely, Bahrain's approach towards sharia governance incorporates the SSB into the corporate governance function of the financial institution. In this way the CBB has created a framework in which the institutionalised safeguards for sharia compliance extend well beyond mandatory requirements for the establishment of an SSB and adherence to AAOIFI standards. The SSB is given an integral role in the governance framework of the financial institution as a whole. Principle 9 of the corporate governance code recommends that the SSB establish a corporate governance committee comprised of at least three members 'to coordinate and integrate implementation of the governance policy framework.'[104] One of the three members should be a sharia scholar of the SSB, who is charged with directing the corporate governance committee with respect to sharia-related matters and to coordinate between 'the complementary roles and functions of the corporate governance committee and the audit committee'.[105] The CBB implemented this recommendation in chapter HC-9 of the rulebook in which it established that a corporate governance committee should comprise at least one sharia scholar of the SSB and that his role should 'link the complementary roles and functions of the corporate governance committee and the SSB'.[106]

[102] *Ibid.*, no. 3. [103] See Central Bank of Bahrain, (n 48) PB-1.1.10.
[104] *Ibid.* [105] *Ibid.*
[106] Central Bank of Bahrain (n 48) HC-9.2.4.

7.6.2 Approved persons criteria

Persons wishing to undertake a controlled function in an IFI must be licensed by the CBB prior to their appointment. Amongst eight categories of controlled functions, which include that of director, chief executive, senior manager and compliance officer, are members of SSBs. Approval is subject to having satisfied 'fit and proper' criteria with respect to the particular position of the licensee concerned, which is provided on a case-by-case basis.[107] As was the case in the UK financial services framework 'fit and proper' criteria concern an individual's personal integrity, honesty and good reputation as well as their professional competence, experience and expertise with regard to the controlled function for which they are applying.[108] Unlike the United Kingdom, however, members of SSBs in Bahrain are categorised as persons undertaking controlled functions, which accordingly require the CBB's authorisation. The difference is attributable to the seriousness with which the CBB treats the function of sharia compliance as well as the consequences of sharia non-compliance for the safety and soundness of the financial institution.

However, the CBB, like most regulators around the world, does not specify the specific qualifications and/or experience necessary for a SSB member to satisfy 'fit and proper' criteria. These are determined on a case-by-case basis. The CBB Law authorises the CBB 'to determine the level of qualifications, experience, and training of a bank's board, officers or employees'.[109] The CBB also considers the particular role or function as well as the size and nature of the licensed institution for which the applicant is applying when examining an applicant's qualifications and experience.[110] The non-disclosure of the specific criteria that applicants must fulfil for authorisation to undertake a controlled function evidently allows the CBB to retain flexibility in determining 'fit and proper' thresholds. Furthermore, AAOIFI governance standard no. 1, which provides standards relating to the appointment, composition and report of an SSB and is mandated by the CBB, stipulates that the board shall consist of three members.[111] The standard makes no reference to specific qualifications and/or experience required of potential sharia board members. In part, this reflects a professionalisation of their role within the financial

[107] *Ibid.*, LR-1A.1.1-1A.1.4. [108] *Ibid.*, LR-1A.2.2.
[109] CBB Law (n 48) Art. 65.
[110] Central Bank of Bahrain (n 48) EN-5.2.3.
[111] AAOIFI (n 69) no. 1.

institution. It may also reflect a lack of industry consensus regarding the necessary qualifications and/or experience an SSB member should possess. At any rate, the CBB does not view the role of SSB members as merely cosmetic. The CBB's process of authorisation ensures that SSB members are professionals undertaking a vitally important controlled function.

7.7 Concluding remarks

Legal trends affecting global markets have a direct impact on regional financial centres including those of the GCC. The analysis above indicates that those trends include a general push to standardise commercial and banking law. There is also a regional effort to create a common market and currency union modelled on the European Union. Yet as subsequent chapters show, each jurisdiction in the GCC approaches the regulation of IFIs in a different manner, likely to reflect the legal history of the particular jurisdiction as well as its ambitions to develop a native Islamic finance industry. Despite these disparate efforts, however, such overarching legal trends, because of their fundamental impact on the integration of regional legal systems, affect the nature and type of legal promulgation within jurisdictions. As a result, the process of IFL law making incorporates and circulates these legal trends.

Bahrain, although sharply delimiting the role of sharia in its legal system, stands out as one of the early pioneers of Islamic finance. The country's role in developing the industry is apparent in its approach to developing an industry-specific regulatory framework. An aspect of this concerns the country's large share of Islamic finance infrastructure, which has helped to buttress its reputation as an Islamic financial centre and continues to allow Bahrain to exercise huge influence over the industry. This involves the CBB's use of IINGO standards as binding directives on all IFIs. Another aspect concerns Bahrain's extensive development of industry-specific regulations, which, arguably, allow IFIs to develop commercially on their own terms in ways that a more assimilative strategy would not. Such an approach may also help to mitigate certain risks such as that of sharia non-compliance due to the CBB's willingness to take a more serious approach to the sharia aspects of the industry.

As the industry grows and captures market share Bahrain is well placed to continue to shape its development in advantageous ways. Yet other regional financial centres have been playing catch-up for quite some time and now rival Bahrain both in terms of market share and ambition to develop Islamic financial hubs.

The next chapter examines one such rival, namely the UAE. With a similar approach, the chapter examines the UAE's legal framework and law-making trends in an effort to understand the ways in which they contribute to the development of IFL.

8

The regulation of Islamic financial institutions in the United Arab Emirates

The UAE has become an increasingly important financial centre in recent years. It has also developed a vibrant Islamic finance market, although, contrary to popular assertion, it has not developed a dual financial framework for the industry. The UAE legal system is similar to Bahrain's civil law legal system, albeit the UAE has reserved a much greater role for the sharia in its Civil Code and other foundational laws. However, the similar legal foundation masks critical differences between the two countries' approaches to Islamic finance. As a result of these differences Islamic financial products that originate in the respective jurisdictions will evince characteristics that derive from the particular nexus of law and market forces.

The UAE Central Bank has actively pursued the modernisation of its financial law, particularly since the 2008 global financial crisis. This has led to the introduction of international standards and best practices originating in the world's leading economies and non-governmental organisations. The result of these layers of interactive legal systems is a complex and particularly hybrid legal framework in which civil law, sharia and international standards are the primary sources of law.

Within this legal framework IFIs are generally subject to the same regulatory treatment as conventional institutions, although some special legislative provisions have helped to facilitate the industry. In general, the regulator maintains a fairly neutral approach to the industry, which leaves a wide role for market forces in the continuing development and innovation of Islamic financial products. Yet financial and legal developments largely originating in the leading economies continue to exert considerable influence on the promulgation of laws governing financial institutions, leading to a gradual standardisation of financial law.

This chapter deals with the ways in which Islamic finance is regulated in the UAE. It examines the nexus of laws used to facilitate the industry and focuses on the ways in which such laws have an impact on IFIs and the services they market. These tasks are undertaken, first, by examining the role of the sharia in the legal systems of the UAE. Thereafter, the regulatory systems in which IFIs operate and are regulated are the focus of analysis.

8.1 The role of the sharia in the judicial systems of the UAE

The UAE is a federation of seven emirates established in 1971 and comprising 32,278 square miles. The emirates are known as Abu Dhabi, Dubai, Sharjah, Ras Al Khaimah, Ajman, Fujairah and Umm al-Quwain. The legal system of the UAE is based on the 1971 constitution, which establishes sovereignty in all matters enumerated in the constitution. The emirates have sovereignty over their own territories in all matters not mentioned in the constitution or not in the exclusive jurisdiction of the UAE. Individually, the emirates are governed by hereditary rulers, who exercise considerable sovereignty over their emirate. Together, the seven rulers of the emirates form a supreme council whereby collective sovereignty over the union is exercised. Although individual rulers are endowed with considerable authority, a growing awareness has developed that considerable economic, political and strategic benefits derive from closer union.[1]

Britain exercised extra-territorial jurisdiction over the emirates since it first concluded a maritime treaty known as the General Treaty of Peace in 1821. The Trucial Emirates, as they were henceforth called, were formally placed under British protection in 1892. Under the treaty, Britain handled the external affairs of the emirates, while the rulers dealt with domestic affairs.[2] British jurisdiction over British and other non-native subjects was formally ceded to Britain in 1945, which was formalised in the Trucial States Order-in-Council 1946 and again in April 1949. A result of the Order-in-Council was to delimit the jurisdiction of all local courts, including sharia courts, to cases involving native citizens.[3] The Order-in-Council replaced the Indian Codes, the governing law of the territories, under which the Governor-General of India hitherto had exercised authority.[4] Britain's withdrawal from the Persian Gulf in 1971 presaged the UAE's promulgation of a constitution in the same year.

[1] Bashir Ahmed, Nakul Asthana *et al.*, 'Country Q&A: United Arab Emirates', *Practical Law*, 2009/10), www.practicallaw.com/8-385-5765. Accessed 21 December 2013.

[2] Butti Sultan Butti Ali Al-Muhairi, 'The Development of the UAE Legal System and Unification with the Judicial System' (1996) 11 *ALQ*, 116, 118.

[3] *Ibid.*, 125.

[4] Herbert J. Liebesny, 'British Jurisdiction in the States of the Persian Gulf' (1949) 3 *Middle E.J.*, 330–1.

Whereas Bahrain retained common law in the areas of contract and tort until 2001, British legal influence has retained less direct impact due to the low amount and minor relevance of cases tried under British jurisdiction. The withdrawal of the British was used to construct a broad array of laws modelled on Egyptian, Sudanese and other Arabic countries with some input from the sharia. These laws, similar to the situation in other Middle Eastern jurisdictions, are largely based on the French Civil Code.[5]

The UAE constitution provides for a central federal government with a Western-styled division of authority between executive, legislative and judicial institutions. The executive authorities comprise the supreme council, the presidency and the council of ministers. A national assembly comprises the legislative power of the country while the judiciary is divided into federal and local jurisdictions.[6] The supreme council is the highest authority in the union and is comprised of the rulers of each emirate. The supreme council exercises 'supreme control over the affairs of the union',[7] which includes the sanctioning of all union laws, decrees, treaties and international agreements.[8]

The constitution stipulates that Islam is the official religion of the union and that the sharia 'shall be a main source of legislation in the Union'.[9] As with other Middle Eastern jurisdictions, the courts' difficulty in interpreting this formulation is a source of legal uncertainty, which will be examined in this section.

Until 1950 the emirates were organised along tribal structures whereby hereditary sheikhs governed in an autocratic manner. Since these rulers controlled the executive, legislative and judicial functions of governance, administrative law was virtually non-existent. Indeed, no formal law courts existed, not to mention a civil service or military. Of course, the absence of formal law courts does not mean that anarchy prevailed. In fact, a well-developed system of customary law interspersed with sharia governed the tribes. Disputes were referred to the sheikhs of the tribe or to the local *qadī*. Although not formally trained, the *qadī* was considered a learned man and would have been well versed in a few basic texts including the Quran.[10]

At the beginning of the twentieth century an influx of nomadic desert dwellers (Bedouin) to coastal towns diluted the tribal structures of these

[5] *Ibid.*, 126–7.
[6] Constitution of the United Arab Emirates, Art 45.
[7] *Ibid.*, Art 47, para 7. [8] *Ibid.*, Art 47, paras 2–4.
[9] *Ibid.*, Art 7. [10] Butti Sultan Butti Ali Al-Muhairi (n 2) 121–2.

areas, so that rulers decided to create formal sharia courts to settle an increasing number of disputes. Like the tribal system of justice that preceded them, judicial decisions handed down by sharia courts were not binding. Rather, a type of voluntary justice existed whereby parties were entitled to accept or reject the judge's decision. When they chose the latter, the ruler could refer the case to another sharia court or to a judge selected by the parties.[11] The decision to administer formal sharia courts represents a historical turning point in that it ushered in a new period in which the nation state began to involve itself with matters traditionally left to customary and tribal law. The discovery of oil in the late 1950s added considerable momentum to changes already under way. The social, legal and economic landscape of the emirates was radically transformed: the creation of modern government institutions, the enactment of codified legislation along Western lines and the initiation of a consultative assembly, which established the union, underscore these transformational developments.

The modern judicial systems of the UAE are organised along local and federal lines and host both civil and sharia law courts. In 1978 the emirates of Abu Dhabi, Sharjah, Ajman and Fujairah, which had a local court system in addition to federal courts, transferred the jurisdiction of their local courts to the federal courts of first instance. Umm al-Quwain transferred its local courts to the federal judiciary in 1991.[12] Dubai and Ras Al Kaimah have maintained independent judicial systems. However, in all emirates with the exception of Ras Al Kaimah the court system comprises the following three tiers: courts of first instance; courts of appeal; and a court of cassation.

The move to federalise the judicial system underscores the gradual integration of UAE law. The UAE constitution provides in Article 151 that union laws issued in accordance with the constitution will prevail over local legislation, regulation and other decisions issued by the authorities of the emirates. However, the constitution provided for continuity in the jurisdiction of local laws until such time as the federal law replaced them. It specifies that: 'all matters established by laws, regulations, decrees, orders and decisions in the various member Emirates of the Union in effect upon the coming into force of this Constitution, shall continue to be

[11] *Ibid.*, 123.

[12] Federal Law No. 6/1978 on the Establishment of Federal Courts and Transferral of the Jurisdiction of the Local Judicial Authorities in Some Emirates to Them, Art. 1-1/1.

applicable unless amended or replaced in accordance with the provisions of this Constitution'.[13]

Federal courts of first instance have the jurisdiction to examine: civil, commercial and administrative disputes between the union and individuals; crimes except for those in the jurisdiction of the supreme federal court as enunciated in Article 99 of the constitution; and personal status, civil and commercial cases between individuals.[14] Furthermore, federal sharia courts have been given jurisdiction in some carefully circumscribed areas of law including: crimes of limited penalties; retaliation and blood money crimes; narcotics crimes; and crimes committed by juveniles.[15]

The UAE has also established a Supreme Court, which originally was known as the constitutional court of the union. The court now has a separate cassation division and thus oversees the application by lower federal courts of existing laws:

> The Supreme Court shall apply the provisions of the Islamic Shari'a, the federal laws, and the other laws in force in the Emirates, that are members of the federation, and which are consistent with the provisions of the Islamic Shari'a. Usages, the principles of natural law and of comparative law shall be applied inasmuch as they do not contradict the provisions of this Shari'a.[16]

The law establishing the Supreme Court of the country is at odds with the constitution's provision of the sharia as 'a' source of law in the sense that the sharia has been made 'the' principal source of law. The Supreme Court is thus bound to review the conformity of federal laws and other laws in force in the emirates with reference to the provisions of the sharia. The result is that any measures contrary to the sharia would be deemed invalid.[17]

Furthermore, Federal Law No. 6/1978, which, as mentioned above, transferred local judicial authorities to federal jurisdiction, provides that: 'Federal Courts shall enforce the provisions of the Islamic Shari'a and the Federal Laws and other Laws in force, and shall enforce customary

[13] UAE Constitution (n 6) Art 148.
[14] Federal Law No. 6/1978 (n 12) Art 8.
[15] Federal Law No. 3/1996 on the Jurisdiction of Shari'a Courts in Examining Some Crimes.
[16] Federal Law No. 10/1973 Concerning the Supreme Federal Court, Art 75.
[17] William Ballantyne, 'The States of the GCC: Sources of Law, the Shari'a and the Extent to which it Applies' (1985) 1 *ALQ*,. 3, 11–12.

rules and general legal principles not contradicting the provisions of Al Shari'a.'[18]

The combined result of these measures seems to indicate that the sharia will be applied as the principal source of law in those emirates that transferred local courts to federal authority.[19] It may not have the same effect in those emirates that did not transfer to federal authority, namely Dubai and Ras Al Khaimah, although union law is superior according Article 151 of the UAE constitution. The differences in wording between the two laws will not have any significant effect since the procedure for the right to appeal begins with union courts in the emirates and then proceeds to the Union Supreme Court.[20] Challenges to the constitutionality of these laws on the grounds that their provision of the sharia exceeded the constitutional position of the sharia as a source of legislation would also not succeed. The Supreme Court would be asked to rule that its own legislative mandate is at odds with the UAE constitution.[21] Finally, the result of law no. 6/1978 and law no. 10/1973 indicates that those emirates which have acceded to federal judicial authority will treat the sharia as the principal source of law.[22] The practical result was that several local and federal laws became susceptible to challenge on the grounds of non-conformity with the sharia. Legal uncertainty ensued, which resulted in several lower courts intervening in the area most often affected by these types of question, namely the legality of using interest in commercial banking.[23]

In the controversial *Junatta Bank* case and other cases concerning the payment of interest (1979–80), the constitutional chamber of the Supreme Court ruled that Abu Dhabi local law no. 3/1970 (Articles 61 and 62), which allowed the levying of interest, was valid on the basis of Article 148 of the constitution. The Article saved the local law from the application of Article 151, which renders local law inferior to the laws of the union. The court effectively sidestepped the conflict between the sharia and secular law by ruling that it was the duty of the legislature to issue laws to replace legislation existing prior to the federation.[24] Although convenient

[18] Federal Law No. 6/1978 (n 12) Art 8.

[19] The reader will recall that these are: Abu Dhabi, Sharjah, Ajman, Fujairah and Umm al-Qawain.

[20] William Ballantyne (n 17) 12. [21] *Ibid.* [22] *Ibid.*

[23] Butti Sultan Butti Ali Al-Muhairi, 'The Position of Shari'a within the UAE Constitution and the Federal Supreme Court's Application of the Constitutional Clause Concerning Shari'a' (1996) 11 *ALQ* 219, 232.

[24] *Ibid.*, 235.

for the court and perhaps a necessity for the UAE economy,[25] the decision is widely regarded as incorrect,[26] since Article 75 of Federal Law No. 10/1973 (see above) effectively abrogated Articles 61 and 62 of Abu Dhabi law. As might be expected, legal uncertainty concerning whether interest was legal under the sharia and/or whether the sharia should be regarded as paramount in light of the wording of the legislation examined above demarcated this area of law.[27]

The promulgation of the federal Civil Code in 1985 has not clarified these complex legal conflicts. In Articles 1–3 of the Civil Code the legislator attempted to clarify the rank of legal sources, including the methodology of their application as well as the substance of public policy. Yet the interaction of the Civil Code, including the role it gives to the sharia, exerts an uncertain influence in the way in which UAE courts will resolve disputes involving commercial matters. Article 1 provides that: 'The attached Law shall operate in respect of civil transactions for the UAE. However, commercial transactions shall continue to be governed by the existing laws and regulations relating thereto until the Federal Commercial Law is enacted.'[28]

From this one gathers that the codified civil law will govern civil transactions, while commercial transactions will be governed by commercial law and eventually a commercial code. Yet, Article 2 states that: 'The rules and principles of Islamic jurisprudence (*fiqh*) shall be relied upon in the understanding, construction and interpretation of these provisions.'[29]

The difficulty in this provision is that the Civil Code, like much codified UAE law, sometimes conflicts with Islamic doctrine. For example, Chapter 5, Articles 1012–1013 limit contracts of hazard (*gharar*) to betting and gambling. It is not concerned with the existence of the subject matter of the obligation, which has busied the minds of jurists for centuries; a description of the object and prize suffices. In fact, Article 202 allows the formation of a contract in which the subject matter is non-existent at the time of contracting, which is viewed by the majority as a contravention of the *gharar* prohibition. The secular purposes of the code are underscored in Article 1026, which permits conventional insurance, generally felt to

[25] Federal Supreme Court, 14/9 on 28/06/1981. C.f. Hind Tamimi, 'Interest under the UAE Law and as Applied by the Courts of Abu Dhabi' (2002) 17 *ALQ*, 50.

[26] Hind Tamimi (n 25) 50. See also William Ballantyne (n 17) 14.

[27] William Ballantyne (n 17) 14.

[28] Federal Law No. 5/1985 Promulgating the Civil Transactions Law of the United Arab Emirates State (Civil Code) as Amended by Federal Law No. 1/1987, Art 1.

[29] *Ibid.*, Art 2.

contravene fundamental provisions of the sharia due to the uncertainty of the subject matter of the contract. Should an UAE court interpret these articles as it has been instructed to do in Article 2 according to the rules and principles of Islamic jurisprudence, will they be found to be invalid? Since the sharia is the interpretive guide in civil law, should it in fact be regarded as the primary source of civil transactions? In the UAE much depends on the ways in which courts decide these issues in practice.

Further, Article 3 defines areas of public policy including marriage, inheritance and systems of governance while providing that public policy may not deviate from the 'imperative provisions and fundamental principles of the Islamic Shari'a'.[30] Article 3 therefore equates public policy, in substance, with the sharia, which, again, raises the question of the way in which a court may decide to rule.

In commercial affairs the applicability of the sharia is excluded by Article 1 of the amended Civil Code.[31] However, it is clear that the Civil Code, which consists of the law of obligations including contract and tort and provides rules for specific nominate contracts including *ijarā*, *istisnā'* and *salam* contracts, cannot be separated from commercial matters. As is the case in English law the principle matter arising in commercial disputes concerns the interpretation of a contract. Clearly, the contractual provisions of the Civil Code, including its provisions for the construction of law, will weigh heavily in a commercial dispute, despite the law's assertion to the contrary.

The promulgation of the Commercial Code in 1993 does little to clarify the matter. It affirms by omission, contrary to the Civil Code, that the rules of law in the absence of a specific agreement or law are to give reference to commercial custom with priority given to special over general customs. In the absence of custom, legislation regarding civil matters (Civil Code and civil procedures laws) is to be consulted and then only when not in conflict with 'the general principles of a commercial activity'.[32] In an effort to further demarcate the secularity of commercial matters, Article 3 provides that commercial matters upon which federal law has been enacted are subject to the provisions of such laws as well as provisions of the Commercial Code not in conflict with the said laws.[33] Commercial

[30] *Ibid.*, Art 3.

[31] Federal Law No. 1/1987. For a more detailed analysis see Isam Ghanem, 'The Impact of the UAE Civil Code Upon Commercial Litigation' (1991) 6 *ALQ*, 370.

[32] Federal Law No. 18/1993 Issuing the Commercial Transactions Law (Commercial Code), Arts 1–2.

[33] *Ibid.*, Art 3.

matters are not to be subject to the sharia and yet the basis of commercial law, namely contract law, is a matter dealt with in the Civil Code.

Despite the legal confusion in the UAE's pluralistic legal system, the practice of the highest courts is to affirm the legality of commercial practices that contravene widely understood interpretations of the sharia. For example, Article 409 of the Commercial Code expressly permits the levying of simple interest in a bank loan: 'the borrower shall be bound to repay the loan and its interests to the bank within such time limits and according to such conditions as are agreed'.[34] Article 76 limits the rate of interest to 12 per cent or a lesser rate agreed by the parties until full settlement, meaning that the receipt of compound interest is not permissible,[35] although, in practice, UAE financial institutions deal in compound interest.[36] Furthermore, Articles 88 and 89 provide for compensation in the event of delay whether damages have been sustained as a result of the delay or not. In practice the sharia has been excluded from this aspect of commercial matters. Still, lingering questions remain concerning the way in which courts will decide other legal issues that are less prominent.

For example, the permissibility of *gharar* is an issue that is not entirely resolved despite the Civil Code's basic permissiveness in that regard. Derivative contracts, which are contested from a sharia point of view due to the uncertain exchange of the counter-values, have sometimes been re-characterised as contracts of gambling in UAE courts. Courts may be persuaded that the transaction is speculative in nature particularly in those cases where the parties did not have a specified interest in the reference asset or obligation of the transaction. Although certain derivative contracts such as interest rate swaps have been held to be permissible, the enforceability of some types of derivative contract depends on the facts of the case, the relationship of the parties and the subject matter of the transaction.[37]

All of the above raises questions about how a UAE court may decide a conflict in which a sharia-compliant transaction is at stake. A UAE court is not legally required to consider the sharia pronouncements of a particular SSB in rendering its decision. On the contrary, it would be likely to proceed in the usual way by deciding cases on the basis of the terms and conditions of the contract. In those instances in which the parties have

[34] *Ibid.*, Art 409 para 3.

[35] The UAE Federal Supreme Court confirmed in 85/2009 on 18/11/2009 that the receipt of compound interest is not permissible.

[36] Hind Tamimi (n 25) 51.

[37] James Farn, 'Credit Default Swaps', *Hadef & Partners*, 3 November 2009, www.hadef-partners.com/News/pageid/120-137/default.aspx?mediaid=98. Accessed 22 April 2014.

chosen the sharia as the governing law of the contract, the court are likely to disregard such a choice of law in favour of UAE law.[38] However, while the basic procedure for dealing with such contracts is likely to be the same as conventional commercial disputes, a UAE court may decide that a contract specifically espousing its sharia credentials should also be adjudged on those terms. Indeed, UAE civil law empowers the court to do so. A court's decision to examine the sharia compliance of Islamic financial transactions may result in the re-characterisation of the contract, sometimes with catastrophic consequences. Unlike in Bahrain there is no central authority for the promulgation and enforcement of sharia rules and standards in the UAE despite the drafting of current legislation designed to develop an independent sharia authority.[39] A lack of such centralised standards renders uncertain the way in which a UAE court will interpret the sharia with reference to the terms of an Islamic financial transaction.

Therefore, the position of the sharia in the constitution of the UAE represents a continuing source of legal uncertainty. Further, the prominence given to the sharia in legislation save that of the Commercial Code increases the probability that it will be given effect. The particular legal context of that is uncertain. The role of the sharia in the legal systems of the UAE represents a conflict of interest on the part of the legislator between the desire to modernise the country via the promulgation of western-inspired systems of law and the ever-present Muslim duty to honour and abide by the sharia in all aspects of a believer's life. To have excluded the sharia in the constitution would have been to ignore the universality of God's commands. The continuing role of the sharia in various pieces of legislation, however, reflects a willingness of the legislator to pick and choose from those areas of the sharia that can be easily accommodated while excluding aspects that are no longer acceptable and/or practicable in the modern world. The role of the sharia in the UAE as in the majority of Middle Eastern jurisdictions, save contemporary Tunisia,[40]

[38] Azlin Ahmed, 'Islamic Financing and the Relevant Laws of the UAE', Al Tamimi & Co, 5 June 2011, www.tamimi.com/en/magazine/law-update/section-7/june-5/Islamic-financing-and-the-relevant-laws-of-the-uae.html. Accessed 22 April 2014.

[39] Bernardo Vizcaino, 'UAE Plans Islamic Finance Authority Backed by Legislation', *Reuters*, 30 October 2013, uk.reuters.com/article/2013/10/30/islamic-finance-emirates-idUKL5N0IK3YY20131030. Accessed 22 April 2014.

[40] David D. Kirkpatrick and Carlotta Gall, 'Arab Neighbors Take Split Paths in Constitutions', *International New York Times*, 14 January 2014, www.nytimes.com/2014/01/15/world/middleeast/arab-neighbors-take-split-paths-in-constitutions.html?hp&_r=1. Accessed 22 April 2014.

demonstrates the uneasy tension between the sharia and modern secular law in these states' legal systems.

8.2 The Central Bank of the UAE and its regulatory approach to Islamic finance

In practical terms, the UAE comprises two financial services jurisdictions: the Dubai International Financial Centre (DIFC), which is the subject of the following chapter, and the rest of the UAE, in which the role of the sharia in its legal systems was examined above. For the sake of clarity, it is useful to understand that the DIFC is an onshore 100-acre financial free zone with its own financial regulatory authority, the Dubai Financial Services Authority (DFSA), and its own securities exchange, the Dubai International Financial Exchange (DIFX). It has also developed an independent judicial system comprised of codified civil and commercial laws based on English common law. DIFC courts have exclusive jurisdiction over disputes arising in the DIFC or in connection with companies registered in the DIFC.[41] The following discussion concerns matters pertaining to the UAE and excludes those concerning the DIFC.

UAE financial services law is considerably less detailed than the regulatory systems of the United Kingdom, Bahrain or the DIFC. Financial services law operates on a principles-based system in which legislation is the principal source of regulation. More detailed provisions are included in regulatory circulars, which the Central Bank issues occasionally. Union Law No. 10 of 1980 (hereinafter 'Banking Law') is the governing law of the UAE financial system. The Banking Law establishes the Central Bank as well as the monetary and financial system. It also empowers the Central Bank as the main body responsible for regulating the banking system in the UAE. The Emirates securities and commodities authority (ESCA) is responsible for regulating local securities and commodities exchanges as well as business relating to those exchanges (which includes brokers, financial advisers and analysts). The Ministry of Economy and Planning is responsible for regulating the insurance business.

The Banking Law provides detailed rules for the registration, licensing and operation of commercial banks, investment banks, financial institutions, monetary and financial intermediaries, and representative offices. Article 94 empowers the Central Bank to issue regulatory instructions and/or circulars to safeguard its monetary and credit policies and to 'take

[41] DIFC, 'About: Discover DIFC', n.d., www.difc.ae/discover-difc. Accessed 22 April 2014.

any measures necessary' to ensure the safety and soundness of the banking system.[42] The Banking Law plays a primary role in establishing the regulatory structure of the banking and financial system.

The commercial transactions law also deals with 'the banking, exchange, stock markets and investment companies operations, trust funds, financial establishments and all kinds of other financial brokerage operations'.[43] Unlike the Banking Law, it contains detailed provisions for bank deposits, bank accounts, documentary credits, guarantees, bills of exchange, loans, promissory notes and cheques.

Despite the prominent role of the sharia in the legal systems of the UAE, the Central Bank has not created an industry-specific regulatory framework for the Islamic finance industry. The basic position is that the products of IFIs entail similar risk profiles to those of conventional products and thus should be subject to conventional regulatory standards. The sharia aspects of such transactions, while acknowledged by the authorities, are largely left to individual IFIs. Federal Law No. 6 of 1985 (hereinafter 'Islamic banking law') is the sole piece of legislation that deals with IFIs and its remit is quite limited.[44] The legislation mostly relies on the regulatory provisions of the Banking Law, while carving out several exceptions to the law that are conducive to specific Islamic financial practices. While legislative initiatives designed to spur the growth of Islamic finance are under discussion, the current legal framework indicates that the Islamic finance industry must operate within the conventional financial system with few specific legislative or regulatory provisions.

8.3 The authorisation of IFIs

The Banking Law categorises financial institutions into commercial banks, investment banks, financial institutions, monetary and financial intermediaries and representation offices. This discussion is primarily concerned with commercial banks but will indicate the relevant rules for investment banks when these are germane to the analysis. Article 78 considers commercial banks those that 'receive funds from the public in the form of demand, under notice, or time deposits, or which carries on the placement of debt instruments or deposit certificates to be used, in whole

[42] Union Law No. 10 of 1980 Concerning the Central Bank, the Monetary System and Organisation of Banking, Art 94.

[43] Federal Law No. 18 of 1993 (n 32) Art 5, s 4.

[44] Federal Law No. 6 of 1985, regarding Islamic Banks, Financial Institutions and Investment Companies.

or in part, for its account and at its risk for granting loans and advances'.[45] The law further provides that commercial banks will undertake the 'issue and collection of cheques, the placing of public or private bonds, trade in foreign exchange and precious metals, or any other operations allowed for commercial banks either by law or by customary banking practice'.[46] All commercial banks are subject to the Central Bank's licensing, supervision and inspection regime.

The Banking Law specifies that all commercial banks, including Islamic banks, must be established as joint-stock corporations, while foreign banks in the UAE are exempt from the requirement. All financial institutions including commercial banks must be licensed by the Central Bank and registered in a central register. Notice of such is published in the official gazette.[47] Any entity not licensed by the Central Bank is not able to use the words 'bank', 'banker' or 'banking' as a commercial designation.[48]

Authorised banks are expressly prohibited from engaging in certain activities including but not limited to 'non-banking operations', referring to commercial or industrial activities in which a bank acquires, owns or trades in goods on its own account; acquires immovable property for commercial purposes on its own account; holds or deals in a bank's own shares; or purchases shares in commercial companies or the bonds issued by such companies, which raise the bank's holdings of such above 25 per cent of a bank's own funds.[49] The Islamic banking law provides, on the other hand, that IFIs, including conventional banks with Islamic windows, are expressly authorised to undertake all the services and operations practised by conventional banks, including those conducted on its own account or in partnership with a third party.[50] Furthermore, the UAE legislator has given sharia-compliant financial institutions the right to undertake a number of operations that conventional banks may not. They can establish companies and/or participate in existing companies, so long as these do not contravene the sharia. Most importantly, IFIs may engage in commercial or industrial activities; the acquisition of or trade in goods; and the acquisition of immovable property on their own account.[51] Furthermore, Article 96(e), which stipulates that interest will

[45] Union Law No. 10 of 1980 (n 42) Art 78.

[46] *Ibid.* [47] Union Law No. 10 of 1980 (n 42) Art 83, s 1.

[48] *Ibid.*, Art 85. [49] *Ibid.*, Art 90.

[50] Federal Law No. 6 of 1985 (n 44) Art 3, which provides that 'Islamic banks shall have the right to carry on all or part of banking, commercial and investment services and operations'.

[51] *Ibid.*, Art 4, s 1, which exempts IFIs from clause (a) of Article 90 and clause (e) of Article 96 of Union Law No. 10 of 1980.

be paid on deposits held by banks on behalf of its customers, is not applicable to IFIs.[52] In sum, the legislator has enacted a number of legislative provisions that facilitate the type of Islamic financial intermediation in which assets are bought and sold on credit and/or investment partnerships are formed.

8.4 The regulatory classification of Islamic financial products

The Central Bank has issued a number of regulations in recent years dealing with the banks and the banking system. The circulars underscore the UAE's increasing adoption of international standards in the wake of the 2008 financial crisis, which has had the effect of galvanising financial centres' development of harmonised regulatory standards. Islamic financial practices that originate in the UAE are affected by the influx of international standards to the same extent as conventional transactions. Adopted standards add pressure to market players to innovate financial products that meet both regulatory and market standards. Such standards become a part of IFL, even if indirectly, and therefore constitute a further source of law for the developing legal system.

The Civil and Commercial Codes of the UAE are the principal sources of most rules concerning the classification of contracts in UAE financial markets including those used by IFIs. The Civil Code, for instance, defines in detail a wide range of contractual structures, which the legislator has largely borrowed from classical *fiqh*. Although the contracts are expressed in codified form, reflecting the demands of the nation state, the rules and stipulations associated with them do not differ greatly from the majority's understanding of valid classical contractual structures. A key difference, however, concerns a few important areas of law, where the legislator has overridden the sharia in favour of commercial flexibility. The Civil Code's definition of *gharar*, as examined above, is an example where this has taken place. The Civil Code includes provisions for a wide range of sales-based contracts including the forward sale (*salam*), deferred payment sales (*bay' bithaman ajil*), hire (*ijāra*), and manufacture (*istisnā'*). It also deals with partnerships including the general partnership (*sharikah*) and specific partnerships including labour (*'amal*), credit (*wūjuh*), and silent partnerships (*muḍārabah*). The legislator has also promulgated a modern commercial companies

[52] *Ibid.*, Art 4, s 2.

law, which includes rules for the formation of a wide range of modern company formations.[53]

Interestingly, the Islamic heritage of the Civil Code's contractual provisions is even extended to areas of law, which, from a western perspective, have a quite different purpose and meaning. Article 849, for example, defines a loan as the 'conferring of ownership upon another of the use of a thing without consideration for a specified period or for a specified purpose, with a condition that that thing should be returned after use'.[54] A loan, according to this definition, is not a sum of money, repayable upon demand or after an agreed period of time. It concerns the use of a thing, a tangible subject matter (*'ayn*), underlining the charitable rather than commercial aspects of the transaction. This represents the legislator's determination to retain the tradition of sharia in modern legislation.

The Commercial Code is not generally concerned with the provision of rules for the wide range of contracts elaborated upon in the Civil Code. It provides the rules for banking, exchange, stock markets and investment companies' operations, trust funds, financial establishments and all kinds of other financial brokerage operations, but offers fewer rules for individual contracts. The law's guidance on bank deposits and accounts provides that a deposit is a 'contract by which one person delivers a sum of money, by any means of payment, to the bank that undertakes to return it upon request or according to the agreed conditions'.[55] This definition, unlike the English law definition of a deposit, allows parties to agree their conditions so that a bank accepting a deposit according to UAE law must not necessarily undertake to return the deposit. This latter clause, 'according to the agreed conditions' provides legal space to use *muḍārabah* contracts as deposit-accepting contracts. The reader will recall that the *muḍārabah* does not permit a guaranteed return of the principal investment to the investor (*rabb al-māl*) should a loss arise. The law of the UAE upholds this basic rule,[56] further stipulating that the 'capital [of the *muḍārabah*] must not be a debt or a deposit with the owner of the capital owed by the *mudārib*'.[57] Islamic banks operating in the UAE regularly offer savings and investment deposits on the basis of the *muḍārabah* contract. Finally, deposits are not insured in the UAE, although, in practice, the

[53] Federal Law No. 8 of 1984 as Amended by Federal Law No. 13 of 1988 Commercial Companies.
[54] Federal Law No. 5/1985 (n 28) Art 849.
[55] Federal Law No. 18/1993 (n 32) Art 371.
[56] Federal Law No. 5/1985 (n 28) Art 704.
[57] *Ibid.*, Art. 694, s. 3.

government has intervened occasionally to prevent depositors from suffering a loss.[58]

The Central Bank, in a recent effort to modernise UAE financial law, has issued circular no. 29/2011 concerning the regulation of bank loans and services offered to individual customers. The regulation clarifies the definition of some carefully specified bank loans and other services as well as the relationship between banks and their customers. Such bank loans differ from those discussed above in that they deal specifically with the extension of credit with interest. Nevertheless, the regulation is applicable to Islamic financial products except in the 'matter of computing interest and determining its amount', in which case that 'would be done in accordance with shariah principles'.[59] This surprising formulation indicates that Islamic financial products may deal in interest so long as the process for doing so is clear and transparent. Accordingly, a 'copy of the established rates [interest rates] should be sent to the central bank for publication'.[60] Two conclusions can be drawn from this rule. First, the UAE Central Bank, unlike the Central Bank of Bahrain, has not created an industry-specific classification system for Islamic financial contracts. The Civil Code undertakes this task in part by providing a number of contractual arrangements along the lines of the Islamic nominate contracts. While the Civil Code does not distinguish the structures from those of conventional transactions, they provide useful prototypes of the foundational products IFIs may deal in. However, absent an Islamic financial rulebook or other legislation, both the circular and the Commercial Code permit IFIs to engage in interest-based business. This is rather curious in the sense that Islamic banking has built its reputation as an ethical, interest-free alternative.

The circular describes a personal loan as a 'loan that is given to individual customers, where repayments are made out of salary and end of service indemnity and/or any other verifiable regular income from a well-defined source'.[61] Thus a personal loan concerns a loan of money, which may not exceed twenty times the salary of the income of the borrower and must be repaid within 48 months.[62] The circular provides specific rules

[58] Bashir Ahmed and Aly Shah, 'United Arab Emirates', Afridi and Angell, Getting the Deal Through: Banking Regulation, 2011, www.afridi-angell.com/items/limg/bankingregulation20112.pdf. Accessed 18 August 2014.

[59] UAE Central Bank Circular No. 29/2011, 'Regulations Regarding Bank Loans & Services Offered to Individual Customers', Art 13.

[60] *Ibid.* [61] *Ibid.*, Art 2, s (a).

[62] *Ibid.*, Art 2, ss (b), (c).

for a number of other financial instruments including car loans, overdraft facilities and credit cards, as well as for repayment instalments and a wide range of fees and the determination of interest rates.

Circular no. 31/2013 regarding mortgage loan regulations is another regulatory tool designed to implement effective standards for the granting of mortgage loans. The circular defines a mortgage loan as 'a loan that is collateralised against a residential property granted for the purpose of constructing, purchasing or renovating a house for owner occupier or investment purposes'.[63] The circular provides detailed rules for risk management, ratios, and disclosure and transparency. Sharia-compatible mortgage contracts are treated in the same way as conventional mortgages, reflecting a similar regulatory approach to that of the United Kingdom towards Islamic finance. Specific mortgage loan providers undertaking the provision of sharia-compatible mortgage finance are 'generally exposed to the same types of risks as a conventional mortgage loan provider'[64] and are thus subject to the same rules. The sharia pronouncements of a sharia-compatible mortgage provider's SSB should be observed in addition to complying with the requirements set out in the circular.[65] These provisions reflect the basic approach the Central Bank takes towards the regulation of Islamic finance. Namely, IFIs must comply with the law while also observing the Islamic standards issued by an IFI's SSB. As will be examined below, such standards vary considerably as there is no central sharia authority in the UAE nor does the UAE mandate the use of AAOIFI standards. The result of this approach, from a sharia perspective, is that IFIs are free to undertake whatever types of financial practice their consumers are willing to invest in and that conform to UAE law.

The following section is concerned with a further aspect of the UAE's regulatory framework for IFIs and other financial institutions. The focus involves the way in which the UAE applies prudential regulatory standards, while the impact of such standards on Islamic financial transactions is a primary concern.

8.5 Capital adequacy standards for IFIs

Financial institutions operating in the UAE are subject to capital adequacy and liquidity standards, which the Central Bank has adopted from international best practices. The UAE's general approach to the application of

[63] UAE Central Bank Circular No. 31/2013 Regarding Mortgage Loan Regulations, Art 1.
[64] *Ibid.*, Art 6. [65] *Ibid.*, Art 6.

CARs with respect to IFIs does not differ in any substantial way from their application to conventional financial institutions. Capital adequacy requirements are dealt with in part by the Banking Law, which provides a broad capital adequacy framework for all commercial banks operating in the UAE. Central Bank circulars, however, are used with much greater frequency and provide more detail in relation to the requirements.

The Banking Law specifies that all commercial banks must maintain at least 40 million dirham in paid-up capital, while branches of foreign banks must allocate the equivalent as capital funds for their operations in the UAE.[66] Furthermore, commercial banks and branches of foreign banks must allocate at least 10 per cent of annual net profits for the establishment of a special reserve until the reserve equals 50 per cent of a commercial bank's capital. In the case of a branch of a foreign bank the amount must have been allocated as capital.[67] Branches of foreign banks are also required to maintain separate accounts for all their operations in the UAE including the balance sheet and profit and loss accounts. The accounts of branches and/or agencies of any bank operating in the UAE are to be drawn up on a consolidated basis.[68]

Circular no. 13/93 represents the first modern effort to create capital reserves in the country's fledgling financial system. The standards provided by the circular came into force in July 1993. Like Basel capital adequacy standards, it divides capital into core, tier 1 and tier 2 capital bases. The sum of a bank's capital base is comprised of tier 1 and tier 2 capital minus various deductions. Tier one capital is defined as the paid-up share capital and published reserves of a bank including minority interests. At the discretion of the Central Bank it may include profits from the current period. Goodwill and other intangible assets, own shares held, shortfalls in provisions, current year losses and others as may be prescribed by the Central Bank are to be deducted from tier 1 capital.[69]

Tier 2 capital comprises undisclosed reserves and re-valued assets (limited to a maximum of 45 per cent of the excess of the market value over the net book value). The re-valued reserves of a bank's property holdings are not to be included. Tier 2 capital also comprises hybrid (debt/equity) capital instruments and subordinated term loans. A bank's capital base is calculated by deducting investments in unconsolidated subsidiaries,

[66] Union Law No. 10 of 1980 (n 42) Art 80.

[67] *Ibid.*, Art 82. [68] *Ibid.*, Art 102.

[69] UAE Central Bank Circular No. 13/93 Regarding Capital Adequacy, Art 1.

associate companies and/or other banks or financial institutions from the total of tier 1 and tier 2 capital.[70]

As per the general Basel practice, a bank's assets are risk weighted according to their relative risk as provided by further Central Bank guidelines. All banks active in the UAE must maintain at all times a risk to asset ratio of at least 10 per cent in which tier 1 capital must comprise at least 6 per cent of total risk-weighted assets. Tier 2 capital is usable up to a maximum of 67 per cent of tier 1 capital.[71]

A commercial bank is required to maintain a minimum level of capital of 40 million dirhams at all times. In the event that a commercial bank's capital falls below the minimum required, the shortfall must be rectified within a period determined by the executive committee of the Central Bank. The period will not exceed one year from the date in which the shortfall has been communicated to the Central Bank.[72]

In 2006, the Central Bank implemented the Basel II Accord, the details of which were analysed in Chapter 6. Implementation was undertaken in stages with all banks expected to be compliant with the standardised approach by 31 December 2007 and with the internal ratings-based approach by 1 January 2011.[73] The 2008 global financial crisis prompted the Central Bank to strengthen capital adequacy regulations. Banks were required to increase their capital levels to 11 per cent by 30 September 2009 whereby tier 1 capital could not be less than 7 per cent. A second phase required banks to increase their capital adequacy to 12 per cent by 30 June 2010 whereby tier 1 capital must comprise at least 8 per cent of the total. These provisions, although temporary and due for review at the beginning of 2011, remain effective.[74]

The promulgation of Basel III standards, which were discussed in Chapter 6, will not affect UAE banks' capital adequacy ratios, although its liquidity standards may require adjustment. UAE banks' total capital adequacy ratio averages 22 per cent, while their combined tier 1 capital ratio is 16.7 per cent of risk-weighted assets.[75] Both ratios exceed Basel III

[70] *Ibid.*, Art 1.2–1.3. [71] *Ibid.*, Arts 2–3.

[72] Union Law No. 10 of 1980 (n 42) Art 81.

[73] UAE Central Bank Circular No. 3735/2006 Regarding Basel II Implementation in the UAE.

[74] UAE Central Bank Circular No. 4004/2009 Regarding Capital Adequacy.

[75] Andrew Torchia, 'UAE to Require Banks to Hold 10 per cent Liquid Assets', *Reuters*, 15 July 2012, uk.reuters.com/article/2012/07/15/uk-uae-banks-basel-idUKBRE86E07J20120715. Accessed 22 April 2014.

requirements by a wide margin. Basel III is due to come into effect by 2019 and requires a minimum capital of 10 per cent.

The UAE does not maintain a deposit guarantee scheme, although as previously mentioned, the Central Bank, in practice, has intervened on several occasions to insure depositors against losses. Theoretically, therefore, it may be easier to ensure market discipline in UAE financial markets, because inadequately capitalised banks will be obliged by market forces to obtain adequate capital or to curtail their lending activities. Deposit guarantee schemes reduce market discipline by reducing banks' incentives to monitor other banks.[76] However, 'research indicates that market discipline tends to be weak'[77] in countries in which IFIs generally operate. This fact, coupled with the UAE's occasional intervention in insuring depositors against losses, means that unrestricted PLS accounts used as fund mobilising accounts should be assessed for capital adequacy purposes. Moreover, the profits of unrestricted PLS accounts in UAE banks are almost certainly smoothed, so that the applicability of CARs is justified. Basel standards allow room for the Central Bank to apply CARs according to the needs of financial institutions in its jurisdiction. The economic characteristics of unrestricted PLS accounts in the Islamic banks operating in the UAE will determine the application of CARs.

As was the case with other jurisdictions under study, the UAE's approach to CARs makes considerable use of Basel standards. In contrast, most jurisdictions differ in their treatment of sharia governance systems. The following section analyses the UAE Central Bank's approach to sharia governance.

8.6 Governance standards for IFIs

Unlike states such as Bahrain and Malaysia, which have created centralised systems of sharia governance, the UAE has delegated sharia supervision to individual SSBs, which comprise part of an IFI's governance structure. Federal Law no. 6 of 1985 regarding Islamic banks, financial institutions and investment companies is the primary source of legislation for the governance of SSBs operating in the UAE. Islamic banks, financial institutions and investment companies, according to the law, are those

[76] Simon Archer and Rifaat Ahmed Abdel Karim, 'Measuring Risk for Capital Adequacy: The Issue of Profit-Sharing Investment Accounts', in Simon Archer and Rifaat Ahmed Abdel Karim (eds.), *Islamic Finance: The New Regulatory Challenge* (Singapore: John Wiley & Sons (Asia), 2013), 296.

[77] *Ibid.*, 297.

that indicate a commitment to abide by the sharia in their articles and memorandums of association and to conduct their financial activities in accordance therewith. Furthermore, IFIs are required to incorporate as public joint stock companies and are thus subject to the provisions of the Commercial Companies Law No. 9 of 1984.[78] This requirement does not apply to the branches of foreign IFIs, which are otherwise subject to UAE laws governing the establishment of branches. Financial institutions including banks, financing companies, investment companies, money exchanges and brokerages are excluded from the application of Ministerial Decision No. 518/2009, which is the principal source of corporate governance standards for all publicly listed corporations or institutions in the UAE.[79]

Federal Law No. 6 of 1985 empowers the cabinet to form a 'higher sharia authority' (HSA), which would include sharia, legal and banking experts and be responsible for supervising the sharia legitimacy of all IFIs undertaking transactions in the UAE. The law empowers the HSA to offer binding opinions (fatwas) on matters relating to the activities of IFIs. The HSA would be housed in the ministry of justice and Islamic affairs.[80] However, despite the provisions of this law empowering the cabinet to create a national sharia board, the UAE has not yet created an HSA. This means that there is no central sharia authority to verify the sharia compliance of products and services currently offered by IFIs or to issue standards to which IFIs must adhere so as to be able to market their products as sharia-compliant.

While a national sharia board has not yet been formed, the law requires IFIs to include in their articles and memorandum of association a stipulation that an SSB will be formed of a minimum of three members who are responsible for determining the sharia compliance of an IFI's transactions and practices. The law allows IFIs to determine the way in which the SSB is formed and the ways in which it will undertake its tasks. Further, the names of members of the respective SSB must be submitted to the HSA for prior approval of their membership of the SSB.[81] In the absence of an HSA, this does not take place in practice. Therefore, IFIs are empowered to decide the terms by which sharia scholars are employed as members of a financial institution's SSB, which excludes the application of corporate

[78] Federal Law No. 6 of 1985 (n 44) Arts 1, 2, 3.

[79] UAE Ministerial Decision No. 518/2009 on Governance Restrictions and Corporate Discipline Standards, Art 2, s c(2).

[80] Federal Law No. 6 of 1985 (n 44) Art 5.

[81] *Ibid.*, Art 6.

governance guidelines to the SSB.[82] In sum, the SSBs of individual IFIs have, in practice, almost complete discretion to decide the sharia compliance of the Islamic products and services they market. Despite the theoretical role of the sharia in the legal systems of the UAE, its application in practice is limited.

8.7 Concluding remarks

The regulatory systems of the UAE comprise a hybrid mixture of legal influences that befits both the composition and developmental trend of a globally active IFL. The UAE legal systems are hybrid by virtue of their post-colonial development as well as the role reserved for the sharia in the UAE constitution. On the one hand, this chapter shows that hybridity is generally not conducive to legal clarity or certainty within the UAE. On the other hand, however, the UAE legislator has attempted to enclose commercial law in a secular bubble, wherein the influence of the sharia in commercial matters can be circumvented. Despite the legislator's attempt, it is still uncertain whether the use of interest in financial transactions – not to mention Islamic transactions, which are generally considered to be interest-free – will be found to be lawful in a UAE court. While the Commercial Code clearly provides for the use of interest, the Civil Code and other areas of law, supported by the role given to the sharia in the constitution, endow the sharia with a clearly prominent but uncertain interpretational role. Nonetheless, a number of judicial decisions handed down by the Supreme Court have overturned lower court decisions prohibiting interest. This indicates that commercial usage or custom, which allows the use of interest, will be treated as the most important source of law with respect to the practice.

The Central Bank has promulgated regulations that provide for the use of interest in Islamic financial transactions and yet the legislator has indicated that IFIs are to perform their activities in conformity with the principles of sharia. This legal confusion concerns the appropriate role of the sharia in the UAE's legal systems. While a trend towards modernisation is unmistakeable across a wide range of UAE society (law, economics,

[82] Central Bank corporate governance guidelines for non-executive directors provide that such persons are subject to 'fit and proper' criteria including: honesty, integrity and reputation; competence and capability; and financial soundness. Non-executive directors are also required to remain independent of management and must avoid conflicts of interest. See UAE Central Bank, *UAE Central Bank Corporate Governance Guidelines for UAE Bank Directors* (Draft, June 2006), 8.

culture, architecture, etc.), a strong attachment to the sharia is not easily parted with (at least, in theory). In practice, however, the legislator has given IFIs a wide margin of freedom in which to conduct their financial activities.

Not unlike the UK regulator's approach to Islamic finance, the UAE Central Bank regulates IFIs in the same way it regulates conventional financial institutions. The legislative requirement that requires IFIs to establish an SSB does little more than that in the absence of a functioning higher sharia authority.

The influx of international standards presents a challenge to the UAE's efforts to craft a regulatory system that is in keeping with the historical traditions of the sharia. The way in which IFL in the UAE develops provides an indication of how the country grapples with that challenge. At the moment, the trend is toward regulatory harmonisation with some room for national differences.

9

The regulation of Islamic financial institutions in the Dubai International Financial Centre (DIFC)

The Dubai International Financial Centre (DIFC) is an offshore financial centre that presents a demonstrative example of the ways in which globalisation affects financial markets and the creation of global commercial law. The DIFC comprises a legal and regulatory framework that was constructed on the basis of international best standards and common law principles primarily originating from the leading global financial centres, London and New York. In contrast to the UAE, the DIFC provides a transparent and clear regulatory framework for Islamic finance and actively implements AAOIFI and IFSB standards. The IFL promulgated in the DIFC is a composite legal product resulting from the amalgamation and complex interaction of diverse legal influences and international regulatory standards.

These topics will be examined by first scrutinising the general contours of the legal and regulatory system of the DIFC. This is followed by an examination of Dubai's regulatory approach to Islamic finance. The chapter proceeds to specific analyses of the authorisation of IFIs, the regulatory classification of Islamic financial services, capital adequacy requirements for IFIs and sharia governance standards.

9.1 The legal and regulatory system of the DIFC

Established in 2004 the DIFC is designed to be a financial free zone with its own unique legal and regulatory environment in the UAE. Free zones, also known as special economic zones or offshore financial centres, offer advantageous tax and regulatory policies. They are designed to encourage foreign direct investment in the UAE.[1] The DIFC has established itself as a

[1] Latham and Watkins, 'Doing Business in the United Arab Emirates' (January 2011), www.lw.com/upload/pubContent/_pdf/pub2783_1.PDF. Accessed 22 April 2014.

bridge between financial markets of the East and West and as an *entrepôt* for capital and investment to and within the GCC region.[2]

A number of free zones have been established in the UAE but most are located in the Emirate of Dubai.[3] Free zones can generally be distinguished from domestic or onshore financial centres in three ways. First, they deal in external currencies or in currencies that are not the currency of the host country. Financial transactions originating in the free zone are not directly linked to the domestic banking system. Second, free zones are generally not designed for UAE nationals – they cater to non-resident clients. Third, they are usually free of taxes and exchange controls imposed on domestic financial markets.[4] While the UAE is largely considered to be a tax-free jurisdiction, most emirates have enacted corporate income tax legislation targeting specific industries. At present, only branches of foreign banks and foreign oil companies are taxed. The DIFC, on the other hand, is completely tax free and is not subject to UAE tax legislation.[5] The DIFC has no restrictions on foreign exchange. It also allows 100 per cent foreign ownership, whereas 'in the rest of the UAE a minimum of 51 per cent of a locally incorporated company's shares must be owned by UAE nationals'.[6] Foreign financial institutions are able to establish their institutions within the DIFC without having to locate a suitable local partner.

The ambition of the architects of the DIFC is for the DIFC to become not merely the principal financial centre of the Middle East but to compete with the likes of the leading global financial centres of London, New York and Hong Kong. That ambition extends to Islamic finance. The volume of Islamic financial activity in Muslim-majority countries, including the countries considered to be the most important international drivers of the industry (Qatar, Indonesia, Saudi Arabia, Malaysia, UAE, Turkey and Bahrain) has increased considerably. One-fifth of banking system assets across these countries is now Islamic with Saudi Arabia in the lead with 50 per cent.[7] The Emirate of Dubai, aware of these trends, is laying

[2] Nasser Saidi, *The Success of DIFC as an International Financial Centre* (Dubai International Financial Centre, September 2009).

[3] See www.uaefreezones.com for a lengthy list of free zones located in the UAE.

[4] Y. S. Park 'The Economics of Offshore Financial Centers' in Richard Roberts (ed.), *Offshore Financial Centres*, vol. I (Cheltenham: Edward Elgar, 1994), 4.

[5] KPMG, 'New Dubai International Financial Centre Set Up' (2003–2004) 15 *Int'l Tax Rev*, 42.

[6] Andrew Henderson and Antony Hainsworth, 'Through an Islamic Window', *IFLR*, September 2008, www.iflr.com/Article/2017785/Through-an-Islamic-window.html. Accessed 22 April 2014.

[7] Ernst & Young, 'World Islamic Banking Competitiveness Report' (2013–14), 17.

the foundation to develop Dubai, including the DIFC, into the 'capital of a global Islamic economy'.[8] In 2013, Dubai announced the creation of a Dubai Islamic Economy Development Centre to drive forward this goal. Its subsidiary objectives include: strengthening sharia-compliant economic activities in both financial and non-financial services; promoting Dubai as a regional and international sharia-compatible hub; and encouraging disputes regarding Islamic financial transactions to be solved in arbitration. Furthermore, the centre is charged with developing 'comprehensive and unified standards to judge the extent of compliance of any good, financial or non-financial service with the provisions of the Islamic Sharia', indicating that the emirate is aware that the lack of sharia standardisation in UAE markets undermines the competitiveness and Islamic legitimacy of the industry.[9] The emirate is also positioning itself to develop sharia-compliant industries including *halāl* tourism, hotels, arts and fashion centres as well as other products and services. For that purpose, a system of accreditation is being developed, which will issue market players with certificates of sharia compliance.[10]

Dubai's ambitions have been tested by the impact of the global financial crisis, which led to a dramatic plunge in the emirate's property prices by as much as 50 per cent and exposed UAE banks to a substantial volume of non-performing loans. Yet the DIFC's combination of world-class infrastructure, legal and regulatory systems, its status as a global trade hub and, arguably, the ambitions of the emirate support its competitive position.

The DIFC was established as a separate jurisdiction in the UAE with its own civil and commercial laws. The three constituent bodies of the DIFC, the DIFC Authority, the DIFC judicial authority – the courts of the DIFC – and the Dubai Financial Services Authority (DFSA) were created through a synthesis of federal and Dubai law.[11] The DIFC is legally exempted from the federal civil and commercial laws of the UAE, although the UAE retains jurisdiction over criminal matters. In practice, this means that commercial matters that arise within the DIFC are not subject to the Civil or Commercial Codes of the UAE. The DIFC, although physically located in the Emirate of Dubai (one of the seven emirates of the UAE), is

[8] Dubai Law No. 13/2013 on the Establishment of Dubai Islamic Economy Development Centre, Art 5.

[9] *Ibid.*, Art 6. [10] *Ibid.*, Art 6 (2)–(3).

[11] Dubai Law No. 9 of 2004 in Respect of the Dubai International Financial Centre.

empowered by law to create its own specific legal and regulatory framework.[12] DIFC law is applicable in the DIFC, while Dubai law is applicable in the Emirate of Dubai. Both legal systems are promulgated by the Ruler of Dubai.[13]

Created through a synthesis of federal and Dubai-based civil laws, the laws and regulatory standards of the DIFC are modelled on international standards and the principles of English common law. The DIFC is a clear example of how the globalisation of finance incentivises the establishment of autonomous jurisdictions that act as havens for global financial institutions. The legal frameworks of these offshore centres are comprised of the legal transplants of leading financial centres and international standards and best practices.

In the neoliberal global economy best practices refer to the dominant laws, regulations, institutions and strategies that prevail in the leading economies. Best practices are considered to have been tried and tested in meeting the needs of market economies and as such represent the best strategy for economic development.[14] They represent a neoliberal penchant for discerning an optimal path or model development paradigm. Deliberate, strategic divergence from this optimal path is considered to be plagued with risks and is thus to be sharply circumscribed.[15]

The notion of a universally applicable development paradigm rests on an assumption that, despite the existence of great diversity in relation to history, culture and levels of development, a judgement concerning the best model can be made.[16] Such a notion is considered to be rooted in solely rational or functional considerations about the reasons for the emergence of certain rules and institutions. It allows economic development to be viewed as a mere technical problem, which makes way for the use of the dominant rules and practices of leading economies.[17]

The belief that dominant, functionally superior practices can be used to transcend the differences between countries, histories, cultures and legal systems overlooks the contingencies of power and other circumstances that led to the dominance of these usages in the first place.[18] The dominance of particular institutions and practices is more likely to be the result of dynamic power relationships in which one party is able to impose itself

[12] Federal Law No. 8 of 2004 Regarding the Financial Free Zones in the United Arab Emirates.

[13] DIFC Regulatory Law No. 1 of 2004, Sch. 1 Int. 2 (b)–(c).

[14] Kerry Rittich, *Recharacterizing Restructuring: Law, Distribution and Gender in Market Reform* (The Hague: Kluwer Law International, 2002) 85.

[15] *Ibid.*, 86. [16] *Ibid.*, 87. [17] *Ibid.* [18] *Ibid.*, 94.

on another. It is in this sense that the notion of best practices is self-reinforcing, since it allows foreign usages to be cloaked in technical terms of what is economically best. The fact that such usages embody value postulates concerning a particular paradigm of law and economics is avoided.

In addition to comprising best practices and international standards, IFL has generally flourished in common law legal frameworks. The choice of common law in the DIFC is premised on the certainty, efficiency and flexibility that common law legal systems have historically established. There is reason to believe that the DIFC has benefited from this aspect of its legal and regulatory systems and this seems to also be the case with its facilitation of Islamic finance. Almost all leading global financial centres, in fact, are common law based. These include London, New York, Hong Kong and Singapore. The world's leading Islamic financial centre is Kuala Lumpur, a common law legal system, while Dubai has become the regional leader in the GCC.

Much of the Islamic banking activity taking place in the UAE is based in Dubai, both within and outside the DIFC.[19] The UAE as a whole commanded 17 per cent of global Islamic banking assets, totalling US$83 billion in 2012.[20] Moreover, the industry grew three times faster than conventional finance with a five-year compound annual growth rate of 14 per cent.[21] In 2011 the total number of companies incorporated in the DIFC was 817 of which 382 were engaged in financial intermediation.[22] As of 2013, twenty-three authorised firms were engaged in Islamic finance.[23] NASDAQ Dubai, the UAE's first equity derivatives market, which is located in the DIFC, is the largest exchange in the world for the issuance of *sukuk*.[24]

The legal framework of the DIFC differs markedly from the complex and uncertain aspects of the UAE legal framework. As a free zone with an independent legal system it is not governed by the UAE constitution and so does not face the problems regarding the inclusion of the sharia within that constitution. DIFC laws and regulations are the sole source of judicial and regulatory decision making. The DIFC courts, which are

[19] Dentons, *Legal Framework*, The Report: Dubai 2014 (Oxford Business Group, 2014), 298.
[20] Global Islamic banking assets exclude Iran.
[21] Ernst & Young (n 7) 15.
[22] DIFC, *DIFC Economic Activity Survey 2011*, Economic Note No. 20 (Dubai International Financial Centre, July 2012), 3.
[23] James Brockett, 'DIFC Boss Plans Islamic Finance Expansion', 30 October 2013, www.menafm.com/tag/difc/. Accessed 22 April 2014.
[24] Nasser Saidi (n 2).

established by law no. 12 of 2004, are not charged with interpreting the law according to other sources of law as is usual in Middle Eastern jurisdictions. The courts are divided into a court of first instance and a court of appeal. The court of first instance can hear any civil or commercial claims, transactions and/or actions to which a DIFC establishment is a party, or where claims, transactions and/or actions that arise out of a contract concluded and/or performed wholly or partly within the DIFC.[25] Moreover, the court of first instance may hear and determine the civil and commercial claims of parties who have no relation to the DIFC but have agreed in writing that their claim will be subject to DIFC courts' jurisdiction.[26] Parties may choose another jurisdiction as the proper law of their contract provided that it does not conflict with the public policy or morals of the centre.[27] In the event that no jurisdiction is specified in the contract, DIFC laws are applicable by default.

The influence of English common law on DIFC courts is remarkable. DIFC courts are modelled on the English commercial court. Judges 'must have significant experience as a qualified lawyer or judge in the common law system'.[28] Almost all first instance and appeal court judges have practised in common law jurisdictions.[29] The English law influence is particularly noticeable in the rules of the DIFC Courts 2007,[30] which are modelled on the English Civil Procedures Rules 1998 as well as the Admiralty And Commercial Courts Guide 2006. A number of other provisions in DIFC laws refer DIFC courts to English law in the event that a legislative lacuna exists.[31] For example, the DIFC court law, Article 50, provides that English rules of evidence may be used in DIFC court proceedings. Further, DIFC Law No. 3 of 2004 on the application of civil and commercial laws in the DIFC[32] allows DIFC courts to apply English common law in the event that the parties have not chosen a proper law of their contract.

Financial institutions of the DIFC are regulated, supervised and licensed by the DFSA, the centre's sole regulatory authority. The DFSA, a principles-based regulator, has the power to issue any rules or regulations

[25] Dubai Law No. 12 of 2004 in Respect of the Judicial Authority at Dubai International Financial Centre as Amended, Art 5(1)(a)–(c).

[26] *Ibid.*, Art 5(2). [27] *Ibid.*, Art 6.

[28] DIFC Law No. 10 of 2004, Art 9(3)(b).

[29] Reza Mohtashami and Sami Tannous, 'Arbitration at the Dubai International Financial Centre: A Common Law Jurisdiction in the Middle East' (2009) 25 *Arb Intl*, 173, 176.

[30] DIFC Order No. 1 of 2007 in respect of Rules of DIFC Court Order No. 1 of 2007.

[31] Reza Mohtashami and Sami Tannous (n 29) 176.

[32] DIFC Law No. 3 of 2004 on the Application of Civil and Commercial Laws in the DIFC, Art 8(2).

necessary to fulfil its regulatory objectives or to facilitate the administration of any law that is administered by the DFSA.[33] It may also develop regulatory policies and confer with the president of the centre regarding the promulgation of related legislation. The following section analyses the DFSA's general approach to Islamic finance.

9.2 The DFSA and its regulatory approach to Islamic finance

A document entitled 'The DFSA's Approach to Regulating Islamic Finance in the DIFC' explains in clear language the way in which the architects of the DIFC chose to construct the legal and regulatory framework for Islamic finance from scratch.[34] Several guiding principles characterise the DFSA regulatory approach to Islamic finance. First, the DFSA is a risk-based regulator, meaning that its regulatory approach addresses the substantive economic risks of financial institutions as opposed to regulating their products and services according to their legal form. Legal differences that do not produce substantively different economic risks will be regulated in a similar way.[35] This is the operating principle of nearly every jurisdiction that facilitates Islamic finance. Some jurisdictions, such as Malaysia and Bahrain, provide Islamic finance with a regulatory framework in which the legal characteristics of Islamic structures are legally recognised and given institutional support. However, even this regulatory approach recognises and addresses the real economic risks of Islamic financial transactions.

The second principle concerns the legal nature of the DIFC, in particular its international and hybrid legal composition. Relevant international standards will and have been implemented in the DIFC, and the DFSA actively participates in the process. In terms of Islamic finance, this means that the DFSA is a member of both AAOIFI and the IFSB and that the authority actively implements international standards as they develop.[36] As a result, market players are forced to actively follow the DIFC's implementation of market standards.

The third principle concerns the type of business the DIFC is primarily engaged in, namely, wholesale business. The DIFC mostly deals with institutional investors and high net-worth individuals, so that retail business

[33] DIFC Regulatory Law No. 1 (n 13) Art 23(2).

[34] DFSA, 'The DFSA's Approach to Regulating Islamic Finance in the DIFC' (n.d.), www.dfsa.ae/Documents/Islamic%20finance%20docs%20for%20upload/DFSA%27s%20approach%20to%20regulating%20Islamic%20finance.pdf. Accessed 22 April 2014.

[35] *Ibid.* [36] *Ibid.*

comprises a less important sector for the centre. This means that the DIFC is designed to function as an internationally active financial centre. It is not tailored to the requirements of specific national markets. This latter principle underscores the global focus and offshore composition of the DIFC.[37]

A fourth principle concerns the legal aspects of the DIFC, in particular the architects' concerns for maintaining flexibility. The DIFC was established as a long-term business project, one which was highly attractive to internationally active financial institutions. In terms of Islamic finance this principle allows both standalone and Islamic windows to conduct business. This principle is followed by most jurisdictions that seek to provide Islamic finance with a jurisdictional haven. In 2011 Qatar took the unusual decision to close its Islamic windows. The Qatar Central Bank may have sought to strengthen the sharia aspects of Islamic financial transactions. However, the illiberal policy has not led to a greater market share for Qatar's standalone Islamic banks, which indicates that there are complex reasons for consumers' uptake of Islamic financial products.[38]

The DFSA, similar to the Bahrain Central Bank, has created a detailed rulebook for Islamic finance. The rulebook is complemented by a markets law, a regulatory law and a law regulating Islamic financial business in the DIFC. The following section analyses these sources of legislation with regard to their rules for the authorisation of IFIs in the DIFC.

9.3 The authorisation of IFIs

The Regulatory Law 2004 is the primary source of regulatory rules and standards for financial institutions operating in the DIFC. The law establishes the powers, functions and objectives of the DFSA and deals transparently with areas of financial law that are relevant to a financial institution's licensing, authorisation, business conduct and operation. Article 42(3) provides that a person[39] may carry on financial services originating in the DIFC if they are:[40]

[37] *Ibid.*

[38] Regan Doherty and Bernardo Vizcaino, 'No Windfall from Qatar Ban on Islamic Windows', *Reuters*, 2 May 2012, www.reuters.com/article/2012/05/02/qatar-islamic-banks-idUSL5E8FU0KH20120502. Accessed 22 April 2014.

[39] A 'person' includes any natural person, body corporate or body unincorporated, including a legal person, company, partnership, unincorporated association, government or state.

[40] DIFC Regulatory Law No. 1 (n 13) Art 42(3)(a)–(c).

> (a) an authorised firm whose license authorises it to carry on the relevant financial services; (b) an external fund manager ...; (c) an authorised market institution whose license authorises it to carry on the relevant financial services.

Authorised firms and/or market institutions must act within the scope of their licence, including any condition or restriction thereto.[41] Moreover, the DFSA only accepts applications for a licence from bodies corporate or partnerships.[42] Persons not meeting these requirements as well as that of Article 41(9)[43] cannot carry out a financial service originating in the DIFC.[44]

The Law Regulating Islamic Financial Business 2004 provides specific rules for the authorisation and conduct of financial institutions providing Islamic financial services. It defines Islamic financial business as 'carrying on one or more financial services in accordance with Shari'a'.[45] This means that a person who undertakes a financial activity that constitutes a financial service and who holds that the activity is sharia compliant will be considered Islamic financial business.[46] Accordingly, an authorised IFI must ensure that its constitutional documents state in clear language that its entire business will be conducted according to sharia principles.[47]

The Law Regulating Islamic Financial Business 2004 defines an IFI as an authorised firm 'whose entire business operations are conducted in accordance with Shari'a' or as an Islamic window 'if it conducts Islamic financial business as part of its overall business operations'.[48] An authorised firm may conduct some of its operations as a conventional financial service provider while also offering Islamic products through its Islamic window.[49]

An authorised firm may not hold itself out as an IFI if the DFSA has not granted it an endorsement to its licence allowing it to conduct Islamic

[41] *Ibid.*, Art 42(4)(a)–(b).
[42] DFSA, *DFSA Rulebook: General Module (GEN)* (Dubai Financial Services Authority, July 2013), 7.2.2.
[43] Article 41(9) exempts funds from the financial services prohibition with respect to any financial service carried on for purposes of the fund.
[44] DIFC Regulatory Law No. 1 (n 13) Art 41(1).
[45] DIFC Law No. 13 of 2004 Law Regulating Islamic Financial Business, Art 10(1).
[46] DFSA, *DFSA Rulebook: Islamic Finance Rules (IFR)* (Dubai Financial Services Authority, July 2013), IFR 2.2(1). The definition of what constitutes a financial service as well as the DFSA's regulatory classification of Islamic financial services is examined in the following section.
[47] *Ibid.*, IFR 3.2.1.
[48] DIFC Law Regulating Islamic Financial Business (n 45) Art 10(2)–(3).
[49] DFSA (n 46) IFR 2.3(4).

financial business.[50] Authorised firms, which may include corporate, partnerships or unincorporated associations, must apply to the DFSA for an endorsement or variation to an endorsement to conduct Islamic financial business.[51] If an IFI, whether an Islamic window or a standalone provider, delivers Islamic financial services to retail clients, the authorised firm must have a retail endorsement to its licence.[52] The DFSA, subject to Article 12(3) and (4), may 'impose conditions and restrictions or additional conditions and restrictions in relation to an endorsement'.[53] The DFSA considers applications for authorisation to carry on a financial service if a person is able to demonstrate that it has 'adequate resources, including financial resources; is fit and proper; and has adequate compliance arrangements'.[54]

The DFSA has established a sophisticated approach to regulating the sharia aspects of IFIs and conventional institutions offering Islamic services. Unlike the FSA in the United Kingdom, for example, the DFSA claims that it takes seriously an IFI's representation that its products are Islamic. The DFSA has chosen to be a 'systems regulator' whereby it mandates a wide range of rules and standards with respect to the sharia governance of IFIs and Islamic windows. Instead of arbitrating sharia matters directly, as the Malaysian Central Bank and Bahrain via AAOIFI do, the DFSA approaches the issue by regulating the systems of an IFI for their compliance with sharia. This places the onus of compliance on the IFI in that its systems and controls are at issue.[55] The last section in this chapter examines the DFSA's approach to sharia governance in greater detail.

The following section examines the types of financial services that DFSA-authorised IFIs are able to undertake. As in previous chapters the primary focus is concerned with PLS investment contracts since these structures are viewed as the cornerstone of Islamic financial intermediation.

9.4 The regulatory classification of Islamic financial products

The previous section indicated that only those institutions that the DFSA had authorised to carry on a financial service would be allowed do so. This section is concerned with the way in which the DFSA regulates

[50] DIFC Law Regulating Islamic Financial Business (n 45) Art 9(1).
[51] *Ibid.*, Arts 11(1)–(2) and 12(1).
[52] DFSA (n 46) IFR 2.3(5).
[53] DIFC Law Regulating Islamic Financial Business (n 45) Art 12(2)(a).
[54] DFSA (n 42) 7.2.5. [55] DFSA (n 34).

Islamic financial services. In particular, it deals with the extent to which the DFSA has created regulatory classifications that cater to the legal specificities of such services. The DFSA defines financial services as those activities listed under rule 2.2.2 in the general rulebook and those 'conducted by way of business and not expressly excluded from regulation as a financial service'.[56] By implication this definition includes the financial products that result from such services. The DFSA has created specific rules for several specified Islamic financial services including PLS investment accounts, investments and *takāful*. Most Islamic services fall under conventional classifications (as listed in GEN 2.2.2.) but must be transacted in a sharia-compliant manner. The basic approach to regulating the specified services is one of substance over form, indicating that the DFSA regulates real economic risks irrespective of the nature of an instrument's legal form.

Amongst a long list of permissible financial services for both conventional and Islamic institutions are the core Islamic intermediation activities of accepting deposits, providing credit and managing PLS investment accounts. In addition to listing PLS accounts as a specified investment, the DFSA specifically exempts them from its definition of a deposit, so that IFIs can use the *muḍārabah* as a fund-mobilising instrument. The DFSA defines a deposit as 'a sum of money paid on terms: (a) under which it will be repaid, with or without interest or a premium, and either on demand or at a time or in circumstances agreed by or on behalf of the person making the payment and the person receiving it'.[57] Independent of further guidance this definition does not allow IFIs to use the *muḍārabah* as a fund-mobilising instrument. However, the DFSA made an exception by not considering the receipt of a sum a deposit as long as it was received by an authorised person to manage a PLS investment account.[58]

Although it resembles the characteristics of a collective investment fund the DFSA has excluded PLS accounts from being treated as such.[59] PLS accounts are not categorised as an investment, which, according to the definition, consist of securities and derivatives. PLS accounts are singled out amongst other Islamic financial services such as Islamic funds and *takāful* for specific regulatory treatment, which is laid out in the Islamic finance rulebook.

[56] DFSA (n 46) IFR 2.4(1)–(2). See GEN 2.3.1 for the meaning of 'by way of business'.

[57] DFSA (n 42) APP1 A1.1.1(1)(a). [58] *Ibid.*, APP1 A1.1.3(c)(xii).

[59] See DFSA, *DFSA Rulebook: Collective Investment Rules* (Dubai Financial Services Authority, July 2013), CIR 2.1.13.

DFSA regulatory treatment of PLS accounts differs markedly from the vast majority of jurisdictions that have chosen to facilitate Islamic finance including those under study. The DFSA requires IFIs to provide written notice to clients informing them that they alone will bear any losses that arise from the transaction, unless there has been negligence or malfeasance on the part of the firm. It advises IFIs to ensure that their PLS accounts are not in any way represented as a deposit. In certain circumstances it may conclude that an authorised firm is using the PLS account as a deposit if, for example, the firm made explicit or implicit guarantees to the client that his or her principal investment would be returned. The provision of cheques, ATM cards or debit cards may also indicate the same.

The DFSA mandates a number of further provisions in relation to PLS investment accounts. The client agreement must include a wide range of information that addresses principal–agent risks associated with PLS modes. These risks were analysed in Chapter 6. For example, information relating to:[60]

> how and by whom the funds of the client will be managed; the basis for profit allocation between the firm and the client; a summary of the policies and procedures for the valuation of assets or portfolio; a summary of policies and procedures for the transfer of funds to and from the profit equalisation reserve or investment risk reserve accounts; details of the segregation of client funds from those of the firm and from creditor claims of the firm; information regarding whether funds from one PLS account will be mixed with those of another; and other requirements.

In addition to addressing the direct informational concerns of the client, the DFSA mandates that authorised firms provide further information in their policy and procedures manuals. Such information includes:[61] the firm's basis for determining whether a PLS account is restricted or unrestricted (note that in any PLS account an authorised firm must provide information relating to how and by whom client funds will be invested); the basis for the allocation of profit or loss; the basis for the allocation of expenses; the manner in which a firm's own funds, and those of restricted and unrestricted PLS accounts are to be controlled and managed; and, importantly, how provisions and reserves against equity and assets are to be applied.

These and other informational requirements squarely address the risks associated with PLS modes and would seem to provide a business

[60] DFSA (n 46) IFR 5.2.2. [61] *Ibid.*, IFR 5.2.4.

environment in which the *muḍārabah* can be transacted according to sharia principles.

In addition to financial services that can be carried out according to sharia principles, the DFSA recognises that conventional investments may also be used as Islamic financial products. These include shares, *sukuk*, units of Islamic funds and structured products. Moreover, Islamic derivatives are being increasingly used by modifying conventional derivatives according to sharia principles.[62]

The next section examines the DFSA's approach to CARs for Islamic financial transactions. In particular, it will examine the approach taken toward PLS accounts in light of the regulator's risk-based approach.

9.5 Capital adequacy standards for IFIs

The DIFC regulatory framework is the composite product of best regulatory practices from the leading economies of the world. According to this globalised regulatory model, the DFSA strives to be fully compliant with Basel core principles including the Basel III framework. At the end of 2012 the DFSA implemented new prudential standards designed to give effect to Basel III standards.[63] This section analyses the general contours of DFSA CARs for IFIs and pays special attention to the regulator's treatment of PLS accounts. The importance of Basel standards in the DIFC regulatory framework is apparent, as are IFSB prudential standards. The latter standards are particularly relevant with respect to the way in which the DFSA has chosen to deal with displaced commercial risk (DCR) in PLS accounts.

The basic rules for authorised firms operating in the DIFC are similar to those of the other jurisdictions under study, which is a testament to the international applicability of Basel standards as well as the dissemination of Islamic financial standards. Globalisation, in relation to Basel standards, clearly does initiate a process of legal standardisation. While Basel standards are implemented differently according to jurisdictional specificities, their implementation, in general, affects the nature of financial services and risk management processes, including Islamic finance. DIFC domestic authorised firms must possess and maintain capital resources in

[62] *Ibid.*, IFR 2.4(6). Chapter 4 discussed this process.

[63] DFSA, 'New and Enhanced PIB Module of DFSA Rulebook – Roll-Out and Implementation' (Dubai Financial Services Authority, 6 December 2012), www.dfsa.ae/Documents/SEO%20Letters%202012/PIB%20module%20roll-out%20Dec%206%202012.pdf. Accessed 22 April 2014.

satisfaction of the DFSA's prudential rules as well as the nature, size and complexity of their business. The basic rule is that an authorised firm's capital resources must outweigh a firm's capital requirements.[64]

Authorised firms that are branches, on the other hand, must ensure that they maintain liquid assets and access to financial resources adequate to the 'nature, size and complexity of its business'.[65] Branches must also comply with home state prudential requirements and report to the DFSA its compliance with home state CARs.[66] The DFSA focus is on ensuring that branches are able to meet liabilities as they fall due, whereas the safety and soundness of the institution are mostly the concern of the home state regulator.

The composition of capital is to be maintained according to some general rules. Sixty per cent of the risk capital requirement, which is the general capital requirement of the firm, must comprise common equity tier 1 (CET1) capital. Tier 1 capital, which is the total of CET1 and additional tier 1 capital, must equate to at least 80 per cent of a firm's risk capital requirement.[67] The CET1 used for meeting these requirements may not form part of the capital conservation buffer, according to Basel III reforms to firms' prudential requirements.[68] The result of these rules is that tier 2 capital may not be used to meet more than 20 per cent of a firm's risk capital requirement.

In addition to the risk capital requirement examined above, a firm has to maintain a so-called base capital requirement, which requires IFIs to maintain CET1 of not less than US$10 million at all times. An authorised firm is required to implement the higher of the two options.[69] This determination should be made on the basis of assessing the component risks of the risk capital requirement, which includes the credit risk capital requirement (CRCOM), the market risk capital requirement, the operational risk capital requirement and the DCR capital requirement.[70] The latter requirement is only applicable to firms operating PLS accounts such as IFIs or Islamic windows. Islamic contracts are treated differently for the calculation of credit and market risks.

The DFSA requires authorised firms managing PLS accounts to calculate a DCR capital requirement in relation to such business. The reader will recall that DCR is the risk that a firm may smooth the profits of its

[64] DFSA, *Prudential – Investment, Insurance Intermediation and Banking Business Module (PIB)* (Dubai Financial Services Authority, July 2013), PIB 3.2.2-3.2.3.

[65] *Ibid.*, PIB 3.2.4(a). [66] *Ibid.*, PIB 3.2.4(b).

[67] *Ibid.*, PIB 3.2.7(2)(a)(i)–(ii). [68] *Ibid.*, PIB 3.2.7(3).

[69] *Ibid.*, PIB 3.3.2. [70] *Ibid.*, PIB 3.8.2.

account holders due to commercial pressures to provide a rate of return that is commensurate with retaining them as a client. Profit smoothing depletes shareholders' equity and a firm's own capital and may thus weaken the commercial position or even solvency of the financial institution. The requirement to calculate a DCR capital requirement reflects the DFSA's estimation that firms managing such accounts engage in profit smoothing.

The DCR capital requirement is equal to 35 per cent of the credit risk capital requirement (CRCOM) and market risk capital requirement of assets funded by unrestricted PLS accountholders. All Islamic contracts funded by unrestricted PLS accounts must be valued to determine the appropriate risk weighting in relation to CRCOM and the market risk capital requirement.[71] The exposure of authorised firms to an Islamic contract and the credit risk weighting or capital charge for the contract are assessed according to DFSA prudential rules.[72]

The binding *murābaḥah* to the purchase orderer (MPO), which was also examined for capital adequacy purposes in the Bahrain regulatory system, provides an example of the way in which these rules are applied. The DFSA treats the MPO by assessing the CRCOM and market risk capital requirements. The CRCOM is assessed in relation to the exposure of assets on the books of authorised firms prior to their purchase by the counterparty (they are owned by the firm and thus constitute a risk to the firm).[73] Such transactions are considered unsettled, which means they remain unsettled after due delivery dates. A specific, rapidly progressive rate applies to the number of days that accrue after the due settlement. For example, 5–15 days is given 100 per cent for calculating the risk-weighted assets. However, 16–30 days is allocated 500 per cent, a very large increase.[74] Moreover, the exposure of accounts receivable under the contract, which are the 'amounts due from the counterparty less any provisions for doubtful debts', are also given a risk-weighted asset.[75] The exposure of a binding MPO should equal the total acquisition cost of the asset (purchase price and other direct costs) less the market value of the asset and any security deposit.[76] The credit risk weighting appropriate to the MPO is also assessed in accordance with sections 4.10, 4.11 and 4.12

[71] DFSA (n 46) IFR 5.4.5, 5.4.6.

[72] See DFSA (n 64) ss 4.9–4.12 of chapter 4.

[73] *Ibid.*, 5.4.7 Table 2. [74] DFSA (n 64) PIB A4.6.5.

[75] See DFSA (n 64) PIB chapter 4.

[76] DFSA (n 46) 5.4.7 Guidance (6).

of the DFSA's Prudential – Investment, Insurance Intermediation and Banking Business Module (PIB).[77]

Upon determining the exposure (E) and credit risk weighting (CRW) of the MPO these figures are applied to a formula depending on whether an Islamic contract is in the trading book[78] or non-trading book[79]. In the non-trading book a firm determines the CRCOM for an Islamic contract by applying the following formula: E x CRW x 10%. CRCOM for a contract in the trading book is determined by referring to PIB methodology in A4.7 and A4.8.[80] The total CRCOM applicable to the authorised firm as a whole can be calculated by totalling the CRCOM requirement applicable to each Islamic contract.[81]

The second necessary variable for calculating an authorised firm's DCR is the market risk capital requirement of assets funded by unrestricted PLS accounts. Market risk 'refers to the risk of incurring losses on positions held by an Authorised Firm with trading intent, due to adverse changes in market prices or in underlying value drivers'.[82] Authorised firms must calculate their market risk capital requirements as the sum of the following components: interest rate risk capital requirement; equity risk capital requirement; foreign exchange capital requirement; commodities risk capital requirement; option risk capital requirement; collective investment fund risk capital requirement; and securities underwriting capital requirement.[83]

Authorised firms such as IFIs may use, with the written approval of the DFSA, an internal model to assess their market risk capital requirement or any component of such requirement.[84] The DFSA prescribes a wide range of requirements that a firm's internal risk model must satisfy to be given approval.[85]

Rules applicable to the measurement of market risk in Islamic financial business require that commodities risk, which is common to Islamic financial business, must be calculated in relation to 'commodities including

[77] *Ibid.*, 5.4.7(4)(c).

[78] The trading book represents a financial institution's proprietary positions in financial instruments or commodities. These instruments are purchased or sold so as to facilitate trading for an institution's customers; to profit in the short term from the actual or expected differences in the bid and asking prices of such instruments; and to hedge against various risks in the trading book.

[79] Positions, exposures, assets and liabilities that are not in the trading book.

[80] DFSA (n 46) 5.4.7(2)–(3). [81] *Ibid.*, 5.4.7(4)(e).

[82] DFSA (n 64) PIB 5 Guidance (1).

[83] *Ibid.*, PIB 5.3.1. [84] *Ibid.*, PIB 5.11.1.

[85] See PIB 5.11.4 Guidance.

precious metals but excluding gold under any Islamic contract'.[86] Further, when executing *murābaḥah*, non-binding MPO, *salam* or parallel *salam*, the commodities sold or leased must be included in the commodities risk capital requirement.[87]

The DFSA has created a detailed framework of prudential requirements for IFIs alongside its provision of rules for conventional institutions. These requirements cater to the specific economic risks of Islamic financial contracts, including its preferred mode of fund mobilisation, the PLS account. The rules are also designed in a way that recognises sharia requirements, though they stop short of mandating the nature of such requirements. The DFSA's approach to sharia governance is similar. It is concerned with policing an IFI's sharia systems and controls while not intervening directly in the sharia aspects of such controls. As a result, authorised IFIs are forced to assume the responsibility for meeting the requirements of sharia. It is an approach to sharia governance that has been heralded as a way forward, particularly for Muslim-minority jurisdictions. The following section examines this topic in greater detail.

9.6 Governance standards for IFIs

The point of departure in relation to sharia governance in the DIFC is the Law Regulating Islamic Financial Business, which requires an authorised firm to appoint an SSB comprised of at least three members and empowers the DFSA to 'make rules prescribing the appointment, formation, conduct and operation of a sharia supervisory board'.[88] The DFSA's rules for sharia governance are modelled in large part from AAOIFI standards, underscoring the growing dissemination amongst GCC jurisdictions of such standards. As a systems regulator, thc DFSA predicates its approach to sharia governance with a general requirement for authorised firms undertaking Islamic financial business to 'establish and maintain systems and controls, which enable it to comply with the applicable sharia requirements'.[89] This very significant rule makes the senior management of an IFI responsible for sharia compliance whereas regulatory guidance in most jurisdictions allows SSBs alone to carry the responsibility of sharia compliance. Further, the governing body of an IFI should include SSB members in decisions involving the objectives and strategies of the firm;

[86] DFSA (n 46) IFR 5.4.12. [87] *Ibid.*, IFR 5.4.13(1).
[88] DIFC Law Regulating Islamic Financial Business (n 45) Art 13 (1)–(2).
[89] DFSA (n 46) IFR 3.3.1.

and persons responsible for a firm's risk control functions should consult with the SSB in relation to sharia matters. In general, SSB members should have 'adequate access to the governing body, senior management and persons undertaking key control functions as appropriate to ensure that their roles can be effectively discharged'.[90]

The importance of these rules is considerable since they illustrate the way in which the DFSA, as a secular financial regulator, understands the role of the sharia in the provision of financial services. The DFSA felt that it could deal with a system of sharia governance, since doing so is merely a technical matter that excludes direct intervention in religious or other qualitative questions. In doing so it could keep religion a private affair, much like the position of religion in the United Kingdom or other secular Western states. The approach is in keeping with the neoliberal conception of markets, which sees markets as value free. The appropriate role of institutions and market players within markets is a technical, almost mechanical issue that can be divorced from subjectivities.

Another important way in which the DFSA institutionalises sharia compliance in authorised firms concerns its requirement that authorised persons must maintain an Islamic financial business policy and procedures manual. The manual should address a lengthy list of matters that are designed to satisfy the general problems of sharia governance including the issues examined in Chapter 6. These include the confidentiality, objectivity, independence, credibility and audit/review processes of SSBs. Due to the importance of establishing policies that mitigate problems relating to sharia governance, they are listed as:

> (a) the manner in which the compliance function will be undertaken, in respect of sharia compliance; (b) the manner in which the SSB will oversee and advise in regard to the Islamic financial business conducted by the authorised person; (c) the manner in which SSB fatwas, rulings and guidelines will be recorded, disseminated and implemented and the internal sharia review undertaken; (d) the manner in which disputes between the SSB and the authorised person in respect of sharia compliance will be addressed; (e) the process for approving those internal systems and controls which are in place to ensure not only that the Islamic financial business is carried out in compliance with sharia, but that information is disseminated, using an appropriate method and manner, to investors and, in the case of an authorised market institution, to persons with access to its facilities; (f) the manner in which conflicts of interest will be identified and managed including where prescribed; and (g) in respect of

[90] *Ibid.*

> authorised person operating an Islamic window, the systems and controls in place to ensure the appropriate separation of the Islamic financial business of the authorised person from its conventional business.[91]

The IFR rulebook provides specific rules concerning SSB members' competency. An IFI must ensure that SSB members are competent to perform their functions as SSB members. This means that an authorised person should examine the experience and qualifications of a person applying to become an SSB member.[92] The governing body of an IFI must approve any appointment, dismissal or other change in relation to the members of an SSB. Furthermore, the DFSA requires authorised firms to maintain transparent records of the appointment, dismissal or other changes made to an SSB for a period of six years. The documentation requirement also includes the process in which the suitability of an SSB candidate was considered and the IFI's assessment of the competency of an SSB member. The factors taken into consideration with respect to a candidate's competency including qualifications and experience should be recorded. The agreed terms of engagement of an SSB member and, finally, the remuneration of SSB members should be documented.[93]

The IFR rulebook is also concerned with information disclosures related to potential conflicts of interest. This includes rules designed to shore up the objectivity of an SSB's fatwas. For example, no SSB member may be a director or controller of the firm.[94] Other rules concern conflicts of interest arising from membership of multiple SSBs. Details of such must be recorded.[95] In general, SSB members are required to notify the firm of any conflict of interest and firms are expected to take steps to mitigate any such conflicts.[96] A firm's inability to do so must result in the dismissal or replacement of the SSB member.[97]

The rules discussed above are designed to deal with problems relating to the disclosure of information, credibility, objectivity and confidence and to allay the potential for conflicts of interest in sharia governance. The DFSA also provides rules concerning the ways in which SSBs fulfil their roles and duties. It stipulates, for example, that all sharia reviews must be conducted in accordance with AAOIFI standard GSIFI No. 2, which deals with sharia governance. Furthermore, the DFSA requires that the IFI commission an annual report from its SSB which complies

[91] *Ibid.*, IFR 3.4.1. [92] *Ibid.*, IFR 3.5 (a)–(b).
[93] *Ibid.*, IFR 3.5.2, 3.5.3. [94] *Ibid.*, IFR 3.5.1(d).
[95] *Ibid.*, IFR 3.5.3(d). [96] *Ibid.*, IFR 3.5.4(1).
[97] *Ibid.*, IFR 3.5.4(2).

with AAOIFI GSIFI No 1. A copy of such report must be delivered to the DFSA within fourteen days of receipt.[98]

In addition to the annual sharia report the DFSA mandates that an authorised firm undertake an internal sharia review to assess the extent to which it complies with its SSB's fatwas, rulings and other guidelines.[99] AAOIFI standard GSIFI No. 3 is the basic template for this and covers the following aspects:

> objectives; internal sharia review; independence and objectivity; professional proficiency; scope of work; performance of the international sharia review; management of the internal sharia review; quality assurance; and elements of an effective internal sharia review control system.[100]

The internal sharia review must be conducted by the internal audit or compliance function of the firm and the persons involved in performing the review must be 'competent and sufficiently independent to assess compliance with sharia'.[101]

While the SSBs of Islamic windows are subject to these requirements, they are also subject to additional rules of disclosure regarding the way in which their funds are stored. In particular, they must disclose to clients or 'any person granted access to its facilities' whether they commingle their conventional and Islamic funds.[102]

The rules and requirements discussed above enable the DFSA to create a system of regulation for IFIs that provides clear and enforceable standards against which an IFI's performance may be measured. As a system's regulator it is not concerned with interpreting the sharia or in creating uniform standards of sharia as would be the case were it to act as a higher sharia supervisory authority. The DFSA approach is a pragmatic one – particularly when viewed within the regulatory capacities of the neoliberal paradigm – in that it recognises that diversity in sharia interpretation exists but refrains from engaging in efforts to standardise the law. Such efforts are conveniently left to sharia scholars.

[98] *Ibid.*, IFR 3.6.1, 3.6.2. [99] *Ibid.*, IFR 3.7.1.

[100] *Ibid.*, IFR 3.7.3.

[101] *Ibid.*, IFR 3.7.4. AAOIFI, *Accounting, Auditing and Governance Standards for Islamic Financial Institutions: Governance Standard for Islamic Financial Institutions: Sharia Review* (Manama: The Accounting and Auditing Organization for Islamic Financial Institutions, 2010), no. 3, paras 9–16 may be consulted for purposes of assessing the competency of personnel or departments performing the review.

[102] DFSA (n 46) IFR 3.8.3(1)–(2). IFR (3) provides that a fund manager of a fund who is making an offer of units of that fund according to Collective Investment Law 2010 requirements, the CIR module and the IFR module does not have to make such a disclosure.

9.7 Concluding remarks

As a financial free zone or offshore financial centre the DIFC epitomises the global development of financial services law and financial market trends. Its hybrid legal structure demonstrates its architects' adoption of legal systems and best practices originating in leading financial centres as well as the standards developed from global regulatory bodies. The DIFC is designed to be globally competitive and its legal and regulatory systems are constructed to attain that objective. These systems are transparent, objective and independent and as such are easily differentiated from the legal uncertainty that characterises the UAE federal jurisdiction.

The DIFC's regulatory treatment of Islamic finance reflects its neoliberal legal and regulatory design. As is the case with other jurisdictions under examination, the DIFC regulates Islamic finance according to economic substance and has created a regulatory system for PLS accounts that takes note of the sharia's requirements with respect to profit- and loss-sharing. However, its basic approach to regulating the sharia does not diverge from the dominant social episteme of neoliberalism, which views markets as a priori, value-neutral, almost self-sufficient entities. Issues concerning sharia interpretation are appropriately treated as private subjectivities in this value-free zone. The DFSA's authorisation of IFIs, its classification and regulatory treatment of Islamic financial services and, finally, its treatment for capital adequacy purposes of Islamic financial services all reflect this approach.

Within the neoliberal paradigm the DIFC's increasing stature as an Islamic financial hub and emerging centre of a global Islamic economy is strengthened by its regulatory approach to sharia governance systems. Comprising Basel, AAOIFI, IFSB and other global regulatory standards and best practices, IFL in the DIFC is a global composite of international best standards and a forerunner of globalisation. The DIFC's approach to Islamic finance sets an influential precedent for other states considering the facilitation of Islamic finance. It provides an example of best practices which other states may wish to emulate in their development of IFL.

10

The enforcement of non-national legal systems: the arbitration of Islamic financial disputes

Almost all types of legal systems require enforcement mechanisms. The power to enforce the law is essential to the authority of a legal system and its ability to coerce actors to adhere to both public and private obligations. In commercial matters the threat of legal enforcement is seen as a necessity as most problems concern the breach of contract and parties' willingness to fulfil contractual obligations is at stake. The threat of the law can induce parties to fulfil their obligations or to seek compromise before formal legal action is taken.

As was examined in Chapter 6, the sharia cannot be used as the governing law of a contract (the exception being Saudi law). This limitation or shortcoming – depending on the perspective – largely derives from the formal aspects of municipal court systems (but more broadly from the ways in which the nation state defines the nature of law). The formal requirements of the state are usefully contrasted with the largely non-national legal practice known as arbitration. Arbitration provides a number of advantageous characteristics for resolving international commercial and financial disputes relative to litigation. Moreover, it consists of an underlying logic that delimits the regulatory capacity of nation states and this has made it controversial, particularly in emerging economies such as those of the GCC. As a global adjudication system built and promoted by leading economies, arbitration should be seen as a legal articulation of the global economy. Its mechanism for resolving disputes and enforcing awards comprises a complex mixture of state-based and non-state-based legal systems. Arbitration is designed to resolve disputes that extend beyond the sovereignty of any one state or that require impartiality, which may not be present in the courts of a particular state. These characteristics make arbitration a natural alternative to litigation for the resolution of Islamic financial disputes.

These ideas are explored by examining the nature of arbitration, its mechanisms and functionality as well as its history and practice in the municipal systems of the Middle East and the United Kingdom. The compatibility of arbitration with the sharia is also discussed.

10.1 Arbitration and Islamic financial transactions

Arbitration allows contracting parties to an Islamic financial transaction the possibility of choosing a non-state body of law or other legal principles as the applicable law of their contract. Theoretically, contracts in which the sharia, the *lex mercatoria* or the general principles of law are the express choice of the parties will be given effect in most jurisdictions around the world. As long as parties have agreed that such rules apply or in circumstances in which the parties have remained silent concerning the governing law, the choice of a non-state law will not affect the validity or enforceability of the arbitral award.[1]

However, in practice, the utility of arbitration in most Arab jurisdictions is limited to some extent by the uncertainty of whether foreign arbitral awards will be recognised and enforced. The municipal courts of Arab states have shown an antipathy towards arbitration, primarily due to an association between the mechanism and the late vestiges of colonialism and in relation to more recent experiences involving FDI. Despite these antipathies, Middle Eastern cultural and legal attributes display affinities for arbitration that presage increased use in regional financial centres.

10.1.1 The nature of arbitration

Arbitration is a process in which parties who are in dispute have agreed, either in their contract or after a dispute has arisen, to submit their dispute to an experienced person who they believe will exercise good judgment and impartiality in resolving their conflict. This person or persons decide the dispute according to the procedures or law of a private tribunal known as the *lex arbitri*. The substantive matters of the dispute may be governed by an entirely different law, or the *lex arbitri* may also be chosen as the law in this instance. However, most international arbitrations are carried out in a neutral country – a country in which the parties are not habitually resident – and the law that governs the enforcement of the award is almost always different from the law chosen to regulate the arbitration proceedings. The arbitrator's decision is both final and binding on

[1] Alan Redfern, Martin Hunter, Nigel Blackaby and Constantine Partasides, *Redfern and Hunter on International Arbitration* (Oxford University Press, 2009), 221.

the parties because the parties have agreed to bind themselves to the tribunal's decision.[2] In effect, the choice to arbitrate is to rescind one's 'right of recourse to the courts of law in respect of any such dispute'.[3]

The possibility of excluding the jurisdiction of municipal courts from adjudicating disputes prevents states from intervening in private contractual relations. Numerous decisions of international case law have upheld the autonomy of the arbitration clause, which enables the arbitration clause to escape the fate of the contract to which it is appended.[4] The autonomy of the arbitration clause does not allow a state party to escape its obligation to arbitrate by unilaterally abrogating this obligation.[5]

Arbitration is made internationally enforceable through the New York Convention. The key characteristics of arbitration, including the neutrality and competence of the arbitral forum, necessarily require broad international recognition and enforcement of arbitral awards to make the system workable. It must rely on municipal courts for the recognition and enforcement of arbitral agreements and awards.

However, competing theories of arbitration dispute the role of the state in the arbitration process. For instance, a contractual theory of arbitration is premised on the parties' mutual consent to arbitrate as embodied in the arbitration agreement. Parties' contractual consent should enable them to determine arbitral procedure and the substantive law of the arbitration without interference from municipal courts.[6] The internationalisation of arbitral agreements disembeds investment agreements from municipal legal systems. An entire private legal order with global validity is established that transcends any one particular commercial transaction. Arbitration clauses refer disputes to arbitration tribunals, such as the International Chamber of Commerce in Paris, which are also responsible for 'legislating' the model arbitration contract. It is this circular relationship between the jurisdiction of arbitration tribunals and the autonomy of arbitration clauses that establishes 'the core of a decision

[2] *Ibid.*, 1–9. [3] *Ibid.*, 17.

[4] *Texaco Overseas Petroleum Co* v. *The Government of the Libyan Arab Republic, Preliminary Award* 53 International Law Reports 389, 408.

[5] Robert B. von Mehren and Nicholas P. Kourides, 'International Arbitration between States and Foreign Private Parties: The Libyan Nationalization Cases' (1981) 75 *A.J.I.L.*, 502.

[6] Katherine Lynch, *The Forces of Economic Globalization: Challenges to the Regime of International Commercial Arbitration* (The Hague: Kluwer Law International, 2003), 66–7.

system', capable of creating a hierarchy of norms and organisational bodies.[7] Hence the creation of global law is process based: it transcends 'the consistency of legal norms structurally secured by the hierarchy of the courts' and is generated via the 'modes of connection between legal operations, which transfer binding legality between even highly heterogeneous legal orders'.[8]

A competing theoretical perspective views arbitration as a geographically rooted dispute resolution process that provides an alternative to municipal courts. This theory, which dominated discussion prior to World War II, views the sovereign state as the sole authority and power from which the process of arbitration draws its legitimacy. The state's authority allows it to determine disputes that cannot be the subject of arbitration. Sovereign authority also allows for judicial review in which the municipal courts retain the right to review the arbitration process and awards rendered in relation to the 'errors of law or fact, abuse of process or public policy'.[9] It does seem, however, that states' sovereign authority over arbitration and other law-making processes has grown weaker or has shifted in the age of globalisation.[10]

Both theories do not fully explain the complex interaction of the transnational nature of arbitration with municipal legal systems and non-governmental organisations. Arbitration is embedded in municipal legal systems to the extent that municipal courts vet parties' agreements and enforce arbitral awards. Yet arbitration is also ambulatory in relation to parties' freedom to choose to remove their dispute from the jurisdiction of a municipal legal system. The legitimacy of an arbitral award is not

[7] Guenther Teubner '"Global Bukowina": Legal Pluralism in the World Society' in Gunther Teubner (ed.), *Global Law Without A State* (Aldershot: Dartmouth Publishing Company 1997), 16–17.

[8] Peter-Gralf Calliess and Peer Zumbansen, *Rough Consensus and Running Code: A Theory of Transnational Private Law* (Oxford: Hart Publishing, 2010), 34.

[9] Katherine Lynch (n 6) 69.

[10] Amr A. Shalakany, 'Arbitration and the Third World: A Plea for Reassessing Bias Under the Specter of Neoliberalism' (2000) 41 *Harv.Int'l. L.J.*, 419, 443. Sovereignty is a complex concept, the meaning of which shifts in relation to context. It basically denotes internal hierarchy and external equality. In the European context, which gave rise to the nation state, the development of sovereignty was closely connected to boundaries or exclusive zones of jurisdiction. Many differences and similarities exist between boundaries in the context of a state and those of frontier zones. By separating centre-periphery relations from inter-system interactions and system-environment interactions useful insights into the nature and patterns of interaction of municipal and transnational systems may be drawn. See Friedrich Kratochwil, 'Of Systems, Boundaries, and Territoriality: An Inquiry into the Formation of the State System' (1986) 39 *Wld. Pol.*, 27.

extinguished in the event that a municipal court decides not to recognise and enforce the award.[11] An empirically grounded observation of global law creation takes note of the complex interactions between state-based and unofficial sources of law. This perspective uncovers the 'governance cocktails' that emerge from a 'pragmatic combination and innovative recombination of governance mechanisms'.[12]

The relevance of arbitration to solving international commercial disputes is shown by the fact that 'international arbitration has become the principal method of resolving disputes between states, individuals, and corporations in almost every aspect of international trade, commerce and investment'.[13] In such disputes huge amounts of money are often at stake. In fact, instances in which large sums are at stake are more likely to be referred to arbitration.[14] It has been commonly used to decide commercial disputes in a much more flexible manner than court proceedings; and has been noted for its capacity to limit the damage or embarrassment of contracting parties in a manner conducive to future constructive business relations.[15] Moreover, a major survey found that corporate counsel preferred arbitration over transnational litigation because it offers a 'private and independent system, largely free from external interference',[16] a reference to the danger of settling commercial disputes when one party is a state.

Yet banks and financial institutions have traditionally shunned arbitration in favour of litigation for the following reasons:[17]

(1) financial disputes typically involve straightforward payment claims and do not involve complex legal questions or fact finding, with the latter more suited to arbitration;

[11] Friedrich Kratochwil (n 10) 67.

[12] Peter-Gralf Calliess and Peer Zumbansen (n 8) 120. See also Ralf Michaels, 'The True Lex Mercatoria: Private Law Beyond the State' (2007) 14 *Ind.J.Global Legal Studies*, 447, 452, who argues that 'the distinction between state and non-state is simply irrelevant; what matters is which laws and institutions are more efficient, regardless of their source'.

[13] Alan Redfern, Martin Hunter, Nigel Blackaby and Constantine Partasides (n 1) 1.

[14] PriceWaterhouseCoopers and Queen Mary University of London, *International Arbitration: Corporate Attitudes and Practices* (London: 2008), 3.

[15] Robert Blackett, 'The Status of Religious "Courts" in UK Law' (2009) *Decisions, Decisions: Disp. Resol. & Int'l Arb. Newsl.*, 12.

[16] PriceWaterhouseCoopers and Queen Mary University of London (n 14) 9.

[17] Audley Sheppard, 'Arbitration of International Financial Disputes', *Kluwer Arbitration Blog*, (Wolters Kluwer, 19 March 2009), kluwerarbitrationblog.com/blog/2009/03/19/arbitration-of-international-financial-disputes/. Accessed 12 April 2014.

(2) arbitration does not provide for the possibility of default judgments or summary judgments, and as a result arbitration is not as efficient and cost effective as court proceedings;
(3) disputes about the tribunal's jurisdiction may lead to unnecessary delays;
(4) arbitrators tend to render more equitable decisions than judges;
(5) the flexibility of the arbitral process creates legal uncertainty;
(6) banks appreciate control of decisions by higher courts on appeal;
(7) arbitration can permit unnecessarily extensive document production (particularly compared with civil law courts);
(8) arbitration is problematic in multi-party disputes;
(9) arbitral confidentiality means that proceedings cause less embarrassment to the debtor; and
(10) awards have limited precedential value.

Moreover, arbitration can be more expensive as the arbitrator must be paid, the venue hired and, in some cases, the fees of an arbitration centre must be borne. However, the relative merits and disadvantages of arbitration versus litigation depend upon the type of transaction, the counterparty and the location of the assets.[18] Furthermore, all courts should not be considered equal; litigation in one country might be more favourable than in another. For example, arbitration is favoured in transactions with counterparties in emerging markets.[19] Finally, all arbitral processes should not always be considered more costly or less efficient than litigation.[20] The next section examines other aspects of modern arbitration practices and considers their compatibility with the sharia.

10.1.2 The compatibility of sharia and modern arbitration

Middle Eastern cultures display a preference for a mediation-like form of dispute resolution. Their communitarian make-up instils individuals with a strong sense of respect to those persons who are senior to themselves, and a duty to protect those who they perceive as more vulnerable. People attempt to save face and take care not to inflict shame on others. A clear preference for informal methods of dispute resolution is viewed as a means of safeguarding peace and harmony within the professional or social group.[21]

[18] *Ibid.* [19] *Ibid.* [20] *Ibid.*
[21] Nabil Antaki, 'Muslims' and Arabs' Practice of ADR' (2009) 2 *NYSBA N.Y. Disp. Res. Lawyer*, 113–14.

Despite this cultural affinity, arbitration has a long and sometimes troubled history in the Arab world. Pre-Islamic Arabs were not familiar with a formal system of justice in which parties settled disputes and ensured their rights. Justice centred on the organisation of the tribe and was largely based on a system of personal vengeance. Resort to arbitration, which was optional and non-binding, offered parties or tribes a way of settling their disputes under the moral authority of an arbitrator.[22] Islam has also supported the resolution of disputes by arbitration. The Treaty of Medina in 622 CE, which established a security pact between the city's Muslims, non-Muslim Arabs and Jews, referred disputes to the Prophet Muhammad. Further, in his conflict with the tribe of Banu Qurayza the Prophet is said to have resorted to arbitration.[23] Indeed, the enduring division between the Sunni and Shiite branches of Islam resulted from the arbitration between Muʿāwiyah, the governor of Syria, and the Caliph ʿAli, the son-in-law of the Prophet in 659 CE concerning the succession and location of the caliphate. Although ʿAli was unwilling to accept the arbitrators' decision in favour of Muʿāwiyah, his acceptance of the principle of arbitration damaged his stature amongst some of his followers.[24]

In commercial affairs, however, it is widely known that early Muslim traders often resorted to arbitrators in settling disputes. The arbitrator was recognised for his prestigious social status, deep knowledge, impartiality and honesty in finding solutions to disputes, which disputants felt morally bound to honour.[25]

Both the Quran and the Sunna provide numerous proofs of the lawfulness of arbitration and indicate that it is a highly recommended,[26] even imperative,[27] practice. The resolution of disputes or settlement is,

[22] Abdul Hamid El-Ahdab, *Arbitration with the Arab Countries* 2nd edn (Alphen aan den Rijn: Kluwer Law International, 1999), 11.

[23] Charles N. Brower and Jeremy K. Sharpe, 'International Arbitration and the Islamic World: The Third Phase' (2003) 97 *A.J.I.L.*, 643.

[24] Philip K. Hitti, *History of the Arabs: From the Earliest Times to the Present* 10th edn (London: Macmillan St Martin's Press, 1970), 181–2. ʿAli's acceptance of arbitration alienated some of his followers known as the Khārijites. It was this early sect of Islam that eventually had ʿAli assassinated.

[25] See Minas Khatchadourian, *Arbitration and Mediation between Europe and the Gulf* (Sharm El-Sheikh: Sharm El-Sheikh International Arbitration Center 2010), 12.

[26] Quran, trans. by M. A. S. Abdel Haleem (Oxford University Press, 2008), 4:35, which states: 'And if you fear a breach between them [husband and wife], send an arbitrator out of his family and an arbitrator out of her family; if they shall desire a conciliation, God will cause them to agree'.

[27] Quran (n 26) 4:59, provides: 'O true believers, obey God, and obey the Apostle and those who are in authority among you; and if you differ in anything, refer it unto God and the Apostle, if you believe in God and the last day; this is best and fairer determination'.

according to the Malikīs, classified in two categories: those disputes which are absolved through the dropping of claims; and those absolved for compensation. Both types of settlement are viewed as noble means of avoiding further conflict and strife in a court of law.[28] While the framework for arbitration in Islam enjoys a firm legal foundation, some of the sharia's rules have posed problems for the process of modern arbitration. In broad terms these include the nature and scope of arbitration, the choice of law, the scope of judicial review and enforcement, and the uncertainty in the rules and regulations regarding arbitration.[29]

The schools of law debated whether the nature of Islamic arbitration is, in fact, nearer to the modern concept of conciliation, which lacks formal legal standing. Even within the schools no clear opinion was held on the matter.[30] An aspect of this debate continues to reverberate in the contemporary world in relation to the lawfulness of the arbitration clause in an investment contract. Contemporary practice provides for an arbitration clause concerning a future dispute to be settled in arbitration. According to the sharia, however, an agreement to arbitrate is equated with a contract of agency, which as a permissible contract (*jāʿiz*) may be revoked by the principal at any time. Parties may not be bound to such an arbitration clause. A further complication concerns the requirement to agree to submit a dispute to arbitration that has not yet arisen. Under sharia an arbitration clause can only be made irrevocable when confirmed by a court or after having remunerated arbitrators. Yet the non-existence of a dispute prevents an arbitration clause from being made a valid and binding arbitration agreement.[31]

Nevertheless, there is agreement amongst modern legal practitioners that an arbitration clause can be enforced as an ordinary contractual agreement in line with the Islamic commitment to contractual sanctity. Yet this seems to be an easy solution forged by 'Western concepts and Western statute law'.[32]

[28] Wahbah Al-Zuhayli, *Financial Transactions in Islamic Jurisprudence*, Vol. II (Damascus: Dar al-Fikr, 2007), 200.

[29] Faisal Kutty, 'The Shari'a Factor in International Commercial Arbitration' (2006) 28 *Loy.L.A.Int'l & Comp.L.Ann.* 565, 596. This section provides only a general overview of some of the most pressing concerns.

[30] Abdul Hamid El-Ahdab (22) 17.

[31] Samir Saleh, *Commercial Arbitration in the Arab Middle East* (London: Graham & Trotman, 1984), 49.

[32] *Ibid.*, 50.

Other problems with arbitral clauses concern the non-existent subject matter. This issue as well as the contingent aspects of the clause are generally considered to contravene the *gharar* prohibition. As was examined in Chapter 3, contingent contracts – two sales in one – are considered to obscure the parties' obligations under the principal contract, sometimes resulting in illicit practices (*ribā*).

Modern jurisprudence has largely disregarded this analysis in favour of the general principle of *pacta sunt servanda*. Invoking the jurisprudence of Ibn Taymīyyah, modern scholars argue that any contract is binding unless it is contrary to public order or deals with a subject matter forbidden by God. Noting that classical *fiqh* did not grapple with arbitration clauses, these writers agree that nothing contrary to public order or the specific prohibitions of the Lawgiver is evident in such clauses.[33]

The majority of Middle Eastern jurisdictions have adopted arbitration laws modelled on Western legal systems to avoid these problems and others, which distinguish Islamic arbitration and sometimes conflict with contemporary arbitration practice.[34] Despite widespread adoption of such laws and nearly every Middle Eastern state's commitment to the New York Convention, the Muslim world's modern experience with arbitration has been troubled. This is the focus of the next section.

10.1.3 Arbitration in the Arab world

Middle Eastern courts' sceptical, sometimes hostile view of arbitration dates back to some famous arbitrations: *Sheikh Abu Dhabi* v. *Petroleum Ltd*,[35] *Ruler of Qatar* v. *International Marine Oil Company Ltd*,[36] and the well-known 1958 *Aramco* v. *Government of Saudi Arabia*.[37] Five decades on these cases continue to colour the perspective with which modern arbitration is viewed in the Islamic world.[38] The view that arbitration is Western, biased and historically exploitative is still represented today.[39]

33 Abdul Hamid El-Ahdab (n 22) 24–6.
34 Samir Saleh (n 31) 25. Saleh notes the closed character, i.e. procedural and substantive laws must be sharia, the revocability of arbitrators and the ancillary character of arbitration under sharia.
35 [1952] 1 Int Comp LQ 247. 36 [1953] 20 Int LR 534.
37 [1958] 27 Int LR 117.
38 Charles N. Brower and Jeremy K. Sharpe (n 23) 644–5.
39 Perhaps the best example of these views is Muthucumaraswamy Sornarajah, 'The Climate of International Arbitration' (1990) 8 *Journ.Int'l. Comm.Arb.*, 47; see also Muthucumaraswamy Sornarajah, *International Commercial Arbitrations: The Problem of State Contracts* (Singapore: Longman, 1990).

In *Sheikh Abu Dhabi v. Petroleum Development (Trucial Coast) Ltd*, Lord Asquith of Bishopstone acted as an umpire for an arbitration in which two arbitrators had been unable to agree on a dispute arising out of a written contract. The dispute concerned the rights of Petroleum Development to the underwater areas owned by the Sheikh or over which he had jurisdiction or mineral oil rights.[40] A principal question to be ascertained by Lord Asquith concerned the law governing the contract. His pronouncement is worth quoting at length because it illustrates a trend in modern legal history in which the sharia has been disparaged:

> This is a contract made in Abu Dhabi and wholly to be performed in that country. If any municipal system of law were applicable, it would prima facie be that of Abu Dhabi. But no such law can reasonably be said to exist. The Sheikh administers a purely discretionary justice with the assistance of the Koran; and it would be fanciful to suggest that in this very primitive region there is any settled body of legal principles applicable to the construction of modern commercial instruments.[41]

Lord Asquith's extremely biased statement should be seen as indicative of a larger colonial trend in which peoples' cultures, customs and political organisation were viewed as primitive, immoral and in need of colonial patronage. Acknowledging that English law could not apply, Lord Asquith nonetheless decided that some of its rules are firmly 'rooted in the good sense and common practice of the generality of civilised nations' – a sort of 'modern law of nature', so that they could be used.[42] In applying the principles of English law he decided that the oil company did have the right to extract oil from the subsoil of Abu Dhabi's territorial waters and islands. The Sheikh succeeded in preventing the company from gaining access to the shelf beyond those waters.[43]

A second phase of modern international arbitration[44] is perhaps even more influential in terms of the way in which it has affected perceptions, as well as the practice, of arbitration in the Middle East. The ascendancy of neoliberalism in this phase, together with its fetish with law as the *sine qua non* of economic development, marked a turning point in favour of the Washington consensus over alternative development theories. The private

[40] [1952] 1 Int Comp LQ 247, 247.

[41] *Ibid.*, 250–1. [42] *Ibid.*, 251. [43] *Ibid.*, 260.

[44] Charles N. Brower and Jeremy K. Sharpe (n 23) 645, divide the 'Islamic world's' experience with arbitration in three phases, which is a useful organising tool for the development of modern international arbitration.

law characteristics of arbitration came to be accepted as 'the sanctioned mechanism for resolving international investment disputes'.[45]

The Libyan oil arbitrations have been seen by some scholars as indicative of a broader trend of bias against the rights of developing countries. In 1971 Libya decided to nationalise all of the interests and properties of BP Exploration Company (Libya), a subsidiary of British Petroleum. In September 1973 and again in February 1974 the government of Libya, led by Colonel Muammar el-Qaddafi, announced the nationalisation of nine other international oil companies. Of the nine Libya chose to nationalise were 100 per cent of the interests and properties of three American companies including Texaco Overseas Petroleum Company (TOPCO); California Asiatic Oil Company (CALASIATIC), a subsidiary of Texaco Inc.; and the Libyan American Oil Company (LIAMCO), a subsidiary of Atlantic Richfield Company. The companies affected by these nationalisations, including British Petroleum, became parties to three major international arbitrations.[46] The Libyan government lost all three arbitrations as it was found to have breached its obligations under the deeds of concession. Arbitrators found no legal justification for the nationalisations,[47] and, indeed, the Libyan government itself announced the measures as political reprisals against the United States and the United Kingdom.[48]

The arbitrations have been given an 'almost mythological position in the contemporary study of arbitration practices' in developing countries.[49] It is necessary to examine the historical context to understand the nature of these arbitrations and the way in which they continue to inform contemporary perceptions of arbitration. Members of the Organization of Petroleum Exporting Countries (OPEC) had sought to advance their interests vis-á-vis international oil companies, which for many years had profited from long-term concessions of petroleum-producing land in return for vastly disproportionate royalties.[50] Libya was a very poor

[45] Amr A. Shalakany (n 10) 425.

[46] These are *BP Exploration Co (Libya) Ltd* v. *The Government of the Libyan Arab Republic* [1979] 53 ILR 297; *Texaco Overseas Petroleum Co* v. *The Government of the Libyan Arab Republic* [1979] 53 ILR 389; and *Libyan American Oil Co* v. *The Government of the Libyan Arab Republic* [1981] 20 ILM 1.

[47] *Texaco Overseas Petroleum Co* v. *The Government of the Libyan Arab Republic, Preliminary Award* 53 ILR 389, 391.

[48] An English translation of the 11 June 1973 nationalisation decree can be found at 13 *International Legal Materials*, 58. See, in general, George Winthrop Haight, 'Libyan Nationalization of British Petroleum Assets' (1972) 6 *Int'l L.*, 541.

[49] Amr A. Shalakany (n 10) 425.

[50] Muthucumaraswamy Sornarajah (n 39) 52.

country at the time of its independence in 1951 but like many other Middle Eastern states had achieved unprecedented economic growth since then as a result of the discovery, extraction and exportation of oil.[51] Weighed down with long-term concessions to foreign oil companies, Middle Eastern states viewed these agreements as vestiges of colonial servitude. OPEC and many other countries sought to change the terms of international law with respect to expropriation in this context. This goal was pursued, in part, at the UN General Assembly, where resolutions concerning the concept of permanent sovereignty over natural resources were promulgated.[52] Another means of challenging the terms of international law was the use of oil as an economic weapon against Western industrialised states.[53]

For resolutions of the General Assembly to have legal validity as opposed to qualifying merely as policy declarations, they must meet the threshold of constituting customary international law. The general rule is that states consistently practise a certain rule and that these states believed they were legally obligated to do so.[54] Resolution 1803 of December 1962 is considered to meet this requirement. It reaffirmed the right of permanent sovereignty over natural resources and provided that nationalisation must be undertaken on the grounds of public utility or national interest. Nationalisation of private interests must also provide for compensation.[55]

The position of the Libyan government was to argue that resolution 3201 and 3281 had 'in effect removed any sovereign action relating to permanent sovereignty over natural resources from the standards of international law and conferred exclusive competence upon the legislative and judicial branches of the host country'.[56] Resolution 3201, the Declaration on the Establishment of a New International Economic Order, affirmed states' sovereignty over their natural resources and economic activities including their rights to control and exploit them. This included 'the right to nationalization or transfer of ownership to its nationals'.[57] Resolution 3281, the Charter of Economic Rights and Duties of States, sought to

[51] Robert B. von Mehren and P. Nicholas Kourides, (n 5) 477.

[52] Charles N. Brower and Jeremy K. Sharpe (n 23) 645.

[53] In November 1973, Arab leaders issued a joint resolution, which called for the 'use of oil as an economic weapon'. See Jordan J. Paust and Albert P. Blaustein, 'The Arab Oil Weapon: A Threat to International Peace' (1974) 68 *A.J.I.L.* 410, 411.

[54] Robert B. von Mehren and P. Nicholas Kourides (n 5) 522.

[55] United Nations, General Assembly Res 1803 (XVII) (14 December 1962).

[56] Robert B. von Mehren and P. Nicholas Kourides (n 5) 523.

[57] United Nations, General Assembly Res 3201 (S-VI) 1 May 1974, Art 4(e).

'constitute an effective instrument towards the establishment of a new system of international economic relations based on equity, sovereign equality and interdependence of the interests of developed and developing countries'.[58] It further proclaimed each state's right to 'nationalise, expropriate or transfer ownership of foreign property, in which case appropriate compensation should be paid by the State adopting such measures'.[59]

Sole arbitrator René-Jean Dupuy, Secretary General of the Hague Academy of International Law and Professor of Law at the University of Nice, determined, on the basis of the voting patterns for the resolutions, that no general consensus of their legal validity existed.[60] There is broad agreement amongst legal scholars that resolutions of the General Assembly are not considered as having a binding legal nature.

The resolutions highlight the efforts of developing countries to overturn the international legal order established for the exploitation and distribution of petroleum including the process of dispute resolution specifically developed for foreign investment.[61] Moreover, because the rules of international arbitration had their origin in the development of international law, Asian, African and Middle Eastern states have viewed international law with suspicion. Like international law, arbitration has been seen as an instrument of Western subjugation and dominance.[62]

The discussion above highlights the historical context in which competing claims of law and ideology were advanced in the period immediately following developing states' independence from the colonial powers. However, the legal impact of the UN resolutions in the Libyan arbitrations was insignificant relative to the choice of law clause and the so-called stabilisation clauses used in the deeds of concession. In disputes involving government entities foreign investors may wish to settle their dispute in a neutral forum, including both the location and the applicable law of the arbitration. Desirous of avoiding possible bias in Libyan municipal courts, the Libyan deeds of concession were to be governed by 'the principles of Libyan law in so far as they were common to principles of international law and, in the absence of such conformity, by general principles of law.'[63] This represents a situation in which the parties sought to avoid

[58] United Nations, General Assembly Res 3281 (XXIX) 12 December 1974.

[59] *Ibid.*, Art 2(c).

[60] Robert B. von Mehren and P. Nicholas Kourides (n 5) 523. Western industrial countries as well as a number of developing countries rejected the resolutions.

[61] *Ibid.*, 645.

[62] Muthucumaraswamy Sornarajah (n 39) 50.

[63] *Texaco Overseas Petroleum Co v. The Government of the Libyan Arab Republic, Preliminary Award* (n 47) 391.

Libyan law, which may be 'very costly, slow, unreliable, corrupt, weak, or simply absent' and to employ private governance mechanisms.[64] The choice of law clause, which basically made the principles of international law the proper law of the arbitration, was shored up by the inclusion of a stabilisation of rights provision, which guaranteed the concession holders their contractual rights created by the concession and which could not be altered except by the mutual consent of the parties.[65] Stabilisation clauses are used by foreign investors to insure themselves against the risk that states arbitrarily, in their sovereign capacity, are not allowed unilaterally to alter or abrogate their contractual rights. The effect of these clauses ousts the jurisdiction of the municipal courts to settle disputes arising from the concession contracts. They also buttress the international legal order by preventing states from exercising their sovereignty to disregard commitments that they have freely undertaken.[66]

The principal argument against arbitration concerns the way in which it bolsters the perceived unfairness of the regime of concession agreements. Some critics argue that the municipal law of the state should not be able to be displaced by a foreign party to a contract that has its legal basis within the host state.[67] Should developing states wish to alter the distributional outcomes associated with neoliberal development policies, this transnational feature of arbitration impedes regulatory intervention.[68] Based on this, critics contend that arbitration is unsuitable for deciding disputes in which foreign interests are able to 'obstruct the national interest and development of the state', especially in relation to a state's natural resources.[69] 'Political' investment disputes should be solved via negotiation and not in a private contractual forum.[70]

The following section examines contemporary arbitration practices by indicating some general trends in the enforcement of arbitral awards in the municipal legal systems under study. Initial focus is placed on English arbitration law and its incorporation of the New York Convention, given

64 Peter-Gralf Calliess, 'The Making of Transnational Contract Law' (2007) 14 *Ind.J.Global Legal Studies* 469, 471.

65 Robert B. von Mehren and P. Nicholas Kourides (n 5) 479.

66 *Ibid.*, 518.

67 Muthucumaraswamy Sornarajah (n 39) 52.

68 Amr A. Shalakany (n 10) 465.

69 Augustus Asante Agyemang, 'The Suitability of Arbitration for Settling "Political" Investment Disputes Involving African States' (1988) 22 *J World Trade*, 123, 124.

70 *Ibid.*, 123.

its prominence as a governing law of international commercial and financial transactions including those of Islamic finance.

10.2 The enforcement of arbitral awards

Arbitration agreements are generally recognised and enforced in England, Wales and Northern Ireland.[71] The United Kingdom is a signatory to the Convention on the Recognition and Enforcement of Foreign Arbitral Awards (the New York Convention)[72] so that arbitral judgments involving cross-border disputes are recognised and enforced in the United Kingdom. Article (2), section (1) provides that 'each contracting state shall recognize an agreement in writing under which the parties undertake to submit to arbitration all or any differences which have arisen or which may arise between them in respect of a defined legal relationship, whether contractual or not, concerning a subject matter capable of settlement by arbitration'.[73] The treaty binds signatory states to recognise awards made outside their national borders unless the government has specifically opted to recognise only certain national jurisdictions.[74] As of 31 March 2014, 149 states out of a total of 192 UN member states, had adopted the convention.[75] The convention has been incorporated in the UK Arbitration Act 1996, which provides that:[76]

(1) A New York Convention award shall be recognised as binding on the persons as between whom it was made, and may accordingly be relied on by those persons by way of defence, set-off or otherwise in any legal proceedings in England and Wales or Northern Ireland.
(2) A New York Convention award may, by leave of the court, be enforced in the same manner as a judgment or order of the court to the same effect.

The UK Arbitration Act 1996 comprises almost all English arbitration law.[77] Unlike conflict of laws principles, which stipulate that only a state

[71] These are the jurisdictions that are subject to the UK Arbitration Act 1996.
[72] New York Convention on the Recognition and Enforcement of Foreign Arbitral Awards [1958].
[73] New York Convention [1958]. [74] *Ibid.*
[75] UNCITRAL, 'Convention on the Recognition and Enforcement of Foreign Arbitral Awards' (New York, 1958) <www.uncitral.org/uncitral/en/uncitral_texts/arbitration/NYConvention_status.html> Accessed on 31 March 2014.
[76] Arbitration Act 1996, s 101.
[77] Arbitration Act 1996; see Robert Blackett (n 15) 12.

law can be used as the governing law of a contract, section 46 provides that:[78]

> The arbitral tribunal shall decide the dispute: (a) in accordance with the law chosen by the parties as applicable to the substance of the dispute; or (b) if the parties so agree, in accordance with such other considerations as are agreed by them or determined by the tribunal.

Thus parties possess the legal right to settle a dispute according to 'such other considerations as are agreed by them', which enables the sharia or other non-state law to be chosen as the law of the arbitration.

Arbitration in the area of consumer banking is limited in the European Union by the terms of the Unfair Terms in Consumer Contracts Directive.[79] The directive proscribes pre-dispute arbitration clauses in consumer contracts that have not been individually negotiated and are thus deemed unfair, i.e. those instances in which a significant imbalance between the rights and obligations of the contracting parties disadvantage the consumer.[80] Any dispute that arises in conjunction with such clauses cannot be the subject of arbitration.[81]

As financial institutions have increased transactions with developing countries the role of arbitration has become more important. Still, it is uncertain whether arbitral awards will be recognised and enforced in these jurisdictions. For example, financial institutions often include arbitration clauses in international loan transactions with counterparties based in the Middle East and Asia, South America, Russia and the CIS. In London this is done by referring disputes to English courts with an option, exercisable by the bank in the event a dispute arises, to initiate arbitral proceedings instead of litigation. This approach was sanctioned in *Law Debenture Trust Corp plc* v. *Elektrim Finance BV*.[82] The following section examines the way in which English courts treat arbitration awards that are the subject of challenge by the losing party. An examination of

[78] Arbitration Act 1996, s 46(1)(a) and (b).

[79] Council Directive 93/13/EEC of 5 April 1993 on unfair terms in consumer contracts [1993] OJ L95/29, Art 3(3). See UK statutory instrument: The Unfair Terms in Consumer Contracts Regulations 1999, SI 1999/2083, para 4(2)(a).

[80] EC (European Council) 'Summary: Unfair Terms in Consumer Contracts' (1993), europa.eu/legislation_summaries/consumers/protection_of_consumers/l32017_en.htm. Accessed 23 March 2014.

[81] Ilias Bantekas, 'Arbitrability in Finance and Banking' in Loukas A. Mistelis and Stavros L. Brekoulakis (eds.), *Arbitrability: International & Comparative Perspectives* (The Netherlands: Wolters Kluwer, 2009), 312.

[82] [2005] EWHC 1412(Ch). See Audley Sheppard (n 17).

the ways in which the municipal courts of GCC states deal with arbitral awards follows thereafter.

10.3 The enforcement of arbitral awards in English courts

Sanghi Polyesters Ltd v. *The International Investor KCSC*[83] offers an example of how arbitral awards involving Islamic financial transactions will be enforced in English courts. The case demonstrates that the right to appeal arbitral awards will be very limited under English law. The case concerned a financing agreement based on an *istiṣnāʿ* contract (purchase or hire agreement) in which The International Investor KCSC (TII) furnished Sanghi Polyesters Ltd (SPL) with US$5 million to produce and export polyester yarn. SPL failed to pay sums due under the contract and subsequently failed to perform under various extension agreements created to assist SPL. Thereafter, TII began arbitration proceedings according to the agreement's arbitration clause, which provided: 'This dispute shall be governed by the Laws of England except to the extent it may conflict with Islamic sharia, which shall prevail'.[84] The arbitrator awarded TII the principal and profit it had claimed but disallowed some additional damages of approximately US$600,000.[85]

The arbitration was held under the auspices of the ICC based in London. The parties had chosen the Arbitration Act 1996 as the law of the forum, which permits parties 'to appeal against a question of law arising out of the Award in certain circumstances but only if the parties have not 'otherwise agreed''.[86] The court found that the parties, in deciding to submit their dispute to arbitration, had waived their right to appeal in accordance with Article 24 of the ICC (the *lex arbitri*). They had clearly 'otherwise agreed' and Mackie J dismissed this argument.

According to section 69, the following issues would enable a party to appeal an arbitral award:

a) that the determination of the question will substantially affect the rights of one or more of the parties;
b) that the question is one which the tribunal was asked to determine;
c) that on the basis of the findings of fact in the award (i) the decision of the tribunal on the question is obviously wrong, or (ii) the question is

[83] [2000] All ER (D) 93. [84] *Ibid*., transcript.
[85] *Ibid*. The sharia only allows damages on the basis of actual loss. Expectation damages do not apply, because only God knows what the future holds.
[86] Arbitration Act 1996, s 69.

one of general public importance and the decision of the tribunal is at least open to serious doubt;

d) that, despite the agreement of the parties to resolve the matter by arbitration, it is just and proper in all the circumstances for the court to determine the question.[87]

The court summarily dismissed SPL's applications which sought to make effect of section 69(3) on the basis of procedural errors committed by the arbitrator and thus confirmed the high threshold necessary for gaining leave to appeal.

Another case, *Halpern* v. *Halpern*,[88] provides insight into the complex conflict of law considerations judges must make in resolving arbitral disputes that parties seek to enforce under English law. While the case addresses a number of contractual issues, including duress, just one subject of the appeal will be examined below; namely, whether Jewish law can be the applicable law of a contract. In this light *Halpern* is important in terms of the way in which the court interpreted section 46(1)(b) of the Arbitration Act 1996. As noted above, section 46(1)(b) allows the arbitral tribunal to decide the dispute, if the parties so agree, in accordance with 'such other considerations' as are agreed by them. Since the court ruled that the seat of arbitration was in England, it decided that 'such other considerations' would permit the tribunal to apply the parties' choice of Jewish law or other non-national law to govern a certain part of the contract[89] 'under which matters of interpretation can be assisted by rules or a law different from the applicable law of the contract'.[90] Because the dispute involved an arbitration, which applied Jewish law, the application of Jewish law was material to the contract.

The claimants in this appeal sought the enforcement of an arbitral award, which had taken place before a Zurich-based Beth Din composed of three Rabbis. The arbitration had sought to resolve issues concerned with the status of an inheritance dispute. All the parties were devout orthodox Jews and had agreed to submit their inheritance disputes to arbitration. The compromise took the form of a written agreement, which did not expressly state which law was to govern the contract.[91] The defence challenged the validity of the award on the basis that under Jewish law it would be unlawful. The defence 'pleaded that Jewish law (*halakha*) was

[87] *Ibid.*, s 69(3). [88] [2007] EWCA Civ 291.

[89] Alan Redfern, Martin Hunter, Nigel Blackaby and Constantine Partasides (n 1) 227.

[90] *Halpern* (n 88) [35].

[91] Juliette Levy, 'Under Duress' (2006) 156 *N.L.J.*, 936.

intended to be the *lex causa* as well as the *lex curia*, and would regulate procedure,' the result of which would render the compromise agreement void.[92]

In the event that a law has not been chosen to govern the agreement, section 46(3) of the Arbitration Act 1996 provides that the court must have reference to the conflict of laws rules which it considers applicable.[93] Furthermore, Article 4 of the Rome Convention provides that:

> To the extent that the law applicable to the contract has not been chosen in accordance with Article 3, the contract shall be governed by the law of the country with which it is most closely connected. Nevertheless, a severable part of the contract which has a closer connection with another country may by way of exception be governed by the law of that other country.[94]

The circumstances of the case involved English law, Swiss Law and Jewish law – the laws of countries as well as a non-state law. The absence of the parties' choice or consent as to the substantive law of the compromise agreement made the consideration of Jewish law as the applicable law of the agreement redundant. *Beximco* established that Article 1(1) of the Rome Convention 'makes it clear that the reference to the parties' choice of "the law" to govern a contract is a reference to the law of a country. It does not sanction the choice or application of a non-national system of law'.[95] The court affirmed the supremacy of states' municipal legal systems in citing the well-known case of *Amin Rasheed Shipping Corp* v. *Kuwait Insurance Co.*[96] In that judgment Lord Diplock said that:

> contracts are incapable of existing in a legal vacuum. They are mere pieces of paper devoid of all legal effect unless they were made by reference to some system of private law which defines the obligations assumed by the parties to the contract by their use of particular forms of words and prescribes the remedies enforceable in a court of justice for failure to perform any of those obligations.[97]

In applying the Rome Convention, the court concluded that the contract had been reached under the auspices of a Beth Din in Switzerland; and the parties resided in England and brought their claim to an English court. Further, the parties to the compromise did not propose the application of Swiss law to the agreement. Therefore, the court found that

[92] *Halpern* (n 88) [14] subpara vii.

[93] Arbitration Act 1996, s 46(3).

[94] *Halpern* (n 88) [27]. [95] *Ibid.*, [21]. [96] [1984] AC 50.

[97] *Ibid.*, 66.

England and hence English law represented the 'closest connection' to the circumstances of the case.[98]

In effect, the Court of Appeal resolved the matter by recognising that the dispute was initially an arbitral dispute and therefore required the court to apply the Arbitration Act 1996. In particular, the court's reference to section 46(1)(b) of the Arbitration Act convinced the court that 'such other considerations' could make the provision of Jewish law material. The finding reaffirms the judgment in *Musawi* v. *Re International Ltd*[99] that paragraph 46(1)(b) entitled the parties to an arbitration to employ Shia sharia law as the substantive law of the dispute.[100] The court in *Halpern* said that the 'solution under which matters of interpretation can be assisted by rules or a law different from the applicable law of the contract, but matters affecting the contract as a whole must be dealt with by the applicable law is ... consistent with the Convention'.[101] Apparently, the court sees its approach to this matter as one of determining the extent to which the applicable law would enable the provision of Jewish law to influence a part of the contract.[102]

The ways in which English municipal courts, on the basis of modern arbitration legislation, will treat arbitral awards provides a useful demonstration of the state-based and non-state-based aspects of this dispute resolution mechanism. The following section examines some general trends concerning the municipal courts of GCC states' approach to recognising and enforcing arbitral awards.

10.4 The enforcement of arbitral awards in GCC states

Arbitration, although still viewed with suspicion in the Islamic world, is now treated more favourably than just two or three decades ago. This is evidenced by the fact that all GCC states are now party to the New York Convention and, in fact, only Iraq and Libya remain outside the convention in the wider Middle Eastern region.[103] Other indications of this changed perspective include the large number of states that have sought to modernise their arbitration laws and even to develop new regional arbitration centres.[104] This attitudinal shift may be due to the increased importance of arbitration as a global adjudication system. Middle Eastern

[98] *Halpern* (n 88) [29]. [99] [2007] All ER (D) 222 (Dec).
[100] *Ibid.*, [46](1)(b). [101] *Halpern* (n 88) [35]. [102] *Ibid.*, [36].
[103] UNCITRAL, 'Convention on the Recognition and Enforcement of Foreign Arbitral Awards' (New York, 1958).
[104] Faisal Kutty (n 29) 593.

states, whose oil wealth has transformed them into capital exporters, increasingly see the utility in a system of international arbitration that acts as a substitute for municipal court litigation of international investment and commercial disputes.[105]

Cross-border Islamic financial transactions stand to benefit from the global arbitration system. Further, key industries in the Middle East such as shipping, energy, oil and gas, and insurance have shown themselves most likely to take advantage of international arbitration.[106]

Despite this, there is still uncertainty as to whether the municipal courts of many Middle Eastern jurisdictions will enforce arbitral awards. Theoretically, signatories to the New York Convention should enforce arbitral awards without re-examination of the award.[107] In practice, enforcement has proved to be uncertain. Article V2 of the Convention establishes an important legal basis for the intervention of municipal courts in the arbitral process. It provides that the recognition and enforcement of the award can be refused on the basis that the subject matter of the dispute is not subject to arbitration in the country in which enforcement is sought or that contravenes a country's public policy.[108] The latter part of this provision concerning public policy is of particular concern to legal practitioners. As was examined earlier, public policy in most Middle Eastern jurisdictions is the sharia and as such is open to a broad spectrum of legal interpretation. This legal diversity, as well as the tendency of the municipal courts of the region to invoke sharia in an ad hoc, arbitrary manner, engenders legal uncertainty. This affects nearly every aspect of arbitration in many Middle Eastern jurisdictions including 'the applicable law, the validity of the arbitration agreement, procedural rules, the arbitrability of the dispute and the choice and capacity of arbitrators'.[109]

The most important article of the Convention for parties in the process of selecting a site for their arbitration is Article V1(e). The article allows a court to refuse to recognise and enforce an arbitral award when it 'has

[105] Charles N. Brower and Jeremy K. Sharpe (n 23) 646–7.

[106] PriceWaterhouseCoopers and Queen Mary University of London (n 14) 9.

[107] Linklaters, 'Recent Developments in Enforcement of Arbitral Awards in the United Arab Emirates', 12 May 2011, www.linklaters.com/Publications/GCC/May/Pages/Recent_Developments_Enforcement_Arbitral_Awards_United_Arab_Emirates.aspx. Accessed 9 April 2014.

[108] United Nations, Convention on the Recognition and Enforcement of Foreign Arbitral Awards (United Nations Conference on International Commercial Arbitration 1958), Art V2.

[109] Steven Finizio and Christopher Howitt, 'When International Arbitration Meets Sharia' (March–April 2013) *CDRJ*, 49.

been set aside or suspended by a competent authority of the country in which, or under the law of which, that award was made'.[110] The recognition of judicial set-aside as a valid reason for a court to refuse to recognise an arbitral award confers the power to set aside or suspend an arbitral award on the courts of the country in which the arbitration took place or the courts of the country whose law the parties chose to govern the arbitration. The Convention does not provide guidance on when the power to suspend or set-aside an arbitral award can be exercised, which incentivises the choice of arbitration in jurisdictions with well-established judicial traditions for exercising restraint in relation to their power to set aside arbitral awards.[111] Many transnational corporations have avoided sitting arbitrations in the Middle East for fear that arbitral awards may be set aside or that the municipal courts of the region are unwilling to recognise and enforce arbitration awards.[112]

Bahrain may be the first jurisdiction in the region to change this perception. One of the first Gulf countries to accede to the New York Convention, Bahrain's infrastructure for international arbitration has become much more favourable to foreign investors in the past three decades.[113] Bahrain houses the GCC Commercial Arbitration Centre, the region's leading commercial arbitration body, and, in 1993, established the Bahrain International Commercial Arbitration Centre. However, Bahrain's infrastructural advantage is mostly attributable to recently enacted legislation, which circumvents its municipal courts. The legislation, Legislative Decree No. 30, allows parties to an international arbitration agreement to agree to hold their arbitration in Bahrain without concern that Bahraini municipal courts will interfere or set aside the arbitral award. The only conditions are that a law other than Bahraini law is chosen to govern the dispute; the parties agree not to challenge an award before the Bahraini courts; and any challenge will only be brought before the municipal courts of the country under whose law the parties have chosen to govern

110 United Nations (n 108) Art V1(e).

111 John M. Townsend, 'The New Bahrain Arbitration Law and the Bahrain "Free Arbitration Zone"' (2010) 65 *Disp.Resol.J.* 74, 77.

112 *Ibid.*, 78.

113 Law No. 12 of 1971, Bahrain Civil and Commercial Procedure, formerly governed all commercial arbitration. Under it Bahraini law was the applicable law of the arbitration when it was held in Bahrain unless the parties agreed otherwise. However, unless the parties unanimously agreed otherwise and, apparently, after the dispute had arisen, the choice of a foreign law was proscribed. See Samir Saleh (n 31) 282.

their dispute.[114] In accordance with Bahrain's obligations under the New York Convention, the legislation permits Bahraini municipal courts to retain jurisdiction in the matter of award enforcement when parties seek to enforce an award in Bahrain.[115]

Legislative Decree No. 30 foresaw the establishment of the Bahrain Chamber for Dispute Resolution (BCDR-AAA), which is a joint venture between the Bahrain Ministry of Justice and the American Arbitration Association (AAA). The law confers jurisdiction upon the BCDR-AAA in two ways: the first is 'jurisdiction by party agreement' (which was discussed above) and the second is known as 'jurisdiction under the law'. Disputes referred to the BCDR-AAA are governed by arbitration rules developed by the BCDR and the AAA. Such rules are virtually identical to the International Arbitration Rules of the AAA/International Centre for Dispute Resolution (ICDR),[116] reflecting significant cross-pollination of international legal rules and expertise.

Jurisdiction under the law may portend an important and constructive development in alternative dispute resolution, particularly in countries in which legal and regulatory systems are not viewed as legally certain or commercially sophisticated. This jurisdiction is open to disputes brought by or against financial institutions licensed by the Central Bank; or in relation to international commercial disputes as defined by the law. The amount in controversy must exceed 500,000 Bahraini dinars (approximately US$1,327 million) for both types of dispute.[117] In its role as administrator of the jurisdiction, the decree provides that BCDR-AAA appoint a panel of three arbitrators to hear a dispute. Two of the three must be judges of the Bahraini courts who receive special training from the BCDR and the AAA.[118] The third arbitrator is appointed according to the rules of the BCDR-AAA, which allows the appointment of international commercial judges, professors, legal practitioners or other professions. The resulting hybrid dispute resolution mechanism offers parties a fusion between arbitration and commercial litigation in which the many advantages of

[114] Bahrain Legislative Decree No. (30) for the Year 2009 with respect to the Bahrain Chamber for Economic, Financial and Investment Dispute Resolution, Art 25.

[115] *Ibid.*, Art 24. The Convention's list of grounds on which recognition and enforcement of an award may be refused are included in this article of the legislation.

[116] John Sykes, 'Bahrain Significantly Heightens its Attraction as a Commercial Dispute Resolution Centre in the Gulf', *Charles Russell*, February 2010, www.charlesrussell.co.uk/UserFiles/file/pdf/International%20Arbitration/bahrain_commercial_dispute_resolution_centre.pdf. Accessed 4 April 2014.

[117] Legislative Decree No. (30) (n 114) Art 9(1).

[118] *Ibid.*, Art 1.

arbitration are available.[119] These advantages render arbitral awards a degree of finality wholly foreign to the judgments given by first instance courts across the globe. This is evidenced by the fact that the court of cassation, Bahrain's high court, is the final instance to which challenges to such awards may be submitted.[120]

Bahrain's modern and commercially specialised arbitration legislation contrasts with the UAE's somewhat outdated arbitration legislation.[121] The UAE, as examined in Chapter 8, is governed by an opaque, hybrid and conflicting civil law regime. Perhaps as a result, arbitration has become more prevalent in the UAE in the past decade. While courts no longer interfere in the arbitral process to the extent they did in the past, considerable risk remains that they will do so. Awards may be challenged in UAE courts on the basis of defects in relation to the arbitration agreement and the tribunal's jurisdiction; defects in relation to the tribunal; procedural defects; and where the award is contrary to public policy.[122] Despite the UAE's accession to the New York Convention, UAE courts are known for taking a broad and formalistic approach to ensuring compliance with Article 216 of the civil procedure code[123] as a pretext for undertaking a quasi review of the merits of a foreign award. A well-known example is *International Bechtel Co Ltd* v. *Department of Civil Aviation of the Government of Dubai*, in which the Dubai Court of Cassation set aside an award in favour of the plaintiff on the ground that the arbitrator had neglected to administer the oath to witnesses according to the UAE civil procedures code.[124] This general approach to arbitration was indicative of UAE courts' historical distrust of arbitration or their reluctance to cede jurisdiction to foreign arbitrators. It was compounded by a lack of specific procedures in the Civil Procedures Code for the enforcement of foreign awards, which led UAE courts to utilise the ratification process

119 These include: the choice of law; the choice of the language of the dispute; a panel of arbitrators specialised in international commercial disputes; limited grounds of challenge; and the exclusion of appeals on judicial merits.

120 John Sykes (n 116) 4–5.

121 The UAE Civil Procedure Code, Federal Law No. (11) of 1992, ch. 3.

122 *Ibid.*, ch. 3, Art 216.

123 Reza Mohtashami, Antonia Birt and Lee Rovinescu, *Arbitration Guide: United Arab Emirates* (International Bar Association February 2013), 14, 17.

124 *International Bechtel Co Ltd* v. *Department of Civil Aviation of the Government of Dubai*, petition no 503/2003, judgment dated 15 May 2005. The annulled award was subsequently enforced in France. For an English translation of the judgment of the Paris Court of Appeal, see (2006) XXXI *Yearbook Commercial Arbitration*, 629.

for domestic awards instead.[125] In an effort to comply with the New York Convention to which the UAE acceded in 2006, and to make itself attractive to foreign investment, the UAE is said to be in the process of drafting a new federal arbitration law.

In recent years, several foreign arbitral awards have been enforced in accordance with the New York Convention, which has led to greater confidence in the business community.[126] This optimism is qualified by the fact that legal systems in the Middle East do not base decisions on precedent and the possibility exists that another court may reach a different decision in any subsequent action, thus compounding the uncertainty of enforceability.[127]

The common law legal framework and custom-built financial services regulation of the DIFC make the free zone a much more attractive location for arbitration than the wider UAE. The DIFC, in contrast to the UAE's troubled historical relationship to arbitration, is specifically designed to attract foreign investment to the free zone with few strings attached. As a legal manifestation of the modern global economy with no historical roots, its architects are under no compulsion to consider the types of issue that a nation state must countenance when deciding to develop its legal systems. Quite simply, a free zone is established to attract foreign investment and generate economic activity. In principle, it is only accountable to its architects and international norms.

In 2008 the DIFC enacted an arbitration law,[128] based on the UNCITRAL model law on international commercial arbitration,[129] which is designed to make the DIFC the leading arbitration centre in the Middle East. The 2008 law replaces the 2004 arbitration law, which was limited to disputes arising within or in connection with the DIFC, and 'where at least one party was entitled to bring an action before the DIFC courts'.[130] Unlike the 2004 law, the 2008 law has been written to cater to all parties notwithstanding any particular connection to the DIFC. In keeping with Article

[125] Gordon Blanke and Soraya Corm-Bakhos, 'Enforcement of Foreign Awards in the UAE', *The In-House Lawyer*, 2011, www.inhouselawyer.co.uk/index.php/united-arab-emirates/9657-enforcement-of-foreign-awards-in-the-uae. Accessed 31 March 2014.

[126] Linklaters (n 107).

[127] Fitch Ratings, 'Fitch's Approach to Rating Sukuk' (Fitch Ratings, 2007), 3.

[128] DIFC Arbitration Law No. 1 of 2008.

[129] The UNCITRAL Model Law represents an international standard for modern arbitration statutes. United Nations, UNCITRAL Model Law on International Commercial Arbitration 1985 with Amendments as Adopted in 2006.

[130] Reza Mohtashami and Sami Tannous, 'Arbitration at the Dubai International Financial Centre: a Common Law Jurisdiction in the Middle East' (2009) 25 *Arb Intl*. 173, 177.

5 of the model law, the 2008 arbitration law curtails the role of court intervention in the arbitration process so that only matters of law are grounds for intervention.[131]

A potential source of uncertainty in the arbitration law concerns its provision for DIFC courts to refuse recognition and enforcement of arbitral awards on the ground that enforcement of the award would be contrary to UAE public policy.[132] Although UAE public policy includes or is commensurate with the sharia (depending on the judge), it is difficult to determine the way in which common-law-trained judges of DIFC courts will interpret the provision.[133] It also raises an important question about the independence of the DIFC from the federal jurisdiction of the UAE.

The question of DIFC independence has been confirmed with an amended version of the judicial authority law, which provides that 'judgments, decisions and orders rendered by the courts and the arbitral awards ratified by the courts shall be executed by the competent entity having jurisdiction outside DIFC in accordance with the procedure and rules adopted by such entities in this regard'.[134] Dubai courts, according to the law, 'may not reconsider the merits of the judgment, decision or order' subject only to procedural conditions.[135] Prior to the amendment, Dubai courts were empowered to determine whether 'the judgment, award or order is final and is "appropriate for enforcement"'.[136] The amended version of the law no longer permits Dubai courts to determine the 'appropriateness' of the judgment, decision or order and thus allows awards to be enforced without being subjected to UAE law regarding the recognition and enforcement of arbitral awards. In principle, an award, which is enforceable in Dubai, should be enforceable throughout the UAE. However, due to the absence of similar legal arrangements with respect to other emirates in the UAE, it is uncertain whether DIFC awards will be directly enforced.[137]

131 *Ibid.*, 178–9. 132 DIFC Arbitration Law (n 128) Art 44(b)(vii).

133 Reza Mohtashami and Sami Tannous (n 130) 182.

134 DIFC Law No. 12 of 2004 in respect of the Judicial Authority at Dubai International Financial Centre as amended, Art 7(2).

135 *Ibid.*, Art 7(3)(c).

136 Article 7(2)(a) was amended on 31 October 2011.

137 Reema Ashraf, Jonathan Brown and Valeria Lysenko, 'Enforcement of Foreign Arbitral Awards Against UAE Counterparties: DIFC-LCIA Awards Versus New York Convention Awards', Hadef & Partners, 12 March 2012, www.hadefpartners.com/News/pageid/120-137/default.aspx?Mediaid=215. Accessed 8 April 2014. The case law is undeveloped. Public records indicate that one DIFC arbitral award was enforced by a UAE court in 2011.

Article 41 of the arbitration law, which allows a losing party to challenge an arbitral award on the grounds that the award conflicts with UAE public policy, is the Achilles heel of DIFC arbitration legislation. Even awards which are to be enforced within the DIFC or in a third country outside the UAE, are subject to the provision. It would seem that even a financial free zone cannot escape the multifaceted histories of sovereign nation states.

In Saudi Arabia, which comprises the largest volume of Islamic banking assets in the GCC, the enforcement of arbitral awards involving financial transactions is highly uncertain due to the sharia, in general, and its prohibitions of *ribā* and *gharar*, in particular. None of the sharia courts in Saudi Arabia would even entertain a dispute involving a prohibited financial activity, let alone approve an arbitral award that involved the payment of interest.[138] Furthermore, any arbitral award governed by a law other than the sharia or Saudi law would be reviewed for its sharia compatibility. While there have been cases in which the Diwān al Mazalim[139] has upheld foreign arbitral awards,[140] parties must countenance considerable legal uncertainty. Where both parties are Saudi nationals, Saudi courts will always apply Saudi law as both the substantive law and *lex arbitri*.[141] Awards found to contradict with the sharia are subject to an exclusion of the prohibited activity from the award or re-submitting the dispute to a different authority.[142]

10.5 Concluding remarks

The non-national legal elements of arbitration make it amenable to the stateless aspects of the sharia. Arbitral awards can also be enforced in states' municipal courts. Arbitration, however, is not without its challenges. It has a troubled history in the Middle East mostly due to the fact that the Arab world's experience with arbitration has been perceived as a vestige of colonial oppression and exploitation. Moreover, modern arbi-

[138] Abdulrahman Yahya Baamir, *Shari'a Law in Commercial and Banking Arbitration: Law and Practice in Saudi Arabia* (Farnham: Ashgate 2010), 154–8.

[139] Also known as the Board of Grievances, the Diwān al-Mazalim is an important administrative and judicial authority, which is responsible for the supervision of arbitral proceedings.

[140] See Diwān al-Mazalim, Decision No. 43/T/4 of 1416 H (1996).

[141] Abdulrahman Yahya Baamir and Ilias Bantekas, 'Saudi Law as Lex Arbitri: Evaluation of Saudi Arbitration Law and Judicial Practice' (2009) *25 Arb Intl* 239, 255.

[142] *Ibid.*, 262.

tration practices introduce dispute resolution practices that challenge classical notions of the sharia.

A manifestation of the global economy, the increasing influence of arbitration as a dispute resolution mechanism is indicative of the ideological, legal and economic spectrum within which nearly every state operates. Perhaps recognising the constraints and driving forces of the global economy the municipal courts of some Gulf states have decided to finally play along and have begun enforcing international arbitral awards. GCC states have modernised or are in the process of modernising arbitration legislation. The Islamic finance industry, which is a product of this economic landscape, gains an important and accommodative means of enforcing transactions from this change of heart.

More broadly, arbitration represents a global legal practice that threatens to unbundle states' sovereignty. Its non-national attributes contribute to legal diversity but the nation state jealously guards its sovereign prerogatives. This push-and-pull between the state and private legal actors is indicative of a larger struggle for diversity and local authority in a world beset by increasing homogenising trends.

11

Conclusion

The traditional, textualist approach to deriving sharia is grounded in a philosophy of law in which human reason was not to pollute or tamper with God's law, whether in revelation or via the Prophet's sayings, deeds and omissions. And yet the *'ulemā'* understood that human reason necessarily had to play a central role, since the sources of law required interpretation and human understanding (*fiqh*) for their legal aspects to be revealed and applied. This methodological conundrum was solved by underscoring contingency in legal interpretation: although a *mujtahid* is highly valued and respected for his knowledge, Islamic learning and erudition, his interpretation represented only one of many probable interpretations of God's law. The balance between the immutable and the exercise of human reason represents an essential compromise in the sharia as it permits legal dynamism.

Theorisers of contemporary IFL place emphasis on developing legal structures that are meant to embody 'authentic' value postulates of the sharia. Their approach is to situate IFL's development within the dominant textualist methodology of the classical age (*usūl al-fiqh*) and the ancient discourse of renowned scholars. The underlying premise is that classical contracts can be modified to give effect to classical values or at a minimum not to transgress 'timeless' rules and religious prohibitions. The implicit claim made by the industry is that IFL, by virtue of its association with the sharia, produces fairer, more equitable, intrinsically 'better' products (from an Islamic perspective) than those of conventional markets.

Notions of what constitutes Islamic commercial law centre on 'universal', 'timeless' concepts such as those of equality, fairness, justice and equity. These concepts are deeply interwoven in human history; they predate Islam or any other monotheistic religion by thousands of years as they resonate with individual quests for moral definition and certainty. In modern scholarly circles, particularly those of Islamic finance, they are synonymous with 'authentic' sharia qualities. These qualities are considered to represent the true objectives or principles of the sharia (particularly in a commercial sense) and as such should be given continuing relevance in the law. And yet 'authentic', 'original' or 'pure' notions of the sharia or some other concept or value postulate cannot be mined from the past to be rehabilitated in the present. Such concepts will always be laden with the idiosyncratic baggage of the presently situated interpreter for the reason that human beings' interpretation of activities or statements is contingent upon a 'field of historically bound conventions and practices mediated by ordinary language'.[1] As interpreters we are 'always implicated within, and must always draw upon, the universe of linguistically structured activities'[2] within which our subjectivity has been formed. Language places limits upon the interpreter, so that our understanding of the different aspects of life (work, family, socialising, etc.) shapes our perceptions, judgments and opinions of the subject matter and the ways in which it can be organised, categorised and made intelligible for an audience.[3] This condition of inter-subjectivity or ingrained bias is simply impossible to overcome; it is a condition of life.

Modern scholars of IFL have not carefully examined this condition. 'Authentic' legal solutions continue to be sought in ancient legal treatises while the role of context in determining the trajectory of the law is neglected. This legalistic focus wilfully ignores the fundamental dynamism inherent in all legal systems; the ways in which context continually informs the substance and letter of the law. Its proponents hold fast to a false sense of certainty in the dynamic global system. Divorced from the contextual environment, scholars' understandings of the sharia will not contribute to the development of distinctively different, ethical financial services.

A contextual perspective of legal systems focuses attention on a field of action or frame in which a particular event or focus is embedded and which provides resources for its interpretation.[4] Context, too, is subject to interpretation. For instance, there is no single definition of the concept, merely a range of ways of using it as an analytical focus to solve different problems. However, the concept arguably represents a more accurate approximation of the relations between causal conditions and their

[1] John Keane, 'More Theses on the Philosophy of History' in James Tully (ed.) *Meaning and Context: Quentin Skinner and His Critics* (Cambridge: Polity Press, 1988) 210.

[2] *Ibid.* [3] *Ibid.*

[4] Alessandro Duranti and Charles Goodwin, 'Rethinking Context: An Introduction' in Alessandro Duranti and Charles Goodwin (eds.) *Rethinking Context: Language as an Interactive Phenomenon* (Cambridge University Press, 1992) 3.

effects. For the performance of any action a set of conditions can be ascertained 'such that the action … might have been different or might not have occurred in their absence, or even such that the occurrence of the action might have been predicted from their presence'.[5] An examination of the causal conditions underlying the transformation of Islamic law in modern financial markets exposes a complex network of scholars, practitioners, states, regulatory authorities, IINGOs and market forces, which together have transformed the structure and meaning of the sharia in the modern world.

The findings of this book indicate that numerous actors (and market forces) contribute to the articulation of IFL in heterogeneous, complex ways. The actors and processes involved in creating IFL differ from traditional notions of the ways in which sharia is to be derived and applied. Yet it is the relationship between actors and social systems, the ways in which they mutually inform one another to generate a larger whole that is the most salient feature in the transformation of the law. The complex interaction between actors (field of action) and subject (sharia principles) indicates that context is never static. Rather it is self-generating. As actors take part in reproducing sharia principles, environment, history and imagination are woven into new contexts in which new material and social understandings are produced ad infinitum.[6]

The context of economic globalisation accelerates this already complex process of legal, economic and social production. In liberalised, deregulated markets the role of global capital in relation to human social systems has assumed awesome proportions. States attempt to nationalise it, INGOs attempt to deal with its de-territorialising, supranational characteristics, and a global adjudication system has been specially erected to safeguard and buttress its flow. From a legal perspective, the numerous sites in which legal processes interact in the production of IFL, more generally, in the production of global commercial law, indicate complex fields of action driven by power dynamics, neoliberal paradigms and the institutional momentum of the global economy.

The North Atlantic states are the primary drivers behind the globalisation of the economy. Aside from the economic statistics of globalisation such as those of FDI flows, this general predominance is apparent in other,

[5] Quentin Skinner, 'Meaning and Understanding in the History of Ideas' in James Tully (ed.) *Meaning and Context: Quentin Skinner and His Critics* (Cambridge: Polity Press, 1988) 59.

[6] Arjun Appadurai, *Modernity at Large: Cultural Dimensions of Globalization* (Minneapolis University Press, 2005) 185.

often less considered ways. Some telling examples include: the worldwide preponderance of English law in commercial and financial transactions; the presence of English and American law firms across the globe;[7] and the production and global dissemination of Western regulatory standards and best practices. While the North Atlantic region is no longer overwhelmingly dominant but rather predominates in the processes of economic globalisation[8] (as China, India and others begin to catch up), its centuries-old ascendance has established the structures and social epistemes of the global economy.[9]

Although inestimable differences exist between municipal legal systems and the economic processes of national economies (as was illustrated in the municipal legal systems examined in this book), the mental equipment, the collective ways of imagining, articulating and reproducing the global economy are squarely embedded within a neoliberal economic episteme. Perhaps one of the most interesting observations in this regard concerns these jurisdictions' development of financial centres – two of the three are financial free zones (DIFC and Bahrain) – and the implications for the development of Islamic finance. Although London is an old and highly developed financial centre (with deep and liquid markets, abundant professional skills and expertise), GCC states have embarked on developing gateway financial centres as a way of attracting global capital and diversifying their oil-dependent economies. These regional hubs in-the-making underscore the power and dominance of finance in the global economy. They reflect a global shift and prioritisation toward the superprofit-making of finance over the lesser returns of manufacturing.[10] Islamic finance is the product of this landscape; it flourishes in the reciprocity of global capital flows, the emergence of gateway financial centres and states' facilitation and regulation of global Islamic capital. Yet its theoretical design is meant to do the opposite of these financialisation trends – namely finance the tangible, real economy.

[7] Steven Mark, 'Harmonization or Homogenization? The Globalization of Law and Legal Ethics – An Australian Viewpoint' (2001) 34 *Vand. J. Transnat'l L.* 1173, 1183.

[8] Domination, according to Foucault, is 'a general structure of power whose ramifications and consequences can sometimes be found descending to the most recalcitrant fibres of society'. See Michel Foucault, 'The Subject and Power' (1982) 8 *Crit. Inq.* 777, 795.

[9] I take the notion of social episteme from John Gerard Ruggie, 'Territoriality and Beyond: Problematizing Modernity in International Relations' (1993) 47 *IO* 139, 157.

[10] Paul Krugman, 'Profits Without Production', *International Herald Tribune*, 20 June 2013, www.nytimes.com/2013/06/21/opinion/krugman-profits-without-production.html?_r=0. Accessed 24 April 2014.

Every municipal legal system studied in this book approaches the facilitation and regulation of Islamic finance in different ways. Some jurisdictions (e.g. Bahrain) have developed industry-specific frameworks for the industry, while others (e.g. United Kingdom, DIFC, UAE) approach it in a more or less assimilative fashion. The greatest differences between jurisdictions concern their approach to the governance of SSBs and the classification of Islamic financial services. These differences originate, in large part, due to the role, if any, given to the sharia in their legal systems. Other regulatory processes including authorisation and CARs are remarkably similar, since these requirements are either fundamental (authorisation) or increasingly global (CARs, liquidity requirements). The linkage between all jurisdictions is their determination to forge facilitative legal structures and to erect sufficient and competitive regulatory apparatuses within a neoliberal policy paradigm. The ideological paradigm of neoliberalism delimits macro-policy choices to the pursuit of competitiveness: financial market reforms (modernisation), labour market deregulation, dismantling or redirecting national welfare systems and the privatisation of public infrastructure. The macro-similarities between jurisdictions are unmistakeable: the financial services produced by these legal exertions are substantively similar to those of conventional financial services.

At first glance economic globalisation seems to be self-contradicting in that it generates global trends toward cultural, legal and economic harmonisation, while providing opportunities for articulating difference, particularly at the local level. In fact, this perception overlooks the self-generative nature of context in which the global and the local are increasingly linked. Take neighbourhoods as an example of viewing globalisation from the ground up. Neighbourhoods, in addition to the spatial and temporal realities of location and history are conceived 'within a historically produced spatiotemporal neighbourhood and with a series of localized rituals, social categories, expert practitioners and informed audiences'.[11] Neighbourhoods are, in part, a product of our individual and social imaginations, fed by our experiences, practices and conventions. But these imaginings of locality must be produced, maintained and reproduced against a necessarily foreign background or context, which in turn infuses notions of locality with new ideas and influences.[12] So, the construction of locality requires ongoing imaginings of the foreign in both discourse and practice.

[11] Arjun Appadurai (n 6) 185. [12] *Ibid.*, 184.

This methodology for understanding context underscores a dynamic fluidity of linkages between the global and the local. It underscores the increasing challenges brought on by the effects of globalisation (the unbundling of territory, the dissemination of mass media, disjunctures between space, subjectivity and social movements, etc.) in producing locality, particularly when it is conceived as a feeling of belonging, a social recognition or an ideological commonality.[13] The municipal legal systems under study are an apt example of this dynamic. Their different approaches to Islamic finance, their varied efforts to modernise legal systems, to restructure their economies are not only challenged by the forces of globalisation but represent a localised interpretation thereof.

Globalisation ushers in a plurality of interactive legalities in municipal legal systems; diverse ways in which states choose to react to the unbundling of their territories; and more generally, to the ways in which modernity continues to find new and unforeseen ways of articulating itself. Yet the engines of modernity remain genetically tied to the power structures of the North Atlantic and its predominant social episteme, i.e. neoliberalism. Beyond law and economics, the North Atlantic's myriad influences are unmistakeable across a range of social interaction (language hegemonies, clothing styles, advertising techniques, armaments, etc.).[14]

And yet power relationships, while providing a general framework for conduct and possible outcomes, are conducive to entire fields of reactions and inventions.[15] At their core power relationships prompt insubordination or obstinacy, which are nothing other than means of escape. The desire for freedom, which is intrinsic to every human being, implies 'a strategy of struggle, in which the two forces are not superimposed, do not lose their specific nature, or do not finally become confused'.[16] Heterogeneity represents ongoing struggle, similar to the life cycle, which continues indefinitely to exert itself within the dynamism of power relationships.

Since its beginnings Islamic finance has represented a challenge to the global economic system, a struggle against the injustices and inequalities of the dominant economic system. The legal pluralistic context illustrates the ways in which notions of the sharia are transformed into dynamic power relations of overlapping legal systems. It provides a critical basis for examining the trajectories of globalisation and the possibilities of change in the global economy.

[13] *Ibid.*, 189. [14] *Ibid.*, 42.
[15] Michel Foucault (n 8) 789. [16] *Ibid.*, 794.

BIBLIOGRAPHY

AAOIFI, 'AAOIFI Publishes New Standards' (The Accounting and Auditing Organization for Islamic Financial Institutions, 2011), www.aaoifi.com/AAOIFI%20-%20PR-Click%20Jordan%20-%20New%20Standards.pdf. Accessed 12 July 2013

'AAOIFI Statement on Sukuk' (The Accounting and Auditing Organization for Islamic Financial Institutions, February 2008), islamicbankers.files.wordpress.com/2008/09/aaoifi_sb_sukuk_feb2008_eng.pdf. Accessed 8 April 2014

Accounting, Auditing and Governance Standards for Islamic Financial Institutions (Manama: The Accounting and Auditing Organization for Islamic Financial Institutions, May 2001)

Accounting, Auditing and Governance Standards for Islamic Financial Institutions: Financial Accounting Standards (Manama: The Accounting and Auditing Organization for Islamic Financial Institutions, 2010)

Accounting, Auditing and Governance Standards for Islamic Financial Institutions: Governance Standard for Islamic Financial Institutions: Sharia Review (Manama: The Accounting and Auditing Organization for Islamic Financial Institutions, 2010)

Shari'a Standards (Manama: The Accounting and Auditing Organization for Islamic Financial Institutions, 2004–2005)

Shari'a Standards for Islamic Financial Institutions (English Version) (Manama: The Accounting and Auditing Organization for Islamic Financial Institutions, 2010)

Sukuk Standard (Manama: The Accounting and Auditing Organization for Islamic Financial Institutions, 2008), http://islamicbankers.files.wordpress.com/2008/09/aaoifi_sb_sukuk_feb2008_eng.pdf. Accessed 15 August 2014

Abdullah D V, 'Liquidity Management in Institutions Offering Islamic Financial Services', Paper Presented at Second Islamic Financial Stability Forum (Jeddah, 2010), www.ifsb.org/docs/David_Vicary_IFSF_paper_FINAL.pdf. Accessed 25 March 2014.

Aghnides N P, *Mohammedan Theories of Finance* (Lahore: Premier Book House, 1961)

Agyemang A A, 'The Suitability of Arbitration for Settling "Political" Investment Disputes Involving African States' (1988) 22 *J World Trade*, 123

Ahmad A U F, *Theory and Practice of Modern Islamic Finance: The Case Analysis from Australia* (Boca Raton, FL: Brown Walker Press, 2010)

Ahmed A, 'Islamic Financing and the Relevant Laws of the UAE', Al Tamimi & Co., 5 June 2011, www.tamimi.com/en/magazine/law-update/section-7/june-5/Islamic-financing-and-the-relevant-laws-of-the-uae.html. Accessed 22 April 2014

Ahmed B, Asthana N, Afridi and Angell, 'Country Q&A: United Arab Emirates', *Practical Law*, 2009/10, www.practicallaw.com/8-385-5765. Accessed 21 December 2013

Ahmed B and Shah A, 'United Arab Emirates', Afridi and Angell, Getting the Deal Through: Banking Regulation, 2011, www.afridi-angell.com/items/limg/bankingregulation20112.pdf. Accessed 18 August 2014

Ahmed H., 'Islamic Law, Adaptability, and Financial Development' (2006) 13 *Islam. Econ. Stud.*, 79

Ahmed H, *Product Development in Islamic Banks* (Edinburgh University Press, 2011)

Ahmed T E, 'Accounting Issues for Islamic Banks' in Archer S and Karim R A A (eds.), *Islamic Finance: Innovation and Growth* (London: Euromoney Books; AAOIFI, 2002)

Ainley M, Mashayekhi A, Hicks R, Rahman A and Ravalia A, *Islamic Finance in the UK: Regulation and Challenges* (London: Financial Services Authority, 2007)

Al-Amine M and Al-Bashir M, 'Istisna' and its Application in Islamic Banking' (2001) 16 *ALQ*, 22

Al-Fahad A H, 'Ornamental Constitutionalism: The Saudi Basic Law of Governance' (2005) 30 *Yale J.Int'l L.*, 375

Al-Ghazzālī A H, *al-Mustaṣfā* min 'Ilm al-Usūl, vol. II (1904)

Al-Khalifa A B M, *The Progress of Islamic Banking and Finance in Bahrain* (Cambridge: Proceedings of the Fifth Harvard University Forum on Islamic Finance, 'Islamic Finance: Dynamics and Development', 2000)

Al-Muhairi B S B A, 'The Development of the UAE Legal System and Unification with the Judicial System' (1996) 11 *ALQ*, 116

'The Position of Shari'a within the UAE Constitution and the Federal Supreme Court's Application of the Constitutional Clause Concerning Shari'a' (1996) 11 *ALQ* 219

Al-Suwailem S, 'Towards an Objective Measure of Gharar in Exchange' (2000) 7 *Islam.Econ.Stud.*, 61

Al-Zuhayli W, *Financial Transactions in Islamic Jurisprudence*, trans. by Mahmoud A. El-Gamal, vol. I (Damascus: Dar al-Fikr, 2003)

Financial Transactions in Islamic Jurisprudence, trans. by Mahmoud A. El-Gamal, vol. II (Damascus: Dar al-Fikr, 2007)

Alchaar M N, Khan A A, Khan A *et al.*, 'Islamic Finance Debate: Prospects and Problems of Shari'ah-Compliant Finance', *Euromoney*, December 2008, www.euromoney.com/Article/2060693/Islamic-finance-debate-Prospects-and-problems-of-Shariah-compliant-finance.html. Accessed 23 March 2014

Ali S S, *Islamic Banking in the MENA Region* (Jeddah: Islamic Development Bank, Islamic Research and Training Institute, 2011)

ALI, 'ALI Overview', 2012, www.ali.org/index.cfm?fuseaction=about.overview. Accessed 6 April 2014

Allot A, *The Limits of Law* (London: Butterworths, 1980)

Alvi S, 'Introduction to IIFM', International Islamic Financial Market, 2009, www.iifm.net/media/PDF/presentation-paper/introduction%20to%20iifm%20by%20ijlal%20a.%20alvi%20-%206th%20dec%2009.pdf. Accessed 23 August 2013

Amin M, 'British Government Policy on Islamic Finance', 3 April 2010, www.mohammedamin.com/Islamic_finance/British_Government_Policy_on_Islamic_finance.html. Accessed 23 March 2014

'Liquidity Management at UK Islamic Banks', 2011, www.mohammedamin.com/Islamic_finance/Liquidity-management-at-UK-Islamic-banks.html. Accessed 25 March 2014

'The New UK Tax Law on Sukuk', *New Horizon*, Jan–March 2008, www.kantakji.com/media/8018/m173.pdf. Accessed 23 March 2014

'Why Has Retail Islamic Banking Not Taken Off in the UK?', 21 June 2010, www.mohammedamin.com/Islamic_finance/Why_has_retail_Islamic_banking_not_taken_off_in_the_UK.html. Accessed 23 March 2014

Anderson J N D, *Islamic Law in the Modern World* (London: Stevens & Sons Limited, 1959)

Anderson N, *Law Reform in the Muslim World* (London: Athlone Press, 1976)

Antaki N, 'Muslims' and Arabs' Practice of ADR' (2009) 2 *NYSBA N.Y. Disp. Res. Lawyer*, 113

Appadurai A, *Modernity at Large: Cultural Dimensions of Globalization* (Minneapolis University Press, 2005)

Arabi O, 'Contract Stipulations (Shurut) in Islamic Law: The Ottoman Majalla and Ibn Taymiyya' (1998) 30 *IJMES*, 29

Archer S and Karim R A A, 'Measuring Risk for Capital Adequacy: The Issue of Profit-Sharing Investment Accounts', in Archer S and Karim R A A (eds.), *Islamic Finance: The New Regulatory Challenge* (Singapore: John Wiley & Sons (Asia), 2013)

'Supervision of Islamic Banks and Basel II: The Regulatory Challenge' in Archer S and Karim R A A (eds.), *Islamic Finance: The Regulatory Challenge* (Singapore: John Wiley & Sons (Asia), 2007)

Ashraf R, Brown J and Lysenko V, 'Enforcement of Foreign Arbitral Awards Against UAE Counterparties: DIFC-LCIA Awards Versus New York Convention

Awards', Hadef & Partners, 12 March 2012, www.hadefpartners.com/News/pageid/120-137/default.aspx?Mediaid=215. Accessed 8 April 2014

Askari H, Iqbal Z, Mirakhor A, *New Issues in Islamic Finance and Economics: Progress and Challenges* (Singapore: John Wiley & Sons (Asia), 2009)

Atallah C C and Ghoul W A, 'The Wa'd-Based Total Return Swap: Sharia Compliant or Not?' (2011) 19 *JOD*, 71, 71

Baamir A Y, *Shari'a Law in Commercial and Banking Arbitration: Law and Practice in Saudi Arabia* (Farnham: Ashgate, 2010)

Baamir A Y and Bantekas I, 'Saudi Law as Lex Arbitri: Evaluation of Saudi Arbitration Law and Judicial Practice' (2009) 25 *Arb Intl*, 239

Baba R, 'Islamic Financial Centres' in Hassan M K and Lewis M K (eds.), *Handbook of Islamic Banking* (Cheltenham: Edward Elgar, 2007)

Bahrain Financial Exchange, 'The Exchange Business: An Insight' (2010), www.bfx.bh/Media/Download/BFXExchangeHandbook1.pdf. Accessed 23 March 2014

Bahrain, Kingdom of, 'The Corporate Governance Code of the Kingdom of Bahrain' (Central Bank of Bahrain, 1 January 2011)

Bakar M D, 'The Shari'a Supervisory Board and Issues of Shari'a Rulings and Their Harmonisation in Islamic Banking and Finance' in Archer S and Karim R A A (eds.), *Islamic Finance: Innovation and Growth* (London: Euromoney Books, 2002)

Bakr D A, *Basel II Enhances Islamic Banks* (Islamic Finance Asia, 2008), www.iefpedia.com/english/wp-content/uploads/2009/11/Basel-II-Enhances-Islamic-Banks.pdf. Accessed 17 August 2014

Balala M, *Islamic Finance and Law: Theory and Practice in a Globalized World* (London: I. B. Tauris, 2011)

Ballantyne W, *Commercial Law in the Arab Middle East: The Gulf States* (London: Lloyd's of London Press, 1986)

'Commercial Law: The Conflict in Shari'a and Secular Law', in Behdad S and Nomani F (eds.), *International Review of Comparative Public Policy* (Greenwich, CT: JAI Press, 1997)

Essays and Addresses on Arab Laws (Richmond, VA: Curzon, 2000)

'Note on the New Commercial Code of Bahrain (Decree Law 7/1987)' (1987) 2 *ALQ*, 3

'The Shari'a and Its Relevance to Modern Transnational Transactions' in *Arab Comparative & Commercial Law: The International Approach*, Proceedings IBA First Arab Regional Conference: Cairo 15–19 February 1987, vol.I (London: Graham & Trotman, 1987)

The Shari'a: The Use of Money (London: Serle Court, 2010)

'The States of the GCC: Sources of Law, the Shari'a and the Extent to which it Applies' (1985) 1 *ALQ*, 3

Ballard R, 'Coalitions of Reciprocity and the Maintenance of Financial Integrity within Informal Value Transmission Systems: The Operational Dynamics of Contemporary Hawala Networks' (2005) 6 *J.B.R.*, 319

Bälz K, 'A Murabaha Transaction in an English Court' (2004) 11 *I.L.& S.*, 117

'Islamic Law as Governing Law under the Rome Convention' (2001) 6 *Unif.L.Rev.*, 37

'Sharia Risk? How Islamic Finance Has Transformed Islamic Contract Law', Occasional Publications no. 9, Islamic Legal Studies Program, Harvard Law School, September 2008), www.law.harvard.edu/programs/ilsp/publications/balz.pdf. Accessed 25 March 2014

Bantekas I, 'Arbitrability in Finance and Banking' in Mistelis L A and Brekoulakis S L (eds.), *Arbitrability: International & Comparative Perspectives* (The Netherlands: Wolters Kluwer, 2009)

Barzilai D, *Syndicated Financing* (London: Islamic Project Financing: 2nd Annual One-Day Workshop, Institute for Islamic Banking and Insurance, 2010)

BCBS, *An Assessment of the Long-Term Economic Impact of Stronger Capital and Liquidity Requirements* (Basel Committee on Banking Supervision, 2010)

'Basel Committee on Banking Supervision Reforms – Basel III', www.bis.org/bcbs/basel3/b3summarytable.pdf. Accessed 8 April 2014

Basel II and Revisions to the Capital Requirements Directive, remarks by Stefan Walter, Secretary General, Basel Committee on Banking Supervision, to the European Parliament Committee on Economic and Monetary Affairs on the BCBS's reform programme (Basel Committee on Banking Supervision, May 2010)

'Basel III: A Global Regulatory Framework for More Resilient Banks and Banking Systems', Bank for International Settlements, June 2011, www.bis.org/publ/bcbs189.pdf. Accessed 22 March 2014

Belder R T de, *Shari'ah-Compliant Project Financing Securitisation Structures* (London: Islamic Project Financing: 2nd Annual One-Day Workshop, Institute of Islamic Banking and Insurance, 2010)

Benston G J, Bromwich M, Litan R E and Wagenhofer A, *Worldwide Financial Reporting: The Development and Future of Accounting Standards* (Oxford University Press, 2006)

Bergsträsser G, 'Anfänge und Charakter des Juristischen Denkens Im Islam. Vorläufige Betrachtungen' (1925) 14 *Der Islam*, 76

Bhambra H, 'Supervisory Implications of Islamic Finance in the Current Regulatory Environment' in Archer S and Karim R A A (eds.), *Islamic Finance: The Regulatory Challenge* (Singapore: John Wiley & Sons (Asia), 2007)

Bi F, *Islamic Project Finance: Project Finance Sukuk* (London: Islamic Project Financing: 2nd Annual One-Day Workshop, Institute of Islamic Banking and Insurance, 2010)

Bieling HJ and Jäger J, Global Finance and the European Economy: The Struggle over Banking Regulation' in van Apeldoorn B, Drahkoupil J and Horn L (eds.), *Contradictions and Limits of Neoliberal European Governance: From Lisbon to Lisbon* (New York: Palgrave Macmillan, 2009)

BIS, *Recent Innovations in International Banking* (Basel: Bank for International Settlements, April 1986)

The Group of Governors and Heads of Supervision Reach Broad Agreement on Basel Committee Capital and Liquidity Reform Package (Basel: Bank for International Settlements, 2010)

Black J, *Rules and Regulators* (Oxford: Clarendon Press, 1997)

Blackett R, 'The Status of Religious "Courts" in UK Law' (December 2009) *Decisions, Decisions: Disp. Resol. & Int'l Arb. Newsl.*, 11

Blanke G and Corm-Bakhos S, 'Enforcement of Foreign Awards in the UAE', *The In-House Lawyer*, 2011,www.inhouselawyer.co.uk/index.php/united-arab-emirates/9657-enforcement-of-foreign-awards-in-the-uae. Accessed 31 March 2014

Board J and el-Tahrir H, 'Risk and the Need for Capital' in Archer S and Karim R A A (eds.), *Islamic Finance: The New Regulatory Challenge* (Singapore: John Wiley & Sons (Asia), 2013)

Bowen J R, 'How English Courts Recognize Shariah?' (2010) 7 *Univ. St. Thomas L.J.*, 411

Brockett J, 'DIFC Boss Plans Islamic Finance Expansion', 30 October 2013, www.menafm.com/tag/difc/. Accessed 22 April 2014

Brower C N and Sharpe J K, 'International Arbitration and the Islamic World: The Third Phase' (2003) 97 *A.J.I.L.*, 643

Brown K, 'Wider Appeal Battles with Signs of Inefficiency', *Financial Times*, 7 December 2009

Buang A H, *Studies in the Islamic Law of Contracts: The Prohibition of Gharar* (Kuala Lumpur: International Law Book Services, 2000)

Burrough B, 'Bringing Down Bear Stearns', *Vanity Fair*, 1 August 2008

Cabral dos Santos J, 'Bank Capital Regulation in Contemporary Banking Theory: A Review of the Literature' (2001) 10 (2) *Financial Markets, Institutions & Instruments*, 4

Çağatay N, 'Riba and Interest Concept and Banking in the Ottoman Empire' (1970) 32 *Stud.Islamica*, 53

Calliess G P, 'The Making of Transnational Contract Law' (2007) 14 *Ind.J.Global Legal Studies*, 469

Calliess G P and Zumbansen P, *Rough Consensus and Running Code: A Theory of Transnational Private Law* (Oxford: Hart Publishing, 2010)

Caruana J, *Basel III: Towards a Safer Financial System* (Madrid: Paper presented at the 3rd Santander International Banking Conference, 2010)

Central Bank of Bahrain, 'CBB Factsheet 2013', www.cbb.gov.bh/page-p-financial_sector_fact_sheet.htm. Accessed 1 May 2014

'CBB Rulebook' (2005), cbb.complinet.com/cbb/microsite/cbb_rulebook.html. Accessed 1 May 2014

'CBB Welcomes Innovation by Financial Firms' (2013) June *Rev 1*

'Profile', www.cbb.gov.bh/page-p-profile.htm. Accessed 1 May 2014

Chapra M U and Khan T, *Regulation and Supervision of Islamic Banks*, Occasional Paper no. 3 (Jeddah: Islamic Development Bank, Islamic Research and Training Institute, 2000)

Chatham House, *The Gulf as a Global Financial Centre: Growing Opportunities and International Influence* (London: Royal Institute for International Affairs, June 2008)

Christou R, *Boilerplate: Practical Clauses*, 4th edn, Commercial Series (London: Sweet & Maxwell, 2005)

Chuah J C T, 'Islamic Principles Governing International Trade Financing Instruments: A Study of the Morabaha in English Law' (2006–2007) *Nw.J.Int'l L.& Bus.*, 137

CIA World Factbook, 'Bahrain', www.cia.gov/library/publications/the-world-factbook/geos/ba.html. Accessed 1 May 2014

City of London, 'Global Financial Centres 7' (2010), www.zyen.com/PDF/GFC%207.pdf. Accessed 7 April 2014

Claessens S and Underhill G, 'The Political Economy of Basel II in the International Financial Architecture' in Underhill G, Blom J and Mügge D (eds.), *Global Financial Integration Thirty Years On: From Reform to Crisis* (Cambridge University Press, 2010)

Clancy P, 'Legal Structure of Cash and Synthetic Transactions' in Watson R and Carter J (eds.), *Asset Securitisation and Synthetic Structures: Innovations in the European Credit Markets* (London: Euromoney, 2006)

Clode M, 'Regulatory Issues in Islamic Finance' in Archer S and Karim R A A (eds.), *Islamic Finance: Innovation and Growth* (London: Euromoney Books, 2002)

Cohen H, 'The Economic Background and the Secular Occupations of Muslim Jurisprudents and Traditionists in the Classical Period of Islam' (1970) 13 *J. Econ.& Soc.Hist.Orient*, 16

Collins L, *Dicey, Morris and Collins on the Conflicts of Laws*, vol. II (London: Sweet & Maxwell, 2006)

Comair-Obeid N, *The Law of Business Contracts in the Arab Middle East* (London: Kluwer Law International, 1996)

Comaroff J and Comaroff J L, 'Millennium Capitalism: First Thoughts on a Second Coming' in Comaroff J and Comaroff J L (eds.), *Millennial Capitalism and the Culture of Neoliberalism* (Durham NC: Duke University Press, 2001)

Cooper F, 'What Is the Concept of Globalization Good For? An African Historian's Perspective' (2001) 100 *Afr. Aff.*, 189

Cotterrell R, *Law's Community: Legal Theory in Sociological Perspective* (Oxford: Clarendon Press, 1995)

Coulson N J, *Commercial Law in the Gulf States* (London: Graham & Trotman, 1984)

'The Concept of Progress and Islamic Law' (Jan–Mar 1964) 40 *Quest*, 16

Cox S, 'The Role of Capital Markets in Ensuring Islamic Financial Liquidity' in Archer S and Karim R A A (eds.), *Islamic Finance: The Regulatory Challenge* (Singapore: John Wiley & Sons (Asia), 2007)

Crawford A, 'Germany to Temporarily Ban Naked Short Selling, Some Swaps of Euro Bonds', *Bloomberg*, May 2011, www.bloomberg.com/news/2010-05-18/germany-to-start-temporary-ban-on-naked-short-selling-of-euro-bonds-banks.html. Accessed 21 March 2014

Crone P, *Roman, Provincial and Islamic Law* (Cambridge University Press, 1987)

Cunningham A, 'Role of Sharia Boards Needs Modernisation', *Financial Times*, 21 April 2010, www.ft.com/cms/s/0/a5a6e474-4d54-11df-baf3-00144feab49a.html#axzz1WK1rhXTO. Accessed 12 April 2014

'custom', *Merriam-Webster's Online Dictionary*, 2009, www.merriam-webster.com/dictionary/custom. Accessed 24 March 2014

Dalhuisen J H, *Dalhuisen on International Commercial, Financial, and Trade Law* (Oxford: Hart Publishing, 2000)

Davies H and Green D, *Global Financial Regulation* (Cambridge, UK and Malden, MA: Polity Press, 2008)

Davies P L, *Gower and Davies' Principles of Modern Company Law*, 8th edn (London: Sweet & Maxwell, 2008)

DeLorenzo Y T, 'Shari'a Supervision in Modern Islamic Finance' (2009), www.guidanceresidential.com/wp-content/uploads/2013/10/shariah_supervision_in_modern_islamic_finance.pdf. Accessed 3 May 2014

'Shari'ah Compliance Risk' (2006–2007) 7 *Chi. J. Int'l L.*, 397.

'The Total Return Swap and the "Shari'ah Conversion Technology" Stratagem', in Beard C (ed.), *Conventional? The Relationship Between Islamic Finance and the Financial Mainstream* (London: Arab Financial Forum, 2008)

DeLorenzo Y T and McMillen M J T, 'Law and Islamic Finance: An Interactive Analysis' in Archer S and Karim R A A (eds.), *Islamic Finance: The Regulatory Challenge* (Singapore: John Wiley & Sons (Asia), 2007)

Dentons, 'Legal Framework', *The Report: Dubai 2014* (Oxford Business Group, 2014)

Deutsche Bank, 'Pioneering Innovative Shari'a Compliant Solutions', Deutsche Bank Academic Paper, London, 2007, www.eurekahedge.com/news/07_mar_DB_Pioneering_Innovative_Sharia_Compliant_Solutions.pdf. Accessed 2 April 2014

DFSA, *DFSA Rulebook: Collective Investment Rules* (Dubai Financial Services Authority, July 2013)

DFSA Rulebook: General Module (GEN) (Dubai Financial Services Authority, July 2013)

DFSA Rulebook: Islamic Finance Rules (IFR) (Dubai Financial Services Authority, July 2013)

'New and Enhanced PIB Module of DFSA Rulebook – Roll-Out and Implementation' (Dubai Financial Services Authority, 6 December 2012), www.dfsa.ae/Documents/SEO%20Letters%202012/PIB%20module%20roll-out%20Dec%206%202012.pdf. Accessed 22 April 2014

Prudential – Investment, Insurance Intermediation and Banking Business Module (PIB) (Dubai Financial Services Authority, July 2013)

'The DFSA's Approach to Regulating Islamic Finance in the DIFC' (Dubai Financial Services Authority, n.d.), www.dfsa.ae/Documents/Islamic%20finance%20docs%20for%20upload/DFSA%27s%20approach%20to%20regulating%20Islamic%20finance.pdf. Accessed 22 April 2014

Dien M I, 'Maslaha in Islamic Law: A Source or a Concept?' in Netton I R (ed.), *Studies in Honour of Clifford Edmund Bosworth* (Leiden: Brill, 2000)

DIFC, 'About: Discover DIFC' (Dubai International Financial Centre, n.d.), www.difc.ae/discover-difc. Accessed 22 April 2014

DIFC Economic Activity Survey 2011, Economic Note No. 20 (Dubai International Financial Centre, July 2012)

'Laws and Regulations' (Dubai International Financial Centre), www.difc.ae/laws-regulations. Accessed 26 March 2014

DirectGov, 'Budget March 2010 – Tax Changes', The National Archives, 25 June 2010, webarchive.nationalarchives.gov.uk/20121015000000/http://www.direct.gov.uk/en/Nl1/Newsroom/Budget/Budget2010/DG_186638. Accessed 22 March 2014

DiVanna J and Sreith A, *A New Financial Dawn: The Rise of Islamic Finance* (Cambridge: Leonardo and Francis Press, 2009)

Dockey D S, Hirschey M and Jones E, 'Information and Contagion Effects of Bank Loan-Loss Reserve Announcements' (1997) 43 *JFE*, 219

Doherty R and Vizcaino B, 'No Windfall from Qatar Ban on Islamic Windows', *Reuters*, 2 May 2012, www.reuters.com/article/2012/05/02/qatar-islamic-banks-idUSL5E8FU0KH20120502. Accessed 22 April 2014

Drezner D, *All Politics is Global: Explaining International Regulatory Regimes* (Princeton University Press, 2007)

Duranti A and Goodwin C, 'Rethinking Context: An Introduction' in Duranti A and Goodwin C (eds.) *Rethinking Context: Language as an Interactive Phenomenon* (Cambridge University Press, 1992), 3

Dusuki A W, 'Commodity Murabahah Programme (CMP): An Innovative Approach to Liquidity Management' in Bakar M D and Ali E A E (eds.), *Essential Readings in Islamic Finance* (Kuala Lumpur: CERT, Centre for Research and Training, 2008)

Dworkin R, 'Liberalism' in Hampshire S (ed.), *Public and Private Morality* (London: Cambridge University Press, 1978)

Eatwell J and Taylor L, *Global Finance at Risk* (Cambridge: Polity Press, 2000)

Edge I, 'Islamic Finance, Alternative Dispute Resolution and Family Law: Developments towards Legal Pluralism?' in Griffith-Jones R (ed.), *Islam and English Law* (Cambridge University Press, 2013)

Edwardes W, *Key Financial Instruments: Understanding and Innovating in the World of Derivatives* (London: Pearson Education Limited, 2000)

Eedle S, *A Global Bank's View of the Evolution of Islamic Finance* (London: Euromoney Yearbooks, 2009–2010)

Eisenberg D M, 'Derivatives and Islamic Finance', in Nethercott C and Eisenberg D (eds.) *Islamic Finance: Law and Practice* (Oxford University Press, 2012)

El-Ahdab A H, *Arbitration with the Arab Countries*, 2nd edn (Alphen aan den Rijn: Kluwer Law International, 1999)

El-Gamal M A, *An Economic Explication of the Prohibition of Gharar in Classical Islamic Jurisprudence* (Houston, TX: Rice University, 2001)

An Economic Explication of the Prohibition of Riba in Classical Islamic Jurisprudence (Houston, TX: Rice University, 2001)

An Introduction to Modern Islamic Economics and Finance, Proceedings of the Fourth Harvard University Forum on Islamic Finance, 'Islamic Finance: The Task Ahead' (Cambridge, 2000)

Islamic Finance: Law, Economics, and Practice (Cambridge University Press, 2006)

El-Hawary D, Grais W and Iqbal Z, *Regulating Islamic Financial Institutions: The Nature of the Regulated*, World Bank Policy Research Working Paper (Washington, DC: The World Bank, 2004)

El Qorchi M, Maimbo S M and Wilson J F, *Informal Funds Transfer Systems: An Analysis of the Informal Hawala System*, IMF/World Bank Occasional Paper 222 (2003)

Ellinger E P, Lomnicka E and Hooley R, *Ellinger's Modern Banking Law* (Oxford University Press, 2006)

Engelen E, Ertürk I, Leaver A, Froud J, Williams K, 'Reconceptualizing Financial Innovation: Frame, Conjuncture and Bricolage' (2010) 39 *Econ. Soc.* 33

Ernst & Young, 'The Islamic Funds & Investments Report' (2008), www.ncusar.org/programs/09-02-17-materials/EY_Islamic_funds_investment_report_2008.pdf. Accessed 25 March 2014

'World Islamic Banking Competitiveness Report' (2013–14), www.ey.com/Publication/vwLUAssets/EY_-_World_Islamic_Banking_Competitiveness_Report_2013-14/$File/EY-World-Islamic-Banking-Competitiveness-Report-2013-14.pdf. Accessed 18 August 2014

European Commission, *Commission Staff Working Document* (Brussels: European Union, 2010)

Communication from the Commission to the Council and the European Parliament of 11 July 2001 on European Contract Law [2001] COM 398 final

Communication from the Commission to the European Parliament and the Council of 12 February 2003 on a more coherent European contract law: an action plan [2003] COM 68 final

European Financial Stability and Integration Report 2012 (Brussels: Commission Staff Working Document, April 2013)

European Council, 'Summary: Unfair Terms in Consumer Contracts' (1993), europa.eu/legislation_summaries/consumers/protection_of_consumers/l32017_en.htm. Accessed 23 March 2014

Evans M and Hnatkovska V, 'International Capital Flows Returns and World Financial Integration', National Bureau of Economic Research, Working Paper 11701 (October 2005)

Fadlallah I, 'Arbitration Facing Conflicts of Culture: The 2008 Annual School of International Arbitration Lecture Sponsored by Freshfields Bruckhaus Deringer LLP' (2009) 25 *Arb Intl*, 303

Farn J, 'Credit Default Swaps', Hadef & Partners, 3 November 2009, www.hadef-partners.com/News/pageid/120-137/default.aspx?mediaid=98. Accessed 22 April 2014.

Farook S, 'Do We Really Need Standardization in Islamic Finance? (Part 1 of 2)', *Islamic Finance News*, 20 January 2010, www.Islamicfinancenews.com. Accessed 23 August 2013

'Do We Really Need Standardization in Islamic Finance? (Part 2 of 2)', *Islamic Finance News*, 27 January 2010), www.Islamicfinancenews.com. Accessed 23 August 2013

Fazio S, *The Harmonization of International Commercial Law* (Alphen aan den Rijn: Kluwer Law International, 2007)

Feldman D, *Civil Liberties and Human Rights in England and Wales*, 2nd edn (Oxford University Press, 2002)

Fincher C, 'British Gilt Issuance to Hold Broadly Steady in 08/09', *Reuters*, London, 7 March 2008, uk.reuters.com/article/2008/03/07/britain-budget-gilts-idUKL0776505020080307. Accessed 25 March 2014

Finizio S and Howitt C, 'When International Arbitration Meets Sharia' (March–April 2013) *CDRJ*, 49

Firoozye N, 'Featured Structure: Wa'd and the Completeness of Islamic Markets', *Opalesque Islamic Finance Intelligence*, 31 August 2009, www.opalesque.com/OIFI116/Featured_and_the_completeness_of_Islamic16.html. Accessed 6 May 2014

Fischer-Lescano A and Teubner G, 'Regime-Collisions: The Vain Search for Legal Unity in the Fragmentation of Global Law' (2004) 25 *Mich.J.Int'l L.*, 1000

Fitch Ratings, 'Fitch's Approach to Rating Sukuk' (2007)

Foster N H D, 'Comparative Commercial Law: Rules or Context' in Nelken D and Örücü E (eds.), *Comparative Legal Studies: A Handbook* (Oxford: Hart Publishing, 2007)

'Islamic Finance Law as an Emergent Legal System' (2007) 21 *ALQ*, 170

'Transfers of Rights and Obligations in the UAE: A Comparative Analysis in the Light of English Law, French Law and the shari'a' in Cotran E (ed.), *Yearbook of Islamic and Middle Eastern Law*, vol. VII (The Hague: Brill, 2000–2001)

'Using Comparative Commercial Law in the Study of Legal Transformation: Commercial Aspects of the Early Stages of Ottoman Legal Transition' in Shaham R and Layish A (eds.), *Islamic Law Facing the Challenges of the 21st Century* (The Van Leer Jerusalem Institute, 2011)

Foucault M, 'The Subject and Power' (1982) 8 *Crit. Inq.*, 777

Freshfields Bruckhaus Deringer, *The New Regulatory Architecture: The Changing Role of the FSA* (London: Freshfields Bruckhaus Deringer, 2009)

Fry M J, *Emancipating the Banking System and Developing Markets for Government Debt* (New York: Routledge, 1997)

FSA, *Strengthening Liquidity Standards* (London: Financial Services Authority, 2008)

'The Fit and Proper Test for Approved Persons (FIT)' in *FSA Handbook* (London: Financial Services Authority, 2011), fshandbook.info/FS/html/handbook/FIT. Accessed 24 March 2014

UK Implementation of the New Basel and EU Capital Adequacy Standards (London: Financial Services Authority, 2002)

FSA and Her Majesty's Treasury, *Consultation on the Legislative Framework for the Regulation of Alternative Finance Investment Bonds (Sukuk)* (London: Financial Services Authority, 2008)

FSCS, 'Compensation Limits', Financial Services Compensation Scheme, 2010, www.fscs.org.uk/what-we-cover/eligibility-rules/compensation-limits/. Accessed 24 March 2014

Furneaux P, Hijazi S, Lee J and Fakhro J, *Cross-Border Development in Islamic Banking* (Islamic Finance Review, Euromoney Yearbooks, 2008/09)

Galbraith J K, *A Short History of Financial Euphoria*, reprint edn (New York: Penguin Books Ltd, 1994)

GCC, *Economic Agreement Between the Gulf Cooperation Council States* (Oman: Cooperation Council for the Arab States of the Gulf, December 2001)

'Economic Indicators' (n.d.), www.gcc-sg.org/eng/. Accessed 1 May 2014

'Foundations and Objectives' (n.d.), www.gcc-sg.org/eng/index895b.html?action=Sec-Show&ID=3. Accessed 1 May 2014

Geertz C, *Local Knowledge: Further Essays in Interpretive Anthropology* (New York: Basic Books, 1983)

Gerber H, 'Sharia, Kanun and Custom in the Ottoman Law: The Court Records of 17th Century Bursa' (1981) 2 *Int'l Journ.Turk.Stud.*, 132

Ghanem I, 'The Impact of the UAE Civil Code Upon Commercial Litigation' (1991) 6 *ALQ*, 370

Giddens A, *The Consequences of Modernity* (Stanford, CA: Polity Press, 1990)

Gill S and Law D, 'Global Hegemony and the Structural Power of Capital', in Gill S (ed.) *Gramsci: Historical Materialism and International Relations* (Cambridge University Press, 1993)

Gluckman M, *The Judicial Process among the Barotse of Northern Rhodesia* (University of Manchester Press, 1955)

Goetzmann W N and Rouwenhorst K G, 'Financial Innovations in History' in Goetzmann W N and Rouwenhorst K G (eds.), *The Origins of Value: The Financial Innovations That Created Modern Capital Markets* (Oxford University Press, 2005)

Goitein S D, *A Mediterranean Society*, vol. I, *Economic Foundations* (Berkeley, CA: University of California Press, 1967)

'Commercial and Family Partnerships in the Countries of Medieval Islam' (September 1964) 3 *Islam.Stud.*, 315

'The Birth-Hour of Muslim Law? An Essay in Exegesis' (1960) 50 *Mus. World*, 23

'The Cairo Geniza as a Source for the History of Muslim Civilisation' (1955) 3 *Studia Islamica*, 75

Goldziher I, 'Muhammedanisches Recht in Theorie Und Wirklichkeit' (1888) 8 *Zeit vergl Rechtswiss.*, 406

Goode R M, *Commercial Law in the Next Millennium* (London: Sweet & Maxwell, 1998)

Goode on Commercial Law, ed. by McKendrick E, 4th edn (London: Penguin Books, 2010)

Goode R, Kronke H and McKendrick E, *Transnational Commercial Law* (Oxford University Press, 2007)

Goodhart C, Hartmann P, Llewellyn D T, Suarez L R and Weisbrod S, *Financial Regulation: Why, How and Where Now?* (London: Routledge, 1998)

Grais W and Pellegrini M, *Corporate Governance and Sharia Compliance in Institutions Offering Islamic Financial Services*, World Bank Policy Research Working Paper 4054 (Washington, DC: The World Bank, 2006)

Corporate Governance in Institutions Offering Islamic Financial Services: Issues and Options, World Bank Policy Research Working Paper (Washington, DC: The World Bank, 2006)

Gray R and Ismail A, 'Regulating Islamic Capital Markets' in Archer S and Ahmed R (eds.), *Islamic Finance: The Regulatory Challenge* (Singapore: John Wiley & Sons (Asia), 2007)

Greif A, 'Reputation and Coalitions in Medieval Trade: Evidence on the Maghribi Traders' (1989) 49 *J.Econ.Hist*, 857

Greuning H V and Iqbal Z, 'Banking and the Risk Environment' in Archer S and Karim R A A (eds.), *Islamic Finance: The Regulatory Challenge* (Singapore: John Wiley & Sons (Asia), 2007)

Risk Analysis for Islamic Banks (Washington, D.C.: The World Bank, 2008)

Gubler Z J, 'The Financial Innovation Process: Theory and Application' (2011) 55 *Del.J.Corp.L.*, 72

Haight G W, 'Libyan Nationalization of British Petroleum Assets' (1972) 6 *Int'l L.*, 541

Hallaq W B, *An Introduction to Islamic Law* (Cambridge University Press, 2009)

Authority, Continuity, and Change in Islamic Law (Cambridge University Press, 2001)

'Contracts and Alliances' in McAuliff J D (ed.), *Encyclopedia of the Qur'an* (Brill Online, 2008)

Islamic Legal Theories (Cambridge University Press, 1997)

Shari'a: Theory, Practice, Transformations (Cambridge University Press, 2009)

The Qadi's Diwan (sijill) before the Ottomans (London: Bulletin of the School of Oriental and African Studies, 1998)

'Was the Gate of Ijtihad Closed?' (1984) 16 *Int'l J.Mid.E.Stud*, 3

Halliday T C and Carruthers B G, 'The Recursivity of Law: Global Norm Making and National Law-making in the Globalization of Corporate Insolvency Regimes' (2007) 112 *Am.J.Soc.*, 1189

Hamilton D S and Quinlan J P, *The Transatlantic Economy 2013*, vol. I (Washington, DC: Paul H. Nitze School of Advanced International Studies, 2013)

Hammond E, 'Construction: Investors Transform UK Horizon', *Financial Times*, 11 May 2011, www.ft.com/cms/s/0/3dbd26fe-7aa1-11e0-8762-00144feabdc0.html#axzz1WKYWWLm7. Accessed 25 March 2014

Hamoudi H A, 'Jurisprudential Schizophrenia: On Form and Function in Islamic Finance' (2006–2007) 7 *Chicag.Journ.Int'l.Law.*, 605

'Muhammad's Social Justice or Muslim Cant?: Langdellianism and the Failures of Islamic Finance' (2007) 89 *Cornell Int.L.J*, 89

'The Death of Islamic Law' (2010) 38 *Ga.J.Int'l.& Comp.L.* 293

'You Say You Want a Revolution: Interpretive Communities and the Origins of Islamic Finance' (2007–2008) 48 *Va.J.Int'l L.*, 249

Haneef M R M, 'Recent Trends and Innovations in Islamic Debt Securities: Prospects for Islamic Profit and Loss Sharing Securities', Paper presented at Harvard University Forum on Islamic Finance, 'Islamic Finance: Current Legal and Regulatory Challenges' (Cambridge, MA, 2005)

Hanna N, 'The Administration of Courts in Ottoman Cairo', in Hanna N (ed.) *The State and Its Servants: Administration in Egypt from Ottoman Times to the Present* (Cairo: American University in Cairo Press, 1995)

Haque Z, *Islam and Feudalism: The Economics of Riba, Interest and Profit* (Lahore: Vanguard Books, 1985)

Hardy N, 'Shari'a Compliance: Understanding the Contributions of Shari'a Boards' in Schneider I and Hanstein T (eds.), *Beitraege Zum Islamischen Recht* (Frankfurt am Main: Peter Lang Verlag, 2006)

Hargreaves C, Davidson P and Perfect S, 'Accidentally Alternative? Scope of the Alternative Finance Arrangements Provisions, Part II', Freshfields Bruckhaus Deringer, *Tax J*, 2008, www.taxjournal.com/tj/articles/accidentally-alternative-20916. Accessed 23 March 2014

Härle P, Heuser M, Pfetsch S and Poppensieker T, *Basel III: What the Draft Proposals Might Mean for European Banking* (Munich: McKinsey & Company, 2010)

Harvey D, *A Brief History of Neoliberalism* (Oxford University Press, 2005)

Hasan A, 'An Introduction to Collective Ijtihad' (2003) 20 *AJISS*, 26

Hassan H, 'Contracts in Islamic Law: The Principles of Commutative Justice and Liberality' (2002) 13 *Journ.Islam.Stud.*, 257

Hegazy W, 'Fatwas and the Fate of Islamic Finance: A Critique of the Practice of Fatwa in Contemporary Islamic Financial Markets', Paper presented at the Harvard University Forum on Islamic Finance, 'Islamic Finance: Current Legal and Regulatory Issues' (Cambridge, 2005)

Henderson A, 'Islamic Financial Institutions' in Nethercott C and Eisenberg D (eds.), *'Islamic Finance: Law and Practice* (Oxford University Press, 2012)

'Islamic Financial Services' in Blair M, Walker G and Purves R (eds.), *Financial Services Law*, 2nd edn (Oxford University Press, 2009)

Henderson A and Hainsworth A, 'Through an Islamic Window', *IFLR*, September 2008, www.iflr.com/Article/2017785/Through-an-Islamic-window.html. Accessed 22 April 2014

Henry C M, 'Islamic Finance in the Dialectics of Globalisation: Potential Variations on the "Washington Consensus"' in Akbarzadeh S (ed.), *The Economy and the Law* (New York: Routledge, 2006)

Her Majesty's Treasury, *Alternative Finance Products, Regulatory Impact Assessment* (London: HM Treasury, 2007)

Government Sterling Sukuk Issuance: A Consultation (London: HM Treasury, 2007)

Government Sterling Sukuk Issuance: A Response to the Consultation (London: HM Treasury, 2008)

The Development of Islamic Finance in the UK: The Government's Perspective (London: HM Treasury, 2008)

Her Majesty's Treasury and Foreign & Commonwealth Office, 'Government Launches First Islamic Finance Task Force' (11 March 2013), www.gov.uk/government/news/government-launches-first-islamic-finance-task-force. Accessed 7 April 2014

Herring R and Schuermann T, 'Capital Regulation for Position Risk in Banks, Securities Firms, and Insurance Companies' in Scott H S (ed.), *Capital Adequacy Beyond Basel: Banking, Securities, and Insurance* (New York: Oxford University Press, 2005)

Hijazi F, 'Global Sukuk Issuance: 2008 Slowdown Mainly Due to Credit Crisis, but Some Impact from Shari'ah Compliance Issues', *International Structured Finance Special Report*, 2009, www.kantakji.com/media/7753/f156.pdf. Accessed 25 March 2014

Hill M and Sandberg R, 'Is Nothing Sacred? Clashing Symbols in a Secular World' (Autumn 2007) *P.L.*, 488

Hitti P K, *History of the Arabs: From the Earliest Times to the Present*, 10th edn (London: Macmillan St Martin's Press, 1970)

HMRC, *Impact Assessment for Stamp Duty Land Tax, Capital Gains Tax & Capital Allowance Tax Reliefs for Alternative Finance Investment Bonds* (London: HM Revenue & Customs, 2009)

Impact Assessment of Sukuk (Islamic Bonds) Legislation (London: HM Revenue & Customs, 2008)

Stamp Duty Land Tax: Commercial Sukuk (London: HM Revenue & Customs, 2008)

Stamp Duty Land Tax: Commercial Sukuk: A Response to the Consultation (London: HM Revenue & Customs, 2009)

Hodgson M G S, *The Venture of Islam*, vol. I. (The University of Chicago Press, 1961)

Horii S, 'Reconsideration of Legal Devices (Hiyal) in Islamic Jurisprudence: The Hanafis and Their "Exits" (Makharij)' (2002) 9 *I.L.& S.*, 312

Hourani A, *The Emergence of the Modern Middle East* (London: Macmillan Press in association with St. Antony's College, Oxford, 1981)

Housby E, *The Development of the Islamic Financial Tradition in Contemporary Britain* (Open University Ph.D. Thesis, 2005)

Howells P and Bain K, *Financial Markets and Institutions*, 5th edn (Harlow: Pearson Education Limited, 2007)

HSBC Amanah, 'Important Notice' (2013), www.hsbcamanah.com. Accessed 7 April 2014

Hurgronje C S, 'Islamic Law and Custom' in Bousquet G H and Schacht J (eds.), *Selected Works* (Leiden: E. J. Brill, 1957)

IBB, *Annual Report and Financial Statements* (London: Islamic Bank of Britain, 2009)

Articles of Association of the Islamic Bank of Britain (London: Islamic Bank of Britain, 2008)

Ibrahim A A, 'Regulation of Shari'ah Governance' (2012) 30 *Rev*, 8

IFSB, 'Capital Adequacy Requirements for Sukuk, Securitisations and Real Estate Investment' (January 2009), www.ifsb.org/standard/ifsb7.pdf. Accessed 25 March 2014

'Guiding Principles on Corporate Governance for Institutions Offering Only Islamic Financial Services (Excluding Islamic Insurance (Takaful) Institutions and Islamic Mutual Funds)' (Kuala Lumpur: IFSB, 2006), www.ifsb.org/standard/ifsb3.pdf. Accessed 25 March 2014

'Guiding Principles on Liquidity Risk Management for Institutions Offering Islamic Financial Services' (March 2012), www.ifsb.org/standard/eng_IFSB-12%20Guiding%20Principles%20on%20Liquidity%20Risk%20Mgmt%20(Mar2012).pdf. Accessed 25 March 2014

'IFSB-15: Revised Capital Adequacy Standard for Institutions Offering Islamic Financial Services (Excluding Islamic Insurance (Takāful) Institutions and Islamic Collective Investment Schemes)' (December 2013), www.ifsb.org/standard/2014-01-28_eng_IFSB15%20Revised%20Capital%20Adequacy_(Jan%202014).pdf. Accessed 25 March 2014

IFSL, *Islamic Finance 2010* (London: International Financial Services London, 2010)

IIFM, 'Published Standards' (n.d.), www.iifm.net. Accessed 25 March 2014

'Sukuk Report: A Comprehensive Study of the International Sukuk Market' (2010), www.kantakji.com/media/7465/c9.pdf. Accessed 25 March 2014

IMF, 'Offshore Financial Centers', IMF Background Paper (Monetary and Exchange Affairs Dept., 2000)

IOSCO, *Analysis of the Application of IOSCO's Objectives and Principles of Securities Regulation for Islamic Securities Products* (Madrid: Executive Committee of the International Organization of Securities Commissions, 2008)

Isard P, *Globalization and the International Financial System* (Cambridge University Press, 2005)

ISDA, 'About ISDA' (2012), www2.isda.org/about-isda/. Accessed 6 April 2014

Islamic Finance Resource, 'AAOIFI Shariah Council's Proposals for Amendments in Contemporary Sukuk Issues' (May 2008), ifresource.com/2008/05/21/aaoifi-shariah-councils-proposals-for-amendments-in-contemporary-sukuk-issues/. Accessed 25 March 2014

Islamic Fiqh Academy, 'Resolution No. 63/1/7 on Financial Markets' (Jeddah: Council of the Islamic Fiqh Academy, 1992)

Islamic Globe, The, 'S&P: Record High Sukuk Issuance 2010' (2010), www.theislamicglobe.com/index.php?option=com_content&view=article&id=112:sap-record-high-sukuk-issuance-2010&catid=6:article&Itemid=38. Accessed 24 March 2014

Jackson S, 'Fiction and Formalism: Toward a Functional Analysis of Usul Al-Fiqh' in Weiss B (ed.), *Studies in Islamic Legal Theory* (Leiden: Brill, 2002)

Islamic Law and the State: The Constitutional Jurisprudence of Shihab Al-Din Al-Qarafi (Leiden: E. J. Brill, 1996)

Jennings R C, 'Loans and Credit in Early 17th Century Ottoman Judicial Records: The Sharia Court of Anatolian Kayseri' (1973) 16 *J.Econ.& Soc.Hist. Orient*, 168

Jobst A, Kunzel P, Mills P and Sy A, *Islamic Bond Issuance – What Sovereign Debt Managers Need to Know*, IMF Policy Discussion Paper (Washington, DC: International Monetary Fund, 2008)

Johansen B, *Contingency in a Sacred Law: Legal and Ethical Norms in the Muslim Fiqh*, vol. VII, *Studies in Islamic Law and Society*, ed. by Peters R and Weiss B (Leiden: Brill, 1999)

'Die Sündige, Gesunde Amme. Moral Und Gesetzliche Bestimmung (Hukm) Im Islamischen Recht' (1998) 28 *Die Welt des Islams*, 264

Johnston D L, 'Maqasid Al-Shari'a: Epistemology and Hermeneutics of Muslim Theologies of Human Rights' (2007) 47 *Die Welt des Islams*, 149

Joint Forum, The, *Risk Management Practices and Regulatory Capital: Cross Sectoral Comparison* (Basel Committee Joint Publication, 2001)

Jones G, 'International Financial Centres in Asia, the Middle East and Australia: A Historical Perspective' in Roberts R (ed.), *International Financial Centres: Concepts, Development and Dynamics*, vol. I (Cheltenham: Edward Elgar, 1994)

Junius A, 'Islamic Finance: Issues Surrounding Islamic Law as a Choice of Law under German Conflict of Laws Principles' (2007) 7 *Chicag.Journ.Int'l. Law*, 537

Juynboll T W, *Handbuch Des Islamischen Gesetzes* (Leipzig: Otto Harassowitz, 1910)

Kahf M, 'Islamic Banks: The Rise of a New Power Alliance of Wealth and Shari'a Scholarship' in Henry C M and Wilson R (eds.), *The Politics of Islamic Finance* (Edinburgh University Press, 2004)

Kamali M H, *Islamic Commercial Law: An Analysis of Futures and Options* (Cambridge: Islamic Texts Society, 1999)

Principles of Islamic Jurisprudence (Cambridge: Islamic Texts Society, 2003)

Kapstein E B, 'Resolving the Regulator's Dilemma: International Coordination of Banking Regulations' (1989) 43 *Int'l Org*, 323

Karasik T, Wehrey F and Strom S, 'Islamic Finance in a Global Context: Opportunities and Challenges' (2007) 7 *Chicag.Journ.Int'l.Law*, 379

Kay J, 'The Forms of Regulation' in Seldon A. (ed.), *Regulation or over-Regulation?* (London: Institute of Economic Affairs, 1988)

Keane J, More Theses on the Philosophy of History' in Tully J (ed.) *Meaning and Context: Quentin Skinner and His Critics* (Cambridge: Polity Press, 1988), 210

Kern S, *Current Issues: Global Financial Markets* (Frankfurt am Main: Deutsche Bank, 2012)

Khan S A, 'Two Paths to Development: Capitalist vs. Islamic Approach' in Al-Roubaie A and Alvi S (eds.), *Islamic Banking and Finance* (London: Routledge, 2010)

Khatchadourian M, *Arbitration and Mediation between Europe and the Gulf* (Sharm El-Sheikh International Arbitration Center, 2010)

Kindleberger C P, 'The Formation of Financial Centers: A Study in Comparative Economic History' in Roberts R (ed.), *International Financial Centres: Concepts, Development and Dynamics*, vol. I (Cheltenham: Edward Elgar, 1994)

Kirkpatrick D D and Gall C, 'Arab Neighbors Take Split Paths in Constitutions', *International New York Times*, 14 January 2014, www.nytimes.com/2014/01/15/world/middleeast/arab-neighbors-take-split-paths-in-constitutions.html?hp&_r=1. Accessed 22 April 2014

Koendgen J, 'Regulation of Banking Services in the European Union: A Comparative View' in Basedow J, Baum H, Hopt K J, Kanda H and Kono

T (eds.), *Economic Regulation and Competition* (The Hague: Kluwer Law International, 2002)

Koendgen O, 'Shari'a and National Law in the Sudan', in Otto J M (ed.), *Sharia Incorporated: A Comparative Overview of the Legal Systems of Twelve Muslim Countries in Past and Present* (Leiden University Press, 2010)

Kourides P N, 'The Influence of Islamic Law on Contemporary Middle Eastern Legal Systems: The Formation and Binding Force of Contracts' (1970) 9 *Colum.J.Transnat'l L.*, 384

KPMG, 'New Dubai International Financial Centre Set Up' (2003–2004) 15 *Int'l Tax Rev*, 42

Kratochwil F, 'Of Systems, Boundaries, and Territoriality: An Inquiry into the Formation of the State System' (1986) 39 *Wld.Pol.*, 27

Krawietz B, 'Cut and Paste in Legal Rules: Designing Islamic Norms with Talfiq' (2002) 42 *Die Welt des Islams*, 3

Kreutzberger K, 'Shari'a Compliant Finance' (Interview 7 June 2012)

Krippner G R, 'The Financialization of the American Economy' (2005) 3 *Socio Econ. Rev.*, 173

Krugman P, 'Profits Without Production', *International Herald Tribune*, 20 June 2013, www.nytimes.com/2013/06/21/opinion/krugman-profits-without-production.html?_r=0. Accessed 24 April 2014

Kuran T, *The Long Divergence: How Islamic Law Held Back the Middle East* (Princeton University Press, 2011)

Kutty F, 'The Shari'a Factor in International Commercial Arbitration' (2006) 28 *Loy.L.A.Int'l & Comp.L.Ann.*, 565

Labib S, 'Geld Und Kredit: Studien Zur Wirtschaftsgeschichte Aegyptens Im Mittelalter' (1959) 2 *J.Econ.& Soc.Hist.Orient*, 225

Lanchester J, *Whoops: Why Everyone Owes Everyone And No One Can Pay* (London: Allen Lane, 2010)

Larosiere J d, 'Basel Rules Risk Punishing the Wrong Banks', *Financial Times*, 26 October 2010

Lastra R, 'The Governance Structure for Financial Supervision and Regulation in Europe' (Fall 2003) 10 *Colum.J.Eur.L.*, 49

Latham and Watkins, 'Doing Business in the United Arab Emirates' (January 2011), www.lw.com/upload/pubContent/_pdf/pub2783_1.PDF. Accessed 22 April 2014

Layish A, 'The Contribution of the Modernists to the Secularisation of Islamic Law' (1978) 14 *Middle E.Stud.*, 263

Leff A A, 'Economic Analysis of the Law: Some Realism About Nominalism' (1974) 60 *Va.L.Rev.*, 451

Levy J, 'Under Duress' (2006) 156 *N.L.J.*, 936

Lewis M K and Algaoud L M, *Islamic Banking* (Cheltenham: Edward Elgar, 2001)

Libson G, 'On the Development of Custom as a Source of Law in Islamic Law' (1997) 4 *I.L.& S.*, 131

Liebesny H J, 'British Jurisdiction in the States of the Persian Gulf' (1949) 3 *Middle E.J.*, 330

Linklaters, 'Recent Developments in Enforcement of Arbitral Awards in the United Arab Emirates' (12 May 2011), www.linklaters.com/Publications/GCC/May/Pages/Recent_Developments_Enforcement_Arbitral_Awards_United_Arab_Emirates.aspx. Accessed 9 April 2014

Llewellyn D, 'Regulation of Retail Investment Services' (1995) 15 *Ec.Aff.*, 1

The Economic Rationale for Financial Regulation (FSA Occasional Papers in Financial Regulation, London: Financial Services Authority, 1999)

'Universal Banking and the Public Interest: A British Perspective' in Saunders A and Walter I (eds.), *Universal Banking: Financial System Design Reconsidered* (Chicago, IL: Irwin Professional Publishing, 1996)

LMA, 'Guide to Syndicated Loans' (n.d.), 1, www.lma.eu.com/uploads/files/introductory_guides/guide_to_par_syndicated_loans.pdf. Accessed 12 August 2014

'Users Guide to Islamic Finance Documents' (20 February 2007)

'Users Guide to the Recommended Form of Primary Documents' (January 2012)

LMC, 'Vision & Role' (2011), www.lmcbahrain.com/role.asp. Accessed 25 March 2014

Lomnicka E, 'Collective Investment Schemes' in Blair M, Walker G and Purves R (eds.), *Financial Services Law*, 2nd edn (Oxford University Press, 2009)

Lopez R S and Raymond I W, *Medieval Trade in the Mediterranean World: Illustrative Documents* (London: Oxford University Press, 1955)

Lothian J R, 'The Internationalization of Money and Finance and the Globalization of Financial Markets' (2002) 21 *J.I.M.F.*, 699

LSE, 'Islamic Factsheet' (2013), www.londonstockexchange.com/specialist-issuers/islamic/downloads/london-a-global-hub-for-islamic-finance.pdf. Accessed 23 August 2013

Sukuk List (July 2013)

Luhmann N, *Social Systems* (Stanford University Press, 1995)

Soziologische Aufklaerung 3, 2nd edn (Opladen: Westdeutscher Verlag GmbH, 1991)

Soziologische Aufklaerung: Aufsaetze Zur Theorie Sozialer Systeme (Koeln und Opladen: Westdeutscher Verlag GmbH, 1970)

Lynch K, *The Forces of Economic Globalization: Challenges to the Regime of International Commercial Arbitration* (The Hague: Kluwer Law International, 2003)

Maine H S, *Ancient Law: Its Connection with the Early History of Society and Its Relation to Modern Ideas*, 10th edn (London: John Murray, 1885)

Majid S, 'Application of Islamic Law in the Middle East' (2003) 20 *I.C.L.R.*, www.mondaq.com/x/52976/international+trade+investment/Application+Of+Islamic+Law+In+The+Middle+East. Accessed 1 May 2014.

Malik M, 'Faith and the State of Jurisprudence' in Oliver P, Scott S D and Tadors V (eds.), *Faith in Law: Essays in Legal Theory* (Oxford: Hart Publishing, 2000)

Mallat C, 'Commercial Law in the Middle East: Between Classical Transactions and Modern Business' (2000) 48 *Am.J.Comp.L.*, 81

'From Islamic to Middle Eastern Law: A Restatement of the Field (Part I)' (2003) 51 *Am.J.Comp.L.*, 699

Marcus A, *The Middle East on the Eve of Modernity: Aleppo in the Eighteenth Century* (New York: Columbia University Press, 1989)

Mark S, 'Harmonization or Homogenization? The Globalization of Law and Legal Ethics – An Australian Viewpoint' (2001) 34 *Vand. J. Transnat'l L.*, 1173

Masmoudi F and Belabed T, *Islamic Finance in the Face of the Financial Turmoil: Opportunities and Challenges* (Paris: CAPmena, March 2010)

Masters B, 'Stability Priority in Finance Rules Shake-up', *Financial Times*, 26 July 2010, www.ft.com/cms/s/0/e22d16ce-98be-11df-a0b7-00144feab49a.html?siteedition=intl#axzz3AjOVrmpS. Accessed 17 August 2014

Mayer A E, 'Law and Religion in the Muslim Middle East' (1987) 35 *Am.J.Comp.L.*, 127

'The Shari'ah: A Methodology or a Body of Substantive Rules?' in Heer N (ed.), *Islamic Law and Jurisprudence* (Seattle, WA: University of Washington Press, 1990)

MCB, *Islamic Finance Transparency Standard: A Consultation* (London: The Muslim Council of Britain, 2008)

McKeen-Edwards H and Porter T, *Transnational Financial Associations and the Governance of Global Finance* (Abingdon: Routledge, 2013)

McKendrick E, 'Harmonisation of European Contract Law: The State We Are In' in Voguenauer S and Weatherill S (eds.), *The Harmonisation of European Contract Law: Implications for Private Laws, Business and Legal Practice* (Oxford: Hart Publishing, 2006)

The Creation of a European Law of Contracts: The Role of Standard Form Contracts and Principles of Interpretation (Nijmegen: Kluwever-Deventer, 2004)

McKenzie D, 'Islamic Finance', *TheCityUK*, London, May 2011, www.thecityuk.com/assets/Uploads/Islamic-finance-2011.pdf. Accessed 23 March 2014

Meadows P, *Access to Financial Services* (London: National Institute of Economic and Social Research, 2000)

Melchert C, 'The Formation of the Sunni Schools of Law' in Hallaq W B (ed.), *The Formation of Islamic Law* (Aldershot: Ashgate, 2004)

Menski W, *Comparative Law in a Global Context: The Legal Systems of Asia and Africa* (Cambridge University Press, 2006)

Merry S E, 'Legal Pluralism' (1998) 22 *Law.Soc.Rev.*, 869

Meyer J W, Boli J and Thomas G M, 'Ontology and Rationalization in the Western Cultural Account' in Meyer J W, Boli J and Thomas G M (eds.), *Institutional Structure: Constituting State, Society, and the Individual* (Newbury Park: Sage Publications, 1987)

Michaels R, 'The True Lex Mercatoria: Private Law Beyond the State' (2007) 14 *Ind.J.Global Legal Studies*, 447

Milmo D, 'Banks Win Concessions and Time on Liquidity Rules', *The Guardian*, 7 January 2013

Ministry of Justice, UK, *Rome 1 – Should the UK Opt In?* (London: Ministry of Justice, 2008)

Mishkin F S, *The Economics of Money, Banking, and Financial Markets* (Boston: Pearson, Addison Wesley, 2004)

Moghul U F and Ahmed A A, 'Contractual Forms in Islamic Finance Law and Islamic Inv. Co. of the Gulf (Bahamas) Ltd. v. Symphony Gems N.V. & Ors.: A First Impression of Islamic Finance' (2003–2004) 27 *Fordham Int'l L.J.*, 150

Mohtashami R, Birt A and Rovinescu L, *Arbitration Guide: United Arab Emirates* (Dubai: International Bar Association, February 2013)

Mohtashami R and Tannous S, 'Arbitration at the Dubai International Financial Centre: A Common Law Jurisdiction in the Middle East' (2009) 25 *Arb Intl*, 173

Montanaro E, 'Islamic Banking: A Challenge for the Basel Capital Accord' in Khan M F and Porzio M (eds.), *Islamic Banking and Finance in the European Union* (Cheltenham: Edward Elgar, 2010)

Moore S F, *Law as Process* (London:Routledge & Kegan Paul, 1978)

Muchlinski P T, '"Global Bukowina" Examined: Viewing the Multinational Enterprise as a Transnational Law-Making Community' in Teubner G (ed.), *Global Law without a State* (Aldershot: Dartmouth Publishing Company, 1997)

Multinational Enterprises & the Law (Oxford University Press, 2007)

Murray C, *Schmitthoff's Export Trade: The Law and Practice of International Trade*, 11th edn (London: Sweet & Maxwell, 2004)

Murray-Brown J and Dennis N, 'Ireland Guarantees Six Banks' Deposits', *Financial Times*, 30 September 2008, www.ft.com/cms/s/0/2124f8f4-8eb9-11dd-946c-0000779fd18c.html3#axzz1XkWOA76T. Accessed 25 March 2014

Musa M Y, 'The Liberty of the Individual in Contracts and Conditions According to Islamic Law' (1955) 2 *Islam.Quarterly*, 79

Nadkarni A, 'World Trade Liberalisation: National Autonomy and Global Regulation' in Mitchie J and Smith J G (eds.) *Global Instability* (London: Routledge, 1999)

Nielsen J S, 'Muslims in Western Europe' in Hillenbrand C (ed.), *The New Edinburgh Islamic Surveys Series* (Edinburgh University Press, 2004)

Noibi M, 'Prudential Regulation of Islamic Banks' in Al-Roubaie A and Alvi S (eds.), *Islamic Banking and Finance* (London: Routledge, 2010)

Norton Rose, 'MPs Confirm UK Commitment to Islamic Finance at Norton Rose Event' (27 January 2010), www.nortonrosefulbright.com/news/26132/mps-confirm-uk-commitment-to-islamic-finance-at-norton-rose-event. Accessed 25 March 2014

'The Implications for the Islamic Finance Market of the Investment Dar Company KSCC v Blom Developments Bank SAL [2009] EWHC 3545 (Ch)' (March 2010), www.nortonrose.com/knowledge/publications/27334/the-implications-for-the-islamic-finance-market-of-the-investment-dar-company-kscc-v-blom-developments-bank-sal-ewhc-3545-ch. Accessed 12 April 2014

NS&I, *Shari'a Compliant Savings Review* (London: National Savings & Investments, 2008)

Nyazee I A K, *Islamic Jurisprudence: Usūl al-Fiqh* (Herndon, VA: International Institute of Islamic Thought, 2000)

Islamic Law of Business Organization: Partnerships (Islamabad: The International Institute of Islamic Thought and Islamic Research Institute, 1997)

O'Brien R and Williams M, *Global Political Economy*, 3rd edn (Basingstoke: Palgrave MacMillan, 2010)

Oakley D, 'London Leads in Race to Be Western Hub', *Financial Times*, 7 December 2009

Obaidullah M, 'Financial Engineering with Islamic Options' (1998) 6 *IES*, 73

Ogus A I, *Regulation: Legal Form and Economic Theory* (Oxford: Hart Publishing, 2004)

Opwis F, 'Islamic Law and Legal Change: The Concept of Maslaha in Classical and Contemporary Islamic Legal Theory' in Amanat A and Griffel F (eds.), *Shari'a: Islamic Law in the Contemporary Context* (Stanford University Press, 2007)

'Maslaha in Contemporary Legal Theory' (2005) 12 *I.L.& S.*, 182

Osborne G, 'London Can Lead the World as an Islamic Finance Hub', *Financial Times*, 28 October 2013

Out-Law News, 'UK Signs up to Rome I Rules on Cross-Border Contract Disputes' (2008), www.out-law.com/page-9337. Accessed 8 April 2014

Park Y S, 'The Economics of Offshore Financial Centers' in Roberts R (ed.), *Offshore Financial Centres*, vol. I (Cheltenham: Edward Elgar, 1994)

Parker G and Masters B, 'FSA to Be Abolished in Osborne Shake-Up', *Financial Times*, 17 June 2010

Parker M, 'Islamic Bank Enters Germany', *Arab News*, 26 April 2010, www.arabnews.com/node/343397. Accessed 25 March 2014

'Islamic Finance Gaining Major Support in Britain', *Arab News*, 14 February 2010, www.arabnews.com/node/337075. Accessed 25 March 2014

Paust J J and Blaustein A P, 'The Arab Oil Weapon: A Threat to International Peace' (1974) 68 *A.J.I.L.*, 410

Peirce L P, *Morality Tales: Law and Gender in the Ottoman Court of Aintab* (Berkeley, CA: University of California Press, 2003)

Pelaez C M and Pelaez C A, *Financial Regulation after the Global Recession* (Basingstoke: Palgrave Macmillan, 2009)

Peters R, 'From Jurists' Law to Statute Law or What Happens When the Shari'a Is Codified' in Robertson B A (ed.), *Shaping the Current Islamic Reformation* (London: Frank Cass, 2003)

Popper N, 'Global Sell-off Shows Fed Reach Beyond the U.S.', *The New York Times*, 20 June 2013, www.nytimes.com/2013/06/21/business/economy/global-sell-off-shows-fed-reach-beyond-the-us.html. Accessed 1 August 2014

Posner E, 'Changing Transatlantic Financial Regulatory Relations' in Underhill G, Blom J and Mügge D (eds.), *Global Financial Integration Thirty Years On: From Reform to Crisis* (Cambridge University Press, 2010)

'Making Rules for Global Finance: Transatlantic Regulatory Cooperation at the Turn of the Millennium' (Fall 2009) 63 *Int'l Org.*, 665

Posner E A, *Law and Economics* (Aldershot: Ashgate/Dartmouth, 2001)

Posner R A, 'The Law and Economics Movement' in Posner R A and Parisi F (eds.), *Law and Economics* (Cheltenham: Edward Elgar Publishing, 1997)

Posner R A and Parisi F, 'Wealth Maximization Revisited' in Posner R A and Parisi F (eds.), *Law and Economics* (Cheltenham: Edward Elgar Publishing, 1997)

PRA, 'Prudential Regulation Authority', Bank of England (2013), www.bankofengland.co.uk/PRA. Accessed 27 July 2013

PRA and FCA, 'Handbook' (n.d.), http://fshandbook.info/FS/html/handbook. Accessed 7 April 2014

Prasad E S, *The Dollar Trap: How the U.S. Dollar Tightened its Grip on Global Finance* (Princeton University Press, 2014)

PriceWaterhouseCoopers and Queen Mary University of London, *International Arbitration: Corporate Attitudes and Practices* (London, 2008)

Qatar Financial Centre Authority, 'Why QFC', 1 July 2013, www.qfc.com.qa/en-US/About-qfc/Why_QFC.aspx. Accessed 26 March 2014

Quaglia L, 'The European Union in Regulating Global Finance', EUSA Conference Paper (Boston: 2011), euce.org/eusa/2011/papers/12e_quaglia.pdf. Accessed 2 April 2014

Quran, trans. by M A S Abdel Haleem (Oxford University Press, 2008)

Radhi H A, *Judiciary and Arbitration in Bahrain: A Historical and Analytical Study* (Boston: Kluwer Law International, 2003)

Rahim A, *The Principles of Islamic Jurisprudence* (New Delhi: Kitab Bhavan, 1994)

Rahman F, 'Riba and Interest' (1964) 3 *Islam.Stud.*, 1

Ramadan T, *Western Muslims and the Future of Islam* (Oxford University Press, 2004)

Ray N D, 'The Medieval Islamic System of Credit and Banking: Legal and Historical Considerations' (1997) 12 *ALQ*, 43

Rayner S E, *The Theory of Contracts in Islamic Law, Arab and Islamic Laws Series* (London: Graham & Trotman, 1991)

Redfern A, Hunter M, Blackaby N and Partasides C, *Redfern and Hunter on International Arbitration* (Oxford University Press, 2009)

Richardson E, *The Integration of Islamic Finance into the Irish Legal System* (Dublin: Trinity College, 2011)

Rittich K, *Recharacterizing Restructuring: Law, Distribution and Gender in Market Reform* (The Hague: Kluwer Law International, 2002)

Rodinson M, *'Islam and Capitalism'* (London: Allen Lane, 1974)

Rose P S and Marquis M H, *Money and Capital Markets: Financial Institutions and Instruments in a Global Marketplace*, 10th edn (New York: McGraw-Hill Irwin, 2008)

Rosen L, 'Law and Custom in the Popular Legal Culture of North Africa' (1995) 2 *I.L.& S.*, 194

Ruggie J G, 'Continuity and Transformation in the World Polity: Toward a Neorealist Synthesis' (1983) 35 *Wld.Pol.*, 261

'International Regimes, Transactions, and Change: Embedded Liberalism in the Postwar Economic Order' (1982) 36 *Int'l Org.*, 379

'Territoriality and Beyond: Problematizing Modernity in International Relations' (1993) 47 *IO*, 139

Rushd I, *The Distinguished Jurist's Primer, a Translation of Al-Bidayat Al-Mujtahid*, trans. by Imran Ahsan Khan Nyazee, vol. II (Reading: Garnet Publishing Limited, 1996)

Saeed A, 'Islamic Banking and Interest' in Peters R and Weiss B (eds.), *Studies in Islamic Law and Society*, vol. II (Leiden: E. J. Brill, 1996)

Saidi N, *The Success of DIFC as an International Financial Centre* (Dubai International Financial Centre, September 2009)

Saillon A, 'Islamic Banking Finally Starting in France', *IFN Reports*, vol. 8, issue 27, 13 July 2011, ddata.over-blog.com/4/08/16/46//IFN-report-July-2011.pdf. Accessed 25 March 2014

Saleh N, 'Are the Validity and Construction of Legal Acts Affected by Cause (Sabab)?' (1992) 7 *ALQ*, 116

'The Role of Intention (Niyya) Under Saudi Arabian Hanbali Law' (2009) 23 *ALQ*, 469

Saleh N A, *Unlawful Gain and Legitimate Profit in Islamic Law* (Cambridge University Press, 1986)

Saleh S, *Commercial Arbitration in the Arab Middle East* (London: Graham & Trotman, 1984)

Sassen S, *A Sociology of Globalization* (New York: W. W. Norton & Co., 2007)

Cities in a World Economy (Thousand Oaks, CA: Pine Forge Press, 2006)

'Global Financial Centers' (Jan/Feb 1999) 78 *Foreign Aff.*, 75

Globalization and Its Discontents (New York: New Press, 1998)

Saudi Arabia, Kingdom of, 'The Basic Law of Governance', *Saudi Embassy*, Ministry of Affairs, 1 March 1992, www.saudiembassy.net/about/country-information/laws/The_Basic_Law_Of_Governance.aspx. Accessed 26 March 2014

Schacht J, *An Introduction to Islamic Law* (Oxford: Clarendon Press, 1964)

'Die Arabische Hijal-Literatur: Ein Beitrag Zur Erforschung Der Islamischen Rechtspraxis' (1926) XV *Der Islam*, 211

'Fiḳh' in Bearman P, Bianquis Th., Bosworth C E, Donzel E V and Heinrichs W P (eds.), *Encyclopaedia of Islam*, 2nd edn (Brill, 2014), referenceworks.brillonline.com/entries/encyclopaedia-of-islam-2/fikh-SIM_2364. Accessed 25 March 2014

'Foreign Elements in Ancient Islamic Law' (1950) 32 *J.Comp.Leg.*, 9

'From Babylonian to Islamic Law' (1994) 1 *Yrbk Islam Mid East L*, 29

'Pre-Islamic Background and Early Development of Jurisprudence' in Khadduri M and Liebesny H J (eds.), *Law in the Middle East* (Washington, DC: The Middle East Institute, 1955)

'Problems of Modern Islamic Legislation' (1960) 12 *Studia Islamica*, 99

'Ribā' in Houtsma M Th, Arnold T W, Bassett R, Hartmann R (eds.), *Encyclopaedia of Islam, First Edition* (1913–1936) (Brill Online, 2014), referenceworks.brillonline.com/entries/encyclopaedia-of-islam-1/riba-SIM_3700. Accessed 25 March 2014

The Origins of Muhammadan Jurisprudence (Oxford: Clarendon Press, 1950)

'Zur Soziologischen Betrachtung Des Islamischen Rechts' (1935) XXII–XXIII *Der Islam*, 207

(tr.), *Das Kitab Al-Hijal Fil-Fiqh (Buch Der Rechtskniffe) Des Abu Hatim Mahmud Ibn Al-Hasan Al-Qazuini* (Hanover: Orient-Buchhandlung Heinz Lafaire, 1924)

Schoenmaker D, 'Contagion Risk in Banking', LSE Financial Markets Group Discussion Paper (London School of Economics, 1996), www.imes.boj.or.jp/cbrc/cbrc-03.pdf. Accessed 25 March 2014

Schoon N, *Islamic Banking and Finance* (London: Spiramus Press, 2009)

Shachar A, *Multicultural Jurisdictions: Cultural Differences and Women's Rights* (Cambridge University Press, 2001)

Shakil M, 'The Impact of Basel II on the Future of Islamic Banking' in Ali N (ed.), *Islamic Finance: Current Legal and Regulatory Issues* (Cambridge, MA: Islamic Finance Project, Harvard Law School, 2005)

Shalakany A A, 'Arbitration and the Third World: A Plea for Reassessing Bias Under the Specter of Neoliberalism' (2000) 41 *Harv.Int'l. L.J.*, 419

Shaukat M, *Sale of Goods and Sale of Debt: A Comparative Analysis*, INCEIF Paper (INCEIF, 2010)

Sheppard A, 'Arbitration of International Financial Disputes', *Kluwer Arbitration Blog*, London: Wolters Kluwer, 19 March 2009, kluwerarbitrationblog.com/blog/2009/03/19/arbitration-of-international-financial-disputes/. Accessed 12 April 2014

Shikder M N, 'Placing Faith in Islamic Finance', *New Horizon*, January–March 2009, www.islamic-banking.com/resources/7/NewHorizon%20Previouse%20Issues/NewHorizon_JanMar09.pdf. Accessed 25 March 2014

Simmons B A, 'The International Politics of Harmonization: The Case of Capital Market Regulation', in Vogel D and Kagan R A (eds.), *Dynamics of Regulatory Change: How Globalization Affects National Regulatory Policies* (Berkeley, CA: University of California Press, 2004)

Singh H, 'Absence of Shariah Audit a "Serious Loophole"', *Malaysian Reserve* (Kuala Lumpur, 29 June 2009), 2.bp.blogspot.com/_PGH0ddCyO7U/Skrsjw4GpsI/AAAAAAAAAZw/q-ro7fBbfi4/s1600-h/090629-TMR-ShariahAudit-MASB-IssamRasameel-p32.JPG. Accessed 25 March 2014

Skinner Q, 'Meaning and Understanding in the History of Ideas' in Tully J (ed.) *Meaning and Context: Quentin Skinner and His Critics* (Cambridge: Polity Press, 1988), 59

Slater S, Jones H, Felsenthal M *et al.*, 'Factbox: Basel III Banking Agreement' (*Reuters*, London, 12 September 2010) <www.reuters.com/article/2010/09/12/us-basel-banks-fb-idUSTRE68B1ZG20100912> Accessed on 25 March 2014

Sloane P D, 'The Status of Islamic Law in the Modern Commercial World' (1988) 22 *Int'l L.*, 743

Smith K, *Islamic Banking and the Politics of International Financial Harmonization*, Paper Presented at Harvard University Forum on Islamic Finance, 'Islamic Finance: Current Legal and Regulatory Issues' (Cambridge, 2005)

Sole J, 'Introducing Islamic Banks into Conventional Banking' in Al-Roubaie A and Alvi S (eds.), *Islamic Banking and Finance* (London: Routledge, 2010)

Sorenson B, 'Ethical Money: Financial Growth in the Muslim World' (2008) 23 *Am.U.Int'l L.Rev.*, 647

Sornarajah M, *International Commercial Arbitrations: The Problem of State Contracts* (Singapore: Longman, 1990)

'The Climate of International Arbitration' (1990) 8 *Journ.Int'l. Comm.Arb.*, 47

Sousa Santos B de, 'Law: A Map of Misreading. Toward a Postmodern Conception of Law' (1987) 14 *J.L.& Soc.*, 279

Toward a New Common Sense (New York: Routledge, 1995)

Toward a New Legal Common Sense: Law, Globalisation, and Emancipation (London: LexisNexis Butterworths, 2002)

Stein P, *Legal Institutions: The Development of Dispute Settlement* (London: Butterworths, 1984)

Stiglitz J E, 'Capital-Market Liberalization, Globalization, and the IMF' (2004) 20 *Oxf. Rev. Econ. Policy*, 57

Stoneman P, *The Economic Analysis of Technological Change* (Oxford University Press, 1983)

Strange S, *The Retreat of the State: The Diffusion of Power in the World Economy* (Cambridge University Press, 1996)

Sundararajan V, 'Risk Characteristics of Islamic Products: Implications for Risk Measurement and Supervision' in Archer S and Karim R A A (eds.),

Islamic Finance: The Regulatory Challenge (Singapore: John Wiley & Sons (Asia), 2007)

Sundararajan V and Errico L, *Islamic Financial Institutions and Products in the Global Financial System: Key Issues in Risk Management and Challenges Ahead* (Washington, D.C.: International Monetary Fund, 2002)

Suratgar D, 'The Development of the Legal Systems of the Middle East; Islamic Law and the Importance of Civil Law to the Process of Modernisation' in Russell B (ed.), *An Introduction to Business Law in the Middle East* (New York: Drake Publishers, 1975)

Sykes J, 'Bahrain Significantly Heightens its Attraction as a Commercial Dispute Resolution Centre in the Gulf', *Charles Russell*, February 2010, www.charlesrussell.co.uk/UserFiles/file/pdf/International%20 Arbitration/bahrain_commercial_dispute_resolution_centre.pdf. Accessed 4 April 2014

Tabb W K, 'Financialization in the Contemporary Social Structure of Accumulation' in McDonough T, Reich M and Kotz D M (eds.), *Contemporary Capitalism and Its Crises: Social Structure of Accumulation Theory for the 21st Century* (Cambridge University Press, 2010)

Tameme M E M, *Demand and Supply Conditions of Islamic Housing Finance in the UK: Perceptions of Muslim Clients* (University of Durham, Ph.D. Thesis, 2009)

Tamimi H, 'Interest under the UAE Law and as Applied by the Courts of Abu Dhabi' (2002) 17 *ALQ*, 50

Taylor C, 'Multiculturalism and the Politics of Recognition' in Gutmann A (ed.), *Multiculturalism and the Politics of Recognition* (Princeton University Press, 1992)

Tett G, *Fool's Gold: How Unrestrained Greed Corrupted a Dream, Shattered Global Markets and Unleashed a Catastrophe* (London: Abacus, 2010)

Teubner G, '"Global Bukowina": Legal Pluralism in the World Society' in Teubner G (ed.), *Global Law Without A State* (Aldershot: Dartmouth Publishing Company, 1997)

Law as an Autopoietic System, European University Institute Press Series (Oxford: Blackwell Publishers, 1993)

TheCityUK, 'Financial Services in Emerging Economies' *TheCityUK*, London, July 2012, www.thecityuk.com/research/our-work/reports-list/financial-services-in-emerging-economies-2012/. Accessed 15 August 2014

'Gulf Cooperation Council (GCC) Working Group, Annual Report', *TheCityUK*, London, 2011, www.thecityuk.com/uk-financial-services-overseas/geographical-markets/gulf-cooperation-council-states/. Accessed 21 March 2014

'Islamic Finance', *TheCityUK*, London, May 2011, www.thecityuk.com/research/our-work/reports-list/islamic-finance-2013/. Accessed 26 March 2014

'Key Facts About UK Financial and Professional Services', *TheCityUK*, London, 2012, www.thecityuk.com/research/our-work/reports-list/key-facts-about-uk-financial-and-related-professional-services/. Accessed 21 March 2014

'The UK Retains Position as Key Western Centre for Islamic Finance', *TheCityUK*, London, 4 May 2011, www.thecityuk.com/media/latest-news-from-thecityuk/the-uk-retains-position-as-key-western-centre-for-islamic-finance/. Accessed 7 April 2014

'UK, The Leading Western Centre for Islamic Finance', *UK Islamic Finance Secretariat*, October 2013, www.londonstockexchange.com/specialist-issuers/islamic/downloads/islamic-finance-2013-f.pdf. Accessed 7 April 2014

The Joint Forum, *Risk Management Practices and Regulatory Capital: Cross Sectoral Comparison* (Basel Committee Joint Publication, 2001)

Torchia A, 'UAE to Require Banks to Hold 10 Percent Liquid Assets', *Reuters*, Dubai, 15 July 2012, uk.reuters.com/article/2012/07/15/uk-uae-banks-basel-idUKBRE86E07J20120715. Accessed 22 April 2014

Torrey C C, *The Commercial—Theological Terms in the Koran* (University of Strasbourg, Ph.D. Thesis, 1892)

Townsend J M, 'The New Bahrain Arbitration Law and the Bahrain "Free Arbitration Zone"' (2010) 65 *Disp.Resol.J.*, 74

Tripp C, *Islam and the Moral Economy* (Cambridge University Press, 2006)

Turkey, '*The Mejelle, Being an English Translation of Majallahel-Ahkam-i-Adliya and a Complete Code of Islamic Civil Law*' (Lahore: Law Publishing Company, 1967)

Twining W, *Globalisation and Legal Theory* (London: Butterworths, 2000)

UAE Central Bank, *UAE Central Bank Corporate Governance Guidelines for UAE Bank Directors* (Draft, June 2006)

Udovitch A L, 'At the Origins of the Western Commenda: Islam, Israel, Byzantium?' (1962) 37 *Speculum*, 198

Partnership and Profit in Medieval Islam (Princeton University Press, 1970)

'The Constitution of the Traditional Islamic Marketplace: Islamic Law and the Social Context of Exchange' in Eisenstadt S N (ed.), *Patterns of Modernity: Beyond the West* (London: Frances Pinter Publishers, 1987), 166

'The "Law Merchant" of the Medieval Islamic World' in von Grunebaum G E (ed.), *Logic in Classical Islamic Culture* (Wiesbaden: Otto Harrassowitz, 1970)

Unal M, 'Shariah Scholars in the GCC-A Network Analytic Perspective' (Funds-at-Work, 2009) <www.iefpedia.com/english/wp-content/uploads/2009/09/Shariah-Scholars-in-the-GCC---A-Network-Analytic-Perspective.pdf> Accessed on 25 March 2014

UNCITRAL, 'Convention on the Recognition and Enforcement of Foreign Arbitral Awards' (New York, 1958), www.uncitral.org/uncitral/en/uncitral_texts/arbitration/NYConvention_status.html. Accessed 31 March 2014

'United Nations Convention on Contracts for the International Sale of Goods' (United Nations Commission on International Trade Law, 1980), www.uncitral.org/pdf/english/texts/sales/cisg/V1056997-CISG-e-book.pdf. Accessed 15 August 2014

Underhill G, Blom J and Mügge D, 'Introduction: the Challenges and Prospects of Global Financial Integration' in Underhill G, Blom J and Mügge D (eds.), *Global Financial Integration Thirty Years On: From Reform to Crisis* (Cambridge University Press, 2010), 13

UNIDROIT, *UNIDROIT Principles of International Commercial Contracts 2010*, International Institute for the Unification of Private Law, Rome, 2010, www.unidroit.org/english/principles/contracts/principles2010/blackletter2010-english.pdf. Accessed 26 March 2014

Usmani M T, *An Introduction to Islamic Finance* (Alphen aan den Rijn: Kluwer Law International 2002)

'Sukuk and Their Contemporary Applications' (2008) www.iefpedia.com/english/wp-content/uploads/2009/11/Sukuk-and-their-Contemporary-Applications.pdf. Accessed on 15 August 2014

van Apeldoorn B, 'The Contradictions of "Embedded Neoliberalism" and Europe's Multi-Level Legitimacy Crisis: The European Project and its Limits' in van Apeldoorn B, Drahokoupil J and Horn L (eds.), *Contradictions and Limits of Neoliberal European Governance: From Lisbon to Lisbon* (New York: Palgrave Macmillan 2009)

van Duyn A, 'The US Holds Its Breath on Bonds', *Financial Times*, 7 December 2009

van Eijk E, 'Sharia and National Law in Saudi Arabia' in Otto J M (ed.) *Sharia Incorporated: A Comparative Overview of the Legal Systems of Twelve Muslim Countries in Past and Present* (Leiden University Press, 2010)

Vesey-Fitzgerald S, 'The Alleged Debt of Islamic to Roman Law' (1951) 67 *L.Q.R.*, 81

Vikor K S, *Between God and the Sultan: An Historical Introduction to Islamic Law* (London: Hurst, 2004)

'The Shari'a and the Nation State: Who Can Codify the Divine Law?' in Utvik B O and Vikor K S (eds.),*The Middle East in a Globalized World* (London: C. Hurst & Co., 2000)

Vizcaino B, 'UAE Plans Islamic Finance Authority Backed by Legislation', *Reuters*, London, 30 October 2013, uk.reuters.com/article/2013/10/30/islamic-finance-emirates-idUKL5N0IK3YY20131030. Accessed 22 April 2014

Vogel F E and Hayes S L, *Islamic Law and Finance: Religion, Risk, and Return, Arab and Islamic Laws Series* (The Hague: Kluwer Law International, 1998)

von Mehren R B and Kourides N P, 'International Arbitration between States and Foreign Private Parties: The Libyan Nationalization Cases' (1981) 75 *A.J.I.L.*, 476

Wakin J A, *The Functions of Documents in Islamic Law* (Albany, NY: University of New York Press, 1972)

Walker G A, *International Banking Regulation: Law, Policy and Practice* (The Hague: Kluwer Law International, 2001)

Warsi S, 'The Future of Islamic Finance in a Global Economy', *Foreign & Commonwealth Office*, 7 June 2013, www.gov.uk/government/speeches/the-future-of-islamic-finance-in-a-global-economy. Accessed 7 April 2014

Watson A, *The Nature of Law* (Edinburgh University Press, 1977)

Watt W M, *Muhammad at Mecca* (Oxford University Press, 1953)

Wedderburn-Day, A R, 'Sovereign Sukuk: Adaptation and Innovation' (Fall 2010) 73 *Law.Contemp.Prob.*, 325

Weiss B, 'Interpretation in Islamic Law: The Theory of Ijtihad' (1978) 26 *Am.J.Comp.L.*, 199

'Tawarruq Loans Split Scholars', *Financial Times*, 7 December 2009

The Spirit of Islamic Law (Athens, GA: University of Georgia Press, 1998)

Wigglesworth R, 'Sharia Compliance Rulings Reverse Trend', *Financial Times*, 7 December 2009

Williams R, 'Archbishop's Lecture – Civil and Religious Law in England: A Religious Perspective' (2008), www.archbishopofcanterbury.org/articles.php/1137/archbishops-lecture-civil-and-religious-law-in-england-a-religious-perspective. Accessed 25 March 2014

'Civil and Religious Law in England: A Religious Perspective' in Griffith-Jones R (ed.), *Islam and English Law* (Cambridge University Press, 2013)

Wilson R, 'Challenges and Opportunities for Islamic Banking and Finance in the West: The United Kingdom Experience' in Al-Roubaie A and Alvi S (eds.), *Islamic Banking and Finance* (New York: Routledge, 2010)

'Islamic Banking in the United Kingdom' in Khan M F and Porzio M (eds.), *Islamic Banking and Finance in the European Union* (Cheltenham: Edward Elgar, 2010)

'Overview of the Sukuk Market' in Adam N J and Thomas A (eds.), *Islamic Bonds: Your Guide to Issuing, Structuring and Investing in Sukuk* (London: Euromoney Books, 2004)

'Regulatory Challenges Posed by Islamic Capital Market Products and Services' in Al-Roubaie A and Alvi S (eds.), *Islamic Banking and Finance* (London: Routledge, 2010)

Wood P R, *Conflict of Laws and International Finance* (London: Sweet & Maxwell, 2007)

Woodman G R, 'The Idea of Legal Pluralism' in Dupret B, Berger M and al-Zwaini L (eds.), *Legal Pluralism in the Arab World* (The Hague: Kluwer Law International, 1999)

Y-Sing L, 'Islamic Finance Set for Big China Leap', *Reuters*, 2 October 2009, uk.mobile.reuters.com/article/fundsNews/idUKLNE59101I20091002. Accessed 25 March 2014

Yeandle M, Danev N and Z/Yen Group, *The Global Financial Centres Index 14* (London: Z/Yen Group Limited, 2013)

Zaring D, 'International Law by Other Means: The Twilight Existence of International Financial Regulatory Organizations' (1998) 33 *Tex Int'l LJ*, 282

Zhu H, *Capital Regulation and Banks' Financial Decisions*, BIS Working Papers (Basel: Bank for International Settlements, 2007)

Zubaida S, *Law and Power in the Islamic World* (London: I. B. Tauris, 2003)

Zysow A, 'The Problem of Offer and Acceptance: A Study of Implied-in-Fact Contracts in Islamic Law and Common Law' (1985–1986) 34 *Clev. St.L.Rev.*, 69

INDEX